James G Panneczio

GROUPS
Process and Practice

FIFTH EDITION

GROUPS
Process and Practice

FIFTH EDITION

MARIANNE SCHNEIDER COREY

Private Practice

GERALD COREY

California State University, Fullerton

Diplomate in Counseling Psychology

American Board of Professional Psychology

BROOKS/COLE PUBLISHING COMPANY

I(T)P® An International Thomson Publishing Company

Pacific Grove • Albany • Bonn • Boston • Cincinnati • Detroit • London
Madrid • Melbourne • Mexico City • New York • Paris • San Francisco
Singapore • Tokyo • Toronto • Washington

A CLAIREMONT BOOK

Sponsoring Editor: *Eileen Murphy*
Marketing Team: *Gay Meixel and Margaret Parks*
Editorial Associate: *Patricia Vienneau*
Production Coordinator: *Fiorella Ljunggren*
Production: *Cecile Joyner, The Cooper Company*
Manuscript Editor: *Kay Mikel*
Permissions Editor: *Carline Haga*

Interior and Cover Design: *Jeanne Calabrese*
Cover Illustration: *Martha Walter, David David Gallery, Philadelphia/Super Stock*
Indexer: *Glennda Gilmour*
Typesetting: *Bookends Typesetting*
Cover Printing: *Phoenix Color Corporation*
Printing and Binding: *Quebecor Printing, Fairfield*

For more information, contact:
BROOKS/COLE PUBLISHING COMPANY
511 Forest Lodge Road
Pacific Grove, CA 93950
USA

International Thomson Editores
Campos Eliseos 385, Piso 7
Col. Polanco
11560 México D.F. México

International Thomson Publishing Europe
Berkshire House 168-173
High Holborn
London WC1V 7AA
England

International Thomson Publishing GmbH
Königswinterer Strasse 418
53227 Bonn
Germany

Thomas Nelson Australia
102 Dodds Street
South Melbourne, 3205
Victoria, Australia

International Thomson Publishing Asia
221 Henderson Road
#05-10 Henderson Building
Singapore 0315

Nelson Canada
1120 Birchmount Road
Scarborough, Ontario
Canada M1K 5G4

International Thomson Publishing Japan
Hirakawacho Kyowa Building, 3F
2-2-1 Hirakawacho
Chiyoda-ku, Tokyo 102
Japan

Printed in the United States of America

10   9   8   7   6   5   4   3   2

Library of Congress Cataloging-in-Publication Data

Corey, Marianne Schneider, [date]
    Groups: process and practice / Marianne Schneider Corey, Gerald Corey. — 5th ed.
        p.   cm.
    Includes bibliographical references and index.
    ISBN 0-534-34224-8
    1. Group psychotherapy. 2. Group counseling. I. Corey, Gerald.
    II. Title.
    RC488.C5935   1997
    616.89'152—dc20
                                            95-49750
                                            CIP

To the memory of our fathers,
Heinrich Schneider and Dr. Joseph Corey,
and to the memory of Jerry's nephew,
Jeff Corey

ABOUT THE AUTHORS

MARIANNE SCHNEIDER COREY is a licensed marriage and family therapist in California and is a National Certified Counselor. She received her master's degree in marriage, family, and child counseling from Chapman College. She is a Fellow of the Association for Specialists in Group Work and a clinical member of the American Association for Marriage and Family Therapy. She holds memberships in the California Association of Marriage and Family Therapists, the American Counseling Association, the National Organization for Human Service Education, the Association for Spiritual, Ethical, and Religious Values in Counseling, and the Association for Specialists in Group Work.

Marianne has been actively involved in leading groups for different populations, providing training and supervision workshops in group process, facilitating a self-exploration group for graduate students in counseling, and co-facilitating weeklong residential workshops in personal growth. She is an adjunct faculty member of the Counseling Department at California State University at Fullerton. She sees groups as the most effective format in which to work with clients and finds it the most rewarding for her personally. With her husband, Jerry, Marianne has conducted workshops, continuing-education seminars, and personal-growth groups in Germany, Belgium, Mexico, and China, as well as regularly doing these workshops in the United States. In her free time Marianne enjoys traveling, reading, visiting with friends, and hiking.

Marianne has co-authored several articles in group work, as well as the following books (published by Brooks/Cole Publishing Company):

- *I Never Knew I Had a Choice,* Sixth Edition (1997, with Gerald Corey)
- *Becoming a Helper,* Second Edition (1993, with Gerald Corey)
- *Issues and Ethics in the Helping Professions,* Fourth Edition (1993, with Gerald Corey and Patrick Callanan)
- *Group Techniques,* Second Edition (1992, with Gerald Corey, Patrick Callanan, and J. Michael Russell)

Marianne and Jerry have been married since 1964. They have two adult daughters, Heidi and Cindy, and have made their home in the mountain community of Idyllwild, California. Marianne grew up in Germany and has kept in close contact with her family there.

GERALD COREY is professor of human services and counseling at California State University at Fullerton and a licensed psychologist. He was the Coordinator of the Human Services Department at the above university for nine years. He received his doctorate in counseling from the University of Southern California. He is a Diplomate in Counseling Psychology, American Board of Professional Psychology; a National Certified Counselor; a Fellow of the American Psychological Association (Counseling Psychology); and a Fellow of the Association for Specialists in Group Work.

Jerry received the Outstanding Professor of the Year Award from California State University at Fullerton in 1991 and was the recipient of an honorary doctorate in humane letters from National Louis University in 1992. He teaches both undergraduate and graduate courses in group counseling, as well as courses in experiential groups, the theory and practice of counseling, and professional ethics. With his colleagues he has conducted workshops in the United States, Germany, Belgium, Scotland, Mexico, and China, with a special focus on training in group counseling. He often presents workshops for professional organizations and at various universities. Along with his wife, Marianne, and other colleagues, Jerry offers weeklong residential personal-growth groups and residential training and supervision workshops each summer. In his leisure time, Jerry likes to travel, hike and bicycle in the mountains, and drive his 1931 Model A Ford.

Recent publications by Jerry Corey, all with Brooks/Cole Publishing Company, include:

- *I Never Knew I Had a Choice,* Sixth Edition (1997, with Marianne Schneider Corey)
- *Theory and Practice of Counseling and Psychotherapy,* Fifth Edition (and *Manual*) (1996)
- *Case Approach to Counseling and Psychotherapy,* Fourth Edition (1996)
- *Theory and Practice of Group Counseling,* Fourth Edition (and *Manual*) (1995)
- *Becoming a Helper,* Second Edition (1993, with Marianne Schneider Corey)
- *Issues and Ethics in the Helping Professions,* Fourth Edition (1993, with Marianne Schneider Corey and Patrick Callanan)
- *Group Techniques,* Second Edition (1992, with Marianne Schneider Corey, Patrick Callanan, and J. Michael Russell)

He is also the coauthor (with Barbara Herlihy) of two books: *Dual Relationships in Counseling* (1992) and *Ethical Standards Casebook,* Fifth Edition (1996).

CONTENTS

PREFACE

This book outlines the basic issues and key concepts of group process and shows how group leaders can apply these concepts in working with a variety of groups.

In Part One, we deal with the basic issues in group work. In this edition, we have reorganized the material and made two chapters into three. Chapter 1 presents an overview of various types of groups, as well as our perspective on how theory guides practice and a multicultural perspective on group work. Chapter 2 gives increased coverage of ethical and legal aspects of group counseling. In Chapter 3, we've expanded on the topic of the group counselor as a person and as a professional. This chapter addresses the skills of group leadership, the co-leadership model, and the training of group counselors.

In Part Two, separate chapters deal with group-process issues for each phase in the evolution of a group. A few of these issues are: designing a group and getting one started, working effectively with a co-leader at each stage of a group, member roles and leader functions, problems that can occur at different times in a group, and techniques and procedures for facilitating group process. There is updated material summarizing the practical applications of research literature at the various stages of a group. Numerous examples illustrate a variety of leader interventions in response to the problems often encountered in facilitating a group. In many cases we have provided sample member-and-leader dialogues to demonstrate our own style of working with group members. Each chapter in this section contains a summary of the characteristics of the particular stage, along with member functions and leader functions at each stage of group development. The chapters conclude with several exercises.

The reading list at the end of Part Two has been updated and is offered to help readers round out their knowledge of the topics discussed in the first two parts of the book.

In Part Three, we show how the basic concepts examined in Part Two can be applied to specific types of therapeutic groups. We offer guidelines for group leaders who want to design groups specifically for children, adolescents, adults, and the elderly. We have also updated the discussion of issues in working with these special populations. This edition has updated coverage of a variety of groups that were discussed in the previous edition. New to this edition are groups in a variety of settings: a men's group in a community agency, a domestic violence group, and an elderly bereavement group.

Although we describe a number of techniques, we discourage the reader from using any technique without first developing a sound rationale for doing so in a particular situation. We focus on the unique needs of each age group and how to meet them; we discuss ethical, legal, practical, and professional guidelines; and we present an expanded and updated list of suggested readings for each type of group. In many ways this is a "how to" book, but it is also a book about the "why" of group leadership.

Groups is intended for graduate and undergraduate students majoring in psychology, sociology, counseling, social work, education, and human services who are taking courses in group counseling or group leadership. It is also a practical manual for practitioners involved in leading groups and for counselors training to lead various types of groups. Others who may find this book useful in their work are social workers, rehabilitation counselors, teachers, pastoral counselors, correctional workers, and marriage and family therapists.

An *Instructor's Resource Manual* for this fifth edition of *Groups* is now available. It contains multiple-choice test items, questions for reflection and discussion, additional exercises and activities, reading suggestions for instructors in preparing classes, a survey of current practices in the teaching of group counseling courses, and examples of course outlines. We also describe our approach to workshops in training and supervising group leaders, which can be incorporated into many group courses.

ACKNOWLEDGMENTS

We want to express our appreciation to Patrick Callanan, Helga Kennedy, Mary Moline, J. Michael Russell, and Veronika Tracy. These friends and colleagues have an influence on our style of group leadership that is reflected in the pages of this book.

The reviewers of this fifth edition have been instrumental in making important changes from the earlier editions. We appreciate the comments and suggestions of two of our students who did a most helpful prerevision: Michelle Muratori and Judy VanDerWende. Those who reviewed the revised manuscript and provided us with many constructive suggestions, which found their way into this new edition are: Paul Blisard, of Southwest Missouri State University; Susan Clark, of Abilene Christian University; Jeremiah Donigian, of SUNY College at Brockport; Allan Dye, of Rollins College; Diana Hulse-Killacky, of the University of Maine; Allen Ivey, of the University of Massachusetts; Jean Leary, of Santa Clara University; Carl Rak, of Cleveland State University; Kathleen Ritter, of California State University–Bakersfield; and James and Joanne Wigtil, of The Ohio State University.

Rosemarie Smead, of Indiana University Southeast and Veronika Tracy, of California State University at Fullerton, reviewed the chapters on group work with children and adolescents (Chapters 9 and 10). Keith Morran, of Indiana University–Purdue University at Indianapolis, and Rex Stockton, of Indiana University at Bloomington, reviewed the research summaries that appear in Chapters 4 through 8.

We appreciate Glennda Gilmour's work in compiling the index.

We thank the following people for granting us permission to describe their groups in Part Three: Lupe and Randy Alle-Corliss, Sandi Burns, Nancy Ceraso English, Alan Forrest, Wayne Huey, Paul Jacobson, Deborah Lambert, Stephen Lanzet, Karen Kram Laudenslager, Kathleen McNamara, Michael Nakkula, and Phil Piechowski. We hope that their innovative group programs inspire those who read this book to think of their own special designs for a group.

The dedicated members of the Brooks/Cole team continue to offer support for all our projects. It is a delight to work with a dedicated staff of professionals who go out of their way to give their best. These people include: Claire Verduin, who recently retired after working 25 years at Brooks/Cole; Eileen Murphy, who is the new editor of counseling and psychology; Fiorella Ljunggren, production services manager, who oversees the production of our books; Cecile Joyner, of The Cooper Company, who coordinated the production of this book; and Kay Mikel, the manuscript editor of this edition, whose fine editorial assistance kept this book reader-friendly. We also want to recognize the work of the late Bill Waller, who edited most of the previous editions of *Groups: Process and Practice,* and whose influence has carried over into this edition. We thank Patricia Vienneau, who facilitated the reviewing process and continued to provide us with unconditional positive regard.

Marianne Schneider Corey
Gerald Corey

GROUPS

Process and Practice

FIFTH EDITION

PART ONE

INTRODUCTION
Basic Issues in Group Work

Through the workshops we offer around the country, we have become aware of a growing interest in using group approaches with a wide variety of populations. In these visits to other states, however, we still hear comments like "We are expected to lead many kinds of groups, yet we don't feel adequately trained." Those who are not familiar with groups are often suspicious about the purpose and value of them. Even though the reputation of groups has suffered from some poor practices in the past, we are convinced that groups have much to offer. The effort involved in setting up and leading groups is considerable, yet we think that this commitment is essential if the group movement is to be viewed with respect. In Part One we discuss the fundamentals of group work and provide guidelines for beginning your own work as a group leader.

CHAPTER 1

INTRODUCTION TO GROUP WORK

FOCUS QUESTIONS

1. What are the advantages of using both educational and support groups in schools and community agency settings? How do you think groups address the demand for services in these settings? What kind of group might you be interested in forming and leading?

2. What have been your experiences as a member of a group? What have you learned in other groups that you could apply to a group you lead?

3. If you were applying for a job leading counseling groups, how would you address these questions: "What theoretical orientation guides how you design and lead a group? How would you set up a group? How do you view your role as a leader?"

4. What are the advantages of practicing within a single theoretical perspective? some disadvantages? What value can you see in developing an eclectic stance by drawing on concepts and techniques from diverse theoretical perspectives? Are there any drawbacks to integrating elements from different theoretical models?

5. Do you think groups are suitable for all client populations? How might you modify the group structure to fit the needs of members of a particular group? What are your thoughts about setting up a group composed of culturally diverse members? In organizing such a group, what are some factors you would consider?

INTRODUCTION

Our hope is that, from its very beginning, this book will get you excited about the prospect of leading groups and about the value of group work. This chapter provides an overview of the various types of groups, discusses our perspective and theory of group work, and addresses a multicultural perspective on group work.

WHY WE WROTE THIS BOOK

This book is written primarily for those who want to learn the practical aspects of designing and conducting groups. Based on our teaching of group courses, we are convinced that people learn best about how groups function and how to facilitate them when they become personally and actively involved in all the course activities. Your own experience as a group member, prior to taking your first group course, will provide you with a readiness for learning. But it is difficult to learn about self-disclosure, working with resistance, confrontation, giving and receiving feedback nondefensively, and identifying with others by simply reading about them. The more you can experience a group, especially from the vantage point of being a participant in one, the more the concepts presented here will come alive. This book will provide you with a cognitive map of the unfolding of group process and present an overview of groups and how they can best function.

OUR PERSPECTIVE ON GROUPS

During the 1960s and 1970s, groups reached their zenith; then the group fever declined for a decade. In the 1990s group work is enjoying a resurgence of interest. In the 1960s encounter groups and personal-growth groups were considered one pathway for making human connections and for moving toward greater self-actualization. Today groups are springing up in all kinds of settings. However, these are not unstructured personal-growth groups but short-term groups for specific client populations that are designed to remediate specific problems.

In the July 1995 issue of the American Psychological Association's *Monitor,* Scott Sleek describes an expanding array of group techniques that are affordable and effective in overcoming a range of psychological and medical problems. The crux of the article is that group therapy fits well into the managed care scene because groups can be designed to be brief and cost-effective treatments. Sleek summarizes studies giving evidence that, in general, group therapy is as effective as individual therapy in bringing about change. In addition, groups provide a sense of community, which can be an antidote to the impersonal culture in which many clients live. However, the focus of these groups is definitely time limited, and they have fairly narrow goals. Many of the time-limited groups are aimed at symptomatic relief, teaching participants problem-solving strategies and interpersonal skills that can accelerate personal changes.

From our perspective, groups are the treatment of choice, not a second-rate approach to helping people change. Many of the problems that bring people to counseling are interpersonally rooted and involve difficulties in forming or maintaining intimate relationships. Clients often feel that their problems are unique and that they have few options to get out of deadening ruts. They may be at a loss in knowing how to live well with the ones they love. Groups provide a natural laboratory that demonstrates to people that they are not alone and that there is hope for creating a different life. In many respects, as you will see in the chapters that follow, groups are powerful because they allow participants to experience some of their long-term problems being played out in the group sessions with opportunities to do something different from what they have been doing.

Groups have immense power to move people in creative and more life-giving directions. But if a group is hastily thrown together or if it is led by someone without proper training, there is potential for the group to be more damaging than beneficial. The purpose of our book is to offer some blueprints for forming and conducting groups in a manner that will release the strivings for health within individuals.

THE THEORY BEHIND THE PRACTICE

OUR THEORETICAL ORIENTATION

We are sometimes asked to declare what theory we follow. Neither of us subscribes to any single theory in its totality. Rather, we function within an integrative framework that we continue to develop and modify as we practice. We draw concepts and techniques from most of the contemporary therapeutic models and adapt them to our own unique personalities. Our conceptual framework takes into account the *thinking, feeling,* and *behaving* dimensions of human experience. Thus, our theoretical orientations and leadership styles are primarily a function of the individuals we are and the experiences we see unfolding in the groups we lead.

A Thinking, Feeling, and Behaving Model   We value approaches that emphasize the *thinking* dimension. Many group members can benefit from an emotional catharsis (the release of pent-up feelings), but some kind of cognitive work is also essential if the maximum benefit is to be gained. We typically challenge members to think about the decisions they have made about themselves, some of which may have been necessary for their psychological survival as children but now are clearly out of date. We hope members will eventually be able to make necessary revisions that can lead them to live more fully. We stress paying attention to "self-talk." How are members' problems actually caused by the assumptions they make about themselves, about others, and about life? How do members create their own problems by the thoughts and beliefs they cling to? How can they begin to free themselves by critically evaluating the sentences they repeat to themselves? In other words, many of our group techniques are designed to tap members' thinking processes, to help them think about events in their lives and how they have interpreted these events, and to work on a cognitive level to change certain belief systems.

In working with group members, we emphasize the value of helping members identify and express their *feelings.* In the groups we lead members often are stuck due to unexpressed and unresolved emotional concerns. If allowed to experience the range of their feelings and talk about how certain events have affected them, their healing process is facilitated. If members feel listened to and understood, they are more likely to express feelings they have previously kept to themselves.

Thinking and feeling are vital components in the therapeutic process, but *behaving* (or *doing*) is essential if the goal is behavior or personality change. Members can spend countless hours gaining insights and ventilating pent-up feelings, but at some point they need to get involved in an action-oriented program of change. Bringing feelings and thoughts together by applying them to real-life situations focused on current behavior is emphasized by behavior therapy and reality therapy. Group leaders can ask useful questions such as these: "What are you doing?" "What do you see for yourself now and in the future?" "Does your present behavior have a reasonable chance of getting you what you want now and will it take you in the direction you want to go?" If the focus of group work is on what people are doing, chances are greater that they will also be able to change their thinking and feeling.

In Chapter 8, Ending a Group, we focus on strategies and techniques to assist members in consolidating what they've learned in their group experience and applying new behaviors to situations they encounter every day. We focus on contracts, homework assignments, action programs, self-monitoring techniques, support systems, and self-directed programs of change. These approaches all stress the role of commitment on the members' part to practice new behaviors, to follow through with a realistic plan for change, and to develop practical methods of carrying out this plan in everyday life.

Underlying our integrated focus on feeling, thinking, and behaving is our philosophical leaning toward the existential approach, which places primary emphasis on the role of choice and responsibility in the therapeutic process. We challenge people to look at the choices they *do* have, however limited they may be, and to accept responsibility for choosing for themselves. Most of what we do in our groups is based on the assumption that people can exercise their freedom to change situations. Thus, we encourage members to focus on what they are thinking, feeling, and doing rather than attempting to change others. In those cases where it is not possible to change a difficult situation, we work with members on changing their attitudes toward it or the way they behave or react to it. The group context offers people opportunities to identify and clarify their thoughts, beliefs, feelings, and the ways they are acting.

When we facilitate a group, we use a variety of techniques that flow from many theoretical models. We adapt the techniques to fit the needs of the group participants rather than attempting to fit the members to our techniques. We consider the client's readiness to confront an issue, the client's cultural background, the client's value system, and the client's trust in us as leaders. We also consider the level of cohesion and trust the members have established with each other when deciding on appropriate interventions. Our concern is to help clients identify and experience whatever they are feeling, identify the ways their assumptions influence how they feel and behave, and experiment with alternative modes of behaving.

Of necessity, this discussion of our theoretical orientation has been brief. For a more elaborate discussion of the various theoretical orientations mentioned here, you are referred to *Theory and Practice of Group Counseling* (G. Corey, 1995).

DEVELOPING YOUR OWN THEORY
OF GROUP PRACTICE

Leading groups without having an explicit theoretical rationale is like flying a plane without a flight plan—although you may eventually get there, you're equally likely to run out of gas. If you operate in a theoretical vacuum and are unable to draw on theory to support your interventions, your groups may not reach a productive stage.

Theory is not a rigid set of structures that prescribes, step by step, what and how you should function as a leader. Rather, we see theory as a general framework that helps you make sense of the many facets of group process, provides you with a map giving direction to what you do and say in a group, and helps you think about the possible results of your interventions. We encourage you to look at all the contemporary theories to determine which concepts and techniques you can incorporate in your leadership style.

Ultimately, the most meaningful perspective is one that is an extension of your values and personality. A theory is not something divorced from you as a person; it is an integral part of the person you are and an expression of your uniqueness. If you are currently a student in training, developing an integrated, well-defined theoretical model may take years of extensive reading and practice in leading groups. We encourage you to devote considerable time to thinking about and discussing your ideas about group practice. With increased experience you will develop new questions. Experiments are tried, and clinical hunches are put to the test. By talking to other group leaders, you can exchange ideas for modifying old practices to fit new knowledge, thus, making changes over time.

Throughout this book we stressed that your ability to draw on your life experiences and personal characteristics is a powerful therapeutic tool. Particularly important is your willingness to examine how your personality and behavior either hinder or facilitate your work as a group leader. Although it is essential to be well-grounded in the theories underlying group work, to acquire skills needed for conducting groups, and to gain supervised experience as a group leader, this is not enough to make you an effective leader. It is also essential that you be willing to take an honest look at your own life to determine if you are willing to do for yourself what you challenge group members to do.

AN OVERVIEW OF THE
VARIOUS TYPES OF GROUPS

The Association for Specialists in Group Work (ASGW) has identified a set of core competencies in general group work. The training standards make it clear that mastery of the core competencies does not qualify a group worker to independently practice in any group work specialty. Practitioners must possess advanced competencies relevant to a particular area of group work.

> The ASGW offers an expanded definition of group work as: a broad professional practice that refers to the giving of help or the accomplishment of tasks in a group setting. It involves the application of group theory and process by a capable professional practitioner to assist an interdependent collection of people to reach their mutual goals, which may be personal, interpersonal, or task-related in nature. (ASGW, 1991, p. 9)

Groups differ with respect to goals, techniques used, the role of the leader, training requirements, and the kind of people involved. Definitions for specific group specializations are given by the ASGW (1991) and by Conyne, Wilson, Kline, Morran, and Ward (1993).

Task/Work Groups. The task/work group specialist assists groups such as task forces, committees, planning groups, community organizations, discussion groups, study circles, learning groups, and other similar groups to correct or develop their functioning. The focus is on the application of group dynamics principles and processes to improve practice and foster accomplishment of identified work goals.

Group workers who specialize in promoting the development and functioning of task/work groups assist these groups to enhance or correct their performance. This group specialist might also develop skill in organizational assessment, training, program development, consultation, and program evaluation.

The training for task/work groups involves course work in the broad area of organizational development, consultation, and management. Specialist training in the area of task/work groups requires a minimum of 30 hours (45 hours recommended) of supervised experience in leading or co-leading a task/work group.

Guidance/Psychoeducational Groups. Education and prevention are critically important goals for the contemporary counselor. The guidance/psychoeducational group specialist strives to educate group members who are relatively well-functioning individuals but who may have an information deficit in a certain area. The specialist uses the group medium to educate group participants who are "at risk" but are presently unaffected by a potential threat (such as AIDS), a developmental life event (such as a transition point), or how to cope with an immediate life crisis (such as suicide of a loved one). The goal is to prevent an array of educational and psychological disturbances.

The specialist training for guidance/psychoeducational groups involves course work in the broad area of community psychology, health promotion, marketing, consultation, group training methods, and curriculum design. These specialists should have content knowledge in the topic areas in which they intend to work (such as substance abuse prevention, stress management, parent effectiveness training, assertion training, AIDS). This speciality requires a minimum of 30 hours (45 hours recommended) of additional supervised experience in leading or co-leading a guidance group in field practice.

Counseling/Interpersonal Problem-Solving Groups. The group worker who specializes in counseling/interpersonal problem solving seeks to help group participants resolve the usual, yet often difficult, problems of living through interpersonal support and problem solving. An additional goal is to help participants develop their existing interpersonal problem-solving competencies so they may be better able to handle future problems of a similar nature. Nonsevere career, education, personal, social, and developmental concerns are frequently addressed.

The specialist training for counseling/interpersonal problem-solving groups should include as much course work in group counseling as possible but at least one course beyond the generalist level. Group counselors should have knowledge in the broad areas of human development, problem identification, and treatment of normal personal and interpersonal problems of living. This specialization requires a minimum of 45 hours (60 hours recommended) of supervised experience in leading or co-leading a counseling group.

Psychotherapy/Personality Reconstruction Groups. The group worker who specializes in psychotherapy/personality reconstruction seeks to help individual group members remediate in-depth psychological problems. The scope of practice is focused on individuals with acute or chronic mental or emotional disorders that evidence marked distress, impairment in functioning, or both. Because the depth and extent of the psychological disturbance is significant, the goal is to aid each individual in reconstructing major personality dimensions.

The specialist training for psychotherapy/personality reconstruction groups focuses on courses in abnormal psychology, psychopathology, and diagnostic assessment to assure capabilities in working with more disturbed populations. This specialization requires a minimum of 45 hours (60 hours recommended) of supervised experience in working with therapy groups.

Throughout the book *therapeutic group* is used as a general term to indicate several types of groups. *Therapeutic* does not refer to the treatment of emotional and behavioral disorders. Rather, the broad purpose of a therapeutic group is to increase people's knowledge of themselves and others, help them clarify the changes they most want to make in their lives, and give them some of the tools necessary to make these changes. By interacting with others in a trusting and accepting environment, participants are given the opportunity to experiment with novel behavior and to receive honest feedback from others concerning the effects of their behavior. As a result, individuals learn how they appear to others.

We use the term *therapeutic group* to refer mainly to two categories of group work:

- counseling/interpersonal problem-solving groups, and
- guidance/psychoeducational groups

The structure, content, and processes we discuss refer primarily to groups that have therapeutic and educational aims. We are writing about counseling groups that have an interpersonal orientation and about psychoeducational groups that are structured around some kind of topic or theme. More complete descriptions of the diverse range of groups—group therapy, group counseling, and structured groups—will be presented next.

GROUP THERAPY

Group therapy originated in response to a shortage during World War II of personnel trained to provide individual therapy. At first, the group therapist assumed a traditional therapeutic role, frequently working with a small number of clients with a common problem. Gradually, leaders began to experiment with different roles and various approaches. Over time, practitioners discovered that the group setting offered unique therapeutic possibilities. Exchanges among the members of a therapy group are viewed as instrumental in bringing about change. This interaction provides support, caring, confrontation, and other qualities not found in individual therapy. Within the group context, members are able to practice new social skills and apply some of their new knowledge.

People generally participate in group therapy to try to alleviate specific symptoms or psychological problems, such as depression, sexual difficulties, anxiety, and psychosomatic disorders. Some therapy groups are organized for the purpose of correcting a specific emotional or behavioral disorder that impedes people's functioning. Thus, many individuals in these groups are in need of remedial treatment rather than developmental and preventive work. In group therapy attention is given to unconscious factors and one's past and to reconstruction of major aspects of the personality. Therapy groups are thus typically of longer duration than most other types.

A variety of methods is employed in the conduct of therapy groups, including techniques designed to induce regression to earlier experiences, methods to work with unconscious dynamics, and procedures aimed at helping members reexperience traumatic situations so that catharsis can occur. The therapist is typically interested in creating a climate that fosters understanding and exploration of a problem area. The process of working through psychological blocks rooted in past experiences often involves exploring dreams, interpreting resistance, dealing with transference that emerges, and helping members develop a new perspective on "unfinished business" with significant others.

In writing about the future of group therapy, Dies (1992) claims that projections for the practice of group therapy include expanding applications of short-term and self-help approaches, refinements in matching treatment strategies with clients' needs, and a movement toward more effective integration of treatment modalities. Dies predicts that the trend toward short-term group therapy approaches, along with multimodal approaches, is likely to continue. He writes that, due to a number of factors, there is little doubt that group therapies will continue to play a pivotal role in the mental health field.

GROUP COUNSELING

The counseling group usually focuses on a particular type of problem, which may be personal, educational, social, or vocational. It is often carried out in institutions such as schools, college counseling centers, and community mental-health clinics and agencies. This type of group differs from a therapy group in that it deals with conscious problems, is not aimed at major personality changes, is generally oriented toward the resolution of specific and short-term issues, and is not concerned with treatment of the more severe psychological and behavioral disorders.

Group counseling has preventive and educational purposes as well as remedial aims. The group involves an interpersonal process and problem-solving strategies that stress conscious thoughts, feelings, and behavior. The focus of the group is often determined by the members, who are basically well-functioning individuals who do not require extensive personality reconstruction and whose problems relate to the developmental tasks of the life span or finding means to cope with stresses of a situational crisis. The group is characterized by a growth orientation, with an emphasis on discovering inner resources of personal strength and constructively dealing with barriers that are preventing optimal development. Members are able to develop interpersonal skills that can equip them to better cope with both current difficulties and future problems. The group provides the support and the challenge necessary for honest self-exploration.

Counseling groups offer an intense experience intended to help relatively healthy people function better on an interpersonal level. Rather than being aimed at curing personality problems, such groups are developmental, in that they explore personal issues that most people struggle with at various transition periods in life. The rationale for these groups is that the support and challenge they provide help participants make an honest self-assessment and determine specific ways in which to change their patterns of thinking, feeling, and acting. Although participants can benefit from the feedback they receive from others, it is ultimately up to them to decide what changes they want to make. Participants can compare the perceptions they have of themselves with the perceptions others have of them and then decide for themselves what they will do with this information.

Counseling groups range from those with an open structure, in which participants shape the direction of the group, to those characterized by a specific focus. But they all share the following goals:

- helping people develop more positive attitudes and better interpersonal skills,
- using the group process as a way of facilitating behavior change, and
- helping members transfer newly acquired skills and behavior learned in the group to everyday life.

The group counselor's job is to structure the activities of the group, to see that a climate favorable to productive work is maintained, to facilitate members' interactions, to provide information that will help the members see alternatives to their modes of behavior, and to encourage them to translate their insights into concrete action plans. To a large extent, group leaders carry out this role by teaching the members to focus on the here and now and to establish personal goals that will provide direction for the group.

Participants in group counseling often have problems of an interpersonal nature, that are ideally explored in a group context. Members are able to see a reenactment of their everyday problems unfold before them in the counseling group. The group becomes a microcosm of society, with a membership that is diverse but that shares common problems. The group process provides a sample of reality, with the struggles that people experience in the group resembling their conflicts in daily life. Through feedback, members are encouraged to see themselves as others do. They have a chance to experience themselves as they did in their original family, reliving conflicts they had with parents and siblings. There is also a chance to practice new ways of behaving, for the empathy and support from other members help clients identify what they want to change and how to bring about change. Participants can learn to respect differences in culture and values and can discover that, on a deep level, they are more alike than different. Although their circumstances may differ, their pain and struggles are universal.

Fairly detailed descriptions of counseling groups for clients of various ages are provided in Part Three of this book. In Chapter 9 there is a group program for elementary schoolchildren that is structured along educational and therapeutic lines. A counseling group for adolescents that deals mainly with the normal developmental concerns of this period is found in Chapter 10. There are several examples of group-counseling programs for various adult populations in Chapter 11. In Chapter 12 support groups and counseling groups for the elderly are described, along with guidelines for setting up and facilitating these groups.

STRUCTURED GROUPS

Groups structured to focus on a particular theme are being increasingly used by agencies, schools, and college counseling centers. Although the specific topic varies according to the interests of the leader and the population of the group, such groups share the aim of providing members with increased awareness of some life problem and the tools to better cope with it. Generally, the sessions are about two hours each week, for 4 to 15 weeks. Depending on the population, some group sessions may be as short as 30 to 45 minutes, especially with children or clients with a short attention span.

At the beginning of these structured groups it is common to ask the members to complete a questionnaire on how well they are coping with the area of concern. Such groups make use of structured exercises, readings, homework assignments, and contracts. When the group comes to an end, another questionnaire is often used to assess the members' progress.

This list will give you some idea of the scope of topics for structured groups:

- managing stress
- assertion training
- eating disorders (bulimia and anorexia)
- women in transition
- dealing with an alcoholic parent
- learning coping skills
- managing relationships and ending relationships
- overcoming perfectionism
- support for incest victims

Part Three of this book provides a variety of examples of short-term structured groups. At this time you might skim the passages dealing with a structured group for repeat dieters, in Chapter 11; a group for women with a history of incest, in Chapter 11; groups for children of divorce, conducted in elementary schools, in Chapter 9; and a high school program for children of alcoholics, in Chapter 10.

A MULTICULTURAL PERSPECTIVE ON GROUP WORK

Effective delivery of group-counseling services must take into account the impact of the client's culture. Culture is, quite simply, the values and behavior shared by a group of people. Culture is not just an ethnic or racial heritage but also can refer to age, gender, sexual orientation, or socioeconomic status. Cultural diversity is a fact of life in our contemporary world. As a group practitioner, you cannot afford to ignore the issue of culture, for culture will influence both the clients' behavior and yours, with or without your awareness. As an integral part of your training program, you need to develop an increased awareness of your own cultural values and personal assumptions so you can work sensitively with clients who have many social differences.

Writers in the field often assert that many counseling approaches fail to meet the complex needs of various ethnic and minority clients because of narrow, stereotyped perceptions of those needs. Asian Americans, African Americans, Latinos, Native Americans, and members of other minority groups terminate counseling significantly earlier than do Euro-American clients. This dropout rate is often caused by barriers such as language difficulties and culture-bound values that hinder the formation of a good counseling relationship (Pedersen, 1994; D. W. Sue, 1990). Regardless of your ethnic, cultural, and racial background, if you hope to build bridges of understanding between yourself and group members who are different from you, it is essential for you to guard against rigid and stereotyped generalizations about social or cultural groups. In short, you need to acquire a multicultural perspective in your practice.

Pedersen (1990) views multiculturalism as the "fourth force" in the counseling field, along with the psychodynamic, behavioral, and humanistic perspectives. He believes it to be the most important new idea to shape the profession in 20 years. Some of the basic assumptions Pedersen (1989, 1990, 1994) makes about multiculturalism have a significant impact on techniques in group work:

- Culture is best defined broadly rather than narrowly so that demographic variables (age, gender, and residence), status variables (social, educational, and economic), and affiliations (formal and informal) are considered as potentially salient cultural features.
- The multicultural perspective is relevant to all aspects of counseling practice rather than being limited to exotic populations and special-interest groups.
- Multiculturalism needs to be understood as a continuous theme in all fields of counseling rather than as an attempt to develop a new and separate field of study.
- Multiculturalism can be the basis for people to disagree without one person being "right"and the other being "wrong."

If you intend to be involved in group work with culturally diverse populations, as most populations are, you must be willing to modify your strategies to meet the unique needs of the members. It is clear that no one "right" technique can be utilized across the board with all clients, irrespective of their cultural background. D. W. Sue (1990) contends that there is a need to develop culture-specific strategies for diverse populations.

There are advantages and limitations when using group formats with culturally diverse client populations. On the plus side, members can gain much from the power and strength of collective group feedback. They can be supportive of one another in patterns that are familiar. As members see their peers challenging themselves and making desired changes in their lives, it gives them hope that change is possible for them. You can adapt the structure and process of your group to fit the cultural context of the group's members, but there are also some cautions to note. Some individuals may be reluctant to readily disclose personal material or to share family conflicts. They may see it as shameful even to have personal problems and all the more shameful to talk about them in front of strangers. People from some cultures rely on members of the extended family for help rather than seeking professional assistance. Some individuals may not feel comfortable in a group or even be willing to be part of a counseling group. Some may be hesitant to join a group because of their unfamiliarity with how groups work, or what is expected in a group may clash with their cultural values. Even though groups are a powerful intervention, they are not for everyone.

Working with culturally diverse client populations requires that group workers possess the awareness, knowledge, and skills to effectively deal with the concerns these clients bring to a group. These skills are dealt with in Chapter 3. You must find ways to avoid getting trapped in provincialism, and you need to challenge the degree to which you may be culturally encapsulated (see Wrenn, 1985). Although it is unrealistic to expect you to have an in-depth knowledge of all cultural backgrounds, it is feasible for you to have a comprehensive grasp of the general principles for working successfully amid cultural diversity. This would be a good time to take an inventory of your current level of awareness, knowledge, and skills that have a bearing on your ability to function effectively in multicultural situations. Reflect on the following questions:

- Are you familiar with how your own culture influences the way you think, feel, and act?
- How prepared are you to understand and work with clients of different cultural backgrounds?
- Is your academic program providing the awareness, knowledge, and skills you'll need to work in groups with diverse client populations?
- To what degree are you now able to accurately compare your own cultural perspective with that of a person from another culture?
- What kinds of life experiences have you had that will better enable you to understand and counsel people who have a different worldview?
- Can you identify any areas of cultural bias that could inhibit your ability to work effectively with people who are different from you? If so, what steps might you take to challenge your biases?

You will need to know much more about diversity issues if you hope to become an effective multicultural group counselor. Our purpose here is to underscore the importance of acquiring multicultural competence. We recommend the following sources for educating yourself about these issues: Alonso and Rutan (1988); Atkinson, Morten, and Sue (1993); Johnson, Santos Torres, Coleman, and Smith (1995); Merta (1995); Pedersen (1990, 1994); Pedersen, Draguns, Lonner, and Trimble (1989); D. Sue and D. W. Sue (1993); D. W. Sue (1990, 1992); D. W. Sue and D. Sue (1990); Sue, Ivey, and Pedersen (1996); and Yu and Gregg (1993).

We strongly suggest that you now complete the *Multicultural Awareness, Knowledge, and Skills Survey* at the end of this chapter. After you score this inventory, look over any items you would like to be able to answer differently. When you finish this book toward the end of the course, we encourage you to take time to complete this inventory a second time and compare your results with your initial assessment. Doing this will allow you to determine whether any of your attitudes or beliefs have changed and whether you have acquired new knowledge and skills in multicultural counseling.

WHERE TO GO FROM HERE

We recommend that you take the time to scan the rest of this book to become familiar with the general terrain of group process. As you review the material, do what you can to relate your past experience to the topics. Before you carefully read this book, reflect on your present attitudes, beliefs, and feelings about groups. Have you had any experience in groups either as a member or as a facilitator? If so, what have these experiences been like? How are you approaching this book? And how are you approaching this group course? Your ability to function effectively as a group counselor has a lot to do with your beliefs pertaining to groups. If you believe in the therapeutic power and potential of groups, and if you are willing to commit yourself to the disciplined work it takes to learn about groups, you are already taking significant steps toward becoming a competent group leader. If you are suspicious about groups, and if you approach this course with a great deal of hesitation, we challenge you to talk about your reservations and concerns, either in the class, if this is appropriate, or with your instructor privately. You'll get much more from reading this book and taking a group course or group workshop if you commit yourself to being active, involved, and open to learning about the group process. This is an excellent time to challenge any misconceptions you may have about groups and identify what you need to do to become a productive member of a group. The steps you take now will help you become a vital and creative group leader.

EXERCISES

There are exercises at the end of the chapters in Parts One and Two. These exercises can be done on your own or in class in small groups. The goal is to provide you with an opportunity to experience techniques, issues, group processes, and potential problems that can occur at the various stages of a group's development. We suggest that you read the exercises at the end of each chapter and focus on those most meaningful to you.

In this chapter we stressed the importance of group leaders adopting a multicultural perspective. This implies that practitioners possess certain awareness, knowledge, and skills that will enable them to use group interventions appropriate to the members' backgrounds. We also discussed multicultural counseling competencies relevant for group work with diverse client populations. (See Sue, Arredondo, and McDavis, 1992, and Arredondo and Toporek, 1996; Chapter 3 deals with these multicultural counseling competencies in more detail.)

What follows is the *Multicultural Awareness, Knowledge, and Skills Survey* (MAKSS), which is a 60-item survey designed by Michael D'Andrea, Judy Daniels, and Ronald Heck, all from the University of Hawaii. Respond to all 60 items on the scale, even if you are not working with clients or actively conducting groups. Base your response on what you think at this time. Try to assess yourself as honestly as possible rather than answering in the way you think would be desirable.

Once you've finished the self-assessment inventory, look at the scoring instructions that follow and tally your scores. If possible, bring the results to a small group in class for exploration. Look at specific items you rated as "very limited" and use them to identify areas that need strengthening. The aim of this survey is to assess where you are now with respect to multicultural awareness, knowledge, and skills. Reading in the area of multicultural counseling is one way to begin increasing your ability to work in multicultural situations.

THE MULTICULTURAL AWARENESS, KNOWLEDGE, AND SKILLS SURVEY (MAKSS)*

1. Culture is not external but is within the person.

    Strongly disagree   Disagree   Agree   Strongly agree

2. One of the potential negative consequences about gaining information concerning specific cultures is that students might stereotype members of those cultural groups according to the information they have gained.

    Strongly disagree   Disagree   Agree   Strongly agree

*Developed by Michael D'Andrea, Ed.D., Judy Daniels, Ed.D., and Ronald Heck, Ph.D., Department of Counselor Education, University of Hawaii, Manoa, 1776 University Ave., WA2-222 Honolulu, Hawaii 96822; (808) 956-7904. Used by permission.

3. At this time in your life, how would you rate yourself in terms of understanding how your cultural background has influenced the way you think and act?

Very limited   Limited   Fairly aware   Very aware

4. At this point in your life, how would you rate your understanding of the impact of the way you think and act when interacting with persons of different cultural backgrounds?

Very limited   Limited   Fairly aware   Very aware

5. How would you react to the following statement? While counseling enshrines the concepts of freedom, rational thought, tolerance of new ideas, and equality, it has frequently become a form of oppression to subjugate large groups of people.

Strongly disagree   Disagree   Agree   Strongly agree

6. In general, how would you rate your level of awareness regarding different cultural institutions and systems?

Very limited   Limited   Fairly aware   Very aware

7. The human service professions, especially counseling and clinical psychology, have failed to meet the mental health needs of ethnic minorities.

Strongly disagree   Disagree   Agree   Strongly agree

8. At the present time, how would you generally rate yourself in terms of being able to accurately compare your own cultural perspective with that of a person from another culture?

Very limited   Limited   Good   Very good

9. How well do you think you could distinguish "intentional" from "accidental" communication signals in a multicultural counseling situation?

Very limited   Limited   Good   Very good

10. Ambiguity and stress often result from multicultural situations because people are not sure what to expect from each other.

Strongly disagree   Disagree   Agree   Strongly agree

11. The effectiveness and legitimacy of the counseling profession would be enhanced if counselors consciously supported universal definitions of normality.

Strongly disagree   Disagree   Agree   Strongly agree

12. The criteria of self-awareness, self-fulfillment, and self-discovery are important measures in most counseling sessions.

Strongly disagree   Disagree   Agree   Strongly agree

13. Even in multicultural counseling situations, basic implicit concepts, such as "fairness" and "health," are not difficult to understand.

Strongly disagree   Disagree   Agree   Strongly agree

14. Promoting a client's sense of psychological independence is usually a safe goal to strive for in most counseling situations.

Strongly disagree   Disagree   Agree   Strongly agree

15. While a person's natural support system (i.e., family, friends, etc.) plays an important role during a period of personal crisis, formal counseling services tend to result in more constructive outcomes.

Strongly disagree   Disagree   Agree   Strongly agree

16. How would you react to the following statement? In general, counseling services should be directed toward assisting clients to adjust to stressful environmental situations.

Strongly disagree   Disagree   Agree   Strongly agree

17. Counselors need to change not just the content of what they think, but also the way they handle this content if they are to accurately account for the complexity in human behavior.

Strongly disagree   Disagree   Agree   Strongly agree

18. Psychological problems vary with the culture of the client.

Strongly disagree   Disagree   Agree   Strongly agree

19. How would you rate your understanding of the concept of "relativity" in terms of the goals, objectives, and methods of counseling culturally different clients?

Very limited   Limited   Good   Very good

20. There are some basic counseling skills that are applicable to create successful outcomes regardless of the client's cultural background.

Strongly disagree   Disagree   Agree   Strongly agree

At the present time, how would you rate your own understanding of the following terms:

21. Culture

Very limited   Limited   Good   Very good

22. Ethnicity

Very limited   Limited   Good   Very good

23. Racism

   Very limited   Limited   Good   Very good

24. Mainstreaming

   Very limited   Limited   Good   Very good

25. Prejudice

   Very limited   Limited   Good   Very good

26. Multicultural Counseling

   Very limited   Limited   Good   Very good

27. Ethnocentrism

   Very limited   Limited   Good   Very good

28. Pluralism

   Very limited   Limited   Good   Very good

29. Contact Hypothesis

   Very limited   Limited   Good   Very good

30. Attribution

   Very limited   Limited   Good   Very good

31. Transcultural

   Very limited   Limited   Good   Very good

32. Cultural Encapsulation

   Very limited   Limited   Good   Very good

33. What do you think of the following statements? Witch doctors and psychiatrists use similar techniques.

   Strongly disagree   Disagree   Agree   Strongly agree

34. Differential treatment in the provision of mental health services is not necessarily thought to be discriminatory.

   Strongly disagree   Disagree   Agree   Strongly agree

35. In the early grades of formal schooling in the United States, the academic achievement of such ethnic minorities as African Americans, Hispanics, and Native Americans is close to parity with the achievement of White mainstream students.

   Strongly disagree   Disagree   Agree   Strongly agree

36. Research indicates that in the early elementary school grades girls and boys achieve about equally in mathematics and science.

Strongly disagree   Disagree   Agree   Strongly agree

37. Most of the immigrant and ethnic groups in Europe, Australia, and Canada face problems similar to those experienced by ethnic groups in the United States.

Strongly disagree   Disagree   Agree   Strongly agree

38. In counseling, clients from different ethnic/cultural backgrounds should be given the same treatment that White mainstream clients receive.

Strongly disagree   Disagree   Agree   Strongly agree

39. The difficulty with the concept of "integration" is its implicit bias in favor of the dominant culture.

Strongly disagree   Disagree   Agree   Strongly agree

40. Racial and ethnic persons are underrepresented in clinical and counseling psychology.

Strongly disagree   Disagree   Agree   Strongly agree

41. How would you rate your ability to conduct an effective counseling interview with a person from a cultural background significantly different from your own?

Very limited   Limited   Good   Very good

42. How would you rate your ability to effectively assess the mental health needs of a person from a cultural background significantly different from your own?

Very limited   Limited   Good   Very good

43. How well would you rate your ability to distinguish "formal" and "informal" counseling strategies?

Very limited   Limited   Good   Very good

44. In general, how would you rate yourself in terms of being able to effectively deal with biases, discrimination, and prejudices directed at you by a client in a counseling setting?

Very limited   Limited   Good   Very good

45. How well would you rate your ability to accurately identify culturally biased assumptions as they relate to your professional training?

Very limited   Limited   Good   Very good

46. How well would you rate your ability to discuss the role of "method" and "context" as they relate to the process of counseling?

    Very limited   Limited   Good   Very good

47. In general, how would you rate your ability to accurately articulate a client's problem who comes from a cultural group significantly different from your own?

    Very limited   Limited   Good   Very good

48. How well would you rate your ability to analyze a culture into its component parts?

    Very limited   Limited   Good   Very good

49. How would you rate your ability to identify the strengths and weaknesses of psychological tests in terms of their use with persons from different cultural/racial/ethnic backgrounds?

    Very limited   Limited   Good   Very good

50. How would you rate your ability to critique multicultural research?

    Very limited   Limited   Good   Very good

51. In general, how would you rate your skill level in terms of being able to provide appropriate counseling services to culturally different clients?

    Very limited   Limited   Good   Very good

52. How would you rate your ability to effectively consult with another mental health professional concerning the mental health needs of a client whose cultural background is significantly different from your own?

    Very limited   Limited   Good   Very good

53. How would you rate your ability to effectively secure information and resources to better serve culturally different clients?

    Very limited   Limited   Good   Very good

54. How would you rate your ability to accurately assess the mental health needs of women?

    Very limited   Limited   Good   Very good

55. How would you rate your ability to accurately assess the mental health needs of men?

    Very limited   Limited   Good   Very good

56. How well would you rate your ability to accurately assess the mental health needs of older adults?

Very limited   Limited   Good   Very good

57. How well would you rate your ability to accurately assess the mental health needs of gay men?

Very limited   Limited   Good   Very good

58. How well would you rate your ability to accurately assess the mental health needs of gay women?

Very limited   Limited   Good   Very good

59. How well would you rate your ability to accurately assess the mental health needs of handicapped persons?

Very limited   Limited   Good   Very good

60. How well would you rate your ability to accurately assess the mental health needs of persons who come from very poor socioeconomic backgrounds?

Very limited   Limited   Good   Very good

SCORING INSTRUCTIONS FOR THE MULTICULTURAL AWARENESS, KNOWLEDGE, AND SKILLS SURVEY (MAKSS)

The MAKSS is designed to measure an individual's multicultural counseling awareness, knowledge, and skills. This 60-item survey is divided into three (3) subscales. Items 1 to 20 provide a measure of multicultural counseling awareness; items 21 to 40 provide a measure of multicultural counseling knowledge; items 41 to 60 provide a measure of multicultural counseling skills.

Subjects who complete the survey are provided with four options in responding to each item. These options are ranked on a Likert-type scale from 1 to 4. A score of 1 indicates "very limited" or "strongly disagree," a score of 2 indicates "limited" or "disagree," a score of 3 is "good" or "agree," and a score of 4 corresponds to "very good" or "strongly agree."

Please note, there are five (5) items in which we have reversed this scoring procedure. That is, on items 11 to 16 and item 38, a score of 4 is given if the subject circled "very limited" or "strongly disagree," a score of 3 is given if the subject circled "limited" or "disagree," a score of 2 is given if the subject circled "good" or "agree," and a score of 1 is given if the subject circled "very good" or "strongly agree." These items should be reverse coded when entered into a computer to be consistent with the other items in the subscale (e.g., 4 is coded 1 for these items only).

To calculate the total subscale scores, individual item scores comprising each subscale are summed (items 1 to 20 = awareness; items 21 to 40 = knowledge; items 41 to 60 = skills), and the sum is divided by 20 (the number of items in each subscale) to generate three mean subscale scores.

You may find a published report of the initial validity and reliability findings and an explanation of statistical procedures in comparing the pre- and posttest results in experimental/control group studies in D'Andrea, Daniels, and Heck (1991).

CHAPTER 2

ETHICAL AND LEGAL ISSUES IN GROUP COUNSELING

FOCUS QUESTIONS

Introduction

Ethical Issues in Group Membership
Involuntary Membership
Informed Consent
Freedom to Withdraw from a Group
Psychological Risks for Members

Confidentiality

Uses and Abuses of Group Techniques

The Role of the Leader's Values in the Group

Multicultural Awareness in Group Practice

Ethical and Legal Standards
Legal Liability and Malpractice
Legal Safeguards for Group Practitioners

Summary of Ethical Principles for Group Leaders

Where to Go from Here

Exercises

**Ethical Guidelines for Group Counselors:
ASGW 1989 Revision**

FOCUS QUESTIONS

1. What things will an ethical group leader be sure to tell prospective members about a group? How can informed consent best be secured from members?

2. What measures might you take as a leader to ensure confidentiality in your group? How might you deal with a situation in which one member broke confidentiality?

3. Under what circumstances would you feel compelled to breach confidentiality of a member in a counseling group? How would you handle this situation?

4. If you were working with a group composed of involuntary members, what, if anything, might you do differently from working with a voluntary group?

5. If you were conducting a time-limited, closed group, how might you deal with a member who wanted to withdraw from the group?

6. What psychological risks are associated with group membership? How can these risks be minimized?

7. What is your thinking about the appropriate place for using techniques in a group?

8. What is one value you hold that is likely to influence the manner in which you work with individual members? How might some of your values either help or hinder you in gaining the trust of members?

9. What legal issues might you consider in setting up a group? Can you think of some legal safeguards to help you avoid a malpractice suit?

10. Review the ASGW's (1989) *Ethical Guidelines for Group Counselors* reproduced at the end of this chapter. What are your thoughts about the value of these guidelines for a group practitioner?

INTRODUCTION

For those who are preparing to become group leaders, a thorough grounding in ethical issues is as essential as a solid base of psychological knowledge and skills. Our aim in this chapter is to highlight the ethical issues of central significance to group workers. Professionals and student/trainees must be thoroughly familiar with the ethical standards of their professional specialization. They must also learn to make ethical decisions, a process that can be taught both in group courses and in supervised practicum experiences.

It is our position that group leaders must eventually learn how to apply established ethical codes to a range of dilemmas they will face as group practitioners. Absolute freedom should certainly not be the rule, nor is "going on intuition" an appropriate path to follow. As a practitioner, you will ultimately have to apply the ethical codes of your profession to the many practical problems you will face. You will not be able to rely on ready-made answers or prescriptions given by professional organizations, which typically provide only broad guidelines for responsible practice

Group work practitioners have become more aware of the ethical, professional, and legal issues relevant to group work in recent years. And malpractice awards to clients who were treated unprofessionally and irresponsibly have increased the anxiety level of many mental-health professionals. When groups reached their zenith in the 1960s and the 1970s, there were some excesses in the name of "experimentation." Practitioners who became aware of ethically questionable practices are now attempting to improve the reputation of groups by designing ethical and legal standards.

Becoming an ethical group practitioner involves more than merely avoiding breaking laws or ethical codes. It demands a high level of consciousness by the group leader, both personally and professionally. We assume that the group leader's personal life is a key determinant of how well he or she will function in the role of group facilitator. Rather than focusing on blatant forms of unethical behavior, such as sexual misconduct, incompetence, negligence, and malpractice, we agree with Kottler (1994a), who recommends that all group practitioners focus on their own subtle unethical behaviors. For example, because of the power group counselors possess, it is possible to use this power to stifle group members instead of empowering them. Being aware of your personal biases is the first step toward guarding against unethical practices in your own group work.

Although groups have unique therapeutic power that can be used to empower clients in their life-changing journeys, groups also have the potential to do harm to participants. The group leader's skill, style, personal characteristics, and competence in group work are crucial dimensions that contribute to the quality of the outcomes of a group. Groups designed around ethically and legally sound principles have a far greater chance of being effective than groups designed without such thought and facilitated inadequately.

Your practice should be guided by established principles that have clear implications for group work. The *ethical codes* discussed in this chapter constitute the rules professional members must adhere to in their practices. If you are a member of a professional organization and you don't follow the ethical codes, you can be expelled from the organization and you could also lose your license. Furthermore, you are vulnerable to a malpractice suit, since courts take into account the standard of care that is reflected in the ethical codes. *Ethical guidelines* have a different purpose. They provide practitioners with suggestions aimed at increasing ethical and professional behavior as a group leader.

In this chapter we have drawn heavily on the *Ethical Guidelines for Group Counselors* (Association for Specialists in Group Work [ASGW], 1989) as a general framework for exploring a host of ethical issues. The guidelines are reproduced at the end of this chapter, and we recommend you refer to them frequently. In addition to these guidelines specifically for group work, it is essential that practitioners know and abide by the ethical codes of their respective professions. The following ethical codes are relevant for group practitioners: *Code of Ethics and Standards of Practice* (American Counseling Association [ACA], 1995), *Ethical Principles of Psychologists and Code of Conduct* (American Psychological Association [APA], 1992), *Code of Ethics* (American Association for Marriage and Family Therapy [AAMFT], 1991), and *Code of Ethics* (National Association of Social Workers [NASW], 1990).

Gumaer and Forrest (1995) identify three steps group counselors can take to assure ethical and legal practice:

- obtain knowledge of the ethical codes,
- pursue critical thinking regarding ethical situations in groups and arrive at thoughtful decisions based on professional standards of practice, and
- demonstrate an interest in ethical group practice through supervision and striving for competence.

Part of the ethical decision-making process involves learning about the available resources you can draw on when you are struggling with an ethical question. Although you are ultimately responsible for making ethical decisions, you do not have to do so in a vacuum. You should also be aware of the consequences of practicing in ways that are not sanctioned by organizations in which you are a member or by the state in which you are licensed to practice.

There will be times when you need to make sound decisions that are not simple and clear. Functioning within the broad guidelines of established ethical codes is a beginning, but you will have to base your practice on sound, informed, and responsible judgment. To do this, experience in leading groups is essential, yet it alone is not enough. You can learn much by consulting with colleagues, by getting continued supervision and training during the early stages of your development as a leader, by keeping up with recent trends, and by attending relevant conventions and workshops.

Some beginning group leaders burden themselves with the expectation that they should always know the "right" thing to do for every possible situation. In contrast, we expect that you will gradually refine your position on the issues we raise in this chapter, a process that demands a willingness to remain open and to adopt a questioning yet responsible attitude. We do not think these issues can be resolved once and for all; these complex issues take on new dimensions as you gain experience as a group leader.

We decided to place this chapter early in the book because the guidelines we discuss here pertain to all phases of a group's development as well as to each special group population. In the chapters that follow, we will return to some of these guidelines and explore ethical issues that pertain to a particular period in a group's history or to conducting specific types of groups.

ETHICAL ISSUES IN GROUP MEMBERSHIP

INVOLUNTARY MEMBERSHIP

Voluntary participation is an important beginning point for a successful group experience. Members will make significant changes only to the extent that they actively seek something for themselves. Unfortunately, groups are not always composed of clients who have chosen to be there. In some mental-health facilities, the main therapeutic vehicle is group therapy. People from all wards may be required to attend these sessions, sometimes several times a week. This situation is somewhat akin to compulsory education—people can be forced to attend but not to learn.

For those group leaders who work in institutions in which the policy is to require group treatment, the members should at least be given the opportunity to ventilate their feelings about this requirement. Members may be reluctant to become involved because of misinformation or stereotyped views about the nature of therapy. They may not trust the group leaders or the process involved. They may think that group therapy is a form of indoctrination. Perhaps they view themselves as healthy and the other members of the group as ill. Most likely, many of them are frightened and have reservations about opening themselves up to others. They are likely to be very concerned about others' gossiping or maliciously using information against them. Perceptive leaders will deal with these issues openly. And although the group leaders may not be able to give the members the option of dropping out of the group, they can provide the support necessary to enable the members to fully come to grips with their fears and resistances without turning the group into a mere gripe session. The group members can also be given the freedom to decide how to use the session time. Group leaders can reassure members that it is up to them to decide what personal topics they will discuss and what areas they will keep private. In other words, they should be clearly informed that they have the same rights as the members of any group, with the exception of the right not to attend.

It is crucial that leaders do not start out with the assumption that a mandatory group will automatically be composed of unmotivated clients, for this belief is bound to have a negative effect on the members. Instead, any initial resistance must be treated with respect as this can be the very material for exploration that leads to increased trust.

INFORMED CONSENT

In general, participation in groups is voluntary in that people are not forced either to join a group or, once they are in the group, to participate in activities if they choose not to. As we have explained, however, this is not always the case. Providing adequate information to prospective group members so they are able to make informed choices about their participation is essential for both voluntary and involuntary groups. Especially when group participation is mandatory, much effort needs to be directed toward clearly and fully informing members of the nature and goals of the group, procedures that will be used, the rights of members to decline certain activities, the limitations of confidentiality, and how active participation in the group may have an effect on them personally. For example, in a state mental hospital in which we served as consultants, groups were the basic form of treatment for "those incompetent to stand trial" and for "mentally disordered sex offenders." Further, patients' release from the institution depended in part on their cooperation in treatment and rehabilitation, which included participation in regular group-therapy sessions. In cases such as these, getting the *informed consent* of members implies that leaders explore with the members during a screening or orientation session what the group process consists of and that they are careful to ascertain whether the members understand what may be involved. It would also be essential to inform sex offenders who were required to have group treatment about the consequences of noncompliance. For example, reporting a client's unwillingness to participate in a group program could result in revocation proceedings and eventual imprisonment. It is the therapist's responsibility to report noncompliance, because failure to do so misleads the courts and corrections authorities and may constitute a danger to the public (Aubrey & Dougher, 1990).

Informed consent involves leaders' making members aware of their rights (as well as their responsibilities) as group participants. Thus, in mandatory groups or in required groups that emphasize self-disclosure and personal involvement, leaders are advised to take special care in discussing what the members have a right to expect.

FREEDOM TO WITHDRAW FROM A GROUP

Once members make a commitment to be part of a time-limited and closed group, do they have the right to leave the group at any time they choose? The ASGW's (1989) position on this issue is that provisions are made to assist a group member to terminate in an effective way. Procedures for leaving a group are explained to all members during the initial group session. Ideally, both the leader and the member work in a cooperative fashion to determine whether a group experience is productive or counterproductive for each individual. Although members have the right to leave a group, it is important that they inform both the group leader and the members before making their final decision. It is a good policy for a leader to discuss the possible risks involved in leaving the group prematurely. Before leaving a group, members should generally discuss their reasons for wanting to stop attending. It is essential that the group leader intervene if other members use undue pressure to force any member to remain in the group. Adequate preparation and screening often reduce the risks of members leaving a group prematurely. However, when all is said and done, members ultimately have a right to quit.

We are not in favor of forcing members to remain in a group regardless of the circumstances, but neither do we emphasize to prospective members that they have the freedom to leave whenever they choose. Instead, during the individual screening interview and the orientation session, we take great care to inform prospective members about the nature of the group. In time-limited, closed groups we also stress to participants the importance of a careful commitment to carrying out their responsibilities.

If a person leaves without this careful consideration and explanation, the consequences could be negative to the members remaining as well as to the departing member. Some members may feel burdened with guilt and may blame themselves for saying or doing "the wrong thing" and contributing to an individual's decision to quit. And the person who leaves may have unexpressed and unresolved feelings that could have been worked through with some discussion. With a commitment to discuss the factors related to leaving, there is an opportunity for everyone concerned to express and explore unfinished business.

PSYCHOLOGICAL RISKS FOR MEMBERS

The forces at work in a therapeutic group are powerful ones. They can be constructive, bringing about positive change, but their unleashing always entails some risk. The *Ethical Guidelines for Group Counselors* (ASGW, 1989) specify that leaders have the responsibility to discuss some of the possible risks of participating in groups. It cannot be assumed that participants are aware of these risks. The guideline is: "Group counselors explore with group members the risks of potential life changes that may occur because of the group experience and help members explore their readiness to face these possibilities" (1.e.).* It is imperative that leaders consider ways of reducing these risks. Members of a group may be subjected to scapegoating, group pressure, breaches of confidence, inappropriate reassurance, and hostile confrontation. The group process may

*Citations refer to the ASGW guidelines, which appear at the end of Chapter 2.

even precipitate a crisis in a member's life. A person may enter a group feeling relatively comfortable and leave feeling vulnerable and defenseless. Areas of personal conflict may be exposed for the first time, causing much pain and leading to a new self-awareness that is difficult to cope with. A person's outside life may be drastically affected, for family members may have adverse reactions to changes. Participants may be left, at the conclusion of a group, in no better condition than when they began the group; they may even feel less equipped than ever to cope with the demands of daily life.

These risks should be discussed with the participants during the initial session, and the leader should examine with them how these dangers can be avoided. For example, a leader of a group for women who have been victims of incest might say: "As you begin to uncover painful memories of your childhood and the abuse that took place, you may feel more depressed and anxious for a time than before you entered this group. It is very important to talk about these feelings in the group, especially if you have thoughts about quitting." Group leaders should also help members explore the concerns they have about transferring what they are learning in the group to their everyday lives. Some groups—short-term intensive workshops, in particular—may arouse strong, previously hidden feelings, and it is important that people be given the means of understanding, or even resolving, the issues behind these feelings. Participants sometimes leave a group with conflicting feelings, wanting to continue with individual or group counseling yet afraid of going further. In a follow-up session these members can get the support they need to examine their ambivalence and decide what to do.

Sometimes, rather than being unaware of the concerns of participating in a group, members invent concerns of their own and are very fearful. For example, some members believe that if they allow themselves to feel their pain, they'll go crazy or sink into a depression so deep they won't be able to climb out of it. Some are convinced that if they give up their self-control, they won't be able to function. Others are frightened of letting others know them, because they think they'll be rejected. There are those who are reluctant to experience their anger, because they fear physically hurting another. Such fears should be explored early, so members can determine how realistic they are and try to put some of them to rest.

Not only do certain risks need to be identified and dealt with in the group, but safeguards against these risks also need to be established. The leader should stress that group members have the right to decide for themselves what to explore and how far to go. Counselors must be alert to group pressure and block any attempts by members to get others to do something they choose not to do.

Group members can be invited or asked, rather than ordered, to participate in certain exercises or techniques. Members should be reassured that they have the option of declining to participate in group activities they find extremely threatening. Direct expression of aggression in an exercise could result in another person's being physically hurt. Therefore, we ask members to release feelings of anger in a symbolic way. Symbolic actions, such as beating a pillow, can have therapeutic value. It is essential that group leaders learn how to cope effectively with whatever may arise as the result of an exercise. It may be easy to provoke someone into experiencing rage, but it is another matter to know what to do when this person relaxes long-standing controls.

After an intense group experience, participants may make rash decisions that affect not only their own lives but also the lives of members of their families. What the individual may see as the result of newfound spontaneity or decisiveness may be due merely to a burst of energy generated by the group. For example, a woman who has been married for 20 years and who becomes aware of her extreme alienation from her husband may leave the group with a resolve to get a divorce. The counselor should caution her of the danger of making decisions too soon after an intense group session. If this woman has changed in the group, she may be able to relate to her husband differently; if she acts too soon, she may not give this behavioral change a chance to happen. It is not the leader's responsibility to stand in the way of members' decisions, but the leader is responsible for warning members against acting on a "group high." It is also a good practice to caution members who have done significant cathartic work, such as role playing, to refrain from leaving a session and saying in person everything they may have symbolically said to a significant other in a therapeutic context. Members sometimes burden themselves with the notion that they are expected to unload everything they experienced in a therapeutic session. We caution them to be selective in what they express to other people in real-life situations. If members hope to enhance their relationships with those they love, they cannot afford to bombard them with the "psychological venom" that they may have released in a symbolic sense in the group. The group counselor can assist them in determining what they most want to communicate and also in finding ways to express their thoughts and feelings in a manner that shows concern and is most likely to lead to a successful encounter.

At this point we will summarize some of the other possible risks in therapeutic groups. Later in the book we will expand our treatment of the issue by developing guidelines for making participants aware of risks and for preparing the members in a way that will reduce the chances of their having a negative experience.

1. Self-disclosure is sometimes misused by group members. This issue will be dealt with at greater length in a later chapter, but we do want to mention that action needs to follow self-disclosure. The group ethic has sometimes been misunderstood to mean the more disclosure that takes place, the better. Privacy can be violated by indiscriminate sharing of one's personal life. Self-disclosure is an essential aspect of any working group, but it is a means to the end of fuller self-understanding and should not be glorified in its own right, at the expense of follow-through.

2.   Some of the disclosures made during a session may not remain in the group. Leaders need to continually stress confidentiality in any group, but even when they do so, the possibility remains that members will talk about what they've heard in the group.

3.   Scapegoating may occur in a group, particularly if leaders do not intervene when they see members "ganging up" on one particular individual. When confrontation occurs, we find it useful to ask the member doing the confronting to state what reactions he or she is having to the person being confronted. This usually stops the member from merely throwing judgmental labels at another.

4.   The danger of inadequate leadership is a by-product of the growth of the group movement. Some people attend a few weekend workshops as participants and then decide, with very little additional experience, to lead groups of their own. Because they experienced a "high," they decide that groups are the answer for any seeker of self-fulfillment. Lacking adequate training or experience, they hastily gather a group together without bothering to screen members or even prepare them for the particular group. Such leaders can do extensive damage and, in the process, cause participants to close themselves off from the possibility of seeking any type of therapy or counseling in the future.

As we've suggested, it is not realistic to expect that all personal risks can be eliminated, and to imply that they can is to mislead prospective members. What is essential is that members be made aware of the major risks, that they have an opportunity to discuss their willingness and ability to deal with them, and that as many safeguards as possible be built into the structure of the group. If members experience chronic depression, severe anxiety attacks, and periods of confusion and crisis, for example, and if they lack clarity regarding the effects of the group experience on them, they should have somewhere to turn for further professional assistance. This is true both during the course of the group and once the group has ended.

The "risks" and "terrible things" some people associate with groups are often really misconceptions about the purpose of groups. In conjunction with exploring potential risks, we make it a practice to separate facts from fantasy by discussing with members any preconceptions they may have brought with them to a group.

CONFIDENTIALITY

One of the keystone conditions for effective group work is confidentiality. It is especially important because the group leader must not only keep the confidences of members but also get the members to keep one another's confidences. *Ethical Guidelines for Group Counselors* (ASGW, 1989) specifies that "group counselors protect members by defining clearly what confidentiality means, why it is important, and the difficulties involved in enforcement"(3.).

In certain group situations confidentiality becomes especially critical and also more difficult to maintain. This situation occurs in groups in institutions, agencies, and schools where the members know and have frequent contact with one another and with one another's associates outside of the group. In an adolescent group in a high school, for example, great care must be exerted to ensure that whatever is discussed in the sessions is not taken out of the group. If some members gossip about things that happened in the group, the group process will come to a halt. People are not going to reveal facts about their personal lives unless they feel quite sure they can trust both the leader and the members to respect their confidences.

The group leader should emphasize at various stages of the group's evolution the importance of maintaining confidentiality (ASGW, 1989). This issue should be introduced during the individual screening interview, and it should be clarified at the initial group sessions. At appropriate times during the course of the group, the leader should remind the members of the need for not discussing identities or specific situations. It is a good practice for group counselors to point out that confidences can be broken by carelessness as well as by malicious gossip. If at any time any member gives indications that confidentiality is not being respected, the leader should explore this matter with the group as soon as possible. Some practitioners recommend having members sign a contract in which they agree to honor confidentiality. Paradise and Kirby (1990) think a contract reinforces the importance of confidentiality in groups and that it serves as a useful documentation when dropping a member from a group for violating confidentiality.

We do expect that members will want to talk about their group experiences with significant people in their lives. We caution them, however, about breaking others' confidences in this process. We tell them to be careful not to mention others who were in the group or to talk about what others said and did. Generally, members do not violate confidentiality when they talk about *what* they learned in group sessions. But they are likely to breach confidentiality when they talk about *how* they acquired insights or how they actually interacted in a group. For example, David becomes aware in a session that he invites women to take care of him, only to resent them for treating him like a child. He may want to say to his wife, "I realize I often resent you for the very thing I expect you to do." It is not necessary that he describe the particular exercise, involving several women in the group, that led to his insight. If David talks about these details out of context, he runs the risk that his wife may misunderstand him and that he may inappropriately reveal other members' personal work. Group leaders not only need to establish clear guidelines for maintaining confidentiality but also need to inform group members about the potential consequences of intentionally breaching confidentiality (ASGW, 1989).

Leaders may be tested by some members of the group. For instance, a counselor may tell the participants in a group in a juvenile correctional institution that whatever is discussed will remain in the group. The youths may not believe this and may in many subtle ways test the leader to discover whether in fact he or she will keep this promise. For this reason it is essential that group leaders not promise to keep within the group material they may be required to disclose. Counselors owe it to their clients to specify at the outset the limits on confidentiality, and in mandatory groups they should inform members of any reporting procedures required of them (ASGW, 1989).

A counselor working with children may be expected to disclose some information to parents if they insist on it, or a leader of a group of parolees may be required to reveal to the members' parole officer any information acquired in the group concerning certain criminal offenses. It is a good policy for leaders to let members know that they may be required to testify against them in court. In general, licensed psychologists, psychiatrists, and licensed clinical social workers are legally entitled to privileged communication. In many states, licensed professional counselors also have privileged communication. This means that these professionals cannot break the confidence of clients unless (1) in their judgment, the clients are likely to do serious harm to themselves or to others; (2) abuse of children or the elderly is suspected; (3) they are ordered by a court to provide information; or (4) the clients give specific written permission.

A particularly delicate problem is safeguarding the confidentiality of minors in groups. Parents may inquire about what their child has discussed in a group, and it is the responsibility of the group leader to inform them in advance of the importance of confidentiality. Parents can be told about the purpose of the group, and they can be given some feedback concerning their child, but care must be taken not to reveal specific things the child mentioned. One way to provide feedback to parents is through a session involving one or both parents, the child, and the group leader.

Group leaders have some general guidelines for what disclosures they are required to make. The ACA's (1995) standard of practice regarding the confidentiality requirement is:

> Counselors must keep information related to counseling services confidential unless disclosure is in the best interests of clients, is required for the welfare of others, or is required by law. When disclosure is required, only information that is essential is revealed and the client is informed of such disclosures. (SP-9)

There are some other ramifications of confidentiality that group leaders would do well to consider. Following are some guidelines concerning the issue of confidentiality:

- When working with minors or with clients who are unable to give voluntary and informed consent, it is essential that the professional exert special care to protect these persons' best interests (APA, 1992).
- When working with minors, leaders should specify the limits of confidentiality (ASGW, 1989).
- It is a wise policy to ask participants to sign a contract in which they agree not to discuss or write about what transpires in the sessions or talk about who was present.
- Although confidentiality is crucial to the success of a group, the leader can do little to guarantee that the policy of confidentiality will be respected by all members (Paradise & Kirby, 1990). Leaders can only ensure confidentiality on their part, not on the part of others in the group (ASGW, 1989).
- It is essential that group leaders become familiar with the local and state laws that will have an impact on their practice. This is especially true in cases involving child molestation, neglect or abuse of the elderly and children, or incest.

USES AND ABUSES OF GROUP TECHNIQUES

Some groups make use of nonverbal exercises to facilitate the therapeutic release of pent-up anger. In your role as a group leader, you have a responsibility to exercise caution in using techniques, especially if these methods are likely to result in the release of intense feelings. You should be prepared to intervene in cases where members attempt to act out aggression in a physical way that might harm themselves or others (ASGW, 1989). One way to deflect aggression and pent-up rage is to encourage clients to release anger on a symbolic object. It is important that you be equipped to cope with powerful feelings, including the expression of anger, that can be triggered by certain role-playing activities. As a general rule, it is not a good idea to introduce a technique that will encourage the expression of anger unless you can handle the consequences, both physical and psychological.

Those members who have held in emotions for many years, perhaps out of a fear of negative consequences if they expressed their feelings, would have their fears tragically reinforced if they were to lose control and harm themselves or someone else. We generally avoid involving the entire group in physical techniques for reasons of safety. We employ techniques that are likely to arouse strong emotions only with members with whom we have established a trusting relationship (G. Corey, M. Corey, Callanan, & Russell, 1992).

You should have a rationale for introducing nonverbal exercises, and it is critical that you use them appropriately and sensitively. It is also important to intervene if members attempt to coerce or pressure a reluctant member into participating. The participants should have an opportunity to share their reactions to the activities.

We use the following guidelines in our practice to avoid abusing techniques in a group:

- Techniques must have a therapeutic purpose and be grounded in some framework.
- Techniques are used to promote a client's further self-exploration.
- Techniques are not used to stir up emotions but to work therapeutically with emotional issues the client initiates. They can help members experience feelings that are hidden or only beginning to emerge.
- Techniques are not used to cover up the group leader's discomfort or incompetence.
- Techniques are introduced in a sensitive and timely manner.
- Techniques are used with consideration for the client's background.
- Techniques are abandoned if they prove ineffective.
- Members are given the option of whether to participate in certain techniques; they are not ordered to participate, but invited.

It is important that you use techniques you have some knowledge about, preferably those you have experienced personally or have received supervision in using. The relevant ASGW (1989) guidelines are: "Group counselors do not attempt any technique unless trained in its use or under supervision by a counselor familiar with the intervention" 10.). "Depending upon the type of intervention, group counselors have training commensurate with the potential impact of a technique" (10.b).

You need to be aware of what a technique might potentially lead to as well as be able to deal with intense emotional outcomes. For example, we have observed student leaders with a reading knowledge of guided fantasy techniques who decided to introduce them in their groups. They were surprised and unprepared to work therapeutically with the emotions released in some members. It would be unrealistic for us to expect that leaders should always know *exactly* what will result from an intervention, but they should be able to cope with unexpected outcomes.

THE ROLE OF THE LEADER'S VALUES IN THE GROUP

Your values are a fundamental part of the person you are. Thus, your values cannot help but influence how you lead a therapeutic group. You can increase your effectiveness as a leader by becoming aware of the values you hold as well as the subtle and direct ways in which you might influence the people in your groups. The ASGW's (1989) guideline on the role of the leader's values is: "Group counselors develop an awareness of their own values and needs and the potential impact they have on the interventions likely to be made"(7.).

Your function as a leader is to challenge members to discover what is right for them, not persuade them to do what you think is right. You can be of service to members by encouraging them to assess their behavior so they can determine the degree to which it is working for them. If members acknowledge that what they are doing is not enabling them to get what they want from life, then a group context is an ideal place for them to modify their attitudes and develop new ways of behaving. The group members need to clarify their own values and goals, make informed decisions, choose a course of action, and assume responsibility and accountability for the decisions they make. The ACA (1995) *Code of Ethics* is clear on the ethics of counselors imposing their values on clients: "Counselors are aware of their own values, attitudes, beliefs, and behaviors and how these apply in a diverse society, and avoid imposing values on clients" (A.5.b).

Imposing your values on clients is often not done blatantly; instead, it can be done in a subtle way, even without your conscious awareness. For instance, you may be firmly convinced that there are universal values that are good for all, such as autonomy, freedom to make one's own choice, equality in relationships, and independence. But some of your group members are likely to adhere to a different set of cultural values. The values influencing their behavior might well be interdeenence, cooperation, loyalty to family, duty and obligation to parents, and thinking of what is best for others. If you assume they would be far better off by changing their values, you are likely to do them a disservice. Although you may not directly impose your values on them, your interventions could be aimed at getting them to do what you think is best for them.

At times you may be faced with ethical issues over sharp differences between your own values and certain values of your clients. You need not always express your personal views on value-laden situations during a session, but if members ask about your views, little is gained by refusing to express them. We are particularly inclined to tell members about our values in cases where there is a conflict rather than pretending that no difference of opinion exists. Expressed values are less likely to interfere with the process in a group than are concealed values. In certain cases it might be necessary to refer clients to someone else because the conflict inhibits your objectivity.

We have heard leaders comment that they would not want to make known their personal values concerning religion, abortion, child-rearing, extramarital affairs, and other such controversial areas because of the fear of swaying members to blindly accept their values. It is our position that leaders cannot remain neutral in value-laden areas. It is also important for group leaders to be aware that extremely needy and dependent members may feel a pressure to please the leader at all costs and hence assume the leader's values automatically. This is a useful issue to explore in the sessions.

Consider for a moment the example of a man who is struggling with the decision of whether to file for divorce. He tells the group that he is not sure he is willing to risk the loneliness he fears he'll experience as a divorced man, yet he feels stuck in an unsatisfying marriage and sees little hope for things to change for the better. Surely the values you have as a leader will influence how you relate to him. Nevertheless, it is one thing to challenge him to look at all his alternatives before making his decision and to use the group to help him explore these alternatives, and quite a different matter to persuade him (or to enlist the group to give him advice) to do what you (or they) think he should do. Your own values might include staying with the marriage at all costs, or they might include divorcing if one is unhappy. The key point is that it is not your role as leader to make this man's decision for him, even if he asks you to do so.

As a group counselor, your basic function is to assist members in finding answers that are congruent with their own values. Your role is to provide a context in which members can examine their feelings and values and eventually arrive at solutions that are in their best interests (G. Corey, M. Corey, & Callanan, 1990, 1993).

MULTICULTURAL AWARENESS IN GROUP PRACTICE

The reality of cultural diversity is another area in which the group leader's values can influence the group process. If counselors do not understand how their cultural backgrounds influence their own thinking and behavior, there is little chance they can work ethically and effectively with group members who are culturally different from themselves. Understanding and respecting differences in people is included in the ACA's (1995) code of ethics:

> Counselors will actively attempt to understand the diverse cultural backgrounds of the clients with whom they work. This includes, but is not limited to, learning how the counselor's own cultural, ethnic, racial identity impacts her/his values and beliefs about the counseling process. (A.2.b)

Most of the ethical codes of the various professional organizations now give some attention to applying these principles when working with culturally diverse clients. For instance, the APA's Office of Ethnic Minority Affairs has developed *Guidelines for Providers of Psychological Services to Ethnic, Linguistic, and Culturally Diverse Populations* (APA, 1993). These principles emphasize the practitioner's responsibility to have a general understanding of the cultural values of his or her clients, so interventions are congruent with their worldviews. Even though these guidelines are not specifically designed for group counselors, they can be applied to group work. Here is a sample of some of the APA's guidelines that we modified for working with groups:

- Group counselors acknowledge that ethnicity and culture influence behavior.
- Group counselors consider the impact of adverse social, environmental, and political factors in assessing problems and designing interventions.
- Group counselors acquire the knowledge and skills necessary for effectively working with the diverse range of members in their groups. They seek consultation, supervision, and further education as ways of filling in any gaps or keeping themselves current.
- Group counselors are aware of how their own cultural backgrounds, attitudes, values, beliefs, and biases influence their work, and they make efforts to correct any prejudices they may have. In their practices, they develop sensitivity to issues of oppression, sexism, and racism.
- Group counselors respect the roles of family and community hierarchies within a client's culture.
- Group counselors respect members' religious and spiritual beliefs and values.
- Group counselors assist members in determining those instances when their difficulties stem from others' racism or bias, so they do not inappropriately personalize problems.
- Group counselors inform members about basic values that are implicit in the group process (such as self-disclosure, striving for independence and autonomy, being direct with others, and taking risks).

As group leaders, it is a good practice to inform members about certain values that are inherent in the therapeutic group process. For example, some groups operate on the following assumptions:

- risk-taking behavior is essential for growth and change;
- choosing for oneself is preferable to living by the standards of others;
- expressing emotions is healthier than repressing them;
- self-disclosure and expressing vulnerability are keys to building intimate relationships and trust in the group;
- striving for independence and autonomy is a primary goal; and
- directness in communicating what one wants and needs from others is valued.

Ethical practice implies clarifying the basic assumptions underlying the operation of the group. It is essential that the goals and processes of the group match the cultural values of the members of that group.

If you respect the members in your group, you will demonstrate a willingness to learn from them. You will be aware of hesitation on a client's part and will not be too quick to misinterpret it. It is not necessary for you to have had the same experiences as your clients; what is important is that you be open to a similar set of feelings and struggles. Attempt to enter the world of the client. Your willingness to put yourself in situations where you can learn about different cultures will be most useful. If you model genuine respect for the differences among clients in your groups, all the group members will benefit from this cultural diversity.

In their discussion of culturally diverse counseling groups, Johnson, Santos Torres, Coleman, and Smith (1995) suggest that culture greatly influences the problems members bring to a group. To develop appropriate solutions to these problems, it is essential to understand how culture influences values, decisions, and actions. Johnson and her colleagues write: "Group counselors must be willing to learn and experience that which is necessary to develop their knowledge, clarify their values, and improve their skills as cross-culturally sensitive helpers. This process begins by accepting the fact that individuals operate within a context that is influenced, in part, by their cultural background" (p. 149).

ETHICAL AND LEGAL STANDARDS

Most professional organizations affirm that practitioners should be aware of the prevailing community standards and of the possible impact on their practice of deviation from these standards. Ethical and legal issues are frequently intertwined, which makes it imperative that group practitioners not only follow the ethical codes of their profession but that they also know their state's laws and their legal boundaries and responsibilities.

Those leaders who work with groups of children, adolescents, and certain involuntary populations are especially advised to learn the laws restricting group work. Issues such as confidentiality, parental consent, informed consent, protection of member welfare, and civil rights of institutionalized patients are a few areas in which group workers must be knowledgeable. Since most group leaders do not possess detailed legal knowledge, it is a good idea to obtain some legal information concerning group procedures and practices. Awareness of legal rights and responsibilities as they pertain to group work protects not only the clients but also group leaders from needless lawsuits arising from negligence or ignorance.

In the times in which we live, it is important to be aware of the interface between legal and ethical issues in areas such as the duty to warn, the duty to protect, and controversies surrounding breaking confidentiality in cases involving individuals with contagious diseases. Consider what you might do in the following situation. A man in one of your groups has disclosed that he is HIV-positive, but he says nothing about his sexual practices with a partner or partners. At a later session he discloses that he is not monogamous and that one of his partners is unaware of his condition. Since he has been engaging in unprotected sex with this person for some time, he sees no point in either disclosing his condition or changing his sexual practices. What might you do in such a case? There are both ethical and legal issues to consider in deciding on your course of action. Furthermore, in the context of a group situation, dealing with this man is bound to be more complex than it would be in individual counseling. There are the reactions of other members to consider as well as the impact of this disclosure on the group process itself. This is an example of a dilemma where the legal parameters have yet to be defined. In its 1995 revisions of the *Code of Ethics,* the ACA added a new code dealing with contagious, fatal diseases:

> A counselor who receives information confirming that a client has a disease commonly known to be both communicable and fatal is justified in disclosing information to an identifiable third party, who by his or her relationship with the client is at a high risk of contracting the disease. Prior to making a disclosure the counselor should ascertain that the client has not already informed the third party about his or her disease and that the client is not intending to inform the third party in the immediate future. (B.1.d)

LEGAL LIABILITY AND MALPRACTICE

Group leaders who fail to exercise due care and act in good faith are liable to a civil suit. Professionals leading groups are expected to practice within the code of ethics of their particular profession and to abide by legal standards. Practitioners are subject to civil liability for not doing right or for doing wrong to another. If group members can prove that personal injury or psychological harm is due to a group leader's failure to render proper service, either through negligence or ignorance, then this leader is open to a malpractice suit. Negligence consists of departing from the "standard of care"; that is, breaching the therapist's duty in providing what is determined as commonly accepted practices of others in the profession that leads to injury to the client. In writing about the topic of legal liability for group counselors in private practice, Paradise and Kirby (1990) contend that the three most important legal issues involve confidentiality, duty to protect, and the issue of fee billing practices. Here are some of the bases for malpractice actions against mental-health professionals:

- engaging in sexual relations with a client
- breaching confidentiality inappropriately
- causing physical injuries through the use of group exercises
- striking or physically assaulting a client as a treatment technique
- malicious infliction of emotional distress
- misrepresenting one's professional training and skills
- wrongful death
- violation of civil rights
- improper diagnosis

- failure to consult
- failure to refer a client when it becomes clear that the person needs intervention beyond the worker's level of competence
- a countersuit for fee collection
- providing birth control or abortion information to a minor
- abandonment
- failing to exercise reasonable care before a client's suicide
- failing to warn and protect a potential victim of a client who has made threats

LEGAL SAFEGUARDS FOR GROUP PRACTITIONERS

The key to avoiding a malpractice suit is to maintain reasonable, ordinary, and prudent practices. Here are some guidelines for group leaders that are useful in translating the terms *reasonable, ordinary,* and *prudent* into concrete actions. Many of these suggestions are modified guidelines based on several textbooks, including: *Confronting Malpractice: Legal and Ethical Dilemmas in Psychotherapy* (Austin, Moline, & Williams, 1990); *Professional Liability and Risk Management* (Bennett, Bryant, VandenBos, & Greenwood, 1990); *Ethical and Legal Issues in Group Counseling* (Corey, Williams, & Moline, 1995); *Avoiding Conflict in Group Therapy: Ethical and Legal Issues in Group Training and Practice* (Gumaer & Forrest, 1995); *The Counselor and the Law* (Hopkins & Anderson, 1990); *Protecting Your Mental Health Practice: How to Minimize Legal and Financial Risk* (Woody, 1988); *Business Success in Mental Health Practice* (Woody, 1989); and *The Law and the Practice of Human Services* (Woody & associates, 1984). These guidelines will help you strive for professional practice.

- Take time and exercise care in screening candidates for a group experience. Many potential problems can be averted by effective screening and referral practices.
- Give the potential members of your groups enough information to make informed choices about group participation, and do not mystify the group process. Professional honesty and openness with group members will go a long way toward building a trusting climate.
- Develop written informed consent procedures at the outset of a group. Using contracts, signed by both the leader and the members, is an example of such a procedure.
- Obtain written parental consent when working with minors. This is generally a good practice, even if not required by state law.
- Develop a diagnostic profile and keep relevant notes on each group member.
- Emphasize the importance of maintaining confidentiality before the group begins and at various times in the group. However, inform

group members that confidentiality in group counseling may not be protected under the state laws of privileged communication and that it cannot be guaranteed.

- Be aware of those situations in which you legally *must* break confidentiality. If confidentiality must be violated, discuss it with the group member and obtain a written release.
- Restrict your scope of practice to client populations for which you are prepared by virtue of your education, training, and experience.
- Be aware of your state laws and professional organization ethical guidelines that limit your practice, as well as the policies of the agency for which you work. Practice within the boundaries of these laws and policies. Inform members about these policies and about legal/ethical limitations (such as exceptions to confidentiality, mandatory reporting, and the like). Courts may refer to a group leader's professional organization's code of ethics to determine liability.
- Make it a practice to consult with colleagues or clinical supervisors whenever there is a potential ethical or legal concern. Find sources of ongoing supervision.
- Have a clear rationale for the techniques you employ in group sessions. Be able to intelligently and concisely discuss the theoretical underpinnings of your procedures.
- Keep yourself informed about research findings and apply this information to increase the effectiveness of your groups.
- Have a clear standard of care that can be applied to your services, and communicate this standard to the members.
- Don't promise the members of your group anything you can't deliver. Help them realize that their degree of effort and commitment will be key factors in determining the outcomes of the group experience.
- If you work for an agency or institution, have a contract that specifies the employer's legal liability for your professional functioning.
- Abide by the policies of the institution that employs you. If you disagree with certain policies, first attempt to find out the reasons for them. Then see if it is possible to work within the framework of institutional policies. Realize that you do not always have to agree with such policies to be able to work effectively. If you have strong disagreement with policies and if they interfere with your ability to do your job, do what you can to get them changed or consider resigning.
- Avoid becoming entangled in social relationships with group members.
- Avoid engaging in sexual relationships with either current or former group members.
- Promote an atmosphere of respect for diversity within the group context.

- Make it a practice to assess the general progress of a group, and teach members how to evaluate their individual progress toward their own goals.
- Learn how to assess and intervene in cases in which group participants pose a threat to themselves or others and be sure to document this in your group record.
- Be alert to when it is appropriate to refer a group member for another form of treatment, as well as when group counseling might be inadvisable.
- Adhere to billing regulations and paperwork requirements as prescribed.
- Remain alert to the ways your personal reactions might inhibit the group process, and monitor your countertransference. Be careful of meeting your own needs at the expense of the members of your group. Avoid using the group as a place where you work through your personal problems.
- Incorporate ethical standards in your practice of group work. You might want to give the members of your groups a copy of the ASGW's *Ethical Guidelines for Group Counselors* (1989) and discuss relevant guidelines at appropriate times during the course of a group.
- Take steps to keep up with theoretical and research developments that have a direct application to group work. Update your group leadership skills. Compare your knowledge, skill, and supervised experiences in group work against the ASGW's *Professional Standards for the Training of Group Workers* (1991) found in Chapter 3.
- Carry malpractice insurance. Students are not protected against malpractice suits. (If students join the ACA, they not only receive the benefits of this professional organization but are also entitled to participate in the liability insurance program.)

Be Open to Learning   This discussion of ethical and legal issues relevant for group work is not intended to increase your anxiety level or make you so careful that you avoid taking any risks. Leading groups is a risky as well as a professionally rewarding venture. You are bound to make mistakes from time to time. Making mistakes is not necessarily fatal; what is essential is that you be willing to acknowledge the mistakes and that you learn from them. By making full use of supervision, you not only learn from what may seem like mistakes but you also minimize the chances of harming clients. It is a disservice to treat group members as though they were fragile and, thus, never challenge them. We hope you won't be frozen with anxiety over needing to be all-knowing at all times—or afraid to intervene for fear of becoming embroiled in a lawsuit. Perhaps the best way to prevent a malpractice action is by having a sincere interest in doing what is going to benefit your client. We encourage you to remain willing to ask yourself these questions throughout your professional career: *What* am I doing, and *why* am I doing it?

SUMMARY OF ETHICAL PRINCIPLES
FOR GROUP LEADERS

A mark of professional group leadership is establishing a set of guiding principles. What follows is not a rigid set of policies but, rather, guidelines that we think will help you clarify your values and encourage you to take a position on basic professional issues pertaining to your role as a group practitioner. Many of these guidelines have already been discussed in this chapter; we repeat them here as a summary checklist for the purpose of review and for quick reference as you read the remainder of this book. We have struggled with these issues in our work with groups, and these guidelines make sense to us. You will have to develop principles that are appropriate for you. Our aim in presenting these guidelines is to stimulate you to think about a framework that will guide you in making sound decisions as a leader.

1.   Make the time to reflect on your personal identity, especially as it is influenced by your professional work. Think about your needs and behavior styles and about the impact of these factors on group participants. It is essential for you to have a clear idea of what your roles and functions are in the group, so you can communicate them to the members.
2.   Have a clear idea of the type of group you are designing. Be able to express the purpose of the group and the characteristics of the clients who will be admitted.
3.   Develop a means of screening that will allow you to differentiate between suitable and unsuitable applicants.
4.   Ask potential group members who are undergoing psychotherapy to consult their therapist before becoming involved in a group.
5.   Tell prospective group members what is expected of them, and encourage them to develop a contract that will provide them with the impetus to obtain their personal goals. Tell members that they will be expected to make appropriate self-disclosures, experiment with new behaviors in the group, examine the impact of their interpersonal style on others, express their feelings and thoughts, actively listen to others and attempt to see the world through their eyes, show respect for others, offer genuine support, and try new behaviors outside of the group.
6.   Make prospective participants aware of the techniques that will be employed and of the exercises that they may be asked to participate in. Give them the ground rules that will govern group activities.
7.   Avoid undertaking a project that is beyond the scope of your training and experience. Make a written statement of your qualifications to conduct a particular group available to the participants.
8.   Make clear at the outset of a group what the focus will be. For example, some groups have an educational focus, and so a didactic approach is used. Other groups have a therapeutic focus, and these use an emotive/experiential approach.

9. Protect the members' right to decide what to share with the group and what activities to participate in. Be sensitive to any form of group pressure that violates the self-determination of an individual and to any activity, such as scapegoating or stereotyping, that unfairly undermines a person's sense of self.

10. Develop a rationale for using group exercises, and be able to verbalize it. Use only those exercises that you are competent to employ. It is best if you have experienced as a member the techniques you use.

11. Relate practice to theory, and remain open to integrating multiple approaches into your practice. Keep yourself informed about research findings on group process, and use this information to increase the effectiveness of your practice. Be thoroughly grounded in a number of diverse theoretical orientations as a basis for creating a personalized style of leading groups.

12. Be aware of the danger of meeting your needs at the expense of the members' needs.

13. Point out to members the psychological risks involved in group participation both before they enter and also when it is appropriate throughout the life of the group.

14. Emphasize the importance of confidentiality to members before they enter a group, during the group sessions when relevant, and before the group terminates.

15. When it is appropriate, be open with the group about your values, but avoid imposing them on clients. Recognize the role that the members' culture and socialization play in the formulation of their values. Respect your clients' capacity to think for themselves, and be sure that members give one another the same respect.

16. Be alert for symptoms of psychological debilitation in group members, which may indicate that participation in the group should be discontinued. Make referral resources available to people who need or desire further psychological assistance.

17. Encourage participants to discuss their experience in the group and help them evaluate the degree to which they are meeting their personal goals. Time can be set aside at the end of each session for members to express their thoughts and feelings about that session.

18. Do not expect the transfer of learning from the group to daily life to occur automatically. Assist members in applying what they are learning. Prepare them for the negative responses that they are likely to encounter when they try to transfer their group learning to their daily lives.

19. Schedule follow-up sessions so members are able to see how others in their group have done and so you have a basis for evaluating the impact on the group experience. Individual sessions may sometimes be of value for members who feel a need to confer with you after a group has ended. These sessions can help members see the group as a beginning by getting involved in further growth experiences.

20. Develop some method of evaluation to determine the effectiveness of the procedures you use. Through at least informal research efforts, you are in a better position to make informed judgments about how well your leadership style is working.

WHERE TO GO FROM HERE

This chapter has introduced some of the ethical, professional, and legal issues you may confront as a group practitioner. Ethical decision making is not a matter of seeking ready-made answers that are immune to questioning and revision. It is a never-ending process. At the end of this chapter we present the ASGW's (1989) *Ethical Guidelines for Group Counselors,* which we hope you'll refer to frequently as you work through the remaining chapters.

A professional organization we find of real value for group practitioners is the Association for Specialists in Group Work (ASGW). We encourage you to join professional organizations such as this while you are a student. The ASGW is a division of the American Counseling Association, formerly known as the Association for Counseling and Development (AADC). All ASGW members receive the *Journal for Specialists in Group Work,* a quarterly journal that publishes research, practical, and innovative articles in the field of group work. They also receive *ASGW Together,* published three times a year, which provides both regional and national information and special articles of interest to group practitioners; the monthly *Journal of Counseling and Development*; and the monthly ACA newspaper *Counseling Today.* In addition to the publications listed above, ACA and ASGW membership provides eligibility for professional liability insurance programs, legal defense services, and professional development through workshops and conventions. Each spring the national convention of ACA meets and offers a variety of preconvention workshops. The ACA has 56 state branches and 4 regional branch assemblies. Students enrolled in counseling or human services programs and who have an interest in group work are able to join ASGW and ACA at reduced rates by contacting: ACA Membership Division, 5999 Stevenson Avenue, Alexandria, Virginia 22304-3300. Telephone: (703) 823-9800 or (800) 347-6647. Fax: (703) 823-0252.

EXERCISES

1.   It comes to your attention that certain members have been gossiping about matters that came up in a high school group you're leading. Do you deal with the offenders privately or in the group? What do you say?

2. Assume that you are about to begin leading a high school counseling group and that the policy of the school is that any teacher or counselor who becomes aware that a student is using drugs is expected to report the student to the principal. How do you cope with this situation?

3. You are conducting a self-exploration group with children in a family clinic. The father of one of the children in your group meets with you to find out how his child is doing. What do you tell him? What do you not tell him? Would you be inclined to meet with the father and his child?

4. Assume that you are a private practitioner who wants to co-lead a weekend assertiveness-training workshop. How would you announce your workshop? How would you screen potential members? Whom might you exclude from your workshop, and why?

5. You are employed as a counselor in the adolescent ward of a county mental hospital. As one of your duties you lead a group for the young people, who are required to attend the sessions. You sense resistance on the part of the members. What are the ethical problems involved? How do you deal with the resistance?

6. Assume that you are asked to lead a group composed of involuntary clients. Because their participation is mandatory, you want to take steps to clearly and fully inform them of procedures to be used, their rights and responsibilities as members, your expectations of them, and matters such as confidentiality. If you were to write up an "informed consent document," what would you most want to put into this brief letter?

7. A member in a group you are leading comes to you after one of the group sessions, saying: "I don't want to come back next week. It doesn't seem as if we're getting anywhere in here, because all that ever goes on is people putting each other down. I just don't trust anyone in here!" she has not said any of this in the sessions, and the group has been meeting for five weeks. What might you say or do? Would you attempt to persuade her to stay in the group? Why or why not?

8. Consider some of the following areas in which your values and those of the members might clash. Consider how you might respond in each of these situations that could arise in your group:

- A woman discloses how excited she is over a current affair and then wonders if she should continue staying with her husband.
- Same situation as above, only the client is a man.
- A woman whose cultural background is different from yours and that of the other members in the group says that she is having difficulty expressing what she wants and in behaving assertively (both in the group and at home). She says she has been taught to think of the interests of others and not be concerned about what she wants.

- An adolescent relates that his life feels bland without drugs.
- A pregnant 16-year-old is struggling to decide whether to have an abortion or give up her baby to an adoption agency.
- A chronically depressed man talks about suicide as his way out of a hopeless situation.
- A man says he is very unhappy in his marriage but is unwilling to get a divorce because he is afraid of being alone.
- Same situation as above, only the client is a woman.
- A member who is from a different culture than the other members says he is having difficulty in the group because he is not used to speaking so freely or openly about family problems.

9. Assume that you are on a committee to formulate guidelines to help counseling students learn how to deal effectively with diversity in their groups. When group leaders encounter people of diverse racial, ethnic, and cultural backgrounds in a counseling group, what issues most need to be addressed? What guidelines might you suggest to address these issues? What experiences would help students examine their attitudes and beliefs about diversity? What kind of information do you think students most need, and how might they best acquire this knowledge? What are your recommendations for developing skill in leading culturally diverse groups?

10. Carefully review the *Ethical Guidelines for Group Counselors* (ASGW, 1989) on pp. 52–58. Identify any of the guidelines that you tend to disagree with or would like to argue about. Which guidelines do you think are most important? Are any guidelines not in this document that you think should be added? To what degree do these guidelines adequately address diversity issues? In small groups in class, discuss both the values and the limitations of these guidelines for the practitioner. Select specific guidelines you'd most like to discuss and bring them to your discussion group. [Note: At the April 1996 Executive Board meeting in Pittsburgh, the ASGW formally accepted the ACA's (1995) Code of Ethics and Standards of Practice as their sole code of ethics. ASGW is currently developing a Standards of Best Practice document to assist their members in applying the ACA Code of Ethics to group work. You may consider the ASGW Ethical Guidelines for Group Counselors (reprinted on pp. 52–58) to be the Best Practice document until the new document is developed.]

ASGW 1989 REVISION
Association for Specialists in
Group Work

ETHICAL GUIDELINES FOR GROUP COUNSELORS

PREAMBLE

One characteristic of any professional group is the possession of a body of knowledge, skills, and voluntarily, self-professed standards for ethical practice. A Code of Ethics consists of those standards that have been formally and publicly acknowledged by the members of a profession to serve as the guidelines for professional conduct, discharge of duties, and the resolution of moral dilemmas. By this document, the Association for Specialists in Group Work (ASGW) has identified the standards of conduct appropriate for ethical behavior among its members.

The Association for Specialists in Group Work recognizes the basic commitment of its members to the Ethical Standards of its parent organization, the American Association for Counseling and Development (AACD) and nothing in this document shall be construed to supplant that code. These standards are intended to complement the AACD standards in the area of group work by clarifying the nature of ethical responsibility of the counselor in the group setting and by stimulating a greater concern for competent group leadership.

The group counselor is expected to be a professional agent and to take the processes of ethical responsibility seriously. ASGW views "ethical process" as being integral to group work and views group counselors as "ethical agents." Group counselors, by their very nature in being responsible and responsive to their group members, necessarily embrace a certain potential for ethical vulnerability. It is incumbent upon group counselors to give considerable attention to the intent and context of their actions because the attempts of counselors to influence human behavior through group work always have ethical implications.

The following ethical guidelines have been developed to encourage ethical behavior of group counselors. These guidelines are written for students and practitioners, and are meant to stimulate reflection, self-examination, and discussion of issues and practices. They address the group counselor's responsibility for providing information about group work to clients and the group counselor's responsibility for providing group counseling services to clients. A final section discusses the group counselor's responsibility for safeguarding ethical practice and procedures for reporting unethical behavior. Group counselors are expected to make known these standards to group members.

From "ASGW Ethical Guidelines for Group Counselors," *Journal for Specialists in Group Work*, Volume 15, Number 2, May 1990, 119–126. © American Association for Counseling and Development. Reprinted with permission. These guidelines were approved by the Association for Specialists in Group Work (ASGW) Executive Board, June 1, 1989.

ETHICAL GUIDELINES

1. *Orientation and Providing Information:* Group counselors adequately prepare prospective or new group members by providing as much information about the existing or proposed group as necessary.

   - Minimally, information related to each of the following areas should be provided.

       a. Entrance procedures, time parameters of the group experience, group participation expectations, methods of payment (where appropriate), and termination procedures are explained by the group counselor as appropriate to the level of maturity of group members and the nature and purpose(s) of the group.

       b. Group counselors have available for distribution, a professional disclosure statement that includes information on the group counselor's qualifications and group services that can be provided, particularly as related to the nature and purpose(s) of the specific group.

       c. Group counselors communicate the role expectations, rights, and responsibilities of group members and group counselor(s).

       d. The group goals are stated as concisely as possible by the group counselor including "whose" goal it is (the group counselor's, the institution's, the parent's, the law's, society's, etc.) and the role of group members in influencing or determining the group's goal(s).

       e. Group counselors explore with group members the risks of potential life changes that may occur because of the group experience and help members explore their readiness to face these possibilities.

       f. Group members are informed by the group counselor of unusual or experimental procedures that might be expected in their group experience.

       g. Group counselors explain, as realistically as possible, what services can and cannot be provided within the particular group structure offered.

       h. Group counselors emphasize the need to promote full psychological functioning and presence among group members. They inquire from prospective group members whether they are using any kind of drug or medication that may affect functioning in the group. They do not permit any use of alcohol and/or illegal drugs during group sessions and they discourage the use of alcohol and/or drugs (legal or illegal) prior to group meetings which may affect the physical or emotional presence of the member or other group members.

       i. Group counselors inquire from prospective group members whether they have ever been a client in counseling or psychotherapy. If a prospective group member is already in a counseling relationship with another professional person, the group counselor advises the prospective group member to notify the other professional of their participation in the group.

       j. Group counselors clearly inform group members about the policies pertaining to the group counselor's willingness to consult with them between group sessions.

       k. In establishing fees for group counseling services, group counselors consider the financial status and the locality of prospective group members. Group members are not charged fees for group sessions where the group counselor is not present and the policy of charging for sessions missed by a group member is clearly communicated. Fees for participating as a group member are contracted between group counselor and group member for a specified period of time. Group counselors do not increase fees for group counseling services until the existing contracted fee structure has expired. In the event that the established fee structure is inappropriate for a prospective member, group counselors assist in finding comparable services of acceptable cost.

2. *Screening of Members:* The group counselor screens prospective group members (when appropriate to their theoretical orientation). Insofar as possible, the counselor selects group members whose needs and goals are compatible with the goals of the group, who will not impede the group process, and whose well-being will not be jeopardized by the group experience. An orientation to the group (i.e., ASGW Ethical Guideline #1), is included during the screening process.

   • Screening may be accomplished in one or more ways, such as the following:
      a. Individual interview,
      b. Group interview of prospective group members,
      c. Interview as part of a team staffing, and,
      d. Completion of a written questionnaire by prospective group members.

3. *Confidentiality:* Group counselors protect members by defining clearly what confidentiality means,

why it is important, and the difficulties involved in enforcement.

a. Group counselors take steps to protect members by defining confidentiality and the limits of confidentiality (i.e., when a group member's condition indicates that there is clear and imminent danger to the member, others, or physical property, the group counselor takes reasonable personal action and/or informs responsible authorities).

b. Group counselors stress the importance of confidentiality and set a norm of confidentiality regarding all group participants' disclosures. The importance of maintaining confidentiality is emphasized before the group begins and at various times in the group. The fact that confidentiality cannot be guaranteed is clearly stated.

c. Members are made aware of the difficulties involved in enforcing and ensuring confidentiality in a group setting. The counselor provides examples of how confidentiality can nonmaliciously be broken to increase members' awareness, and help to lessen the likelihood that this breach of confidence will occur. Group counselors inform group members about the potential consequences of intentionally breaching confidentiality.

d. Group counselors can only ensure confidentiality on their part and not on the part of the members.

e. Group counselors video or audio tape a group session only with the prior consent, and the members' knowledge of how the tape will be used.

f. When working with minors, the group counselor specifies the limits of confidentiality.

g. Participants in a mandatory group are made aware of any reporting procedures required of the group counselor.

h. Group counselors store or dispose of group member records (written, audio, video, etc.) in ways that maintain confidentiality.

i. Instructors of group counseling courses maintain the anonymity of group members whenever discussing group counseling cases.

4. *Voluntary/Involuntary Participation:* Group counselors inform members whether participation is voluntary or involuntary.

a. Group counselors take steps to ensure informed consent procedures in both voluntary and involuntary groups.

b. When working with minors in a group, counselors are expected to follow the procedures specified by the institution in which they are practicing.

c. With involuntary groups, every attempt is made to enlist the cooperation of the members and their continuance in the group on a voluntary basis.

d. Group counselors do not certify that group treatment has been received by members who merely attend sessions, but did not meet the defined group expectations. Group members are informed about the consequences for failing to participate in a group.

5. *Leaving a Group:* Provisions are made to assist a group member to terminate in an effective way.

a. Procedures to be followed for a group member who chooses to exit a group prematurely are discussed by the counselor with all group members either before the group begins, during a pre-screening interview, or during the initial group session.

b. In the case of legally mandated group counseling, group counselors inform members of the possible consequences for premature self-termination.

c. Ideally, both the group counselor and the member can work cooperatively to determine the degree to which a group experience is productive or counterproductive for that individual.

d. Members ultimately have a right to discontinue membership in the group, at a designated time, if the predetermined trial period proves to be unsatisfactory.

e. Members have the right to exit a group, but it is important that they be made aware of the importance of informing the counselor and the group members prior to deciding to leave. The counselor discusses the possible risks of leaving the group prematurely with a member who is considering this option.

f. Before leaving a group, the group counselor encourages members (if appropriate) to discuss their reasons for wanting to discontinue membership in the group. Counselors intervene if other members use undue pressure to force a member to remain in the group.

6. *Coercion and Pressure:* Group counselors protect member rights against physical threats, intimidation, coercion, and undue peer pressure insofar as is reasonably possible.

a. It is essential to differentiate between "therapeutic pressure" that is part of any group and "undue pressure," which is not therapeutic.

b. The purpose of a group is to help participants find their own answer, not to pressure them into doing what the group thinks is appropriate.

c. Counselors exert care not to coerce participants to change in directions which they clearly state they do not choose.

d. Counselors have a responsibility to intervene when others use undue pressure or attempt to persuade members against their will.

e. Counselors intervene when any member attempts to act out aggression in a physical way that might harm another member or themselves.

f. Counselors intervene when a member is verbally abusive or inappropriately confrontive to another member.

7. *Imposing Counselor Values:* Group counselors develop an awareness of their own values and needs and the potential impact they have on the interventions likely to be made.

a. Although group counselors take care to avoid imposing their values on members, it is appropriate that they expose their own beliefs, decisions, needs, and values, when concealing them would create problems for the members.

b. There are values implicit in any group, and these are made clear to potential members before they join the group. (Examples of certain values include: expressing feelings, being direct and honest, sharing personal material with others, learning how to trust, improving interpersonal communication, and deciding for oneself.)

c. Personal and professional needs of group counselors are not met at the members' expense.

d. Group counselors avoid using the group for their own therapy.

e. Group counselors are aware of their own values and assumptions and how these apply in a multicultural context.

f. Group counselors take steps to increase their awareness of ways that their personal reactions to members might inhibit the group process and they monitor their countertransference. Through an awareness of

the impact of stereotyping and discrimination (i.e., biases based on age, disability, ethnicity, gender, race, religion, or sexual preference), group counselors guard the individual rights and personal dignity of all group members.

8. *Equitable Treatment:* Group counselors make every reasonable effort to treat each member individually and equally.

a. Group counselors recognize and respect differences (e.g., cultural, racial, religious, lifestyle, age, disability, gender) among group members.

b. Group counselors maintain an awareness of their behavior toward individual group members and are alert to the potential detrimental effects of favoritism or partiality toward any particular group member to the exclusion or detriment of any other member(s). It is likely that group counselors will favor some members over others, yet all group members deserve to be treated equally.

c. Group counselors ensure equitable use of group time for each member by inviting silent members to become involved, acknowledging nonverbal attempts to communicate, and discouraging rambling and monopolizing of time by members.

d. If a large group is planned, counselors consider enlisting another qualified professional to serve as a co-leader for the group sessions.

9. *Dual Relationships:* Group counselors avoid dual relationships with group members that might impair their objectivity and professional judgment, as well as those which are likely to compromise a group member's ability to participate fully in the group.

a. Group counselors do not misuse their professional role and power as group leader to advance personal or social contacts with members throughout the duration of the group.

b. Group counselors do not use their professional relationship with group members to further their own interest either during the group or after the termination of the group.

c. Sexual intimacies between group counselors and members are unethical.

d. Group counselors do not barter (exchange) professional services with group members for services.

e. Group counselors do not admit their own family members, relatives, employees, or personal friends as members to their groups.

f. Group counselors discuss with group members the potential detrimental effects of group members engaging in intimate inter-member relationships outside of the group.

g. Students who participate in a group as a partial course requirement for a group course are not evaluated for an academic grade based upon their degree of participation as a member in a group. Instructors of group counseling courses take steps to minimize the possible negative impact on students when they participate in a group course by separating course grades from participation in the group and by allowing students to decide what issues to explore and when to stop.

h. It is inappropriate to solicit members from a class (or institutional affiliation) for one's private counseling or therapeutic groups.

10. *Use of Techniques:* Group counselors do not attempt any technique unless trained in its use or under supervision by a counselor familiar with the intervention.

a. Group counselors are able to articulate a theoretical orientation that guides their practice, and they are able to provide a rationale for their interventions.

b. Depending upon the type of an intervention, group counselors have training commensurate with the potential impact of a technique.

c. Group counselors are aware of the necessity to modify their techniques to fit the unique needs of various cultural and ethnic groups.

d. Group counselors assist members in translating in-group learnings to daily life.

11. *Goal Development:* Group counselors make every effort to assist members in developing their personal goals.

a. Group counselors use their skills to assist members in making their goals specific so that others present in the group will understand the nature of the goals.

b. Throughout the course of a group, group counselors assist members in assessing the degree to which personal goals are being met, and assist in revising any goals when it is appropriate.

c. Group counselors help members clarify the degree to which the goals can be met within the context of a particular group.

12. *Consultation:* Group counselors develop and explain policies about between-session consultation to group members.

a. Group counselors take care to make certain that members do not use between-session consultations to avoid dealing with issues pertaining to the group that would be dealt with best in the group.

b. Group counselors urge members to bring the issues discussed during between-session consultations into the group if they pertain to the group.

c. Group counselors seek out consultation and/or supervision regarding ethical concerns or when encountering difficulties which interfere with their effective functioning as group leaders.

d. Group counselors seek appropriate professional assistance for their own personal problems or conflicts that are likely to impair their professional judgment and work performance.

e. Group counselors discuss their group cases only for professional consultation and educational purposes.

f. Group counselors inform members about policies regarding whether consultation will be held confidential.

13. *Termination from the Group:* Depending upon the purpose of participation in the group, counselors promote termination of members from the group in the most efficient period of time.

a. Group counselors maintain a constant awareness of the progress made by each group member and periodically invite the group members to explore and reevaluate their experiences in the group. It is the responsibility of group counselors to help promote the independence of members from the group in a timely manner.

14. *Evaluation and Follow-up:* Group counselors make every attempt to engage in ongoing assessment and to design follow-up procedures for their groups.

a. Group counselors recognize the importance of ongoing assessment of a group, and they assist members in evaluating their own progress.

b. Group counselors conduct evaluation of the total group experience at the final meeting (or before termination), as well as ongoing evaluation.

c. Group counselors monitor their own behavior and become aware of what they are modeling in the group.

d. Follow-up procedures might take the form of personal contact, telephone contact, or written contact.

e. Follow-up meetings might be with individuals, or groups, or both to determine the degree to which: (i) members have reached their goals, (ii) the group had a positive or negative effect on the participants, (iii) members could profit from some type of referral, and (iv) as information for possible modification of future groups. If there is no follow-up meeting, provisions are made available for individual follow-up meetings to any member who needs or requests such a contact.

15. *Referrals:* If the needs of a particular member cannot be met within the type of group being offered, the group counselor suggests other appropriate professional referrals.

a. Group counselors are knowledgeable of local community resources for assisting group members regarding professional referrals.

b. Group counselors help members seek further professional assistance, if needed.

16. *Professional Development:* Group counselors recognize that professional growth is a continuous, ongoing, developmental process throughout their career.

a. Group counselors maintain and upgrade their knowledge and skill competencies through educational activities, clinical experiences, and participation in professional development activities.

b. Group counselors keep abreast of research findings and new developments as applied to groups.

CHAPTER 3

THE GROUP COUNSELOR: PERSON AND PROFESSIONAL

FOCUS QUESTIONS

Introduction

The Group Counselor as a Person

Problems and Issues Facing Beginning Group Leaders
Personal Characteristics of the Effective Group Leader

The Group Counselor as a Professional

Survey of Group-Leadership Skills
An Integrated View of Leadership Skills
Developing Skills as a Multicultural Group Counselor

The Co-Leadership Model

The Basis of Co-Leadership
Advantages of the Co-Leadership Model
Disadvantages of the Co-Leadership Model

Professional Competence and Training

The Issue of Leader Competence
Professional Training Standards for Group Counselors
Training and Personal Experience
Ethical Issues in Training Group Counselors

Developing a Research Orientation to Practice

The Current Status of Group Work Research
Obstacles to the Advancement of Research on Group Work
The Challenge of Combining Research and Practice

Exercises

Attitude Questionnaire on Group Leadership
Self-Assessment of Group-Leadership Skills

Points to Remember: Summary of Part One

FOCUS QUESTIONS

1. Beginning group leaders face a number of concerns when setting up and leading groups. What are your concerns about leading a group?

2. What personal characteristics, skills, and specialized knowledge do you associate with effective group leadership? Which of these attributes is crucial to competently lead groups?

3. What skills for leading a group do you already possess? What skills do you need to acquire or strengthen?

4. Are you confident of your ability to conduct groups characterized by culturally diverse membership? What specific knowledge and skills do you most need to acquire to enhance your effectiveness when working with clients who are culturally different from you?

5. How might you modify the techniques you use to suit the specific needs of clients from diverse backgrounds? How can you determine the effectiveness of the techniques you employ in a culturally diverse group?

6. What are some advantages and disadvantages of co-leadership of a group, both for the members and for the co-leaders? In choosing a co-leader, what specific qualities would you most look for?

7. What education and training do you think a person needs to be a competent leader?

8. What experience and supervision would you like to receive as part of your program in group leadership?

9. What is your position on the issue of private psychotherapy for group leaders? Should group membership be part of a leader's background?

10. Should students be required to participate in an experiential and group-counseling class oriented toward personal growth? What are some of the ethical aspects involved when instructors of group counseling courses also function in therapeutic ways as part of teaching the course?

INTRODUCTION

This chapter deals with the influence of the group counselor, both as a person and as a professional, on the direction a group takes. First, we consider the counselor as a person, addressing problems faced by beginning group leaders and the personal qualities of effective leadership. Then, looking at the group counselor as a professional, we consider the specific skills of group leadership, what it means to become an effective multicultural group counselor, and the co-leadership model. We also address issues in training group counselors and highlight the ASGW's professional standards for training.

THE GROUP COUNSELOR AS A PERSON

The professional practice of leading groups is bound up with who the counselor is as a person. Indeed, the leader's ability to establish solid relationships with others in the group is probably the most important tool he or she has in facilitating group process. As a group leader, you bring your personal qualities, values, and life experiences to every group. To promote growth in members' lives, you need to be committed to reflection and growth in your own life. If you hope to inspire others to get out of deadening ruts, it is imperative that you keep yourself vital. You need to be willing to reinvent yourself if you hope to challenge the members of your group to create meaning in their lives. If you are a student, now is a good time to begin this personal quest. How you deal with the stresses and anxieties of a training program have important implications for how you will function as a professional helper. The person you are acts as a catalyst for bringing about change in the groups you lead.

PROBLEMS AND ISSUES FACING BEGINNING GROUP LEADERS

Those who are just beginning to lead groups typically feel overwhelmed by the potential problems they face. New leaders ask themselves questions such as:

- Will I be able to get the group started? How?
- What techniques should I use?
- Should I wait for the group to initiate activity?
- Do I have what it takes to follow through once something has been initiated?
- What if I like some people more than others?
- What if I make mistakes? Can I cause someone serious psychological harm?
- Do I know enough theory? Can I apply whatever I do know in groups?
- Should I share my anxiety with my group?
- What do I do if there is a prolonged silence?
- How much should I participate or involve myself in a personal way in the groups I lead?
- Will I have the knowledge and skills to work effectively with clients who are culturally different from me?
- What if the entire group attacks me?
- How do I know whether the group is helping people change?
- How can I work with so many people at one time?

Whether you are a beginning group leader or a seasoned one, successful groups cannot be guaranteed. Hence, courage is necessary, the courage to function under conditions of uncertainty. You are sure to make mistakes, and if you can admit them, you will learn from them. It is important that you not be harshly critical of yourself, imposing standards of perfection. In supervising group leaders, we tell trainees that the fear of making mistakes can stifle their creativity and their ability to remain in the present.

One problem you will probably face as a beginning group leader is negative reactions from members. On the one hand, if you structure a group by using specific techniques, you may be accused by members of constricting their freedom. The members may rebel by refusing to cooperate with the structure. On the other hand, if you do not provide some degree of structure and direction, members may criticize you for allowing them to flounder, and they may wait passively for you to initiate some exercise. You need to learn how to constructively confront those who have these reactions. If you become tight and defensive, the members may, in turn, become increasingly defensive. Such an undercurrent of unresolved hostility will sabotage any further work. How to deal with these situations will be discussed later in this section and at different places in this book.

Beginning group leaders should realize that it will take time to develop leadership skills. Many feel like quitting after leading only a few sessions. Such people usually want to be accomplished leaders without experiencing the self-doubts and fears that may be necessary to their development as a leader. Some feel devastated if they don't receive an abundance of positive feedback. It probably cannot be mentioned too many times that some struggle and uncertainty are almost always a part of learning how to lead well. Nobody expects to perfect any skill (skiing, playing the guitar, making pottery) in a few introductory lessons. Those who finally experience success at these endeavors are the ones who have the endurance to progress in increments. There is probably no better teacher than experience, but unguided experience is often unsatisfactory. Immediate feedback—from a supervisor, from co-leaders, or from other budding leaders in a training group—enables leaders to profit from their experience.

PERSONAL CHARACTERISTICS OF THE EFFECTIVE GROUP LEADER

In our view who the leader is as a person is one of the most significant variables influencing the group's success or failure. In discussing the personality characteristics of the effective group leader with some of our colleagues, we have found that it is difficult to list all the traits of successful leaders and even more difficult to agree on one particular personality type associated with effective leadership. Following are some personal characteristics that we deem important. As you read about each of these dimensions, reflect on how it applies to you. Consider the degree to which you are at least on the road to acquiring the personal characteristics important for your success as a group leader.

Courage   One of the most important personal traits of effective group leaders is courage. Courage is demonstrated through your willingness (1) to be vulnerable at times, admitting mistakes and imperfections and taking the same risks you expect group members to take; (2) to confront others but to stay "with" them as you work out conflicts; (3) to act on your beliefs and hunches; (4) to be emotionally touched by others and to draw on your experiences to identify with them; (5) to examine your life; (6) to be direct and honest with members; and (7) to express to the members your fears and expectations about the group process. Just as the members of your groups will have fears, so will you as the leader. By the behavior you model, you can teach the members that courage does not mean being without fears; rather, it means acknowledging fears and dealing with them.

Willingness to Model   One of the best ways to teach desired behaviors is by modeling them in the group. Through your behavior and the attitudes conveyed by it, you can create such group norms as openness, seriousness of purpose, acceptance of others, and the desirability of taking risks.

Remember that you teach largely by example—by doing what you expect members to do. Realize that your role differs from that of the group member, but do not hide behind a professional facade. By engaging in honest, appropriate, and timely self-disclosure, you can both participate as a member in the group and fulfill the leadership function of modeling.

Presence   The ability to be emotionally present with group members is extremely important. It involves being touched by others' pain, struggles, and joys. Some members may elicit anger in a group leader, and others may evoke pain, sadness, guilt, or happiness. You become more emotionally involved with others by paying close attention to your own reactions. This does not mean that you will necessarily talk about the situation in your own life that caused you the pain or evoked the anger. It means that you will allow yourself to experience these feelings, even for just a few moments. Fully experiencing emotions gives you the ability to be compassionate and empathic with your clients. At the same time, as you're moved by others' experiences, it is important to remain a separate person and to avoid the trap of overidentifying with your clients' situations.

To increase your ability to be present, spend some time alone before leading a group and block out distractions as much as possible. It is good to prepare yourself by thinking about the people in the group and about ways in which you might increase your involvement with them.

Goodwill and Caring   A sincere interest in the welfare of others is essential in a group leader. It implies that you will not exploit members or use them primarily to enhance your own ego. Your main job in the group is to help members get what they are coming for, not to get in their way. Caring involves respecting, trusting, and valuing people. In some cases it may be exceedingly difficult for you to care for certain group members, but we hope you will at least want to care. It is vital that you become aware of what kind of people you care for and what kind you find it difficult to care for. You can gain this awareness by openly exploring your reactions to members.

There are various ways of exhibiting a caring attitude. One way is by inviting a client to participate but allowing that person to decide how far to go. Or you can observe discrepancies between a client's words and behavior but confront that person in a way that doesn't intensify fear and resistance. Another way to express caring is by giving warmth, concern, and support when, and only when, you feel it toward a person.

Belief in Group Process   Some counselors really don't believe that groups can bring about significant change in clients, but they continue to lead groups. We think that a deep confidence in the value of group process is positively related to constructive outcomes. You need to believe in what you are doing and trust the therapeutic forces in a group. We continue to find that our enthusiasm and convictions are powerful both in attracting a clientele and in providing an incentive to work. Group leaders who do not genuinely believe in the value of therapeutic work and who do it only for money or power are behaving unethically.

Openness   To be effective, it certainly helps to be open with yourself, open to members of the group, open to new experiences, and open to lifestyles and values that differ from your own. At times, you may want to reveal your own experiences or, at least, the meaning that certain experiences have for you. Openness does not mean that you reveal every aspect of your personal life. Rather, it means that you reveal enough of yourself to give the participants a sense of who you are as a person. It can also enhance group process if you appropriately reveal your reactions to the members and to how you are being affected by being with the group.

Your openness tends to foster a corresponding spirit of openness within the group. It allows members to become more open about their feelings and beliefs, and it lends a certain fluidity to the group process. Self-revelation should not be manipulated as a technique; it is best done spontaneously, when it seems appropriate.

Becoming Aware of Your Own Culture   Knowing how your own culture influences your decisions and daily behavior provides a frame of reference for understanding the worldview of those who differ from you. Openness to diversity is the opposite of being entrapped by a narrow existence. Cultural encapsulation, or provincialism, affects not only you but your group members as well. The theme of the ACA's 44th annual convention was Celebrating Diversity Through the Art of Counseling. One of the keynote speakers, Don Locke of North Carolina State University, made the point that we live in three distinct worlds. We are unique beings; each of us is unlike anyone else. But because we belong to the human family, we all share some common traits. And finally, we often respond to other individuals based on the characteristics that bring us together. If you have a sense of your own culture and how your values are influenced by your social environment, you have a basis for understanding the world of those who are different from you in a number of respects. Your willingness to welcome diversity will, to a large extent, determine your effectiveness in bringing energy to a group.

Nondefensiveness in Coping with Attacks   Dealing frankly with criticism is related to openness. If you hope to endure as a group leader, you simply cannot afford to have a fragile ego. Group leaders who are easily threatened, who are insecure in their work of leading, who are overly sensitive to negative feedback, and who depend highly on group approval will encounter major problems when carrying out a leadership function. Members may sometimes accuse you of not caring enough, of being selective in your caring, of structuring the sessions too much, of not providing enough direction, of being too harsh, and so forth. Some of the criticism may be fair—you may be insensitive or uncaring at times—and some of it may be an unfair expression of jealousy, testing authority, power seeking, or projection onto you of feelings for other people. It is crucial for you to nondefensively explore with the group the feelings behind the criticism.

If members take a risk and confront the leader and are chastised for doing this, they are likely to feel scolded for taking a chance and may withdraw. Furthermore, others in the group may receive the message that openness and honesty are not really valued. Even if someone verbally abuses you as a leader, it is not therapeutic for you to respond in kind. Instead, you can give the person your reactions and let him or her know how you are affected by the confrontation. You can model for members an effective and nonaggressive way of expressing your thoughts and feelings.

Personal Power   Personal power does not entail domination of members or manipulation of them toward the leader's end. Rather, it is the dynamic and vital characteristic of leaders who know who they are and what they want. This power involves a sense of confidence in self and a certain charisma. Such leaders' lives are an expression of what they espouse. Instead of merely talking about the importance of being alive, powerful leaders express and radiate an aliveness through their actions.

Power and honesty are closely related. In our view people with personal power are the ones who can show themselves. Although they may be frightened by certain qualities within themselves, the fear doesn't keep them from examining these qualities. Powerful people recognize and accept their weaknesses and don't expend energy concealing them from themselves and others. In contrast, powerless people need very much to defend themselves against self-knowledge. They often act as if they are afraid that their vulnerabilities will be discovered.

Clients often badly need to see leaders not only as powerful but also as having all the qualities that the members are striving for. Such clients may view leaders as perfect. They tend to undercut their own power by giving their leader *all* of the credit for their insights and changes. There is a danger that leaders will become infatuated with clients' perceptions of them as finished products and come to believe this myth. Powerful group leaders can accept credit where it is due and, at the same time, encourage clients to accept their own share of credit for their growth.

Stamina   Group leading can be taxing and draining as well as exciting and energizing. Therefore, you need physical and psychological stamina and the ability to withstand pressure to remain vitalized throughout the course of a group. Some novice counselors begin a group feeling excited and anticipating each session—until, that is, the group becomes resistive, clients begin to drop out, or members complain that the group is going nowhere. If you lose most of your stamina at this point, any possibility that the group will be productive may be lost. This means that you need to be aware of your own energy level. Furthermore, it is good to have sources other than your groups for psychological nourishment. If you depend primarily on the success level of your groups for this sustenance, you run a high risk of being undernourished and thus of losing the stamina so vital to your success as a leader. Unrealistically high expectations can also affect your stamina. Those leaders who cling to such expectations of dramatic change are often disappointed in themselves and in what they perceive as "poor performance" on the part of their group. Faced with the discrepancy between their vision of what the group *should* be and what actually occurs, these leaders often lose their enthusiasm and begin to needlessly blame both themselves and the group members for what they see as failure.

Willingness to Seek New Experiences   Your personhood is largely determined by the variety of your life experiences. A narrow range of experiences restricts your capacity to understand the psychological worlds of clients who have different values resulting from different life experiences. Your willingness to put yourself in situations where you can learn about different cultures will be most useful in helping you work effectively with culturally diverse populations. If you genuinely respect the differences among the members of your groups and are open to learning from them, you will win their trust. By contrast, "culturally encapsulated" counselors tend to make rigid and stereotyped generalizations about individuals within a particular cultural group. As a result, they tend to impose their worldview on the members of their groups. This narrowness demonstrates a lack of respect for the complexity of the human struggles that grow out of various cultural backgrounds.

It is important to learn about human struggles by recognizing and wrestling with your own life issues. If you have lived a fairly sheltered life and have known little pain and strife, how can you empathize with clients who have suffered and have made dramatic life choices? If you have never experienced loneliness, joy, anguish, or uncertainty, what basis do you have for tuning in to the pain that your clients experience? Although it is not possible for you to experience directly everything that you encounter in others, you should at least be willing to identify ways in which you can draw on your own emotions in working with group members. It is unrealistic to expect yourself to have experienced the same problems as all of your clients, but the emotions that all of us experience are much the same. We all experience psychological pain, even though the causes of this pain may be different. One basis for empathizing with clients is being open to the sources of pain in your own life, without becoming swept up by this pain.

Self-Awareness   A central characteristic for any therapeutic person is an awareness of self, including one's identity, cultural perspective, goals, motivations, needs, limitations, strengths, values, feelings, and problems. If you have a limited understanding of who you are, you will surely not be able to facilitate this kind of awareness in clients. As we've mentioned, being open to new life experiences and divergent lifestyles is one way you can expand your awareness. Involvement in your own personal therapy, both group and individual, is another way for you to become more aware of who you are and whom you might become. Awareness of why you choose to lead groups is crucial, including knowing what needs you are meeting through your work. If you are functioning with dim self-awareness, you could keep yourself blinded for fear of what you might discover. How can you encourage others to risk self-discovery if you are hesitant to come to terms with yourself? You have a potentially rich source of information about yourself if you will reflect on interactions you have had with members of your groups.

Sense of Humor   At times, people take themselves so seriously that they miss an opportunity to put the importance of their problems into perspective. Although therapy is serious business, there are many humorous dimensions of the human condition. The ability to laugh at yourself and to see the humor in your human frailties can be extremely useful in helping members keep a proper perspective and avoid becoming "psychologically heavy." Groups occasionally exhibit a real need for laughter and joking simply to release built-up tension. This release should not be viewed as an escape, for genuine humor can heal. If you can enjoy humor and infuse it effectively into the group process, you will have an invaluable asset.

Inventiveness   The capacity to be spontaneously creative, approaching each group with fresh ideas, is a most important characteristic. Freshness may not be easy to maintain, particularly if you lead groups frequently. You must somehow avoid becoming trapped in ritualized techniques or a programmed presentation of self that has lost all life. If you are able to discover new ways of approaching a group by inventing experiments that emerge from here-and-now interactions, you are unlikely to grow stale. Working with interesting co-leaders is another source of fresh ideas. Getting some distance from groups—for example, by conducting fewer of them, doing other things, or taking a vacation—may also help you gain a fresh perspective.

Personal Dedication and Commitment   Being a professional who makes a difference involves having ideals that provide meaning and direction in your life. This kind of dedication has direct application for leading groups. If you believe in the value of group process, and if you have a vision of how groups can empower individuals, you will be better able to ride out difficult times in a group. If you have a guiding vision, you can use it to stay focused and on track with group members when the waters get rough.

Being a dedicated professional also involves humility, which means being open to feedback and ideas and being willing to explore one's self. Humility does not mean being self-effacing. It is the opposite of the arrogance that is implied in convincing ourselves that we have "truly arrived" and that there is nothing more for us to learn. In addition, professional commitment entails staying abreast of changes in the field, reading journals and books, and attending periodic seminars to remain fresh and innovative.

THE GROUP COUNSELOR AS A PROFESSIONAL

SURVEY OF GROUP-LEADERSHIP SKILLS

Although the personality characteristics of the group leader are among the most important determinants of group outcomes, we think it is a mistake to assume that being a person of goodwill and approaching your group enthusiastically are all you need to lead effectively. Some personality attributes seem positively related to effective leadership, but these characteristics by themselves are not sufficient. Basic counseling skills specific to group situations must be developed. Like most skills, counseling skills can be taught to some degree, but there is also an element of art involved in using these skills in a sensitive and timely way. Learning how and when to use these skills is a function of supervised experience, practice, feedback, and confidence.

We will now consider some of the skills you will need to acquire as a competent group leader. As you read, keep in mind that these skills, like your personal qualities, are not sufficient to ensure effective leadership. Unless you are also the kind of person who provides a positive model that your clients can benefit from, your success as a leader will be limited.

Active Listening   It is most important to learn how to pay full attention to others as they communicate, and this process involves more than merely listening to the words. It involves absorbing the content, noting gestures and subtle changes in voice or expression, and sensing underlying messages. Group leaders can improve their listening skills by first recognizing the barriers that interfere with paying attention to others. Some of these roadblocks are not really listening to the other, thinking about what to say next instead of giving full attention to the other, being overly concerned about one's role or about how one will look, and judging and evaluating without putting oneself in the other person's place. Like any other therapeutic skill, active listening exists in degrees. Some leaders are so intent on being in the spotlight that they can't focus on anything outside themselves; other leaders have developed a high degree of perceptivity in discerning others' messages. The skilled group leader is sensitive to the congruence (or lack of it) between what a member is saying in words and what he or she is communicating through body posture, gestures, mannerisms, and voice inflections. For instance, a man may be talking about his warm and loving feelings toward his wife, yet his body may be rigid and his fists clenched. A woman recalling a painful situation may both smile and hold back tears.

Reflecting   Reflecting, a skill that is dependent on active listening, is the ability to convey the essence of what a person has communicated so the person can see it. Many neophyte group leaders find themselves confining most of their interaction to mere reflection. Somehow it seems safe. And, since members continue to talk, leaders continue to reflect. Carried to its extreme, however, reflection can become a hollow echo, empty of any substance:

Member: "I really didn't want to come to the group today. I'm bored, and I don't think we've gotten anyplace for weeks."

Leader: "You didn't want to come to the group because you're bored and the group isn't getting anywhere."

There was plenty of rich material here for the leader to respond to in a personal way, or with some confrontation, or by asking the person and the other members to examine what was going on in the group. Beginning on a reflective level may have value, but staying on that level produces blandness. The leader might have done better to reply "You sound discouraged about the possibility of getting much from this experience." The leader would then have been challenging the member to look at the emotions that lay beneath his words and, in the process, would have been opening up opportunities for meaningful communication.

Clarifying   Clarifying is a skill that can be valuably applied during the initial stages of a group. It involves focusing on key underlying issues and sorting out confusing and conflicting feelings. Thus, a girl might say: "I hate my father, and I wish I didn't have to see him anymore. He hurts me so often. I feel guilty when I feel this way, because I also love him and wish he would appreciate me." The therapist might clarify: "You have feelings of love and hate, and somehow having both of these feelings at once doesn't seem OK." Clarification can help the client sort out her feelings so that she can eventually experience both love and hate without experiencing guilt. However, stronger intervention methods than clarification may have to be used before she can accept this polarity.

Summarizing   When the group process becomes bogged down or fragmented, the skill of summarizing is useful. On the basis of a summary, decisions about where to go next can be made. For example, some members may be arguing that the leader is not providing enough structure and direction while others are maintaining that the leader is handling the group correctly. If the interaction seems to be turning into a debate, the group leader might interrupt and have each person state briefly how he or she feels about the issue. The leader can then summarize and offer possible alternatives.

At the end of a session the leader might make some summary statements or ask each member to summarize. For instance, a leader might say "Before we close, I'd like each of us to make a statement about his or her experience in the group today and tell where he or she is left." It's a good idea for the leader to make the first summary statement, so that the members will have a model for this behavior. Sometimes, however, the leader may want to close the session with his or her own reactions.

Facilitating   The group leader can facilitate the group process by (1) assisting members to openly express their fears and expectations, (2) actively working to create a climate of safety and acceptance in which people will trust one another and therefore engage in productive interchanges, (3) providing encouragement and support as members explore highly personal material or as they try new behavior, (4) involving as many members as possible in the group interaction by inviting and sometimes even challenging members to participate, (5) working toward lessening the dependency on the leader, (6) encouraging open expression of conflict and controversy, and (7) helping members overcome barriers to direct communication. The aim of most facilitation skills is to help the group members reach their own goals. Essentially, these skills involve opening up clear communication among the members and helping them increase their responsibility for the direction of their group.

Empathizing   An empathetic group leader can sense the subjective world of the client. This skill requires the leader to have the characteristics of caring and openness already mentioned. The leader must also have a wide range of experiences to serve as a basis for identifying with others. Finally, the leader must be able to discern subtle nonverbal messages as well as messages transmitted more directly. It is impossible to fully know what another person is experiencing, but a sensitive group leader can make a good guess. It is also important, however, for the group leader to avoid blurring his or her identity by overidentifying with the group members. The core of the skill of empathy lies in being able to openly grasp another's experiencing and at the same time maintain one's separateness.

Interpreting   Group leaders who are highly directive are likely to make use of interpretation, which entails offering possible explanations for certain behaviors or symptoms. If interpretations are accurate and well-timed, they must result in a member's moving beyond an impasse. It is not necessary that the leader always make the interpretation for the client; in Gestalt therapy clients are encouraged to make their own interpretations of their behavior. A group leader can also present an interpretation in the form of a hunch, the truth of which the client can then assess. For instance, an interpretation might be stated as follows: "Harry, I've noticed that, when a person in the group talks about something painful, you usually intervene and become reassuring and in some way try to take that person's pain away. What might that say about you?" It is important that the interpretation be presented as a hypothesis rather than as a fact. Also important is that the person have a chance to consider the validity of this hunch in the group.

Questioning   Questioning is really not much of a skill, and it is overused by many group leaders. Interrogation seldom leads to productive outcomes, and more often than not it distracts the person working. If a member happens to be experiencing intense feelings, questioning is one way of reducing the intensity. Asking "Why do you feel that way?" is rarely helpful. However, appropriately timed "what" and "how" questions do serve to intensify experiencing. Examples are questions such as "What is happening with your body now, as you speak about your isolation?" "In what ways do you experience the fear of rejection in this group?" "What are some of the things you imagine happening to you if you reveal your problems to this group?" "How are you coping with your fear that you can't trust some of the members here?" These questions direct the person to heighten awareness of the moment. Leaders should develop the skill of asking questions like these and avoiding questions that remove people from themselves. Questions that are not helpful include those that search for causes of behavior, probe for information, and the like: "How long have you been seeking your father's approval?" "Why do you feel depressed?" "Why don't you leave home?"

Linking   A group leader who has an interactional bias—that is, who stresses member-to-member rather than leader-to-member communication—makes frequent use of linking. This skill calls on the insightfulness of the leader in finding ways of relating what one person is doing or saying to the concerns of another person. For example, Katherine might be describing her feeling that she won't be loved unless she's perfect. If Pamela has been heard to express a similar feeling, the leader could ask Pamela and Katherine to talk with each other in the group about their fears. By being alert for cues that members have some common concern, the leader can promote member interaction and raise the level of group cohesion.

Confronting   Beginning group leaders are often afraid to confront group members for fear of hurting them, of being wrong, or of inviting retaliation. It doesn't take much skill to attack another or to be merely critical. It does take both caring and skill, however, to confront group members when their behavior is disruptive of the group functioning or when there are discrepancies between their verbal messages and their nonverbal messages. In confronting a member, a leader should (1) challenge specifically the behavior to be examined, avoiding labeling the person, and (2) share how he or she feels about the person's behavior. For example, Danny has been interrupting the group, pelting people with "why" questions and offering interpretations. The leader might intervene: "Danny, I find it difficult to listen to all your questioning and telling people how they are. Most of the time when you enter the group interaction, you interpret others' behavior for them, and I still don't know much about you. I would be interested in getting to know you better."

Supporting   The skill in supportive behavior is knowing when it will be therapeutic and when it will be counterproductive. A common mistake is offering support before a participant has had an opportunity to fully experience a conflict or some painful feelings. Although the intervention may be done with good intentions, it may abort certain feelings that a given member needs to experience. Another mistake is supporting game-playing behavior. For instance, if a woman is playing helpless and trying to convince everyone of how fragile she is, a leader who offers support will, in effect, foster her dependency. What the leader might do instead is confront the member with the fact that she can do for herself what she's pleading for others to do for her. Support is appropriate when people are facing a crisis, when they're venturing into frightening territory, when they attempt constructive changes and yet feel uncertain about these changes, and when they're struggling to rid themselves of old patterns that are limiting. Leaders should remember that too much support can send the message that people are unable to support themselves.

Blocking   Group leaders have the responsibility to block certain activities of group members, such as questioning, probing, gossiping, invading another's privacy, breaking confidences, and so forth. The skill is to learn to block counterproductive behaviors without attacking the personhood of the perpetrator. This requires both sensitivity and directness. Some examples of behavior that need to be blocked are:

- **Bombarding others with questions.** Offenders can be asked to make direct statements out of their questions.
- **Gossiping.** If a member talks *about* another member in the room, the leader can ask the person to speak directly *to* the person being spoken about.
- **Storytelling.** If lengthy storytelling occurs, a leader can intervene and ask the person to say how all this relates to present feelings and events.
- **Breaking confidences.** A member may inadvertently talk about a situation that occurred in another group or mention what so-and-so did in a prior group. This talk should be stopped by the leader in a firm but gentle manner.
- **Invasion of privacy.** If a person pushes another, probing for personal information, this behavior must be blocked by the group leader.

Diagnosing   Diagnostic skills involve more than labeling behavior, identifying symptoms, and figuring out what category a person falls into. They include the ability to appraise certain behavior problems and choose the appropriate intervention. For example, a leader who diagnoses a client as deeply angry must consider the safety and appropriateness of encouraging the client to "let out your pent-up rage." Leaders also need to develop the skill of determining whether a particular group is indicated or contraindicated for a member, and they need to acquire the expertise necessary to make appropriate referrals.

Modeling   One of the best ways for leaders to teach a desired behavior to members is to model it for them. If group leaders value risk taking, openness, directness, sensitivity, honesty, respect, and enthusiasm, it is essential to demonstrate attitudes and behavior congruent with these values. Leaders can best foster these qualities in the members by demonstrating them in the group. A few specific behaviors leaders can directly model include respect for diversity, appropriate self-disclosure, giving feedback in ways that others can hear and accept nondefensively, receiving feedback from members in a nondefensive manner, involvement in the group process, presence, and challenging others in direct and caring ways. In groups that are co-facilitated, the relationship between the co-leaders can set norms for appropriate engagement between members.

Suggesting   Leaders can offer suggestions aimed at helping members develop an alternative course of thinking or action. Suggestions can take a number of forms, such as giving information, asking members to consider a specific homework assignment, asking members to create their own experiments, and assisting members in looking at a circumstance from a new vantage point. Leaders can also teach members to offer appropriate suggestions to each other. Although suggestions can facilitate change in members, there is a danger that suggestions can be given too freely and that advice can short-circuit the process of self-exploration. There is a fine line between suggesting and prescribing; the skill is in using suggestions to enhance an individual's movement toward making his or her own decisions.

Initiating   When the leader takes an active role in providing direction to members, offers some structure, and takes action when it is needed, the group is aided in staying focused on its task. These leadership skills include using catalysts to get members to focus on their personal goals, assisting members in working through places where they are stuck, helping members identify and resolve conflict, knowing how to use techniques to enhance work, providing links among the various themes in a group, and helping members assume responsibility for directing themselves. Too much leader initiation can stifle the creativity of a group, and too little leader initiation can lead to passivity on the part of the members.

Evaluating   A crucial leadership skill is evaluating the ongoing process and dynamics of a group. After each group session it is valuable for the leader to evaluate what happened, both within individual members and among the members, and to think about what interventions might be used next time with the group. Leaders need to get in the habit of asking themselves questions such as: What changes are resulting from the group? What are the therapeutic and antitherapeutic forces in the group?

The leader must also teach participants how to evaluate, so they can appraise the movement and direction of their own group. Once the group has evaluated a session or series of sessions, its members can decide what, if any, changes need to be made. For example, during an evaluation at the close of a session, the leader and the members are in agreement that the group as a whole has been passive. The leader might say: "I feel the burden of initiating and sense that you're waiting for me to do something to energize you. I'm challenging each of you to examine your behavior and to evaluate to what degree you're personally responsible. Then please think about what, specifically, you're willing to do to change this group."

Terminating   Group leaders must learn when and how to terminate their work with both individuals and groups. They need to develop the ability to tell when a group session should end, when an individual is ready to leave a group, and when a group has completed its work, and they need to learn how to handle each of these types of termination. The skill of terminating a single session or a whole group involves (1) providing the members with suggestions for transferring what they've learned in the group to the environment they must return to, (2) creating a climate that will encourage members to make contracts to do work between sessions or after the group, (3) preparing people for the psychological problems they may face on leaving a group, (4) arranging for a follow-up group, (5) telling members where they can get additional therapy, and (6) being available for individual consultation at the termination of a group. Follow-up and evaluation activities are particularly important if the leader is to learn the impact of the group as a therapeutic agent.

AN INTEGRATED VIEW OF LEADERSHIP SKILLS

Some counselor-education programs focus mainly on developing counseling skills and assessing competencies, whereas other programs stress the personal qualities that underlie these skills. Ideally, training programs for group leaders give due weight to both of these aspects. Later in this chapter, when professional standards for training group counselors are described, we will go into more detail about the specific areas of knowledge and the skills that group workers need.

We want to acknowledge that you are likely to feel somewhat overwhelmed when you consider all the skills that are necessary for effective group leadership. It may help to remember that, as in other areas of life, you will become frustrated if you attempt to focus on all aspects of this field at once. You can expect to gradually refine your leadership style and gain confidence in using these skills effectively.

Several points about the skills we have discussed need to be emphasized. First, these skills can best be thought of as existing at varying levels rather than on an all-or-nothing basis. They can be fully mastered and used in a sensitive and appropriate manner, or they can be only minimally developed. Second, these skills can be learned and constantly improved through training and supervised experience. Participating in a group as a member is one good way to determine what a group is about. Leading or co-leading a group under supervision is another excellent way to acquire and refine leadership skills. Third, these skills are not discrete entities; they overlap a great deal. Active listening, reflection, and clarification are interdependent, as are interpreting and diagnosing. Hence, by developing certain skills, a leader automatically improves others. Finally, these skills cannot be divorced from who the counselor is as a person, for the choice of which skills to develop and use is an expression of the leader's personality.

DEVELOPING SKILLS AS A MULTICULTURAL GROUP COUNSELOR

In addition to the group leadership skills already discussed, special knowledge and skills are required when dealing with culturally diverse group members. Most of those writing about the role of culture in the counseling process agree that effective group counselors have some level of understanding of their own cultural conditioning, the cultural conditioning of their clients, and an awareness of the sociopolitical system of which they are a part. If you hope to understand the culture of clients who differ from you, it is imperative that you first understand your own culture.

D. W. Sue, Arredondo, and McDavis (1992) have developed a conceptual framework for multicultural counseling competencies and standards. Their revised and expanded dimensions of multicultural competency involve three areas: beliefs and attitudes, knowledge, and skill. Arredondo, Toporek, and their colleagues (1996) developed a comprehensive set of multicultural competency standards, which were approved by the Association for Multicultural Counseling and Development in 1995. What follows is a condensed version of the multicultural competencies and standards identified by Sue and his colleagues, and also by Arredondo and her colleagues, which we have adapted for use by group practitioners.

Beliefs and Attitudes of Culturally Skilled Group Workers   Effective group leaders recognize and understand their own stereotypes and preconceived notions about other racial and ethnic groups. They do not allow their personal biases, values, or problems to interfere with their ability to work with clients who are culturally different from them. They are aware of how their own cultural background and experiences have influenced attitudes, values, and biases about what constitutes psychologically healthy individuals. They have moved from being culturally unaware to knowing their cultural heritage. They seek to examine and understand the world from the vantage point of their clients. They respect clients' religious and spiritual beliefs and values. They recognize the sources of their discomfort with differences between themselves and others in terms of race, ethnicity, culture, and beliefs. Because these group leaders welcome diverse value orientations and diverse assumptions about human behavior, they have a basis for sharing the worldview of their clients as opposed to being culturally encapsulated. Rather than maintaining that their cultural heritage is superior, they are able to accept and value cultural diversity. They are able to identify and understand the central cultural constructs of the members of their groups, and they avoid applying their own cultural constructs inappropriately with these group members. Group leaders monitor their functioning through consultation, supervision, and further training or education. They realize that group counseling may not be appropriate for all clients or for all problems.

Knowledge of Culturally Skilled Group Workers   Effective culturally skilled group practitioners possess knowledge about their own racial and cultural heritage and how it affects them in their work. In addition, they understand how oppression, racism, discrimination, and stereotyping affect them personally and professionally. They do not impose their values and expectations on their clients from differing cultural backgrounds, and they avoid stereotyping clients. They understand the worldview of their clients, and they learn about their clients' cultural backgrounds. Because they understand the basic values underlying the therapeutic group process, they know how these values may clash with the cultural values of various minority groups. These practitioners are aware of the institutional barriers that prevent minorities from utilizing the mental-health services available in their communities. They possess specific knowledge and information about the group members with whom they are working. They are aware of the values, life experiences, cultural heritage, and historical background of their culturally different group members. Furthermore, they are knowledgeable about the community characteristics and the resources in the community as well as the family. Culturally skilled group leaders view diversity in a positive light, which allows them to meet and resolve the challenges that arise in their work with a wide range of client populations. They know how to help clients make use of indigenous support systems. Where they lack knowledge, they seek resources to assist them. The greater their knowledge of culturally diverse groups, the more likely they are to be effective group leaders.

Skills and Intervention Strategies of Culturally Skilled Group Workers   Culturally skilled group counselors familiarize themselves with relevant research and the latest findings regarding mental health and mental disorders that affect diverse client populations. They are willing to seek out educational, consultative, and training experiences to enhance their ability to work with culturally diverse client populations. Multicultural counseling is enhanced when group leaders use methods and strategies and define goals consistent with the life experiences and cultural values of the group members. Such practitioners modify and adapt their interventions in a group to accommodate cultural differences. They do not force members to fit within one counseling approach. They are able to send and receive both verbal and nonverbal messages accurately and appropriately. To the extent that is possible, culturally skilled practitioners become actively involved with minority individuals outside the group setting (community events, celebrations, and neighborhood groups). They are committed to understanding themselves as racial and cultural beings and are actively seeking a nonracist identity.

Recognizing Your Own Limitations   As a culturally skilled group leader, you are able to recognize the limits of your multicultural competency and expertise. When necessary, you will refer clients to more qualified individuals or to additional resources. It is not realistic to expect that you will know everything about the cultural background of members in your groups. There is much to be said for letting group members teach you about relevant aspects of their culture. Ask members to provide you with the information you will need to work effectively with them. In working with culturally diverse individuals within a group, it helps to assess the degree of acculturation and identity development that has taken place. This is especially true for individuals who have had the experience of living in another culture. They often have allegiance to their own home culture but find certain characteristics of their new culture attractive. They may experience conflicts when integrating the values from the two cultures in which they live. These core struggles can be productively explored in an accepting group if the leader and the other members respect this cultural conflict.

If you are working with clients from a specific ethnic and cultural background different from your own, you can benefit from reading articles addressing group work with diverse client populations. Some resources listed in the References and Suggested Readings for Parts One and Two are: Arredondo and Toporek (1996), Banawi and Stockton (1993), Chu and Sue (1984), Comas-Diaz (1992), DeLucia, Coleman, and Jensen-Scott (1992), Dufrene and Coleman (1992), Fukuyama and Coleman (1992), Gainor (1992), Greeley, Garcia, Kessler, and Gilchrest (1992), Ho (1984), Johnson, Santos Torres, Coleman, and Smith (1995), Lee, Juan, and Hom (1984), Leong (1992), Merta (1995), Rollock, Westman, and Johnson (1992), Sue, Arredondo, and McDavis (1992), Wrenn (1985), and Yu and Gregg (1993).

THE CO-LEADERSHIP MODEL

THE BASIS OF CO-LEADERSHIP

Many who educate and train group leaders have come to favor the co-leadership model of group practice. This model has a number of advantages for all concerned: the group members can gain from the perspectives of two leaders; the co-leaders can confer before and after a group and learn from each other; and supervisors can work closely with the co-leaders during their training and can provide them with feedback. We prefer co-leadership both for facilitating groups and for training and supervising group leaders, and we usually work as a team. Although each of us has independent professional involvements (including leading groups alone at times), we very much enjoy co-leading and continue to learn from each other as well as from other colleagues we work with. Nevertheless, we do not want to give the impression that co-leadership is the only acceptable model, because many people facilitate a group alone quite effectively.

In conducting training workshops with university students, we continually hear how they value working with a partner, especially if they are leading a group for the first time. As we discussed earlier, group leaders preparing to meet their first group tend to experience self-doubt, anxiety, and downright trepidation! The task seems far less monumental if they meet their new group with a co-leader whom they trust and respect. In our in-service workshops for group workers, we find it is useful to observe the trainees as they co-lead so we can discuss what they are actually doing as they facilitate a group. Then, as we offer feedback to them, we frequently ask them to talk with each other about how they felt as they were co-leading and what they think about the session they have just led. The feedback between these co-leaders can be both supportive and challenging. They can make constructive suggestions about each other's style, and the process of exchanging perceptions can enhance their ability to function effectively as co-leaders.

The choice of a co-leader is important. If the two leaders are incompatible, their group is bound to be negatively affected. For example, power struggles between co-leaders will have the effect of dividing the group. If co-leaders are in continual conflict with each other, they are providing a poor model of interpersonal relating. Such conflict typically leads to unexpressed hostility within the group, which gets in the way of effective work. We are not suggesting that co-leaders will never have conflicts. What is important is that they work out any disputes in a decent and direct manner, for doing so can model ways of coping with interpersonal conflict.

A major factor in selecting a co-leader should be mutual respect. Two or more leaders working together will surely have their differences in leadership style, and they will not always agree or share the same perceptions or interpretations. If there is mutual respect and trust between them, however, they will be able to work cooperatively instead of competitively, and they will be secure enough to be free of the constant need to prove themselves.

It is not coincidence that those with whom we lead are also our closest friends. When several of us work together as a team in leading a workshop or presenting as a panel at a convention, we often receive comments about our style of interacting with one another. For example, people at times remark that our differences in personality and style complement one another. They observe enthusiasm, playfulness, a willingness to openly disagree, an absence of competition, and a liking and respect among us. The point we want to make is that the way we work as a team has a definite impact on the people we work with.

It is not essential that you be best friends with your co-leader. What you need is a good working relationship, which you can achieve by taking time to talk with each other. Although we take delight in our personal and professional relationship, we are also willing to engage in the hard work necessary to be a successful team. This relationship reflects our belief that it is essential that co-leaders get together regularly to discuss any matters that may affect their working as a team. We emphasize discussing how we are feeling in regard to our personal life as well as talking about specific group purposes and making plans for an upcoming group. Further, we tell co-leaders in training to arrange to spend time together both before and after each group session to evaluate their leadership and the group's progress, as well as to make plans for future sessions.

ADVANTAGES OF THE CO-LEADERSHIP MODEL

Having acknowledged our clear preference for co-leading groups, we will now present a summary of what seem to us the major advantages of using the co-leadership method:

1.   The chance of burnout can be reduced by working with a co-leader. This is especially true if you are working with a draining population, such as severely disturbed individuals who often simply get up and leave, who hallucinate during sessions, and who may be withdrawn or be acting out. In such groups one leader can attend to certain problem members while the other attempts to maintain the work going on in the group.

2.   If intense emotions are being expressed by one or more members, one leader can pay attention to those members while the other leader scans the room to note the reactions of other members, who can later be invited to share their feelings. Or, if appropriate, the co-leader can find a way to involve members in the work of someone else. Many possibilities exist for linking members, for facilitating interaction between members, and for orchestrating the flow of a group when co-leaders are sensitively and harmoniously working as a team.

3.   If one leader must be absent because of illness or professional reasons, the group can proceed with the other leader. If one of the co-leaders is especially drained on a given day or is temporarily experiencing some emotional pain, the co-leader can assume primary leadership, and the leader having problems can feel less burdened with the responsibility to "be there" for the group members. In such a case it may be appropriate for the co-leader to say to the group that he or she is going through some difficulties personally, without going into great detail. By simply having said this, the leader is likely to feel freer and may be much more present. This admission provides sound modeling for the members, for they can see that group leaders are not beyond dealing with personal problems.

4.   If one of the leaders has been strongly affected by a session, he or she can later explore feelings of anger, depression, or the like in some detail with the co-leader. The co-leader can be used as a sounding board, can check for objectivity, and can offer useful feedback. There is no problem of breaking confidentiality in such instances, for the co-leader was also present at the session. However, we do want to emphasize that it is often necessary for leaders to express and deal with such feelings in the session itself, especially if they were aroused in the group setting. For example, if you are aware that you are perpetually annoyed by a given

member, you might need to deal with your annoyance as a group matter. In certain cases a group member's concerns might touch your own "unfinished business," and you might explore your personal issues in the session. This is a time when a competent and trusted co-leader is especially important.

5.   An important advantage of co-leading emerges when one of the leaders is affected by another member to the degree that countertransference is present. Countertransference can distort one's objectivity so that it interferes with leading effectively. For example, your co-leader may typically react with hostility or some other intense feeling to one member who is seen as a problem. Perhaps you are better able to make contact with this member, and so you may be the person who primarily works with him or her. You can be of valuable assistance by helping your co-leader talk about, and perhaps even resolve, irrational reactions and attachments toward such a client.

DISADVANTAGES OF THE CO-LEADERSHIP MODEL

Even with a co-leader you choose, one whom you respect and like, there are likely to be occasional disagreements. This difference of perspective and opinion need not be a disadvantage or a problem. Instead, it can be healthy for both of you, because you can keep yourself professionally alert through constructive challenges and differences. Moreover, if you deal with your differences or conflicts during the session (rather than pretending that they do not exist), you are providing excellent modeling on how to work with conflicts. Most of the disadvantages in co-leading groups have to do with poor selection of a co-leader, random assignment to another leader, or failure of the two leaders to meet regularly:

1.   Problems can occur if co-leaders rarely meet with each other. The results are likely to be a lack of synchronization or even a tendency to work at cross purposes instead of toward a common goal. For example, we've observed difficulties when one group leader thought that all intervention should be positive, supportive, and invitational, whereas the other leader functioned on the assumption that members need to be pushed and directly confronted and that difficult issues should be brought up. The group became fragmented and polarized as a result of the incompatible leadership styles. The main problem was that the leaders did not take the time to discuss their differences.

2.   A related issue is competition and rivalry. For example, one leader may have an exaggerated need to have center stage, to be dominant at all times, and to be perceived as the one in control; such a leader might even actively put down the co-leader. Obviously, such a relationship between co-leaders is bound to have a negative effect on the group. In some cases members may develop negative reactions toward groups

in general, concluding that all that ever goes on in them is conflict and the struggle for power.

3.   If co-leaders do not have a relationship built on trust and respect or if they do not value each other's competence, they may not trust each other's interventions. Each leader may insist on following his or her own hunches, convinced that the other's are not of value.

4.   One leader may side with members against the other leader. For example, assume that Sue confronts a male leader with strong negative reactions and that his co-leader (a woman) joins Sue in expressing her reactions and even invites the members to give feedback to the co-leader. This practice can divide the group, with members taking sides about who is "right." It is especially a problem if one leader has not previously given negative reactions to the other and uses the situation as a chance to "unload" feelings.

5.   Co-leaders who are involved in an intimate relationship with each other can get into some problematic situations if they attempt to use time in the session to deal with their own relationship struggles. Although some members may support the co-leaders' "working on their issues" in the group, most clients are likely to resent these co-leaders for abdicating their leadership functions.

We think it is important that the two leaders have some say in deciding to work as a team. Otherwise, there is a potential for harm for both the group members and the co-leaders. Careful selection of a co-leader and time devoted to meeting together are essential. We encourage those who co-lead groups to spend some time both before *and* after each session discussing their reactions to what is going on in the group as well as their working relationship as co-leaders.

PROFESSIONAL COMPETENCE AND TRAINING

As a group leader you must provide only those services and use only those techniques for which you are qualified by training and experience. It is your responsibility as you market your professional services to accurately represent your competence. Although we encourage you to think of creative ways of reaching diverse populations, we also emphasize the need for adequate training and supervision in leading groups with such members. If you lead groups that are clearly beyond the scope of your preparation, you are not only practicing unethically but are also wide open to a malpractice suit.

Because various professions have differing training and educational standards for group work and because specializations call for various skills, we will not try to specify an "ideal program" that would produce competent group leaders. Rather, we will outline several general areas of professional experience that we consider basic in the development of a capable leader.

THE ISSUE OF LEADER COMPETENCE

Who is qualified to lead groups? What are some criteria by which to determine the level of competence of group leaders? How can leaders recognize their limits?

Concerning the issue of qualification, several factors must be considered. One is the type of group. Different groups require different leader qualifications. Some professionals who are highly qualified to work with college students are not competent to lead children's groups. Professionals who are trained to lead personal-growth groups may lack either the training or the experience necessary to administer group therapy to an outpatient population. Some may be very successful with groups for alcoholics or drug addicts yet be unequipped to lead couples' groups or to work with families. So we can restate the basic question as: Who is qualified to lead *this type* of group with *this type* of population?

Another issue related to competence is that of licenses, degrees, and credentials. In our judgment the training that leads to attainment of such certification is usually valuable, but degrees alone do not indicate that a person is a qualified leader. During the professional education of counselors who hope to work as group leaders, at least one course in the theory and practice of group counseling is essential. Unfortunately, it is not uncommon to find only one such survey course available to students in a master's degree program in psychology or counseling. A person may hold a Ph.D. in counseling psychology and be licensed to practice psychotherapy yet not be equipped, either by training or by personality, to practice *group* work. At the same time, we can conceive of a paraprofessional, without a degree or a license, who could competently lead or co-lead certain types of counseling groups or structured groups.

Group leaders need to recognize their limitations. Toward this end, they might well ask themselves:

- What kinds of clients am I capable of dealing with?
- What are my areas of expertise?
- What techniques do I handle well?
- How far can I safely go with clients?
- When should I consult another professional about a client?
- When should I refer a client to someone else?

Professional group workers know their limitations and recognize that they can't lead all kinds of groups or work with all kinds of clients. They familiarize themselves with referral resources and don't attempt to work with clients who need special help beyond their level of competence. Furthermore, responsible group workers are keenly aware of the importance of continuing their education. Even licensed and experienced professionals will attend conventions and workshops, take courses, seek consultation and supervision, and get involved in special training programs from time to time.

Truly competent group workers also have reasons for most of the activities they suggest in a group. They are able to explain to their clients the theory behind their group work and how it influences their practice. They can tell the members in clear language the goals of a group, and they can state the relationship between the way they lead the group and these goals. Effective group leaders are able to conceptualize the group process and to relate what they do in a group to this model. They continually refine their techniques in light of their model. In short, they possess the knowledge and skills that are described next.

PROFESSIONAL TRAINING STANDARDS FOR GROUP COUNSELORS

Effective group leadership programs are not developed by legislative mandates and professional codes alone. For proficient group leaders to emerge, a training program must make group work a priority. Unfortunately, in some master's programs in counseling not even one group course is required. In some programs such a course is still an elective. In those programs that do require course work in group counseling, there is typically one course that covers both the didactic and experiential aspects of group process. It is a major undertaking to adequately train group counselors in a single course!

The ASGW (1991) has published expanded *Professional Standards for the Training of Group Workers,* which specify two levels of competencies and related training. A set of core *knowledge* competencies and *skill* competencies provide the foundation on which specialized training is built. At a minimum, one group course should be included in a training program, and it should be structured to help students acquire the basic knowledge and skills needed to facilitate a group. These group skills are best mastered through supervised practice, which should include observation and participation in a group experience. The standards also contain a set of guidelines for integrating the new provisions with the Council for Accreditation of Counseling and Related Educational Programs (CACREP) accreditation standards.

A number of areas of knowledge are considered basic for all group leaders. These include identifying one's strengths and weaknesses, having clarity of one's values, being able to describe the characteristics associated with the typical stages in a group's development, being able to describe the facilitative and debilitative roles and behaviors that group members may take, knowing the therapeutic factors of a group, understanding the importance of group and member evaluation, and being aware of the ethical issues special to group work.

And some basic skill competencies should be possessed by anyone leading a group. Some of these skills include being able to open and close group sessions, modeling appropriate behavior for group members, engaging in appropriate self-disclosure in the group, giving and receiving feedback in the group, helping members attribute meaning to their experience in the group, and assisting members to integrate and apply what they have learned. The ASGW standards state that these group work skills are best mastered through supervised practice, which should include observation and participation in a group experience. Although a minimum of 10 hours of supervised practice is required, 20 hours is recommended as part of the core training.

Once counselor trainees have mastered these core knowledge and skill domains, they can acquire training in group work specializations in one or more of four areas: (1) task/work groups, (2) guidance/psychoeducational groups, (3) counseling/interpersonal problem-solving groups, and (4) psychotherapy/personality reconstruction groups. The standards detail specific knowledge and skill competencies for these specialties and also specify the recommended number of hours of supervised training for each. (Refer to Chapter 1 for a definition of these groups and their specific training requirements.)

The core competencies and experiences delineated in the 1991 ASGW training standards are considered the benchmarks for training group workers. The standards of the Council for Accreditation of Counseling and Related Educational Programs (CACREP, 1994) that deal with group work reflect much of this material (Conyne et al., 1993). Attempts have been made to implement the ASGW recommendations with the CACREP standards, outlining supervised clinical experience obtained in both practicum and internship programs. The CACREP standards require experience in individual and group counseling under supervision and, consistent with the ASGW training standards, indicate that at least one-fourth of direct service practicum be devoted to group work.

The current trend in training group leaders focuses on learning group process by becoming involved in supervised experiences. Certainly, completion of one graduate course in group theory and practice does not equip anyone to competently lead groups. Both direct participation in planned and supervised small groups and clinical experience in leading various groups under careful supervision are needed to equip leaders with the skills to meet the challenges of group work.

TRAINING AND PERSONAL EXPERIENCE

As is clear from our brief review of the ASGW's (1991) professional standards for training, it is essential for prospective group leaders to undergo extensive training appropriate to the general type of group they intend to lead. We highly recommend three types of experience as adjuncts to a training program: personal (private) psychotherapy, group therapy, and participation in a supervised training group.

Personal Psychotherapy for Group Leaders   We encourage trainees to get involved in their own personal counseling, both individual and group. During the course of these sessions, we hope they will come to a greater understanding of their motivation to facilitate groups. They can also explore the biases that might hamper their receptiveness to clients, any unfinished business that might lead to distortions in their perceptions of group members, other needs that might either facilitate or inhibit the group process, current conflicts, and ways they can fully recognize and utilize their strengths. In short, group counselors should demonstrate the courage to do for themselves what they expect members in their groups to do. Our rationale here is that group counselors cannot effectively assist clients to explore conflicts that they have not recognized and dealt with in themselves. We are not implying that therapists must have experienced every personal problem of the clients they work with, but they must have the courage to honestly search within themselves and face what they find.

Self-Exploration Groups for Group Leaders   We have discovered that participation in a self-exploration group (or some other type of interactive process-oriented group) is an extremely valuable adjunct to a group leader's internship training experiences. Beginning group leaders typically experience some anxiety regarding their adequacy, and their interactions with group members frequently lead to a surfacing of unresolved past or current problems. It is generally inappropriate for group counselors to use the groups they are responsible for leading to do their own extensive work. At times, there may be a fine line between being a leader and being a member, but leaders who habitually "become members" of their groups should join a therapeutic group as a member and use that group to explore their problems and continue their growth. Besides being of therapeutic value, such a group can be a powerful teaching tool for the trainee. One of the best ways for leaders to learn how to assist members in their struggles is by working themselves as members of a group.

Training Groups for Group Leaders   The training group can lead to insights and awareness without becoming a therapy group. Trainees can learn a great deal about their response to criticism, their competitiveness, their need for approval, their jealousies, their anxieties over being competent, their feelings about certain members of the group they lead, and their power struggles with co-leaders or members of their group. These are but a few of the issues that are appropriate for work in a training group.

Leaders who have an exaggerated need for approval may avoid being confrontive, may assume a passive stance, or may become inappropriately supportive in their groups. This need for approval can hamper their potential leadership success by preventing them from effectively encountering others. Another example is the person who is attracted to being a group leader primarily by the power inherent in this position. This person's exaggerated need to control and direct others may lead to the mechanical use of a repertoire of techniques designed to impress the group participants with the therapist's prowess. Styles such as these can be detected and worked with during the session of a training group.

ETHICAL ISSUES IN TRAINING GROUP COUNSELORS

One controversial ethical issue in the preparation of group leaders involves combining experiential and didactic methods in training. We consider an experiential component to be essential in teaching group-counseling courses. Struggling with trusting a group of strangers, risking vulnerability, receiving genuine support from others, developing good working relationships with peers, and being challenged to examine the impact of one's behavior on others are all vital learning experiences for future group leaders. If for no reason other than because it provides an understanding of what clients face, we think group experience for leaders is indispensable.

Students have a right to be informed of the specific nature of course requirements before they enter a program, and we find that it is common practice to combine the experiential and didactic domains. In their national survey of the training of group counselors, Merta, Wolfgang, and McNeil (1993) found that a large majority of counselor educators continue to use the experiential group in preparing group counselors. Furthermore, there is significant diversity in using alternative training models, and safeguards vary.

In group classes that are taught both experientially and didactically, the first half of the class typically deals with counseling theories and group-process issues. The content of the discussions may be very similar to the material in this textbook. During the second half of the session, many instructors conduct a group in which the students have an opportunity to be a member. Sometimes students co-lead a small group with a peer and are supervised by the instructor. Of course, this arrangement is not without problems either. Students may fear that their grades will be influenced by their participation (or lack of it) in the experiential part of the class.

Although we admit that there are inherent problems in teaching students how groups function by involving them on an experiential level, we think such difficulties can be resolved. Clear guidelines should be established so students know what their rights and responsibilities are. This arrangement does put a bit more pressure on both the instructor and the students, and it calls for honesty, maturity, and professionalism.

The focus of such a group might well be on here-and-now interactions. Even if members choose not to bring up matters such as their childhood, there is plenty to talk about if they deal with how they are affected by the work of other members and their reactions to other people in the group. If they openly and honestly learn to deal with one another, they are making great strides toward learning how to facilitate a group.

Those who teach group courses often function in multiple roles as group facilitator, instructor, evaluator, and supervisor. Although blending roles presents potential ethical problems, the literature reveals various strategies for limiting the impact of these problems. Merta, Wolfgang, and McNeil (1993) admit that no one training model or combination of safeguards is apt to solve the dilemma of protecting students from adverse dual relationships and at the same time provide them with the best possible training. It is challenging for those who teach group courses to learn ways to differentiate between experiential training workshops and counseling groups. At times it is difficult to draw clear distinctions between training workshops and counseling groups. It is essential that faculty who teach group courses or conduct training workshops for group workers monitor their practices by keeping the purpose of the training workshop clearly in mind. The boundaries between the domains of training workshops and counseling groups can be clarified by discussing relevant issues with colleagues.

It is essential to keep in mind the primary purpose of a group-counseling course, which is teaching students leadership skills and providing an understanding of how group process works. Although the main aim of a group course is not to provide personal therapy for students, participating in such a group can and ought to be therapeutic. Students can make a decision about what personal concerns they are willing to share, and they can also determine the depth of their personal disclosures. A group course is not designed to be a substitute for an intensive self-exploration experience, but learning about how groups function can be enhanced through active and personal participation in the group process.

We have found that most students sincerely interested in becoming effective group practitioners are willing to get involved in both the academic training and the self-exploration that lead to becoming the best possible group counselor. Likewise, as educators, it is our challenge to provide the best training available, keeping in mind the safeguards mentioned above.

DEVELOPING A RESEARCH
ORIENTATION TO PRACTICE

As a group leader, you will be expected to demonstrate the efficacy of your interventions. With the current emphasis on short-term treatments that provide symptom relief or solve clients' problems, familiarity with research in the group work field is becoming an essential part of practice. Along with follow-up group sessions and individual interviews of members of your groups, research can help you come to a better understanding of the specific factors that contributed to the successful outcomes or the failures of your groups. Applied research can help you refine your interventions and identify factors that interfere with group effectiveness. As a practitioner, it is essential that what you do in your groups is informed by research on the process and outcomes of groups. Part of your development as a group leader involves thinking of ways to make evaluation research a basic part of your group practice.

The following sections address the importance of combining research and practice in group work, identify some of the reasons for the gap between researchers and group practitioners, and describe some attitudes of practitioners toward research.

THE CURRENT STATUS OF GROUP WORK RESEARCH

Consumers and funders are increasingly demanding that practitioners demonstrate the value of their therapeutic strategies. Based on empirical investigations of more than four decades of group work, Dies (1992) writes that the general conclusion is that there is relatively little difference in outcome between individual and group treatments. With the pressures to justify the expense of psychotherapy, Dies suggests that clinicians are likely to face increased challenges to explain why the treatment of choice for most clients is not group therapy. In writing of the future of group therapy, Dies states that research on group interventions is expected to reflect growing efforts to link group process and outcome, provide a more congenial collaboration between practitioners and researchers, and offer a more sophisticated blending of research designs to study group process and outcomes.

A survey of more than 40 years of research shows an abundance of evidence that group approaches are associated with clients' improvement in a variety of settings and situations (Bednar & Kaul, 1978, 1979, 1994; Bednar & Lawlis, 1971; Kaul & Bednar, 1978, 1986). But the general consensus among experts is that the current knowledge of the effects of specific group treatments is modest at best. Researchers know little about how group processes mediate change in participants, how members influence group processes, and what dimensions of psychological functioning are most amenable to change in small groups. Quite simply, although researchers know that group treatments can be effective, they don't know much about why this is so. Rosenbaum, Lakin, and Roback (1992) put the challenge to researchers as follows: "Group therapies work, but how, and why, and with whom is still less clear than therapists (and their patients) would wish. The challenge to develop this kind of knowledge grows greater with the rapid increase in the bewildering variety of helping experiences that use group approaches" (p. 720).

Dies (1993) conducted a survey of 156 group psychotherapy investigators representing 29 different countries. Those surveyed agreed that our understanding about the complex interactions that influence treatment outcomes is rather meager. More is known about the general dimensions of group atmosphere, such as cohesion and group climate, than is known about selection of members, group composition, group leader techniques, and underlying group dynamics. Dies believes that the trend toward tailoring interventions to address specific diagnostic issues, along with the pressures to design effective, cost-efficient brief interventions will force researchers to confront these relatively neglected issues in future studies.

OBSTACLES TO THE ADVANCEMENT OF RESEARCH ON GROUP WORK

A gap exists between research and practice in group counseling, and closing it involves overcoming some major obstacles. Practitioners often view researchers as a "strange breed," preoccupied with trivial issues. Practitioners are likely to dismiss research without weighing its potential contributions. Counseling practitioners (as opposed to counselor educators, consultants, and administrators) are least likely to regularly read group research articles or use published research findings in their work with groups (Robison & Ward, 1990). Furthermore, empirical findings are seldom reported in a way that encourages group leaders to translate research into practice (Dies, 1983b).

As Stockton has observed (see Bednar et al., 1987), the lack of collaboration between researchers and practitioners continues to be a key problem in group work. Researchers often do not really understand what can be learned from clinical experience, and practitioners often perceive research as being irrelevant to clinical practice. Only a small percentage of group practitioners use research findings in any consistent manner or engage in research of their own. If this knowledge gap is to be bridged, practitioners and researchers need to develop an increased mutual respect for what each can offer, and they must learn to work cooperatively, accepting the dual role of practitioner/researcher (Morran & Stockton, 1985; Stockton in Bednar et al., 1987).

In their survey of research activities and attitudes among ASGW members, Robison and Ward (1990) found that few respondents conducted research with groups at the time they completed the survey. Research activities, both current and past, were reported most frequently by counselor educators, consultants, and administrators, and reported least by practicing counselors and counseling students. Insufficient time, funds, and employer support were most frequently reported as reasons for not conducting research with groups. Other reasons given for not conducting research on groups included: ethical issues or policies prohibiting research with agency clients, lack of interest, research facilities unavailable, lack of training in research methods, and lack of past success in presenting and publishing findings.

In their article on perspectives on research in group work, seven colleagues comment on overcoming obstacles to the future development of research (Bednar et al., 1987). These authors mention a number of common conceptual, methodological, and attitudinal impediments. They conclude that reducing these obstacles will require a commitment by researchers and other professionals:

- to improve conceptualizations of variables studied in relation to groups,
- to use research designs and methods that can assess the subtle nature of interactions among the leader and members,
- to improve reporting of the characteristics of treatment and control groups that are studied, and
- to focus on the applications of research findings.

These results can only be achieved through meaningful collaboration between researchers and group practitioners.

THE CHALLENGE OF COMBINING RESEARCH AND PRACTICE

Many group workers are not willing to devote time to devising evaluative instruments as part of their clinical practice. Yalom (1995) admits that few group practitioners will ever have the time, funding, and institutional backing to engage in large-scale research, yet he contends "many can engage in intensive single-patient or single-group research, and *all* clinicians must evaluate published clinical research" (p. 529).

It is possible, however, to make systematic observation and assessment basic parts of the practice of group work. Instead of thinking exclusively in terms of rigorous empirical research, practitioners can begin to consider alternatives to traditional scientific methods. One such alternative is evaluative research, which is aimed at gathering and assessing data that can be of value in making decisions about programs and in improving the quality of professional services (Dies, 1983a). In group work, pure research should not be seen as the only type of inquiry that has value. Practitioners and researchers can choose to do good field research instead (Morran & Stockton, 1985).

Whether or not group workers actually conduct research with their groups may be less important than their willingness to keep themselves informed about the practical applications of research on group work. At the very least, group counselors need to be up to date with the research implications for practice. Yalom (1995) claims that group trainees need to know more than how to implement techniques in a group—they also need to know how to learn. Faculty should teach and model a basic research orientation characterized by an open, self-critical inquiring attitude toward clinical and research evidence. He writes that students need to critically evaluate their own work and maintain sufficient flexibility to be responsive to their own observations. Yalom summarizes the challenge well:

> If the group therapy field is to develop coherently, it must respond to responsible, well-executed, relevant, and credible research; otherwise, group therapy will continue its capricious, helter-skelter course, and research will become a futile, effete exercise. (p. 529)

One survey asked practitioners how journal articles reporting research on groups could be made more useful to them in their own work with groups (Robison & Ward, 1990). The suggestions for improving published research with groups were:

- publish more articles on research that attempts to replicate earlier studies,
- increase the specificity of research reports,
- give more information about the experimental and control treatments used,
- describe more fully the rationale for studies,
- emphasize the relevance of research findings to group practice,
- publish more high-quality studies using actual groups in school and agency settings,
- increase the number of literature reviews of research on selected topics on groups,
- define dependent and independent variables more specifically, and
- place more emphasis on behavioral and attitudinal variables in published research.

According to Yalom (1995), a research orientation allows group therapists, throughout their career, to remain flexible and responsive to new evidence. Practitioners who lack a research orientation will have no basis to critically evaluate new developments in the field of group work. Without a consistent framework to evaluate evidence of the efficacy of innovations in the field, practitioners run the risk of being unreasonably unreceptive to new approaches. Or, in contrast, they uncritically embrace one fad after another.

EXERCISES

For those of you who are leading a group for the first time, we encourage you to complete these exercises both before you begin leading and then again toward the end of the semester. The comparison will give you a basis for seeing how your attitudes and ideas may evolve with experience.

ATTITUDE QUESTIONNAIRE
ON GROUP LEADERSHIP

Below are some statements concerning the role and functions of a group leader. Indicate your position on each statement, using the following scale:

1 = strongly agree
2 = slightly agree
3 = slightly disagree
4 = strongly disagree

_____ 1. It is the leader's job to actively work at shaping group norms.

_____ 2. Leaders should teach group members how to observe their own group as it unfolds.

_____ 3. The best way for a leader to function is by becoming a participating member of the group.

_____ 4. It is generally wise for leaders to reveal their private lives and personal problems in groups they are leading.

_____ 5. A group leader's primary task is to function as a technical expert.

_____ 6. It is extremely important for good leaders to have a definite theoretical framework that determines how they function in a group.

_____ 7. A group leader's function is to draw people out and make sure that silent members participate.

_____ 8. Group leaders influence group members more through modeling than through the techniques they employ.

_____ 9. It is generally best for the leader to give some responsibility to the members but also to retain some.

_____ 10. A major task of a leader is to keep the group focused on the here and now.

_____ 11. It is unwise to allow members to discuss the past or to discuss events that occurred outside the group.

_____ 12. It is best to give most of the responsibility for determining the direction of the group to the members.

_____ 13. Leaders should limit their self-disclosures to matters that have to do with what is going on in the group.

_____ 14. If group leaders are basically open and disclose themselves, transference by members will not occur.

_____ 15. A leader who experiences countertransference is not competent to lead groups.

_____ 16. Group leaders should develop a personalized theory of leadership based on ideas drawn from many sources.

_____ 17. To be effective, group leaders must recognize their reasons for wanting to be leaders.

_____ 18. Part of the task of group leaders is to determine specific behavioral goals for the participants.

_____ 19. A leader's theoretical model has little impact on the way
people actually interact in a group.

_____ 20. If group leaders have mastered certain skills and techniques,
it is not essential for them to operate from a theoretical framework.

_____ 21. Leaders who possess personal power generally dominate the
group and intimidate the members through this power.

_____ 22. There is not much place for a sense of humor in conducting
groups, because group work is serious business.

_____ 23. Group leaders should not expect the participants to do anything that they, as leaders, are not willing to do.

_____ 24. In groups with co-leaders there is the potential that the members will play one leader against the other like children
playing one parent against the other.

_____ 25. For co-leaders to work effectively with each other, it is essential that they share the same style of leadership.

_____ 26. In selecting a co-leader, it is a good idea to consider similarity
of values, philosophy of life, and life experiences.

_____ 27. If co-leaders do not respect and trust each other, there is the
potential for negative outcomes in the group.

_____ 28. Those who co-lead a group should be roughly equal in skills,
experiences, and status.

_____ 29. Co-leaders should never openly disagree with each other
during a session, for this may lead to a division within the
group.

_____ 30. The group is bound to be affected by the type of modeling that
the co-leaders provide.

We suggest that after you have completed this self-inventory, your class
break into small groups to discuss the items.

SELF-ASSESSMENT OF GROUP-LEADERSHIP SKILLS

In this chapter we described a set of skills necessary for effective group
leadership. The following self-inventory helps you identify areas of
strengths and weaknesses as a group leader. Read the brief description of
each skill and then rate yourself on each dimension. Think about the
questions listed under each skill. These questions are designed to aid you
in assessing your current level of functioning and identifying specific
ways you can improve on each skill.

You can profit from this checklist by reviewing it before and after
group sessions. If you are working with a co-leader, he or she can provide
you with a separate rating. These questions also provide a framework for

exploring your level of skill development with fellow students and with your supervisor or instructor.

To what degree do you demonstrate the following? (One space is for you to rate yourself early in the term and the other space for later on.) On each skill, rate yourself on this 3-point scale:

3 = I do this most of the time with a high degree of competence
2 = I do this some of the time with an adequate degree of competence
1 = I do this occasionally with a relatively low level of competence

___ ___ 1. **Active listening.** Hearing and understanding both subtle and direct messages, and communicating that one is doing this.
   a. How well do I listen to members?
   b. How attentive am I to nonverbal language?
   c. Am I able to hear both direct and subtle messages?
   d. Do I teach members how to listen and respond?

___ ___ 2. **Reflecting.** Capturing the underlying meaning of what is said or felt and expressing this without being mechanical.
   a. Can I mirror what another says without being mechanical?
   b. Do my restatements add meaning to what was said by a member?
   c. Do I check with members to determine the accuracy of my reflection?
   d. Am I able to reflect both thoughts and feelings?

___ ___ 3. **Clarifying.** Focusing on the underlying issues and assisting others to get a clearer picture of what they are thinking or feeling.
   a. Do my clarifying remarks help others sort out conflicting feelings?
   b. Am I able to focus on underlying issues and themes?
   c. Do members get a clearer focus on what they are thinking and feeling?
   d. Does my clarification lead to a deeper level of member self-exploration?

___ ___ 4. **Summarizing.** Identifying key elements and common themes and providing a picture of the directional trends of a group session.
   a. Does my summarizing give direction to a sesson?
   b. Am I able to tie together several themes in a group session?
   c. Do I attend adequately to summarizing at the end of a session?

d. Do I encourage members to summarize what they heard?

5. **Facilitating.** Helping members to express themselves clearly and to take action in a group.
   a. Am I able to help members work through barriers to communication?
   b. How much do I encourage member interaction?
   c. Am I successful in teaching members to focus on themselves?
   d. Can I steer members into discussing here-and-now reactions?

6. **Empathizing.** Adopting the internal frame of reference of a member.
   a. Are my life experiences diverse enough to provide a basis for understanding members?
   b. Can I maintain my separate identity at the same time as I empathize with others?
   c. Do I communicate to others that I understand their subjective world?
   d. Do I promote expressions of empathy among the members?

7. **Interpreting.** Explaining the meaning of behavior patterns within some theoretical framework.
   a. Are my interpretations accurate and well-timed?
   b. Do I present my interpretations in the form of hunches?
   c. Do I encourage members to provide their own meaning for their behavior?
   d. Do I avoid making dogmatic interpretations?

8. **Questioning.** Using questions to stimulate thought and action but avoiding question/answer patterns of interaction between leader and member.
   a. Do I overuse questioning as a leadership style?
   b. Do I ask "what" and "how" questions instead of "why" questions?
   c. Do I keep myself hidden through asking questions?
   d. Do I use open-ended questions that lead to deeper self-exploration?

9. **Linking.** Promoting member-to-member interaction and facilitating exploration of common themes in a group.
   a. Do my interventions enhance interactions between members?
   b. Do I foster a norm of member-to-member interactions or leader-to-member interactions?
   c. Do I help members find a way to connect with each other?

d. Am I able to orchestrate interactions so several members can be involved in working at the same time?

_____ _____ 10. **Confronting.** Challenging members to look at some aspects of their behavior.
a. Do I model caring and respectful confrontation?
b. How do members generally react to my confrontations?
c. Am I able to confront specific behaviors without being judgmental?
d. In confronting others, do I let them know how I am affected by their behavior?

_____ _____ 11. **Supporting.** Offering some form of positive reinforcement at appropriate times in such a way that it has a facilitating effect.
a. Do I recognize the progress members make?
b. Do I build on the strengths and gains made by members?
c. Do I balance challenge and support?
d. Does my providing support sometimes get in the way of a member's work?

_____ _____ 12. **Blocking.** Intervening to stop counterproductive behaviors in the group or to protect members.
a. Am I able to intervene when necessary without attacking a member?
b. Do I block a member's behavior that is disruptive to the group?
c. Am I aware of when it is necessary for me to protect a member from another member?
d. Can I effectively block counterproductive behaviors?

_____ _____ 13. **Diagnosing.** Getting a clear sense of members without labeling them.
a. Can I understand a member's problem without using a label?
b. Do I help members to assess their own problematic behavior?
c. Am I able to detect members who may not be appropriate for a group?
d. Can I create interventions that fit with my diagnostic impressions?

_____ _____ 14. **Modeling.** Demonstrating to members desired behaviors that can be practiced both during and between group sessions.
a. What kind of behavior do I model during group sessions?
b. Am I able to model effective self-disclosure?

c. Can I model caring confrontations?

d. What is the general effect of my modeling on a group?

_____ _____ 15. **Suggesting.** Offering information or possibilities for action that can be used by members in making independent decisions.

a. Do I differentiate between suggesting and prescribing?

b. Do my suggestions encourage members to take initiative?

c. Do I tend to give too many suggestions?

d. How do I determine when to give suggestions and when to avoid doing so?

_____ _____ 16. **Initiating.** Demonstrating an active stance in intervening in a group at appropriate times.

a. Do I generally get group sessions started in an effective manner?

b. Do I take active steps to prevent a group from floundering in unproductive ways?

c. Am I able to initiate new work with others once a member's work comes to an end?

d. Do I teach members how to initiate their own work in the sessions?

_____ _____ 17. **Evaluating.** Appraising the ongoing group process and the individual and group dynamics.

a. What criteria do I use to assess the progress of my groups?

b. What kinds of questions do I pose to members to help them evaluate their own gains as well as their contributions to the group?

c. Do I make a concerted effort to assist members in assessing their progress as a group?

d. What kind of evaluation instruments do I use in a group?

_____ _____ 18. **Terminating.** Creating a climate that encourages members to continue working after sessions.

a. Do I prepare members for termination of a group?

b. Do I allow adequate time at the end of a session for closure?

c. Do I help members transfer what they learn in group to daily life?

d. Do I take steps to help members integrate their learnings in group?

Once you complete this self-assessment, circle the items where you most need improvement (any items that you rated as "1" or "2"). Circle the letter of the questions that are the most meaningful to you, as well as the questions that indicate a need for attention. Think about specific strategies you can design to work on the skills where you see yourself as being most limited. It is a good idea to take this inventory at least twice—once at the beginning of the course and then again later.

POINTS TO REMEMBER:
SUMMARY OF PART ONE

Following is a list of 15 basic concepts and guidelines that we hope you will remember:

1. It is important to have a theoretical rationale that will help you make sense of what occurs in a group. Because each established group theory stresses a particular dimension of the group process, we encourage a selective borrowing of concepts from each of them. What is important is that you devote time to conceptualizing the group process.

2. We believe that personality and character are the most important variables in making effective group leaders. Techniques cannot compensate for the shortcomings of leaders who lack self-knowledge, who are not willing to do what they ask group members to do, or who are poorly trained. Character traits of effective leaders, in our view, include courage, willingness to model, presence, caring, a belief in the group process, openness, nondefensiveness, personal power, endurance, a sense of humor, imagination, and self-awareness. We ask you to think about your personal characteristics and to try to decide which will be assets and which liabilities to you as a group leader.

3. In addition to having certain personal characteristics, effective group leaders are knowledgeable about group dynamics and have leadership skills. We suggest that you make frequent use of the inventories we have presented as a means of thinking about personal areas you might need to improve and competencies you might need to develop.

4. You will be faced with the need to take a stand on a number of basic issues, including how much responsibility for what goes on in the group belongs to the members and how much to you as the leader, how much and what type of structuring is optimal for a group, what kind of self-disclosure is optimal, what role and function you will assume, and how you will integrate both support and confrontation into group practice.

5. Ethical codes have been established by various professional organizations, and those who belong to such organizations are bound by them. Thus, ethical guidelines governing group practice are not something you decide alone or in a vacuum. You should familiarize yourself with these established codes of ethics and with the laws that may affect group practice. The latter are particularly important if you are working with children or adolescents.

6. A solid academic background is desirable, but also important is an internship experience in which you can get supervised experience in leading and co-leading groups. Ongoing training groups and personal-growth groups are useful adjuncts to your academic program and your practical experience. Personal psychotherapy (both individual and group) is also valuable for you personally and for your development as a practitioner.

7. In developing a proposal for a group, include the selection procedures you plan to use, the composition you plan for the group, and details such as where and when you will hold the group. We recommend an individual screening session for all applicants and a pregroup session.

8. Group approaches to therapy have some distinct advantages over individual approaches, but they also have limitations. It is a mistake to think that groups are for everyone, and in designing a group be able to state clearly why a group is the treatment approach of choice. Such a written rationale should include descriptions of the goals of the group, the means that will be used to accomplish these goals, the role of the members, your function and role, and the means that will be used to assess the outcomes.

9. Psychological risks are associated with participation in a group. It is your responsibility to help the members identify and explore their readiness to deal with these potential risks. It is also your job to develop means of minimizing the risks.

10. A therapeutic group is a means to an end. Participants can use the group to learn more about themselves, to explore their conflicts, to learn new social skills, to get feedback on the impact they have on others, and to try out new behaviors. The group becomes a microcosm of society, in which members can learn more effective ways of living with others. Depending on the type of group, there are some clear advantages to constituting a group that is diverse with respect to age, gender, cultural background, race, and philosophical perspectives.

11. It is a helpful practice to develop guidelines for behavior in groups and teach them to the members. Some of the behaviors you might stress are keeping the group's activities confidential, respecting the differences that characterize the members, taking responsibility for oneself, working hard in the group, listening, and expressing one's thoughts and feelings.

12. Pay attention to the diversity that exists within your group, and use this diversity to accentuate the members' work. Help members recognize the ways in which their cultural background is influencing their values and behavior, and highlight cultural themes as they surface during a session.

13. Throughout the life of a group, continue teaching members how to assess their individual progress so that they have a basis for determining the degree to which they are accomplishing their goals. Also, encourage the members to evaluate the group as a whole and how its time is being used.

14. Be aware of your reactions in the group. You can use them very effectively in enhancing the group process. Remember that they are your most useful therapeutic instrument as a group leader. Be willing to share your reactions to what is occurring within the here and now of the group sessions.

15. Take some time to think about your therapeutic style and its impact on the process and outcomes of your group. Be able to describe its key features in clear terms.

PART TWO | GROUP PROCESS
Stages of Development

The stages in the life of a group do not generally flow neatly and predictably in the order described in the chapters that follow. In actuality, there is considerable overlap between stages, and once a group moves to an advanced stage, it is not uncommon for it to stay at a plateau for a time or to temporarily regress to an earlier stage. Similarly, the fact that certain tasks have been accomplished in a group, such as working through conflicts, does not mean that new conflicts will not erupt. Groups ebb and flow, and both members and leaders need to pay attention to the factors that affect the direction a group takes.

Knowing about typical patterns in the evolution of a group will give you a valuable perspective. You will be better able to predict problems and to intervene in appropriate and timely ways. Knowledge of the critical turning points in a group lets you help the participants mobilize their resources so that they can successfully meet the tasks facing them at each stage.

CHAPTER 4

FORMING
A GROUP

FOCUS QUESTIONS

Introduction

Developing a Proposal for a Group

Working Within the System

Attracting and Screening Members

Guidelines for Announcing a Group and Recruiting
  Group Members

Practical Procedures for Announcements and Recruitment

Screening and Selection Procedures

Practical Considerations in Forming a Group

Group Composition

Group Size

Frequency and Duration of Meetings

Length of a Group

Place for Group Meetings

Open versus Closed Groups

The Uses of a Pregroup Meeting

Clarifying Leader and Member Expectations

Setting Up Basic Ground Rules

Exploring the Advantages of and Misconceptions about Groups

An Integrated Approach to Pregroup Preparation:
Research Findings

Building Evaluation into Group Work

Co-Leader Issues at the Pregroup Stage

Pregroup Stage: Summary

Member Functions and Possible Problems

Leader Functions

Exercises

Exercises in Group Planning

Interviewing Exercises

FOCUS QUESTIONS

1. What issues do you think leaders should consider in organizing a group?

2. How would you go about drafting a written proposal for a group, and how would you "sell" your idea to the agency or institution where you work?

3. How would you announce your group and recruit members? What are some practical ways you can think of to get a group started?

4. What criteria would you use to screen and select members for a group? If you decided to exclude someone who had applied, how would you handle this matter?

5. If you were conducting individual interviews to select group participants, what are some questions you would most want to ask?

6. How would you explain to a potential member the risks and benefits involved in groups? What are some ways of minimizing the psychological risks?

7. What are some misconceptions you think people have concerning the nature and functioning of groups?

8. What are some advantages of a preliminary session in which potential members can determine whether a given group is for them? How would you want to make use of this first meeting?

9. What are the major ethical considerations in organizing and forming a group?

10. Do you have different attitudes about forming a voluntary group than you do regarding an involuntary one?

INTRODUCTION

We cannot overemphasize the importance of the preparatory period during which a group is organized. Careful attention to forming a group is crucial to its outcome. You will spend time wisely by thinking about what kind of group you want and by getting yourself psychologically ready for your leadership role and functions. The more clearly you can state your expectations, the better you will be able to plan and the more meaningful the experience will be for the participants. A lack of careful thought and planning will show up later in a variety of problems that lead to confusion and floundering among the participants. In planning a group, an initial step is clarifying the rationale for it, which entails drafting a detailed proposal.

DEVELOPING A PROPOSAL FOR A GROUP

Many good ideas for groups are never put into practice because they are not developed into a clear and convincing plan. If you are going to create a group under the auspices of an agency, you will probably have to explain your proposed goals and methods. Consider these questions when preparing your proposal:

- What type of group are you forming? Will it be a personal-growth group or one designed to treat people with certain disorders? Will it be long term or short term?
- Whom is the group for? Identify the specific population.
- Is the group composed of voluntary or involuntary members? If it is a mandatory group, what special considerations must you address?
- What are the general goals and purposes of this group? That is, what will members gain from participating in it?
- Why is there a need for such a group?
- What are the basic assumptions underlying this project?
- What are your qualifications to lead this group?
- What screening and selection procedures will be used? What is your rationale for using these particular procedures?
- How many members will be in the group? Where will the group meet? How often will it meet? How long will each meeting last? Will new people be allowed to join the group once it has started?
- How will the members be prepared for the group experience? What ground rules will you establish at the outset?
- What structure will your group have? What techniques will be used? Why are these techniques appropriate? In what ways can you employ your techniques in a flexible manner to meet the needs of culturally diverse client populations?
- How will you handle the fact that people will be taking some risks by participating in the group? What will you tell the members about these dangers, and what will you do to safeguard members from unnecessary risks? Will you take any special precautions with participants who are minors?
- What evaluation procedures do you plan? What follow-up procedures?
- What topics will be explored in this group? To what degree will the topics be determined by group members and to what degree by you?
- What do you expect to be the characteristics of the various stages of the group? What might the problems be at each stage, and how will you cope with them?

Summary Checklist for a Proposal   Five general areas form the basis of a sound and practical proposal. They are:

1. **Rationale.** Do you have a clear and convincing rationale for your group? Are you able to answer questions that might be raised?
2. **Objectives.** Are you clear about what you most want to attain and how you will go about doing so? Are your objectives specific, measurable, and attainable within the specified time?
3. **Practical considerations.** Is the membership defined? Are the meeting time, frequency of meetings, and duration of the group reasonable?
4. **Procedures.** Have you selected specific procedures to meet the stated objectives? Are these procedures appropriate and realistic for the given population?
5. **Evaluation.** Does your proposal contain strategies for evaluating how well the stated objectives were met? Are your evaluation methods objective, practical, and relevant?

WORKING WITHIN THE SYSTEM

If you hope to have your proposal accepted both by your supervisors in an agency and by the potential members, you will need to develop the skills necessary to work within a system. To get a group off the ground, you must use awareness and sensitivity in negotiating with the staff of the institution involved. In all clinics, agencies, and hospitals, power issues and political realities play a role. You may become excited about organizing groups only to encounter resistance from your coworkers or your administrators. You may be told, for example, that only psychologists, social workers, and psychiatrists are qualified to lead groups. The rest of the staff may be as cynical as you are inspired about the prospects of doing groups in your setting. Some of your colleagues may be jealous of your efforts, especially if you have successful groups. They may feel that you are taking "their" clients away from them.

The representatives of institutions need to be educated about the potential value, as well as realistic limitations, of groups for their clients. It is helpful to be able to predict some of the major concerns that administrators and agency directors are likely to have about the proposal you submit. For example, if you are attempting to organize a group in a public high school, the administrators may be anxious about parental complaints and potential lawsuits. If you are able to appreciate their concerns and speak directly to ethical and legal issues, you stand a better chance of getting your proposal accepted. If you are not clear in your own mind about what you hope to accomplish through group work or how you will conduct the meetings, the chances are slim that a responsible administrator will endorse your program. If you have not thought through some questions that you are likely to be asked about your proposal, you are setting yourself up for defeat. Here are a few examples of questions that we've been asked as we were presenting a group proposal:

- How will this institution be covered legally in the event of a lawsuit?
- Will the program be voluntary, and will the parents of minors give written consent?
- What will you do if this group proves to be psychologically disruptive for some of the members?
- Are you prepared to deal with confrontations from parents or from community members?

Regardless of the type of group you wish to form, having a clear and organized written proposal and presenting it personally are key components for translating ideas into action. A variety of sample group proposals are presented in Chapters 9 through 12. As you review these proposals for various age groups, think of specific groups that would be appropriate to the population you serve and the setting in which you work. See if you can adapt any of these proposals to fit your needs.

ATTRACTING AND SCREENING MEMBERS

Assuming that you have been successful in getting a proposal accepted, the next step is to find a practical way to announce your group to prospective participants. How a group is announced influences both the way it will be received by potential members and the kind of people who will join. Although professional standards should prevail over a commercialized approach, we have found that making personal contact with potential members is one of the best methods of recruiting.

GUIDELINES FOR ANNOUNCING A GROUP AND RECRUITING GROUP MEMBERS

Professional issues are involved in publicizing a group and recruiting members. The *Ethical Guidelines for Group Counselors* (ASGW, 1989) state that prospective members should have access to the following information (preferably in writing):*

- a statement of the goals and purposes of the group
- entrance procedures, time limits of the group experience, and termination procedures
- the rights and responsibilities of both group members and the group leader
- techniques and procedures that may be used, especially any specialized or experimental activities in which members may be expected to participate

*Refer to the end of Chapter 2 where these guidelines are reproduced. See guideline 1.

- education, training, and qualifications of the group leader
- fees and any other related expenses
- a statement of whether follow-up service is included in the fee
- a realistic statement of what services can and cannot be provided within a particular group structure
- personal risks involved in the group
- use of any recording of sessions

In writing announcements, it is best to give an accurate picture of the group and to avoid making promises about the outcomes of the group and raising unrealistic expectations. As we've indicated, making direct contact with the population most likely to benefit from the group is an excellent way to follow up printed announcements. These personal contacts, which can include distributing printed information to those interested, lessen the chance that people will misunderstand the purposes and functioning of the group.

Another effective method of announcing and recruiting for a group is to inform your agency colleagues. They can then refer clients to you who are appropriate for the particular group. It is possible that they can also do the preliminary screening, including giving written information on the group to potential members with whom they have contact. Involve your coworkers as much as possible in every phase of organizing your group.

PRACTICAL PROCEDURES FOR ANNOUNCEMENTS AND RECRUITMENT

A specific example of identifying and recruiting a target population is provided by Deborah Lambert and Nancy Ceraso English, at North Allegheny Senior High School in Pennsylvania. They find that some groups are more popular than others with high school students. Groups that tend to have relatively low enrollment because of their nature or the stigma attached to them include those for children of alcoholics and those for clients needing follow-up care after a drug-treatment program. In contrast, groups for dealing with parents and for dealing with sexual relationships have a high appeal. Here is a list of practical strategies and considerations Lambert and English find helpful in overcoming student identification and recruitment difficulties:

> **Classroom Presentations.** Presenting the information to individual classrooms or to homerooms may be one of the most effective means of announcing and recruiting potential group members. Films, lectures, and discussions naturally increase knowledge and sensitivity among the student body.
>
> **Hallway Posters.** Place signs in well-attended areas such as the lunchroom, hallways, and bathrooms. Attractive and eye-catching phrases increase the likelihood of a response. "Tear-off" phone num-

bers or "take-one" business cards allow for discretion and future reference. Remove the signs after three to four weeks, but post new ones at regular intervals (four or five times a year).

PA Announcements. Public-address announcements have limited effectiveness, because students often miss them or tune them out. But they can be made at different times of the day. Give a room number and a main office contact for easy student access.

Newspaper Articles. Advertise in the school paper. Include registration information and key phrases to describe your groups. Supply articles written by past or present members or by facilitators.

Teacher Contacts. Keep the faculty members informed of the groups you are running. Provide them with a brief description of the types of students you hope will participate. Familiarize teachers with the characteristics and behavior that typify the populations you are hoping to reach. Provide homeroom teachers with an announcement to be read to their classes describing the groups and the names of the group facilitators.

Parent Letter or Bulletin. Inform parents of the groups available and the benefits of participating. Provide them with the name of the student-assistance coordinator or counselor who is running the group.

Peer Referrals. Friends are an excellent resource. Follow your school policy on peer referrals. Take steps to ensure that peer reporting does not take on a "narc" quality. At designated "open-house" meetings invite students to bring their friends.

Student Handbook. Include a description of your program and the various groups that will be held in the school handbook.

Counselor Staffing. Meet with the counselors, the school nurse, and administrators to let them know about the groups you will be offering. They may be able to identify appropriate candidates.

The main point is that Lambert and English do not wait passively for students to come in and sign up for the groups they offer. Instead, they use multiple approaches to contact students directly (giving talks in the classrooms) and indirectly (meeting with counselors, teachers, and other school personnel). Because of their own enthusiasm for their groups, they are more likely to attract students who could profit. In Chapter 10 there are descriptions of two groups that English and Lambert offer at North Allegheny Senior High School: a group for children of alcoholics and one for students who are coming out of drug rehabilitation.

SCREENING AND SELECTION PROCEDURES

After announcing a group and recruiting members, the next crucial step is arranging for screening and selecting the members who will make up the group. The ASGW *Ethical Guidelines for Group Counselors* (1989) state: "Insofar as possible, the counselor selects group members whose needs and goals are compatible with the goals of the group, who will not impede the group process, and whose well-being will not be jeopardized by the group experience" (2).

This guideline raises several questions: What screening method should be used? How can you determine who would be best suited for the group, who might have a negative impact on the group process, or who might be jeopardized by the experience? How can you therapeutically deal with those candidates who, for whatever reason, are not included in the group?

The type of group should determine the kind of members accepted. A person who can work well in a structured, short-term group designed to teach social skills or to cope with stress might not be ready for an intensive therapy group. Psychotic individuals would probably be excluded from a counseling group yet might benefit from a weekly group for outpatients at a mental-health center. The question that needs to be considered is: Should *this* particular person be included in *this* particular group at *this* time with *this* group leader?

Preliminary Screening Sessions   We endorse screening procedures that include a private session between the candidate and the leader. During the private session, the leader might look for evidence that the group will be beneficial to the candidate. Some questions to consider are: Is this person motivated to change? Is this a choice of the individual or of someone else? Why this particular type of group? Does he or she understand what the purposes of the group are? Are there any indications that group counseling is contraindicated for this person at this time?

Group applicants should be given the opportunity, at their private sessions, to interview the group leader. They should be invited to ask questions concerning the procedures, basic purposes, and any other aspect of the group. This questioning is important as a means not only of getting information but also of developing a feeling of confidence in the group leader, which is necessary if productive work is to take place. In other words, we believe that screening should be a two-way process and that potential members should be encouraged to form a judgment about the group and the leader. Given enough information about the group, a member can make a better informed decision about whether to enter it.

In addition to the private screening, a session for all the candidates is extremely valuable. At a preliminary session the leader can outline the reason for the group and the topics that might be explored. This introduction can be most helpful for people who are uncertain whether they want to invest themselves in this group. Potential members can meet one another and begin to explore the potential of the group.

We admit that screening and selection procedures are subjective and that ultimately the intuition and judgment of the leader are crucial. We are concerned that candidates benefit from a group but even more concerned that they might be psychologically hurt by it or might drain the group's energies excessively. Certain members, while remaining unaffected by a group, sap its energy for productive work. This is particularly true of hostile people, people who monopolize, extremely aggressive people, and people who act out. The potential gains of including certain of these members must be weighed against the probable losses to the group as a whole. We also believe that group counseling is contraindicated for individuals who are suicidal, extremely fragmented or acutely psychotic, sociopathic, facing extreme crises, highly paranoid, or extremely self-centered.

A leader needs to develop a system for assessing the likelihood that a candidate will benefit from a group experience. Factors that must be taken into consideration are the level of training of the leader, the proposed makeup of the group, the setting, and the basic nature of the group. For example, it might be best not to accept a highly defensive individual into an ongoing adolescent group, for several reasons. A group may be too threatening for a person so vulnerable and may lead to increased defensiveness and rigidity, or such a person may have a counterproductive effect on group members who want to do serious work.

In some cases it may not be practical and realistic to conduct individual interviews, and alternatives will have to be relied on. One alternative is group screening sessions. This method saves time and also has the advantage of providing an idea of how each person reacts to a group situation. Once members meet one another in a group situation, they can better decide if they want to make a commitment to the group.

Personal contact is always best. For example, we offered a personal-growth group in Europe in which it was unrealistic to screen members privately on a personal basis. We did provide the person who had agreed to organize this group with a detailed letter that described relevant information about the workshop. In several personal contacts with the sponsor we discussed our philosophy of group work, the central purposes of the workshop, and who would most benefit from it. In spite of our efforts to spell out the nature of the group and to prepare those who would attend, we met with considerable opposition from some members, who asserted that the group was not what they had envisioned. This experience reinforced our belief in the value of screening and detailed preparation done in a personal way.

There are other instances when screening may not be practical or even possible. If you work in a county facility or a state hospital, chances are you will simply be assigned a group. The basis for assigning members could be their diagnosis or the ward they are on. Even if you are not able to select members for your group, you can make at least brief individual contact with them to prepare them. You will also have to devote part of the initial sessions to preparations, for many of the members may not have the faintest idea why they are in the group or how the group might be of any value to them. In open groups, whose membership changes as some clients leave and new ones are added, it is a good practice to meet individually with incoming members so you can orient them.

Assessing and Choosing Members   We are often asked the questions: "How do you decide who will best fit into the group, who will most benefit from it, and who is likely to be harmed by the experience?" "If you decide to exclude a person from the group, how do you handle this in a tactful and therapeutic manner?" As a group leader you must make the ultimate decision to include or exclude certain clients. Because the groups we typically offer are voluntary, one factor we look for during the interview is the degree to which a candidate wants to make changes and is willing to expend the necessary effort. We consider whether a group seems the appropriate method of intervention to accomplish the desired changes. We also weigh heavily how much the candidate seems to want to become a member of this group, especially after he or she is given information about it.

We sometimes find ourselves reluctant to let certain people into a group in spite of their desire to join. As we've mentioned, we do pay attention to our intuitions concerning a person, so in the last analysis our screening and selection process is a subjective one. A variety of reasons might lead us to exclude a person, but whatever our reservations are, we discuss them with the prospective member. At times, after we've discussed our concerns, we see matters differently. At other times we simply cannot with a clear conscience admit a person.

If we do not accept people, we tend to stress how the group might not be appropriate for them and, in some cases, how they would not be appropriate for the group. We strive to break the news in a manner that is honest, direct, and sensitive and that helps those who are not being accepted to remain open to other options. For example, we might determine that a highly defensive and extremely anxious person who is very frightened in interpersonal relationships is likely to benefit from a series of individual counseling sessions before being placed in a group situation. We would explain our rationale and encourage the person to consider accepting a referral for an appropriate type of intervention. In other words, we do not close the door on people we exclude from a group with no explanation, nor do we convey that there is something intrinsically wrong with them because they were not included in this particular group.

When we do in-service training workshops for group leaders in various agencies and institutions, many leaders tell us that they don't screen people for their groups. They cite any number of reasons: they don't have the time; they don't have much voice in choosing group members, because people are simply assigned to a group; they don't really know how to determine who will or will not benefit or will be negatively influenced by a group experience; they cannot see why screening is really important; they don't want to play the role of expert in deciding who will be included or excluded; or they don't want to make a mistake by turning away people who might gain from a group. In response, we emphasize that we see screening not as a highly objective and scientific process but as a rough device for getting together the best clientele for a given group. As we mentioned earlier, our view of screening entails a dialogue with the prospective members. It is an opportunity to give information to them and to orient them to the group, and it is a way to help them share in the decision of whether it is appropriate for them to become involved.

PRACTICAL CONSIDERATIONS IN FORMING A GROUP

GROUP COMPOSITION

Whether a group should have a homogeneous membership or a heterogeneous one depends on the group's goals. In general, for a specific target population with given needs, a group composed entirely of members of that population is more appropriate than a heterogeneous group. Consider a group composed entirely of elderly people. It can focus exclusively on the specific problems that characterize their developmental period, such as loneliness, isolation, lack of meaning, rejection, deterioration of the body, and so forth. This similarity of the members can lead to a great degree of cohesion, which in turn allows for an open and intense exploration of their life crises. Members can express feelings that have been kept private, and their life circumstances can give them a bond with one another.

Examples of other homogeneous groups are Alcoholics Anonymous, Recovery Inc., Parents without Partners, and Weight Watchers. It is common to hear people claim that, unless one has actually experienced what it is like to be, for example, an alcoholic, one cannot fully understand, and thus cannot help with, an alcoholic's unique problems. We don't accept the premise that the group leader must have experienced every problem of the client. It is important only that group leaders be able to identify with the feelings of clients—their loneliness, fear, and anxiety. When a specific problem exists, however, group cohesion can help, and so homogeneity is appropriate.

A case can sometimes be made, however, for combining people from different populations in a single group. In one of her "Death and Dying" seminars, Dr. Elisabeth Kubler-Ross shared her dream of having children on every hospital ward for the elderly. She maintained that this would give the elderly a chance to share their life and experiences with children and to get the meaning from life that comes from taking care of children. The children would benefit by getting the opportunity to experience older people. Thus, a combination of these two age groups could have some unique therapeutic results for members of both.

Sometimes a microcosm of the outside social structure is desired, and in that case a heterogeneous group is, of course, called for. Personal-growth groups and certain therapy groups tend to be heterogeneous. Members can experiment with new behavior and develop interpersonal skills with the help of feedback from a rich variety of people in an environment that represents out-of-group reality.

GROUP SIZE

What is a desirable size for a group? The answer depends on several factors: the age of the clients, the experience of the leader, the type of group, and the problems to be explored. For instance, a group composed of elementary schoolchildren might be kept to three or four, whereas a group of adolescents might be made up of six to eight people. For a weekly on-going group of adults, about eight people with one leader may be ideal. A group of this size is big enough to give ample opportunity for interaction and small enough for everyone to be involved and to feel a sense of "group."

FREQUENCY AND DURATION OF MEETINGS

How often should a group meet? For how long? Should a group meet twice weekly for one-hour sessions? Or is an hour and a half to two hours once a week preferable? With children and adolescents it may be better to meet more frequently and for a shorter period to suit their attention span. If the group is taking place in a school setting, the meeting times can correspond to regularly scheduled class periods. For groups of college students or relatively well-functioning adults, a two-hour weekly session might be preferable. This two-hour period is long enough to allow some intensive work yet not so long that fatigue sets in. You can choose any frequency and duration that suit your style of leadership and the type of people in your group. For an inpatient group composed of lower-functioning members, it is desirable to meet on a daily basis for 45 minutes. Because of the members' psychological impairment, it may not be realistic to hold their attention for a longer period. Even for higher-functioning inpatient groups, it is a good practice to meet several times a week, but these groups might be scheduled for 90 minutes. (An excellent description of inpatient therapy groups for both higher-level and lower-functioning clients is provided by Irvin Yalom in his 1983 book *Inpatient Group Psychotherapy.*)

LENGTH OF A GROUP

What should the duration of a group be, and is it wise to set a termination date? We believe that with most groups a termination date should be announced at the outset, so members will have a clear idea of the time limits under which they are working. Our college groups typically run about 15 weeks—the length of a semester. With high school students the same length seems ideal, for it is long enough for trust to develop and for work toward behavioral changes to take place but not so long that the group seems to be dragging on interminably. One of our colleagues has several closed groups in his private practice that last 16 weeks. After a few meetings he schedules an all-day session for these groups, which he finds adds greatly to their cohesion. When the group comes to an end, those who wish to join a new group have that option. The advantages of such an arrangement are that the time span allows for cohesion and productive work and that members can then continue practicing newly acquired interpersonal skills with a new group of people. Perhaps a major value of this type of time-limited group is that members are motivated to realize that they do not have forever to attain their personal goals. At different points in this 16-week group, the members are challenged to review their progress, both individually and as a group. If they are dissatisfied with their own participation or with the direction the group is taking, they have the responsibility to do something to change the situation.

Of course, some groups composed of the same members meet for years. Such a time structure allows them to work through issues in some depth and to offer support and challenge in making life changes. These ongoing groups do have the potential for fostering dependency, and thus it is important that both the leader and members evaluate the impact of the group on the clients' daily living.

PLACE FOR GROUP MEETINGS

Where should the group hold its meetings? Many places will do, but privacy is essential; the members must feel that they will not be overheard by people in adjoining rooms. Groups often fail because of their physical setting. If they are held in a day hall or ward full of distractions, productive group work will not occur. We like a group room that is not cluttered up with chairs and tables and that allows for a comfortable seating arrangement. We prefer a setting that enables the group to sit in a circle. This arrangement lets all the participants see one another and allows enough freedom of movement that the members can spontaneously make physical contact. It is a good idea for co-leaders to sit across from each other. In this way the nonverbal language of all members can be observed by one leader or the other and a "we-versus-them" atmosphere can be avoided.

OPEN VERSUS CLOSED GROUPS

Open groups are characterized by changing membership. The group continues, and as certain members are ready to leave, new members are admitted. *Closed groups* typically have some time limitation, and members are expected to remain in the group until it ends; new members are not added. The question of whether a group should be open or closed depends on a number of variables. There are some advantages to incorporating new members as others leave, for this change can provide stimulation. There can be a lack of cohesion, however, particularly if too many clients leave or too many new ones are introduced at once. Therefore, it may be better to bring in new members one at a time as an opening occurs. One colleague who co-leads open groups in an agency stresses reviewing of the ground rules with each incoming member. Rather than taking group time whenever a new person is included, he covers the rules with the new member as part of the intake interview. He also asks other members to teach the new member about a few of the guidelines in an attempt to have them take more responsibility for their own group. If members are dropped and added sensitively, these changes do not necessarily interfere with the cohesiveness of the group.

In some settings, such as mental-health wards in state hospitals or certain day-treatment centers, group leaders do not have a choice between an open and a closed group. Because the membership of the group changes almost from week to week, continuity between sessions and cohesion within the group become difficult to achieve. Nevertheless, cohesion is possible, even in cases where members attend only once or a few times. However, a high level of activity is demanded of inpatient group therapists, for at times the life of the group may be only a single session. These leaders must structure and activate the group. They need to call on certain members, they must actively support members, and they need to interact personally with the participants (Yalom, 1983).

If you are forming an open group, it is essential that you have some idea about the rate of turnover of the members. How long a given member can participate in the group may be unpredictable. Therefore, your interventions need to be designed with the idea in mind that many members may attend for only one or two sessions. In conducting an open group, it is good to remind all the members that this may be the only time they have with one another. The interventions that you make need to have closure within each session. For example, you would not want to facilitate a member's exploration of a painful concern that could not be satisfactorily addressed in that session. You also have a responsibility to facilitate member interactions that can lead to some form of resolution within a given session. This involves leaving enough time to explore with members what they have learned in a session and how they feel about leaving each session.

One of our colleagues regularly conducts several open groups in a community mental-health agency. He finds that trust and cohesion do develop in most of these groups, for even though the membership does change somewhat over a period of time, there is a stable core of members. When new members join, they agree to attend for at least six sessions. Also, members who miss two consecutive meetings without a valid excuse are not allowed to continue. These practices increase the chances for continuity.

THE USES OF A PREGROUP MEETING

We suggested earlier that a preliminary meeting of all those who were thinking of joining the group was a good follow-up to screening and orientation interviews as well as a useful device when individual interviews were impractical. Such a pregroup session provides an excellent way to prepare members and to get them acquainted with one another. This session also provides the members with more information to help them decide if they are willing to commit themselves to what would be expected of them. Busy practitioners sometimes do not make the time for a separate preparation period but, instead, incorporate an orientation to group participation as a part of the initial stage of a group's life. If an individual interview or a pregroup session with all members is impractical, the first group meeting can be used to cover the issues we are discussing in this chapter. Our preference is for a separate individual orientation (which is part of the individual screening interview), followed up by a pregroup meeting for all participants.

At this initial session or the pregroup meeting the leader can explore the members' expectations, clarify the goals and objectives of the group, discuss procedural details, impart some information about group process, and answer members' questions. This is an ideal time to focus on the clients' perceptions, expectations, and concerns. This process does not have to consist of a lecture to the members; it can involve the members and encourage them to interact with one another and the leader from the onset. This interactive model of preparation can reveal interesting information about both the dynamics of the individuals and the "personality of the group." Patterns begin to take shape from the moment a group convenes. Structuring the group, including the specification of procedures and norms, should be accomplished early in the group's history. Some of this structuring should have been done during the individual intake sessions, but a continuation of it should be the focus of the first group session. Group counselors should either establish ground rules or ask the group to do so. Ideally, group rules can be cooperatively developed by the leader and the members as part of the group process.

CLARIFYING LEADER AND MEMBER EXPECTATIONS

The pregroup session is the appropriate time to encourage members to express the expectations they are bringing with them to the group. We typically begin by asking: "What are your expectations for this group? What did you have in mind when you signed up?" The replies give us a frame of reference for how the members are approaching the group, what they want from it, and what they are willing to give to it to make it a success.

We also share *our* expectations by giving the members an idea of why we designed the group, what we hope will be accomplished, and what we expect of ourselves as leaders and them as members. This is a good time for you to reemphasize and clarify what you see as your responsibilities to the group and to further discuss the members' rights and responsibilities. You can explain what services you can and cannot realistically provide within the particular structure offered—for example, private consultations or follow-up sessions.

If you are forming groups in a community agency setting, it is likely that their members will be culturally diverse. Depending on a member's specific heritage, you will need to deal with a variety of expectations of you as a group leader. Some participants may look to you as an authority figure who will direct them, some will view you as an expert, and some may expect you to do most of the talking while they listen. In working with culturally diverse groups, it is essential not to make assumptions based on race, ethnicity, or culture without verifying your assumptions with individual members. Never assume that people who give the appearance of being ethnically different are indeed culturally different. If a person with Asian features applies for your group, do not assume that he or she necessarily adheres to Asian cultural values. It is also a mistake to conclude that merely because certain clients have lived in the United States for a period of time they have become acculturated into the mainstream society. What is important is that you invite the members of your groups to verbally state *their* expectations and that you be willing to explore these expectations during the initial session.

In the article "Who's the Expert Anyway?" George Hunter (1994) describes an informal, peer-facilitated, multicultural group in a prison setting. A doctoral student with little correctional experience working in a federal prison, Hunter was culturally different from most of the inmates in many respects and found he lacked the background to be a credible "expert" as a group leader. Even though he did not share many cultural similarities with these prisoners, he was able to create a climate that could be used to empower the members. In essence, Hunter assisted the inmates in planning their own group. Inmates who had been in prison for a time were informally assigned as sponsors to new inmates and these sponsors assumed a central role in facilitating the group. Hunter found that this approach entailed a sense of altruism that had an empowering benefit. These inmates "experts" were able to reach their peers more effectively than an "outsider" could.

As this illustration demonstrates, even in a prison group composed of culturally diverse members, the process of including members when designing their group increased the meaning of the members' experiences. By having members identify and express their expectations, and by clarifying your expectations as a group leader, members are better able to function successfully in the group. You do not necessarily have to share the culture or the life experience of your members to effectively facilitate a group with them. What is essential is that you understand and respect their experiential world and that you involve members in their own treatment. A great deal can be done to prevent the unnecessary anxiety that results when members are thrown into a group without any idea of what to expect from the situation. You can help alleviate anxiety by:

- allowing members to talk about their reactions to coming to the group and considering ways the group can lead to their empowerment,
- helping members clarify their goals and what they can do in the group to achieve their goals,
- explaining what you expect of members, and
- giving members a general idea of what they can expect from you and from the group.

In some cases your challenge will be to discover ways of designing an informal, peer-facilitated group with you assuming the role of facilitator and consultant.

SETTING UP BASIC GROUND RULES

The pregroup session is the appropriate place to establish some procedures that will facilitate group process. Some leaders prefer to present their own policies and procedures in a nonauthoritarian manner. Other leaders place the major responsibility on the group members to establish procedures that will assist them in attaining their goals. Whatever approach is taken, some discussion of ground rules will be necessary.

Ethical Guidelines for Group Counselors (ASGW, 1989), presented in Chapter 2, can help group leaders establish minimum ground rules and ethical standards. These guidelines state, for example, that group leaders must:

- protect members by defining clearly what confidentiality means, why it is important, and the difficulties involved in enforcing it;
- protect member rights against physical threats, intimidation, coercion, and undue peer pressure;
- discuss with members the risks involved in group participation, especially regarding life changes, and help members explore their readiness to face these risks;
- take steps to ensure informed consent procedures in both voluntary and involuntary groups;
- tell members what will be expected of them; and
- give members a general idea of the techniques and activities that are part of the group process.

Ideally, confidentiality is discussed during the individual interview, but because it is so important to the functioning of a group you cannot assume that once you've addressed the subject members will have no further concerns about it. At the pregroup session it is a good idea to state that confidentiality is not an absolute and to outline the restrictions. Depending on the type of group and the setting, leaders may not be able to guarantee that all member disclosures will be kept within the group. In cases of incest and child abuse and in cases of clients who pose a danger to themselves or to others, confidentiality must be breached. Limitations to confidentiality apply especially to groups with children and adolescents, groups with parolees, groups composed of involuntary populations such as prisoners and sex offenders in an institution, and groups of psychiatric patients in a hospital or clinic. These individuals should be told that certain things they say in the group may go into their chart, which might be available for other staff members to read. It is a good practice to let group members know what kinds of information might be recorded as well as who will have access to it. Leaders should specify what they can and cannot promise to their clients. The members then have a basis for deciding what and how much they will disclose. This kind of honesty about confidentiality will go a long way toward establishing the trust that is absolutely necessary for a working group. Review Chapter 2 for a further discussion of confidentiality.

Other issues to explore with your group at the first (or an early) session include policies about showing up for all group sessions and being punctual; smoking and eating during sessions; bringing friends to a session; obtaining written parental permission, in the case of minors; socializing outside the group with other members; getting involved intimately with other members; and reinforcing member rights and responsibilities. Leaders must be aware of and discuss with the members any additional ground rules and policies particular to the setting in which they are working. You will not be able to fully discuss all the policies and procedures you deem essential to the smooth functioning of your group in one or two sessions, but having an established position on these matters will be an asset when particular issues arise at some point in the development of the group.

In his system of pregroup preparation, Yalom (1995) is guided by the following goals:

- Strive to create an alliance with group members, so they can become collaborators in their own change process. Provide members with a conceptual framework of how group therapy works as a social laboratory.
- Describe how a therapy group helps members enhance their interpersonal relationships.
- Give members guidelines about how to get the most from group therapy. Emphasize the importance of members being honest and direct with their feelings in the context of here-and-now group interactions.

- Anticipate frustrations and disappointments, including predicting stumbling blocks, that participants are likely to encounter.
- Give guidelines pertaining to the duration of group therapy.
- Instill faith in group therapy.
- Discuss ground rules, such as sharing perceptions and reactions about oneself and other members in the group, confidentiality, and sub-grouping.

Underlying everything that Yalom says in preparing individuals for group therapy is the goal of demystifying the therapeutic process. He emphasizes the collaborative nature of group therapy. If certain clinical realities do not allow for a comprehensive cognitive approach to group therapy preparation, Yalom contends that a short preparation is better than none at all.

EXPLORING THE ADVANTAGES OF AND MISCONCEPTIONS ABOUT GROUPS

We typically devote some time at the pregroup session to a discussion of both the advantages of therapeutic groups and certain misconceptions about the group process.

Advantages   Therapeutic groups have certain distinct advantages over other intervention strategies:

- Participants are able to explore their style of relating to others and to learn more effective social skills.
- The group setting offers support for new behavior and encourages experimentation. Members can try out new behaviors and decide whether they want to incorporate them into their outside life.
- There is a re-creation of the everyday world in some groups, particularly if the membership is diverse with respect to age, interests, race, cultural background, socioeconomic status, and type of problem. When this heterogeneity occurs, a member has the advantage of interacting with a wide range of personalities, and the feedback received can be richer and more diverse than that available in a one-to-one setting.
- Certain factors that foster personal growth are more likely to be present in groups. For instance, members have the opportunity to learn about themselves through the experience of others; to experience emotional closeness and caring, which encourage them to be open; and to identify with the struggles of other members.
- The group setting provides an optimal arena for participants to discover how they affect others. A member (Susan) may complain that she feels isolated from people. Through interaction with members in the group, she is likely to become aware of what she is doing to create her loneliness and isolation. If she typically sits apart from the group, rarely

says much, and often appears critical, other members may respond to her by saying that they are afraid of her and that they are staying away from her. She may be rejecting others before they have a chance to reject her.

Exploring Misconceptions   Some misconceptions about groups need to be critically appraised at the pregroup meeting:

• *Groups are for everyone.* Not all people are suited to groups. Some clients are too suspicious, too hostile, or too fragile to benefit from a group experience. Some can be psychologically damaged by attending certain groups. Before a person is accepted into a group, such factors need to be carefully weighed by both the counselor and the client to increase the chances that the person will benefit from such an experience.

• *Working out my problems in the group will automatically solve my problems at home.* Participants need to be aware that acquiring insights and skills in handling their concerns within the group does not mean that they can apply this learning to their everyday lives without facing some obstacles. In the group they may have received positive feedback and support for daring to change. When they return home, they may well meet with resistance and antagonism when they deviate from old and familiar ways. Others may have an investment in keeping them as they were, because that way they're more predictable and more easily controlled. The depression that so often follows the feeling of being able to conquer the world is a reality that participants need to examine.

• *The goal of a group is that members will leave it feeling close and loving toward everyone in the group.* The genuine closeness that can be achieved in an intensive group can be the result of shared struggles, and the worth of this emotional bond is not to be discounted. However, the basic purpose of a group is *not* to create a loving bond among all the members. Rather, intimacy should be considered a by-product of meaningful work in a group that leads to increased intimacy in one's outside life. Unfortunately, some members use groups as a vehicle for expressing their problems, in the hope that they will be understood and totally accepted, and make little or no attempt to do what is necessary to substantially change their lives. It is important to remember that a group experience is not an end in itself.

• *Groups are places where people are attacked and defenses are torn down.* We frequently hear people express the fear that they will leave the group defenseless and emotionally wounded. Leaders must respect necessary defenses and not strip them away. Our hope is that people can learn that rigid defenses are not always necessary and that they can safely remove unnecessary walls that separate them from others. When people become more authentic, even though they may be vulnerable, they discover a core of strength within themselves. We certainly don't support the approach of some groups, in which ruthless attacks are seen as a desirable way of stripping away a person's defenses.

- *Groups tell people how to be.* Instead of merely accepting the dictates or suggestions of others, successful group members acquire an increased ability to look within themselves for their own answers to the present and future problems that life poses. Groups are neither places to dispense advice nor means of indoctrinating people into agreement with a particular philosophy of life. The group experience can challenge members to reexamine their philosophy and make the modifications they desire.
- *Group pressure forces people to lose a sense of identity.* Although it is true that group pressure can be used in destructive ways, it can also be used constructively. Some pressure is almost inevitable, for there are expectations to be honest, to get involved personally, to interact with people in the group in direct and open ways, and to reveal oneself. What is important is how leaders and members deal with the basic pressure that is part of a group experience. Pressure does not have to be viewed as something that "cracks" a person and forces submission. Instead, it can be the impetus for members to face and work through conflicts they might otherwise avoid.
- *Only people who are emotionally disturbed join groups.* There is a misconception that all therapy or counseling, either individual or group, is designed to cure people of mental and emotional illness. It is true that some groups are aimed at helping a disturbed population find some relief; but there are also many groups for developmental purposes—groups designed to help people recognize their potential and remove blocks to personal growth. Healthy people can use the group experience as an aid in viewing themselves more honestly and critically and seeing themselves as others see them. Many groups focus on a well population and use therapy for preventive as well as remedial purposes.
- *Groups are artificial and unreal.* Some criticize groups on the ground that they operate in an unrealistic context. We believe that a group setting can be more real than so-called real life, in the sense that people shed many of the pretenses that characterize their everyday interactions. Certain aspects of this experience may seem artificial, but if the participants can discover ways of putting into practice what was learned in the group, the real value of their experience is undeniable.

For his long-term outpatient groups, Yalom (1995) provides an overview of the interpersonal theory of therapy and shows members that many of their current problems are linked with past personal relationships. He also clears up misconceptions about group therapy by teaching members how to involve themselves in active and responsible ways in the group sessions. In sum, he shows them how group therapy can be a rich arena for learning more about their interpersonal styles and how they can use the group as a place to acquire and practice more effective interpersonal skills. For his short-term inpatient groups, Yalom (1983) modifies his approach to preparation, because most hospital stays are too short to allow for much pretraining. Instead, he does this preparation as an initial part of the therapy group. He invites members who have been in the group for a time to join him in the orientation process for newcomers.

AN INTEGRATED APPROACH TO PREGROUP PREPARATION: RESEARCH FINDINGS

Some practitioners promote member ambiguity and see pregroup structuring as counterproductive to the natural evolution of the group. These practitioners believe that too much advance preparation or teaching members about the process of a group "pollutes" the process and deprives the members of creating their own structure. However, as you can see by the emphasis we give to preparation of individuals for group membership, we endorse the value of pregroup preparation.

The kind of pregroup preparation we advocate is a form of structuring aimed at helping members get focused and expressing their thoughts and feelings pertaining to the here-and-now interactions at the beginning of a group experience. This preparation assists members in deciding what they want from a group and gives them some tools for attaining their goals. This process is important for groups with different forms, such as inpatient and outpatient groups, open and closed groups, and short-term and long-term groups. Although the specific content of pregroup preparation will differ based on the specific kind of group, members stand a better chance of utilizing the group process if they understand how the particular group they will participate in functions and if they know what is expected of them. Some kind of preparation is useful for structured psychoeducational groups and for solution-focused short-term groups as well as for counseling and therapy groups. The basic aim of this preparation is to increase the chances that the group will become a cohesive autonomous unit that will permit individuals to engage in productive work.

Along with preparing members for a group, it is essential that co-leaders prepare themselves for the group. Leaders need to be prepared both individually and as a co-leading team. Too often co-leaders understand little of each others' philosophy and leadership styles before the group begins. If the group leaders are unprepared, it is unlikely that they will be able to effectively prepare members for a meaningful group experience.

Practitioners often give positive reports of their particular approach to pregroup preparation. Reviews of the literature are generally favorable about the benefits of advance preparation. Some research suggests that members who understand what behaviors are expected of them tend to be more successful. When goals, role requirements, and behavior expectations are understood by members from the outset, therapeutic work proceeds more effectively. Unproductive anxiety can be reduced by informing members about group norms in advance. Preparatory training increases the chances of successful outcomes because it reduces the anxiety participants often experience during the initial sessions and provides a framework for understanding group process (Bednar, Melnick, & Kaul, 1974; Borgers & Tyndall, 1982; Bowman & DeLucia, 1993; Burlingame & Fuhriman, 1990; Fuhriman & Burlingame, 1990; Meadow, 1988; Piper & Perrault, 1989; Sklare, Keener, & Mas, 1990; Sklare, Petrosko, & Howell, 1993; Stockton & Morran, 1982; Yalom, 1995).

Based on their review of the literature, Bednar and Kaul (1994) concluded that pregroup training is a potent factor in creating successful therapeutic groups, having a substantial impact on group process and member outcomes. Although the value of pregroup preparation is established, it is not precisely clear how pregroup training works. Preparing members for a group through cognitive instructions, behavioral rehearsal, or by watching models all contribute to effective group treatment.

Borgers and Tyndall (1982) and Bowman and DeLucia (1993) describe three ways of preparing members for a group experience: cognitive learning, vicarious experiencing, and behavioral practice. With cognitive methods, members acquire information through reading handouts that describe the purpose of the group, member performance expectations, common stumbling blocks, and typical group phenomena. Vicarious experiencing includes the use of tape recordings, videotapes, and films to model desired group behavior in a working group. Behavioral practice involves members' participating in structured activities such as giving and receiving feedback, confrontation, self-disclosure, and identifying resistance. Borgers and Tyndall conclude that perhaps the most useful form of pregroup preparation consists of a combination of these approaches. Their conclusions have some research support; studies have consistently shown that groups receiving both instruction and modeling do better than those receiving only one treatment or neither (Stockton & Morran, 1982).

A good deal of research has been conducted into the value of pretherapy preparation for both individual and group psychotherapy. The overwhelming consensus of both dyadic and group reviewers is that role preparation appears to affect early therapeutic processes positively and also seems to be linked to later client improvement (Fuhriman & Burlingame, 1990). Pregroup orientation appears to be a standard practice for members of short-term therapy groups. A number of factors make such orientation sessions necessary for these clients: the diversity of members in a typical group, the range of personal concerns, the different settings, the time-limited framework, and the unfamiliarity of the group format. The content of this pregroup orientation reflects the perspective of leaders who conduct short-term group therapy. It sets the stage for later development of the leader/member and member/member therapeutic relationships. Preparation activities in short-term groups are directed toward facilitating the most effective use of the time that is available (Burlingame & Fuhriman, 1990).

Meadow (1981) contends that preparing clients for a group before the first meeting is essential. She stresses that this preparatory activity should include informing clients about the purpose, process, and rules of the group and clarifying any inaccurate expectations potential clients may have about being members. In an empirical study assessing the preparation of members through a series of pregroup interviews, Meadow (1988) found that clients who participated in pregroup interviews had more realistic expectations and perceptions of group membership and had a clearer understanding of the group's purpose than those who did not participate in pregroup interviews.

In a review of the literature on pretherapy preparation for group members, Piper and Perrault (1989) found that practitioners had a core of long-term objectives. These goals included maintaining attendance, enhancing the process and outcome of a group, and increasing the level of satisfaction within a group. To obtain these objectives, leaders used a variety of cognitive, affective, and behavioral strategies in pregroup preparation. The cognitive procedures involved creating accurate expectations about desirable behavior by members, customary roles of therapists, typical events in therapy, and realistic outcomes. The affective strategies had the aim of reducing anxiety and establishing positive interpersonal bonds. Increasing clients' participation, self-disclosure, and interpersonal feedback are examples of behavioral strategies.

Piper and Perrault's review involved 20 studies during the period from 1962 to 1987. Despite the widespread positive endorsement found in the clinical literature, their survey did not show impressive benefits in process and outcome stemming from such preparation. They concluded that there were not enough methodologically strong research studies to clearly answer questions about the relationship between particular forms of pretraining and specific process and outcome effects. Although they assert that the effects of pretherapy preparation on outcome have been overstated, they concede that there are benefits with respect to attendance, remaining in the group, and enhancing the therapy process.

In conducting this discussion of pregroup preparation, we want to caution you against bombarding the members with too much information at the preliminary meeting. Many of the topics that relate to participation in the group can be handed out in written form to the members, and clients can be encouraged to raise any questions or concerns they have after they have read this material.

The theoretical and research literature generally supports the value of systematically preparing members for a group experience (Meadow, 1988). Many groups that get stuck at an early developmental stage do so because the foundations were poorly laid. What is labeled as "resistance" on the part of group members is often the result of a failure on the leader's part to adequately explain what groups are about, how they function, and how members can become actively involved. In addition to preparing members for a group, it is a good idea for leaders to periodically review with the members some of the guidelines on how they can make the best use of group time. Throughout the life of a group, there are critical times when structuring and teaching can assist members in becoming actively involved in the group process.

BUILDING EVALUATION INTO GROUP WORK

If you do group work in a community agency or an institution, you may be required to demonstrate the efficacy of your treatment approach. Federal and state grants typically stipulate measures for accountability. Thus, it is essential in most settings that you devise procedures for assessing the degree to which clients benefit from the group experience. In your proposals for groups, we suggest that you include the procedures you intend to use to evaluate both the individual member outcomes and the outcomes of the group as a unit.

There is no need to be intimidated by the idea of incorporating a research spirit into your practice. Nor do you have to think exclusively in terms of rigorous empirical research. Various qualitative methods are appropriate for assessing a group's movement, and these methods may be less intimidating than relying exclusively on quantitative research techniques. One alternative to the traditional scientific method is evaluation research, which aims at gathering data that can be useful when making improvements within the structure of a group. *Member-specific measures* are used to assess changes in attitudes and behaviors of individual clients. It is possible to develop your own devices for evaluating the degree to which members attain their goals. *Group-specific measures* assess the changes common to all members of the group, such as increased self-awareness, decreased anxiety, and improved personal relationships. Many of these measures are available in standardized form, or you can adapt them to suit your needs. The practice of building evaluation into your group programs is not only a useful procedure for accountability purposes but it can also help you sharpen your leadership skills and see more clearly changes you might want to make in the format for future groups. (The problems of combining research and practice are addressed in Chapter 3.)

CO-LEADER ISSUES AT THE PREGROUP STAGE

If you are co-leading a group, the central issue at this early stage is that you and your co-leader have equal responsibility in forming the group and getting it going. Both of you need to be clear about the purpose of the group, what you hope to accomplish with the time you have, and how you will meet your objectives. Cooperation and basic agreement between you and your co-leader will be essential in getting your group off to a good start.

This cooperative effort might well start with your meeting to develop a proposal, and ideally both of you will present it to the appropriate authority. This practice ensures that designing and originating the group are not solely one leader's responsibility. This shared responsibility for organizing the group continues with the various tasks that we've outlined in this chapter. You and your co-leader will be a team when it comes to matters such as announcing and recruiting for membership; conducting screening interviews and agreeing on whom to include and exclude; agreeing on basic ground rules, policies, and procedures and presenting them to the members; preparing members and orienting them to the group process; and sharing in the practical matters that must be handled to form a group.

It may not always be possible to share equally in all the responsibilities. Although it is *ideal* that both leaders interview the applicants, time constraints may make this impractical. Tasks may have to be divided, but both leaders should be involved as much as possible in making the group a reality. If one leader does a disproportionate share of the work, the other can easily develop a passive role in the leadership of the group once it begins.

If co-leaders do not know each other or if they don't have much sense of how the other works professionally, they are likely to get off to a poor start. Simply walking into a group unprepared, without any initial planning or acquaintance with your co-leader, is to invite future problems. Just as it is critical that members be prepared for entering a group, the leaders must be psychologically prepared and oriented to each other's style. We have a few suggestions that co-leaders can consider before the initial session:

- Make the time to at least get to know something about each other personally and professionally before you begin leading together.
- Talk about your theoretical orientations and how each of you perceives groups. What kind of group work has each of you experienced? In what ways will your theory and leadership styles influence the direction the group takes?
- Is either of you concerned or having reservations about leading with the other? What might get in your way in your dealings with each other? How can you use your separate talents productively as a team? How can your differences in leadership style have a complementary effect and actually enhance the group?
- Each of you can talk about your own strengths and weaknesses, with implications for how they will affect your leading together. With this knowledge you may be able to forestall some potential problems.
- For the two of you to work together well as team, you should be in agreement on the ethical aspects of group work. What does each of you consider to be unethical practice, and are there differences? The ethical issues touched on both in this chapter and in the preceding chapter need to be discussed.

Although these suggestions do not represent all the possible areas that co-leaders can explore in getting to know each other, they do provide a basis for focusing on significant topics.

PREGROUP STAGE: SUMMARY

MEMBER FUNCTIONS AND POSSIBLE PROBLEMS

It is important that members joining a group possess the knowledge necessary to make an informed decision concerning their participation. Members should be active in the process of deciding if a group is right for them. Following are some issues that pertain to the role of members at this stage:

- Members should know all the specifics about a group that might have an impact on them.
- Members need to learn how to screen the group leader to determine if this group with this particular leader is appropriate for them at this time.
- Members need to be involved in the decision to include or exclude them from the group.
- Members need to prepare themselves for the upcoming group by thinking about what they want from the experience and how they can attain their goals.
- Members can be given pretests, which can be either standardized instruments or devices designed by the leader, to assess values, perceptions, attitudes, and personal problems.

Problems can arise if potential members:

- are coerced into a group,
- do not have adequate information about the nature of the group and thus do not know what they are getting themselves into, or
- are passive and give no thought to what they want or expect from the group.

LEADER FUNCTIONS

The main tasks of group leaders during the formation of a group include:

- developing a clearly written proposal for the formation of a group
- presenting the proposal to the proper authorities and getting the idea accepted
- announcing the group in such a way as to inform prospective participants

- conducting pregroup interviews for screening and orientation purposes
- making decisions concerning selection of members and composing the group
- organizing the practical details necessary to launch a successful group
- getting parental permission, if necessary
- preparing psychologically for leadership tasks, and meeting with the co-leader (if any)
- arranging for a preliminary group session for the purposes of getting acquainted, orientation to ground rules, and preparation of the members for a successful group experience

EXERCISES

EXERCISES IN GROUP PLANNING

Select a particular type of group (personal-growth, counseling, or other) and a target population (children, adolescents, or adults). Keeping in mind the group you've selected, answer the following questions. The purpose of the exercise is to give you an idea of the questions you need to ask yourself while planning your group.

1. What is your role in this group?
2. What do you most want to occur in your group? State your purposes simply and concretely.
3. Would you form a contract with your group, and, if so, what would be the essence of the contract? Would you expect each member to develop a contract?
4. Mention a few ground rules or policies you feel would be essential for your group.
5. How can you determine whether you have the skills necessary to lead this particular type of group?
6. What is the focus of your group? (Is it didactic? experiential? remedial? developmental?)
7. Would you accept only volunteer group members? Why or why not?
8. What characteristics would people have to have to be included? What is the rationale?
9. What procedures and techniques would you use in your group? Are your procedures practical? Are they related to the goals and the population of the group?
10. What evaluation methods might you use to determine the effectiveness of your approaches? Are your evaluation procedures appropriate to the purposes of your group?

INTERVIEWING EXERCISES

1.   Screening-Interview Exercise. One person in the class volunteers to play the role of a group leader conducting a screening interview for members for a particular type of group. The group leader conducts a ten-minute interview with a potential member, played by another member. Then the prospective client tells the group leader how he or she felt and what impact the group leader made. The group leader shares his or her observations about the prospective group member and tells whether the person would have been accepted into the group and why or why not. This exercise can be repeated with another client so that the group leader can benefit from the feedback and try some new ideas. Several students can experience the role of the interviewer and the role of the interviewee. It is essential that feedback be given so that people can improve their skills in conducting screening interviews. The rest of the class can offer feedback and suggestions for improvement after each interview.

2.   Group-Member Interview. We have recommended that prospective group members examine the leader somewhat critically before joining a group. This exercise is just like the preceding one, except that the group members ask the questions of the leader, trying to learn things about the leader and the group that will allow a wise decision about whether to join. After ten minutes the leader shares observations and reactions, and then the member tells whether he or she would join this leader's group and explains any reservations. Again, the class is invited to make observations.

CHAPTER 5

INITIAL STAGE
OF A GROUP

FOCUS QUESTIONS

Introduction

Group Characteristics at the Initial Stage
Some Early Concerns
Initial Resistance
Hidden Agendas
Self-Focus versus Focus on Others
Here-and-Now Focus versus There-and-Then Focus
Trust versus Mistrust

Creating Trust: Leader and Member Roles
The Importance of Modeling
Attitudes and Actions Leading to Trust

Identifying and Clarifying Goals
General Goals for Group Members
Helping Members Define Personal Goals

Group-Process Concepts at the Initial Stage
Group Norms
Group Cohesion

**Helping Members Get the Most
from a Group Experience**
Leader Guidelines for Members
Avoid Too Much Teaching

Leader Issues at the Initial Stage
Division of Responsibility
Degree of Structuring
Opening and Closing Group Sessions

Initial Stage: Summary
Stage Characteristics
Member Functions and Possible Problems
Leader Functions

Exercises

FOCUS QUESTIONS

1. What guidelines might you offer to help members get the most from a group experience?

2. What ways can you think of to assist members in creating trust in the leader and among themselves? What role do you see yourself as having in establishing trust during the initial stage of a group?

3. What are some specific ways to help members identify and clarify their goals for group participation?

4. What cultural factors would you consider in assessing a client's readiness to participate in a group?

5. What sort of resistance behaviors might you encounter during the first few sessions?

6. What group norms, or standards, would you most want to establish?

7. What are some ways to help a group develop cohesion at the first few meetings?

8. What are a few things you would attend to in opening each group session?

9. What ideas do you have for effectively bringing each session to closure?

10. How much structuring do you think is helpful for a group to accomplish its tasks? To what degree might you assume the responsibility for providing structure in a group you lead or co-lead?

INTRODUCTION

This chapter contains many examples of teaching members about how groups function. We describe the characteristics of a group in its early stages, discuss the importance of creating trust as the foundation for a group, explore the topic of establishing goals early in the life of a group, provide guidelines for helping members get the most from a group, and discuss formation of group norms and the beginnings of group cohesion. We also suggest some guidelines for opening and closing group meetings.

GROUP CHARACTERISTICS AT THE INITIAL STAGE

The central process during the initial stage of a group is orientation and exploration. Members are getting acquainted, learning how the group functions, developing spoken and unspoken norms that will govern group behavior, exploring their fears and hopes pertaining to the group, clarifying their expectations, identifying personal goals, and determining if this group is a safe place. This stage is characterized by members' expressing fears and hesitations as well as hopes and expectations. The manner in which the leader deals with these reactions determines the degree of trust that can be established in the group.

SOME EARLY CONCERNS

It is common at these early sessions for the participants to be tentative and vague about what they hope to get from a group experience. Most members are uncertain about group norms and expected behavior; thus, there may be moments of silence and awkwardness. Some may be impatient and ready to work, while others may appear hesitant and uninvolved; others may be eager to find quick solutions to their problems. If your leadership style involves very little structure, the level of anxiety is likely to be high because of the ambiguity of the situation, and there will probably be considerable floundering and requests from members for direction. Members may say: "What are we supposed to be doing here?" "I really don't know what we should be talking about."

If someone does volunteer a problem for discussion, chances are that other members will engage in problem solving. Rather than encouraging the person to fully explore a struggle, some members are likely to offer suggestions and what they consider to be helpful advice. This may seem like progress, for there is the appearance of group interaction, but too much advice giving bypasses the necessity for people to work through their problems and discover their own solutions.

Trust can be lost or gained by the manner in which the leader handles the initial expression of any negative reactions. A member's internal dialogue might be: "I'll take a chance and say what I am thinking, and then I'll see how this leader and others in here respond. If they are willing to listen to what I don't like, perhaps I can trust them with some deeper feelings." The group leader must be aware of the tentative nature of discussion in these early sessions and treat negative comments with openness and acceptance.

INITIAL RESISTANCE

During the initial phase of a group, members typically appear rather hesitant to get involved. In some cases the participants are intimidated by the leader and may view the leader with some degree of suspicion. Some members may doubt that counseling groups can be of any real value in helping them solve their problems. Others will not believe they have the freedom to talk about personally significant matters, and they may sit back, silently observe, and wait for something to happen.

Cultural factors may also influence clients' readiness to participate in a group. You may see members as "resistant" when they are only being true to their cultural heritage. Such members may believe that it is distasteful to talk publicly about private matters such as sexuality, family problems, and religious conviction. Those members who have cultural injunctions against talking about their family in a group may be reluctant to take part in role playing involving symbolically talking to their parents. You would do well to explore with these members how they could work with personal concerns in a way that would not violate their cultural norms. You can help such members by being aware of their cultural context and at the same time respectfully challenging them to consider modifying their values enough to allow them to explore personal issues. An important leadership function is assisting members in understanding how some of their initial resistance to self-disclosure relates to their cultural conditioning.

Regardless of the type of group, some initial resistance is to be expected in the early stage, even if people are eager to join in. This resistance can be manifested by complaints about the place of meeting or about what appear to be inconsequential matters. What members do talk about is likely to be less important than what they keep hidden: their real fears about being in this group at this moment. Because resistance often arises from fearful expectations, identifying and discussing these fears at the early stage will benefit the whole group.

The following are some common fears that participants identify:

- Will I be accepted or rejected in here?
- Can I really say what I feel, or do I have to couch my words carefully so that others won't be offended?
- How will this group be any different from my interactions in daily situations?
- I'm afraid that others will judge me.
- Am I like other people in here?
- Will I feel pressured and pushed to perform?
- Will I be able to take risks in here?
- I'm afraid I'll look stupid.
- Will I tell too much about myself?
- I fear being hurt.
- What if the group attacks me?
- I'm afraid I'll become dependent on the group.
- What if I find out things about myself that I can't cope with?
- I'm afraid that I'll change and that those I'm close to won't like my changes.
- What if I'm asked to do something I don't want to do?

Because we recognize that such anxieties exist, we begin by encouraging the members to share and explore them. It sometimes helps in building a trusting atmosphere to ask people to split up into pairs and then to join to make groups of four. In this way members can choose others with whom to share their expectations, get acquainted, and talk about their fears or reservations. For some reason, talking with one other person and then merging with others is far less threatening to most participants than talking to the entire group. This subgroup approach is an excellent icebreaker, and when the entire group gets together again, there is generally a greater willingness to interact.

Members are testing the waters at the early sessions to see if their concerns are being taken seriously and if the group is a safe place to express what they think and feel. If their reactions, positive or negative, are listened to with respect and acceptance, they have a basis to begin dealing with deeper aspects of themselves. A good way for you to start dealing with members' resistance is by listening to their fears and encouraging full expression of them. It is not helpful to say to an anxious member: "You don't need to be afraid in here. Nobody will hurt you." You cannot honestly make such promises, because some members may very well feel hurt by someone's response to them. What is far more important is that members know that you want them to say when they feel hurt and that you will not abandon them but will help them deal with whatever they are feeling.

HIDDEN AGENDAS

A common form of resistance in the group relates to the presence of a hidden agenda; that is, an issue that affects the way the group is progressing but is not openly discussed. If encouragement to face these issues is lacking, the group process gets bogged down because the norm of being closed, cautious, and defensive replaces the norm of being open. We find that when there are unspoken reactions (by one member, several members, or the entire group), a common set of features emerges: trust is low, hostility emerges, people are guarded and are unwilling to take risks, we feel that we are working harder than the members, and there is a vague feeling that something just does not make sense.

In one group a member said, "There's someone in this room I don't like." The entire group was affected by this comment, and several members later disclosed that they had wondered if they were the disliked person. It wasn't until the member was willing to deal directly with the conflict that he was having with another participant that the atmosphere in the room cleared up.

A training workshop we conducted included a member of military personnel as well as civilians. The military trainees held different ranks and included both officers and enlisted personnel. One participant discovered that his wife was working with the wife of another person in the group. The hidden agenda in this group consisted of reactions related to the two men's different ranks and concerns over repercussions of what might be said in the group and how it might be used outside the group. Others wondered if confidentiality would be honored. The concerns that members had were not initially discussed, in spite of our invitations. The polite and hesitant interactions eventually led to a high level of frustration among the participants. Not until one member took the risk of disclosing her real fears did others acknowledge what was really going on in the room.

In another group, the adolescent group members displayed a great unwillingness to talk. The hidden agenda was the concern over rumors that some gossiping was taking place. The members who had the concern over confidentiality were reluctant to express their feelings because of a fear that others might condemn them for their lack of trust.

In our training and supervision workshops we have sometimes made an erroneous assumption that all the participants were there voluntarily. In several cases in various agencies, resistance was initially high because some members felt pressured by their superiors to attend. We encouraged them to express their grievances, after which they were more willing to become involved. Even though we were not able to remove the pressure they felt over having to attend, our willingness to nondefensively hear what they had to say did help them overcome their reluctance to participate. If we had not facilitated an exploration of their feelings, little learning would have occurred.

Groups do not move forward unless hidden agendas are uncovered and fully discussed. This process often requires patience on our part and a willingness to continually check with members to find out if they are saying what they need to say. We point out to them that what bogs groups down is not so much what people *are* saying but what they *are not* saying. It is not comfortable for us to deal with these undercurrents, yet we continue to learn about the value of respectfully, yet firmly, challenging members to express persistent thoughts and feelings about what is emerging in the group.

SELF-FOCUS VERSUS FOCUS ON OTHERS

One characteristic we observe in members of most beginning groups is a tendency to talk about others and to focus on people and situations outside of the group. Storytelling participants will at times deceive themselves into believing that they are really working, when in fact they are resisting speaking about and dealing with their own feelings. They may talk about life situations, but they have a tendency to focus on what other people are doing to cause them difficulties. Skilled group leaders help such members examine their own reactions to others.

During the initial phase of a group, the demanding job is to get group members to focus on themselves. Of course, trust is a prerequisite for this openness. When members use a focus on others as a method of resisting deeper exploration of themselves, your leadership task is to steer them back. For example, you might say, "I'm aware that you're talking a lot about several important people in your life. They're not here, and we won't be able to work with them. But we are able to work with your feelings and reactions toward them and how their behavior affects you." An awareness of proper timing is essential. The readiness of a client to accept certain interpretations or observations must be considered. You must be skilled not only in helping people recognize that their focus on others can be defensive but also in giving them the courage to work through their resistance.

HERE-AND-NOW FOCUS VERSUS THERE-AND-THEN FOCUS

Some groups have a primary focus on what is occurring at the time in the room. The predominant theme these groups explore is present member/member interactions. The material for discussion emerges from these encounters. Other groups focus largely on outside problems that members bring to the session, as well as problems associated with past experiences.

We have both a here-and-now focus and a there-and-then focus. We find that members are not ready to deal with significant issues pertaining to their lives away from the group until they first deal with their reactions to one another in the room. To meaningfully explore personal problems, members must first feel safe and trusting. During the initial sessions we ask members to make connections between personal problems they are facing in their world and their experience in the group. If a member discloses that she feels isolated in her life, for instance, we ask her to be aware of how she may be isolating herself in the group setting.

TRUST VERSUS MISTRUST

If a basic sense of trust and security is not established at the outset of a group, serious problems can be predicted. People can be said to be developing trust in one another when they can express any feelings without fear of censure; when they are willing to decide for themselves specific goals and personal areas to explore; when they focus on themselves, not on others; and when they are willing to risk disclosing personal aspects of themselves.

In contrast, a lack of trust is indicated by an undercurrent of hostility and suspicion and an unwillingness to talk about these feelings. Other manifestations of lack of trust are participants' taking refuge in being abstract or overly intellectual and being vague about what they expect from the therapeutic group. Before a climate of trust is established, people tend to wait for the leader to decide for them what they need to examine. Any disclosures that are made tend to be superficial and rehearsed, and risk taking is at a low level.

CREATING TRUST: LEADER AND MEMBER ROLES

THE IMPORTANCE OF MODELING

Your success in creating a climate of trust within a group has much to do with how well you've prepared both yourself and the members. If you've given careful thought to why you are organizing the group, what you hope to accomplish, and how you'll go about meeting your objectives, the chances are greatly increased that you'll inspire confidence. The members will see your willingness to think about the group as a sign that you care about them. Furthermore, if you've done a good job with the pre-group issues (such as informing members of their rights and responsibilities, giving some time to teaching the group process, and preparing the members for a successful experience), the members will realize that you are taking your work seriously and that you are interested in their welfare.

Establishing trust is a central task for the initial stage of a group. It is not possible to overemphasize the significance of the leader's modeling and the attitudes expressed through the leader's behavior in these early sessions. In thinking about your role as a leader, ask yourself these questions: Do I feel energetic and enthusiastic about this group? Do I trust myself to lead and am I able to inspire confidence? To what degree do I trust the group members to work effectively with one another? Am I able to be psychologically present in the sessions, and am I willing to be open about my own reactions to what is going on in the group?

The person who you are, and especially the attitudes about group work and clients that you demonstrate by the way you behave in the sessions, may be the crucial factor in building a trusting community. (Refer to our discussion of the personal characteristics of the effective leader in Chapter 3.) You teach most effectively through your example. If you trust in the group process and have faith in the members' capacity to make significant changes in themselves, they are likely to see value in their group as a pathway to personal growth. If you listen nondefensively and respectfully and convey that you value members' subjective experience, they are likely to see the power in active listening. If you are genuinely willing to engage in appropriate self-disclosure, you will foster honesty and disclosure among the members. If you are truly able to accept others for who they are and avoid imposing your values on them, your members will learn valuable lessons about accepting people's right to differ and to be themselves. In short, what you model through what you do in the group is one of the most powerful ways of teaching members how to relate to one another constructively.

If you are co-leading a group, you and your colleague have ample opportunities to model a behavioral style that will promote trust. If the two of you function harmoniously with a spontaneous give and take, for example, members will feel more trusting in your presence. If your relationship with your co-leader is characterized by respect, authenticity, sensitivity, and directness, the members will learn about the value of such attitudes and behaviors. Furthermore, the way in which the two of you interact with the members obviously contributes to or detracts from the level of trust. If one co-leader's typical manner of speaking with members is sharp, short, and sarcastic, for example, the members are likely to quickly pick up this leader's lack of respect for them and tend to become closed or resistant. Therefore, it is wise for co-leaders to examine each other's style of interacting.

It is a mistake to assume that as a leader or a co-leader you have sole responsibility for the development and maintenance of trust. The level of trust is engendered by your attitudes and actions, yet it also depends to a large degree on the level of investment of the members. If they want very little for themselves, if they are unwilling to share enough of themselves so that they can be known, if they simply wait passively for you to "make trust happen," and if they are unwilling to take risks in the sessions, trust will be slow to develop. In the last analysis, however, the tone set by your leadership will influence their willingness to disclose themselves and to take those steps necessary to establish trust.

ATTITUDES AND ACTIONS LEADING TO TRUST

We value Carl Rogers's (1970) emphasis on the "facilitative dimensions of the therapeutic relationship," and we see certain attitudes and actions as enhancing the level of trust in a group. We will discuss these important themes next.

Attending and Listening   Careful attending to the verbal and nonverbal messages of others is necessary for trust to occur. If genuine listening and understanding are absent, there is no basis for connection between members. If members feel that they are being heard and deeply understood, they are likely to trust that others care about them.

There are numerous ways in which both leaders and members may demonstrate a lack of attending, including not focusing on the speaker but thinking of what to say next, asking many closed questions that have the effect of probing for information, doing too much talking and not enough listening, giving advice readily instead of encouraging the speaker to explore a struggle, paying attention only to what people say explicitly and thus missing what they express nonverbally, and engaging in selective listening (hearing only what one wants to hear).

We don't think that most group members possess natural listening skills, nor do they have the ability to respond effectively to what they perceive. Therefore, teaching basic listening and responding skills is a part of the trust process. Pay attention to whether members feel that they are being listened to with understanding. If they don't feel that they are, why should they speak about deeply personal matters? Why should they reveal themselves to those who do not care?

Understanding Nonverbal Behavior   Inexperienced group workers frequently make the error of focusing exclusively on what members are saying and miss the more powerful nonverbal messages. People often express themselves more honestly nonverbally than they do through their words. Detecting discrepancies between verbal and nonverbal behavior is an art. Examples of clients displaying these discrepancies include a member who is talking about a painful experience while smiling; a member who speaks very softly and proclaims that nobody listens to him; a client who is verbally expressing positive feelings yet is hitting the floor with clenched fists; a person who says that she really wants to work and to have group time but consistently waits until the end of a session before bringing up her concerns; a participant who claims that she feels comfortable in the group and really likes the members yet sits with her arms crossed tightly and tends to face away from the group; and a member who displays facial expressions and gestures but denies having any reactions.

What are some guidelines for understanding and dealing with nonverbal behavior? Even though you may have a clear idea of what a nonverbal behavior means, it is crucial not to confront the client with an interpretation. It is best to describe the behavior: "I notice that you're smiling, yet you're talking about painful memories, and there are tears in your eyes. What do you want me to believe, your words or your body?" After describing what you are seeing, invite the participant to offer the meaning of the nonverbal behavior. At times you may misunderstand nonverbal information and even label it as resistance. The behavior may well be a manifestation of a cultural injunction. For example, a leader is role-playing Javier's father and asks Javier to make eye contact with him as he is talking. In spite of many invitations, Javier continues to look away or at the floor as he talks to his symbolic father. The leader is unaware that Javier would have felt disrespectful if he looked directly at his father or another authority figure.

In summary, it is essential that you avoid making assumptions about what members are experiencing and, instead, assist members to recognize and explore the possible meanings of their nonverbal behavior. If you misread or ignore nonverbal messages or if you abrasively confront certain behavior, the level of trust in the group will surely suffer.

Empathy   Empathy is the ability to tune in to what others are subjectively experiencing and to see their world through their eyes. When people experience this understanding without critical judgment, they are most likely to reveal their real concerns, for they believe that others are understanding and accepting them as they are. This kind of nonjudgmental understanding is vitally related to trust.

One of your leadership functions is to help members develop greater empathy by pointing out behaviors that block this understanding. Examples of these counterproductive behaviors include responding to others with pat statements, not responding to others at all, questioning inappropriately, telling others how they should be or should feel, responding with critical judgments, and being defensive.

Empathy is an avenue of demonstrating support. For example, Judy benefits when others are able to understand her. If she talks about going through an extremely painful divorce, Clyde can let her know the ways in which he identifies with and understands her pain. Though their circumstances are different, he empathizes with her pain and is willing to share with her his feelings of rejection and abandonment when his wife left him. What helps Judy is Clyde's willingness to tell her about his struggles rather than providing her with quick answers. Instead of giving her ready-made solutions or offering her reassurance, he helps her most by sharing his life with her. Our colleague, Patrick Callanan, often says that people learn more from hearing how others are engaged in a struggle than from hearing their solutions to their problems.

Genuineness and Self-Disclosure   Genuineness implies a congruence between a person's inner experience and what he or she projects externally. Applied to your role as a leader, genuineness means that you don't pretend to be accepting when internally you are not feeling accepting, you don't give out dishonest responses, you don't rely on behaviors that are aimed at winning approval, and you avoid hiding behind a professional role as a leader. Through your own authenticity, you offer a model to members that inspires them to be real in their interactions.

Consider a couple of examples in which you might be challenged to provide authentic responses rather than expected ones. A member who is new to your group might spontaneously ask you, "What do you think of me?" You could politely respond with, "I think you're a very nice person." A more honest response could be: "I don't know you well enough to have strong reactions to you. I'm sure that as I get to know you better, I'll share my perceptions with you." You might want to ask this person what prompted her question and discover that she is intimidated by your position in the group and needs quick reassurance. By helping her identify the reason for her question, you can help her be more authentic with you. In another case a member says to you in the middle of a conflict with him: "Oh, give me a hug; I don't like this tension between us." Chances are that you don't really feel like hugging him at this moment. It is nevertheless important that you give an honest reply to his request. You could say, "I'm very much struggling with you right now, and I'm willing to continue working this through. I'm not willing to hug you now, but that doesn't mean that at some later point, when we've resolved our conflict, I won't feel close enough to hug you. I don't think a hug now will alleviate the tension between us."

Related to being real is the matter of self-disclosure. As a leader you can invite members to make themselves known by letting others in the group know you. As we have pointed out before, this openness does not have to entail an indiscriminate sharing of your private life with the participants, but you can reveal your thoughts and feelings related to what is going on within the group. If you are authentic and appropriately self-disclosing and if you avoid hiding behind defenses, you will encourage the rest of the group to be open about their concerns. Sometimes group participants will challenge you by saying, "We tell you all of our problems, but we don't know any of yours." You could surrender to this pressure to prove that you are "genuine" and end up with a problem. A genuine disclosure is: "Yes, in this group, due to my role, I'm likely to learn more about the nature of your problems than you will learn about my personal concerns, but this doesn't mean that I don't have difficulties in my life. If you and I were members in another group, I expect that you'd learn more about me. While I'm not likely to bring my outside problems into this group, I'm very willing to let you know how I'm being affected in these sessions."

Respect   Respect is shown by what the leader and the members actually do, not simply by what they say. Attitudes and actions that demonstrate respect include avoiding critical judgments, avoiding labeling, looking beyond self-imposed or other-imposed labels, expressing warmth and support that is honestly felt, being genuine and risking being yourself, and recognizing the rights of others to be different from you. If people receive this type of respect, they are supported in their attempts to talk about themselves in open and meaningful ways.

Nancy may express her fear of being judged by others and talk about how she is reluctant to speak because of this fear of criticism. Members are not offering her respect when they too quickly reassure her that they like her just as she is and that they would not judge her. It would be more helpful to encourage her to explore her fear of being judged, both in past situations and in the group. It is important to let her feelings stand and to work with them, rather than discounting them. Most likely her feelings of being judged reside within her and are projected onto others. If the leader allows the members to reassure Nancy, she may momentarily feel reassured. However, as soon as she is away from the group, her internal judge will speak up again.

Caring Confrontation   A crucial factor in the development of trust is the way in which confrontations are handled in the sessions. A confrontation can be an act of caring that takes the form of an invitation for members to examine some discrepancy between what they are saying and what they are doing or between what they are saying and some nonverbal cues they are manifesting. If confrontations are made in an abrasive, "hit-and-run" fashion and if the leader allows people to be verbally abusive, trust is greatly inhibited. You can teach members directness coupled with sensitivity, which results in their seeing that confrontation can be handled in a caring yet honest manner. Challenging members is just as important as supporting them, for a timely challenge can inspire them to look at aspects of themselves that they have been avoiding.

Whereas hostile attacks have the result of closing people up by making them defensive, caring confrontations can actually increase the trust in a group. Members learn that they can express even negative reactions in a way that respects those they are confronting. For example, Claire is very willing to speak on everything and constantly brings herself in on others' work. An ineffective confrontation is: "I want you to be quiet and let others in here talk." An effective confrontation is: "Claire, I appreciate your willingness to participate and talk about yourself. However, I'm concerned that I have heard very little from several others in the group, and I want to hear from them too."

The attitudes and behaviors described here have an important bearing on the level of trust established within a group. Although trust is the major task to be accomplished at the initial stage of a group's development, it is a mistake to assume that once trust has been established it is ensured for the duration of that group. We want to emphasize that it ebbs and flows, and new levels of trust must be established as the group progresses toward a deeper level of intimacy. A basic sense of safety is essential for the movement of a group beyond the initial stage, but this trust will be tested time and again and take on new facets in later stages.

IDENTIFYING AND CLARIFYING GOALS

In the absence of a clear understanding about the purpose of a group and meaningful goals of members, much needless floundering can occur. Members will have real difficulty making progress until they know why they are in the group and how they can make full use of the group to achieve their goals.

One of the major tasks of the initial stage is to establish both group goals and individual goals. Examples of general group goals include creating a climate of trust and acceptance, promoting self-disclosure in significant ways, and encouraging the taking of risks. It is essential that these goals (and norms, which we will discuss later) be explicitly stated, understood, and accepted by the members early in the group. Otherwise, considerable conflict and confusion are certain to occur at a later stage. What follows are some general goals common to most therapeutic groups and some examples of goals for specialized groups.

GENERAL GOALS FOR GROUP MEMBERS

Although the members must decide for themselves the specific aims of a group experience, some broad goals common to most group therapy include:

- to increase self-esteem
- to accept the reality of one's limitations
- to reduce behavior that prevents intimacy
- to learn how to trust oneself and others
- to become aware of how one's culture affects personal decisions
- to increase self-awareness and thereby increase the possibilities for choice and action
- to learn the distinction between having feelings and acting on them
- to free oneself from the inappropriate early decisions that keep one less than the person one would like to be
- to recognize that others struggle too
- to clarify the values one has and to decide whether and how to modify them
- to become both independent and interdependent
- to learn to make choices in a world where nothing is guaranteed
- to find ways to resolve personal problems
- to increase one's capacity to care for others
- to become more open and honest with selected others
- to deal with other members in a direct manner in the here-and-now group situation
- to support and challenge others
- to confront others with care and concern
- to learn how to ask others for what one wants
- to become sensitive to the needs and feelings of others
- to provide others with useful feedback

These are general goals, and they must be narrowed down to apply to what each member expects to gain from group participation.

In addition, specialized groups often have specific goals for members beyond the broad goals common to most groups. For example:

- **Goals for an incest group** are to assist people in talking about incidences of incest; to discover common feelings of anger, hurt, shame, and guilt; and to work through unfinished business with the perpetrator.
- **Goals for people with disabilities group** are to express anger, grief, and resentment about their disability; to learn to deal with the reduced privacy caused by the disability; to learn to work within the limitations imposed by the handicap; and to establish a support system.
- **Goals for a substance-abuse group** are to help the abuser confront difficult issues and learn to cope with life stresses more effectively; to

provide a supportive network; and to learn more appropriate social skills.

- **Goals for elderly people** are to review life experiences; to express feelings over losses; to improve members' self-image; and to continue finding meaning in life.
- **Goals for acting-out children** are to accept feelings and at the same time learn ways of constructively expressing them and dealing with them; to develop skills in making friends; and to channel impulses into constructive behavior.

Regardless of the type of therapeutic group, it is important to consider some methods of assisting participants in developing concrete goals that will give them direction. Participants in groups do not automatically formulate clear goals. It is the responsibility of group leaders to use their skills to help members make their goals specific so that others present in the group will understand them (ASGW, 1989).

HELPING MEMBERS DEFINE PERSONAL GOALS

Participants are typically able to state only in broad terms what they expect to get from a group. For instance, Carol, who says she'd like to "relate to others better," needs to specify with whom and under what conditions she encounters difficulties in her interpersonal relationships. She also needs to learn to state concretely what part of her behavior she needs to change. The leader's questions should help her become more specific. With whom is she having difficulties? If the answer is her parents, then what specifically is causing her problems with them? How is she affected by these problems? How does she want to be different with her parents? With all this information the leader has a clearer idea of how to proceed with Carol.

Here are some examples of how leaders can intervene to help members make a global goal more specific:

Member: "I want to get in touch with my feelings."
Leader: "What kind of feelings are you having difficulty with?"

Member: "I want to work on my anger."
Leader: "With whom in your life are you angry? What do you most want to say?"

Member: "I have very low self-esteem."
Leader: "List some of the ways in which you put yourself down."

Member: "I have trouble with intimacy."
Leader: "Whom in your life are you having trouble getting close to, and what might you be doing to prevent the intimacy you want?"

Defining goals is an ongoing process, not something that is done once and for all. Throughout the course of a group it is important to help members assess the degree to which their personal goals are being met and, if appropriate, to help them revise any of their goals (ASGW, 1989). As members gain more experience, they are in a better position to know what they want from a group, and they also come to recognize additional goals that can guide their participation. Their involvement in the work of other members can act as a catalyst in getting them to think about ways in which they can profit from the group experience.

Once members have a general idea of what they want to get from being a group member, establishing a contract is one excellent way for them to be more precise in their personal goals. Basically, a contract is a statement by participants of what problems they want to explore and what behaviors they are willing to change. It is a way of encouraging clients to think about the group and about their role in it. In the contract method, group members assume an active and responsible stance. Of course, contracts can be open-ended in that they can be modified or replaced as appropriate. Contracts can be used in most of the groups discussed in this book.

Contracts and homework assignments can be combined fruitfully. In Carol's case a beginning contract could commit her to observe and write down each time she experiences difficulties with her parents. If she discovers that she usually walks away at times of conflict with them, she might pledge in a follow-up contract to stay in one of these situations rather than avoiding it.

As another example, consider a man in an assertiveness-training group who decides that he would like to spend more time on activities that interest him. He might make a contract that calls for him to do more of the things he would like to do for himself, and he might assign himself certain activities to be carried out during the week as experiments. At the next group session he would report the results. Partly on the basis of these results, he could decide how much and in what ways he really wanted to change. Then he could do further work in the group toward his chosen ends.

GROUP-PROCESS CONCEPTS AT THE INITIAL STAGE

The group process, as we have said, involves the stages that groups tend to go through, each characterized by certain feelings and behaviors. Initially, as the members get to know one another, there is a feeling of anxiety. Each waits for someone else to begin the work. Tension, conflict, or even boredom build up. If things go well, however, the members learn to trust one another and the leader, and they begin to openly express feelings, thoughts, and reactions. Thus, included under the rubric *group process* are activities such as establishing norms and group cohesion, learning to work cooperatively, establishing ways of solving problems, and learning to express conflict openly. We'll now discuss in depth two of these group-process concepts—group norms and group cohesion—that are especially important during the initial stage. *Group norms* are the shared beliefs about expected behaviors aimed at making groups function effectively. *Group cohesion* is a sense of togetherness, or community, within a group. A cohesive group is one in which members have incentives for remaining in the group and share a feeling of belongingness and relatedness.

GROUP NORMS

Norms and procedures that will help the group attain its goals can be developed during the early stage. If the norms—standards that govern behavior in the group—are vague, valuable time will be lost, and tensions will arise over what is appropriate and inappropriate. There are, however, implicit (or unspoken) norms as well as those that are explicitly stated.

Implicit norms may develop because of preconceived ideas about what takes place in a group. Members may assume, for example, that a group is a place where everything must be said, with no room for privacy. Unless the leader calls attention to the possibility that members can be self-disclosing and still retain a measure of privacy, members may misinterpret the norm of openness and honesty as a policy of complete candor, with no secrets. Another example of an implicit norm that we sometimes see in our groups is pressure to experience catharsis and crying. In most of our intensive therapeutic groups, there is a fair amount of crying and expression of pent-up feelings. Certain members wrongly assume that we judge the quality of their personal work by the volume of tears shed or the intensity of catharsis.

Implicit norms may also develop because of modeling by the leader. If a leader curses and uses abrasive language, members are more likely to adopt this pattern of speech in their group interactions, even though the leader has never expressly encouraged people to talk in such a manner. Another example of an implicit norm pertains to changes in members' everyday lives. If an unassertive member reports that she is being perceived as more assertive at work, she may receive applause from the group. Even though behavior change outside of the group is not specifically stated as a norm, this implicit norm can have a powerful effect on shaping the members' responses and behaviors. Implicit norms do affect the group. They are less likely to have an adverse influence if they are made explicit.

The following explicit norms are examples of standards of behavior that are common in many groups:

• Members are expected to attend regularly and show up on time. When they attend sessions only sporadically, the entire group suffers.

Members who regularly attend will resent the lack of commitment of those who miss sessions.

• Members are encouraged to be personal and share meaningful aspects of themselves, communicating directly with others in the group and, in general, becoming active participants.

• Members are expected to give feedback to one another. They can evaluate the effects of their behavior on others only if the others are willing to say how they have been affected. It is important for members not to withhold their perceptions and reactions but, rather, to let others know what they perceive.

• Members should focus on feelings and express them, rather than talking about problems in a detached and intellectual manner.

• Members are encouraged to focus on here-and-now interactions within the group. Immediacy refers to being genuine in one's relationships. Members focus on being immediate by expressing and exploring conflicts within the group. Immediacy is called for when there are unverbalized thoughts and feelings about what is happening in a session, particularly if these reactions are having a detrimental effect on the group process. There is little need to dwell in the group on the details of how members behave in various social situations, because this behavior becomes apparent in the here and now of group interaction. Thus, one of your leadership functions is to ask questions such as "How is it for you to be in this group now?" "With whom do you identify the most in here?" "What are some of the things that you might be rehearsing to yourself silently?" "Whom in this room are you most aware of?" You can also steer members into the here and now by asking them to reveal what they think and feel about what is going on in the group.

• Members are expected to bring into the group personal problems and concerns that they are willing to discuss. They can be expected to spend some time before the sessions thinking about the matters they want to work on. This is an area in which unspoken norms frequently function. In some groups, for example, the participants may get the idea that they are not good group members unless they bring personal issues from everyday life to work on during the sessions. Members may get the impression that it is not acceptable to focus on here-and-now matters within the group itself and that they should be willing to work on other problems.

• Members are encouraged to provide therapeutic support. Ideally, this support facilitates both an individual's work and the group process, rather than distracting members from self-exploration. But some leaders can implicitly "teach" being overly supportive or, by their modeling, can demonstrate a type of support that has the effect of short-circuiting painful experiences that a member is attempting to work through. Leaders who are uncomfortable with intense emotions (such as anger or the pain associated with past memories) can actually collude with members by fostering a pseudosupportive climate that prevents members from fully experiencing and expressing intense feelings of any kind. Some groups are so supportive that challenge and confrontation are ruled out. An unverbalized norm in this area is the focus on expressing only positive feelings and favorable reactions. If this practice becomes a pattern, members can get the idea that it is not acceptable to express any criticism, even if it is constructive.

• The other side of the norm of support is providing members with challenges to look at themselves. Confrontation is the process that involves expressing in a direct and caring manner a challenge for members (or leaders) to look at some discrepancy between what they are saying and doing. Members need to learn how to confront others without arousing defensiveness. Early in our group, for example, we establish a norm that it is not acceptable to dismiss another in a hostile and labeling way, such as by saying "You're an idiot!" Instead, we teach members to directly and cleanly express the anger they are feeling, avoiding name calling. Members are asked to express the source of their anger, including what led up to their feelings. For example, if Ann says to Rudy "You're an idiot," the leader can ask her to let Rudy know how she has been affected by him. She can also be encouraged to express the stored-up reactions that led her to label him. In contrast, some leaders model harsh confrontations, and members soon pick up the unexpressed norm that the appropriate way to relate to others in this group is with attacks. Some groups even specialize in confrontation on the assumption that the only way people change is by having their defenses stripped away through unrelenting verbal attacks.

• Groups can operate under either a norm of exploring personal problems or a norm of problem solving. In some groups, for example, as soon as members bring up situations that they'd like to understand better, they are bombarded by suggestions for how they can "solve" these problems. The fact of the matter is that solutions are often not possible, and what members most need is an opportunity to talk about what they are feeling. Of course, problem-solving strategies are of use in teaching members new ways of coping with their difficulties. But it is important that clients have an opportunity to explore their concerns before suggested solutions are presented.

• Members can be taught the norm of listening without thinking of a quick rebuttal and without becoming overly defensive. Although we don't expect people to merely accept all the feedback they receive, we do ask them to really hear what others are saying to them and to seriously consider these messages—particularly ones that are repeated consistently.

These are a few examples of group norms. The important point is that the group's norms be discussed as the group unfolds and develops.

Many groups become bogged down because members are unsure of what is expected of them. This is a further rationale for the importance of preparing members to assume an active role in attaining their personal goals (which we emphasized in Chapter 4). For instance, a member may want to intervene and share her perceptions while a leader is working with another client, but she may be inhibited because she is not sure whether she should interrupt the group leader at work. Another member may feel an inclination to support a fellow group member at the time when that member is experiencing some pain or sadness but may refrain because he is uncertain whether his support will detract from the other's experience. Another member who is bored, session after session, may keep this feeling to herself because she is not sure of the appropriateness of revealing it. Perhaps if she were told that it was permissible to experience her boredom and valuable to express it, she might be more open with her group and, consequently, less bored.

If group norms are clearly presented and if the members see the value of them and cooperatively decide on some of them, they will be potent forces in shaping the group. Part of the orientation process consists of identifying and discussing norms that are aimed at developing a cohesive and productive group

GROUP COHESION

During the early stage of a group the members do not know one another well enough for a true sense of community to be formed. There is an awkwardness and a period of becoming acquainted. Though participants talk about themselves, it is likely that they are presenting more of their public selves rather than deeper aspects of their private selves. Genuine cohesion typically comes after groups have struggled with conflict, have shared pain, and have committed themselves to taking significant risks. But the foundations of cohesion can begin to take shape during the initial stage.

Some indicators of this initial degree of cohesion are cooperation among members; a willingness to show up for the meetings and be punctual; an effort to make the group a safe place, including talking about any feelings of lack of trust or fears of trusting; support and caring, as evidenced by being willing to listen to others and accept them for who they are; and a willingness to express reactions to and perceptions of others in the here-and-now context of the group interactions. Genuine cohesion is not a fixed condition arrived at automatically. Instead, it is an ongoing process of solidarity that members earn through the risks they take with one another. Group cohesion can be developed, maintained, and increased in a number of ways. Here are some suggestions for enhancing group cohesion.

• Trust must be developed during the early stage of a group. One of the best ways of building trust is to create a group climate characterized by respect for the opinions and feelings of the members. It is essential that members openly express their feelings concerning the degree of trust they are experiencing. An opportunity can be provided at the outset for members to share their reservations, and this open sharing of concerns will pave the way for productive work. (Creating a trusting environment will be discussed in detail in the next section.)

• If group members share meaningful aspects of themselves, they both learn to take risks and increase group cohesiveness. By modeling—for instance, by sharing their own reactions to what is occurring within the group—leaders can encourage risk-taking behavior. When group members do take risks, they can be reinforced with sincere recognition and support, which will increase their sense of closeness to the others.

• Group goals and individuals goals can be jointly determined by the group members and the leader. If a group is without clearly stated goals, animosity can build up that will lead to fragmentation of the group.

• Cohesion can be increased by inviting (but not forcing) all members to become active participants. Members who appear to be passive or withdrawn can be invited to express their feelings toward the group. These members may be silent observers for a number of reasons, and these reasons ought to be examined openly in the group.

• Cohesion can be built by sharing the leadership role with the members of the group. In autocratic groups all the decisions are made by the leader. A cooperative group is more likely to develop if members are encouraged to initiate discussion of issues they want to explore. Also, instead of fostering a leader-to-member style of interaction, group leaders can promote member-to-member interactions. This can be done by inviting the members to respond to one another, by encouraging feedback and sharing, and by searching for ways to involve as many members as possible in group interactions.

• Conflict is inevitable in groups. It is desirable for group members to recognize sources of conflict and to deal openly with them when they arise. A group can be strengthened by acceptance of conflict and by the honest working through of differences.

• Group attractiveness and cohesion are related. It is generally accepted that the greater the degree of attractiveness of a group to its members, the greater the level of cohesion. If the group deals with matters that interest the members, if the members feel that they are respected, and if the atmosphere is supportive, the chances are good that the group will be perceived as attractive.

• Members can be encouraged to disclose their ideas, feelings, and reactions to what occurs within their group. The expression of both positive and negative reactions should be encouraged. If this is done, an honest exchange can take place, which is essential if a sense of group belongingness is to develop.

HELPING MEMBERS GET THE MOST FROM A GROUP EXPERIENCE

Some behaviors and attitudes promote a cohesive and productive group—that is, a group in which meaningful self-exploration takes place and in which honest and appropriate feedback is given and received. We begin orienting and preparing members during the preliminary session, but we typically find that time allows only an introduction to the ways in which clients can get the most from their group experience. Consequently, during the initial phase of the group's evolution we devote some time to teaching members the basics of group process, especially how they can involve themselves as active participants. We emphasize that they will benefit from the experience in direct proportion to how much they invest of themselves, both in the group and in practicing on the outside what they are learning in the sessions.

We do not present the following guidelines as a lecture in one sitting. We begin by giving members written information about their participation in the group. We also allocate time to discuss these topics as they occur naturally within the sessions, which increases the odds that members will be receptive to thinking about how they can best participate.

We encourage you to use these guidelines as a catalyst for thinking about your own approach to preparing members. Reflecting on this material may help you develop an approach that suits your own personality and leadership style and that is appropriate for the groups you lead. The following suggestions are written from the leader's point of view and directed to the members.

LEADER GUIDELINES FOR MEMBERS

Learn to Help Establish Trust   Participants often wait for some other person to take the first risk or to make some gesture of trust. Members can enhance their experience in the group by helping to create a trusting climate. They can do this, paradoxically, by revealing their lack of trust. Members can gain from initiating a discussion that will allow genuine trust to develop.

Example: Harold was older than most of the other group members, and he was afraid that they would not be able to empathize with him, that they would exclude him from activities, that they would view him as an outsider—a parent figure—and that he would not be able to open up. After he disclosed these fears, many members gave Harold praise for his willingness to reveal his mistrust. His disclosure, and the response to it, stimulated others to express some of their concerns. This sharing stimulated trust in the entire group by making it clear that it was appropriate to express fears. Instead of being rejected, Harold was accepted and appreciated, for he was willing to make a significant part of himself known to the rest of the group.

Express Persistent Feelings   There are times when members keep their feelings of boredom, anger, or disappointment a secret from the rest of the group. It is most important that persistent feelings related to the group process be aired. We often make statements to members such as "If you are feeling detached and withdrawn, let it be known" or "If you are experiencing chronic anger or irritation toward others in this group, don't keep these feelings to yourself."

Example: In a group of adolescents that met once a week for ten weeks, Margaret waited until the third session to disclose that she didn't trust either the members or the leader, that she was angry because she felt pressured to participate, that she was scared to express what she felt because she might look foolish, and that she really didn't know what was expected of her as a group member. She had experienced these feelings since the initial session but had withheld them from the group. The leader let Margaret know how important it was for her to reveal these persistent feelings of distrust so they could be explored and resolved.

Beware of Misusing Jargon   It is unfortunate that the group movement offers another way of being dishonest. Some people learn a new language that can remove them from their direct experiences. Take, for example, phrases such as "I can really relate to you," "I want to get closer to my feelings," "I get good vibes from you," "I'd like to stop playing all these games with myself," "Let me be in the present moment," and "I have to be spontaneous." If terms such as *relate to, get closer to,* and *vibes* aren't clearly defined and reserved for certain circumstances, the quality of communication will be poor. People who learn to use this vague language may deceive themselves into thinking that they are self-actualized. What a refreshing experience it is to talk with people who have had no group experience and who are able to say in plain English what it is they want and why they decided to get involved in a group.

We encourage members to use descriptive language by asking them what they mean by "really relating to that" or by asking them to clarify what feelings they want to express. When members speak in hazy terms and use jargon, we are likely to ask them to repeat what they said in terms that a 10-year-old child could understand.

Related to misusing jargon is the way in which members' use of language sometimes distances them from themselves and from others. For example, when people say "I can't" instead of "I won't" or when they use many qualifiers in their speech ("maybe," "perhaps," "but," "I guess"), we ask them to be aware of how they are contributing to their powerlessness by their choice of words. This practice also applies to the use of a generalized "you" or "people" when "I" is what is meant. The more members can assume responsibility for their speech, the more they can reclaim some of that power they have lost through impersonal modes of expression.

Example: "People are usually afraid to talk openly in the group," Valerie said. "They feel threatened and scared." The leader intervened by asking Valerie to repeat everything she had just said but to substitute "I" for the general impersonal words "people" and "they." The leader asked her whether using "I" was closer to the truth of what she really wanted to convey. After all, she could speak with authority about her own feelings, but she could not be an expert about others' feelings.

Decide for Yourself How Much to Disclose   Group members are sometimes led to believe that the more they disclose about themselves, the better. They are asked not to think about the need for privacy. Though self-disclosure is an important tool in the group process, it is up to each participant to decide what aspects of his or her life to reveal. This principle cannot be stressed too much, for the idea that members will have to "tell everything" contributes to the resistance of many people to becoming participants in a group.

The most useful kind of disclosure is unrehearsed. It expresses present concern and may entail some risk. As participants open up to a group, they have fears about how other people will receive what they reveal. If a member shares that he is shy, often quiet, and afraid to speak up in the group, the other members will have a frame of reference for more accurately interpreting and reacting to his lack of participation. Had he not spoken up, both the leader and other members would have been more likely to misinterpret his behavior.

Members should be cautioned, however, about the dangers of "paying membership dues" by striving to reveal the biggest secret. Self-disclosure is not a process of "letting everything hang out" and of making oneself psychologically naked. Let members know time and again that they are responsible for deciding what, how much, and when they will share personal conflicts pertaining to their everyday life.

Example: In a weekly group in an agency, Luis, a minority client, did not want to talk about his sexual relationship with his wife. One of the cultural values he grew up with was to keep such personal concerns private. He did talk about how difficult it was for him to identify what he felt, let alone express feelings to others. Although he did not feel comfortable in discussing sexuality, he was willing to share with the group his difficulties in letting himself experience feelings of sadness, compassion, jealousy, and fright. Luis did not want to go through life as an unfeeling person. Other group members respected him for his willingness to tell them why he was not ready to talk about his sexual relationship. Because of this understanding that he felt from other members, he was encouraged to share more of his feelings of fear and sadness.

Be an Active Participant, Not an Observer   A participant might say: "I'm not the talkative type. It's hard for me to formulate my thoughts, and I'm afraid I don't express myself well. So I usually don't say anything in the group. But I listen to what others are saying, and I learn by observing. I really don't think I have to be talking all the time to get something out of these sessions." Although it is true that members can learn by observing interactions and reacting nonverbally, their learning will tend to be limited. If they assume the stance of not contributing, others will never come to know them, and they can easily feel cheated and angry at being the object of others' perhaps flawed observations.

Another way in which some members keep themselves passively on the fringe of group activity is by continually saying "I have no real problems in my life at this time, so I don't have much to contribute to the group." We attempt to teach these members to share their reactions to their experience in the group as well as to let others know how they are being affected. Members who choose to share little about events outside of the group can actively participate by keeping themselves open to being affected by other clients. Leaders can contribute to group cohesion by helping those members who feel that they have nothing to contribute recognize that they are depriving fellow members if they do not at least share how they are reacting to what others are saying.

Example: When Thelma was asked what she wanted from the group, she replied: "I haven't really given it that much thought. I figured I'd just be spontaneous and wait to see what happens." The leader let Thelma know that sometimes other people's work might indeed evoke some of her own issues and that she might spontaneously react. However, the leader taught her that it was important for her to think about and to bring up the concerns that initially brought her to the group. As the sessions progressed, Thelma did learn to let the other members know what she wanted from them. Instead of being a passive observer without any clear goals who would be content to wait for things to happen to her, she began to take the initiative. She showed that she wanted to talk about how lonely she was, how desperate and inadequate she frequently felt, how fearful she was of being weak with men, and how she dreaded facing her world every morning. As she learned to focus on her wants, she found that she could benefit from her weekly sessions.

Expect Some Disruption of Your Life   Participants in therapeutic groups should be given the warning that their involvement may complicate their outside lives for a time. As a result of group experiences, members tend to assume that the people in their lives will be both ready and willing to make significant changes. It can be shocking for members to discover that others thought they were "just fine" the way they were, and the friction that results may make it more difficult than ever to modify familiar patterns. Therefore, it is important for members to be prepared for the fact that not everyone will like or accept some of the changes they want to make. Perhaps some relationships will be discontinued and some new ones formed.

Example: Ron came away from his group with the awareness that he was frightened of his wife, that he consistently refrained from expressing his wants to her, and that he related to her as he would to a protective mother. He feared that if he asserted himself with her, she would leave. In the group he not only became disgusted with his dependent style but also decided that he would treat his wife as an equal and give up his hope of having her become his mother. Ron's wife did not cooperate with his valiant efforts to change the nature of their relationship. The more assertive he became, the more disharmony there was in his home. While he was trying to become independent, his wife was struggling to keep their relationship the way it was; she was not willing to respond differently to him.

Realize That You Don't Have to Be Sick to Benefit from a Group   It is not uncommon to find members questioning the value of the group and being somewhat skeptical about its ability to help them. Some people shy away from counseling groups because they believe that groups are only for people with severe emotional problems. Members should be taught that a minor "tune-up" is possible without a major overhaul. Groups can offer the opportunity to examine how past decisions are influencing one's present life. Effective groups provide both the support and the challenge necessary for evaluating one's direction and for making changes if desired.

Example: Sid was embarrassed over having joined a group. He accepted the notion that any kind of therapy was for people with serious emotional and mental disorders. Gradually, through the example of fellow group members, he found that struggling for change was not sick but, rather, courageous. He then felt freer to use the group as a place to try out new behavior, and he became open to working with internal blocks that were preventing him from forming close ties with those he cared about.

Expect to Discover Positive Aspects of Yourself   A common fear about therapy is that you will discover how unlovable, how empty, how hopeless, or how powerless you are. More often than not, though, people in groups begin to realize that they're lovable, that they can control their own destiny, and that they have talents they never knew about. Members often explore intense feelings of pain in a group. Unrecognized and unexpressed pain is blocking them from living a truly joyous life. It is through releasing and working through these painful experiences that they begin to reclaim a joyful dimension of themselves. For instance, many participants experience an inner strength, discover a real wit and sense of humor, create moving poetry or songs, or dare for the first time to show a creative side of themselves that they have kept hidden from others and from themselves. A group experience, then, can show people a positive and creative side of themselves.

Example: Frank expressed the positive side of the group experience rather poetically when he said: "I have learned that there are lots of beautiful rose bushes with pretty flowers, and on those bushes are thorns. I'd never trade the struggle and pain I had to go through to appreciate the joy of smelling and touching those roses. Both the roses and the thorns are a part of life."

Listen Closely and Discriminatingly   Group members should listen carefully to what the other members say about them, neither accepting it wholesale nor rejecting it outright. Members should listen discriminatingly, deciding for themselves what does and what doesn't apply to them. Before they respond, they can be asked to quiet down, to let what is being said to them sink in, and to take note of how it is affecting them. Members are sometimes busy formulating responses while others are still speaking to them. They cannot fully comprehend what is being communicated to them if they are not totally engaged in listening.

Example: In an adolescent group, members told Jack that it was hard for them to listen to his many stories. Although some of his stories were interesting, they gave no clue to the nature of his struggles, which were why he was in the group. Other members told him that it was easier to hear what he was saying when he talked about himself. When Jack became defensive and angry and denied that he had been acting that way, he could have been asked by the leader or members to think over the feedback before he so rigorously rejected it.

Pay Attention to Consistent Feedback   A person may get similar feedback from many people in different groups yet may still dismiss it as invalid. Although it is important to discriminate, it is also important to realize that a message that has been received from a variety of people is likely to have a degree of validity.

Example: In several groups Dan heard people tell him that he didn't seem interested in what they had to say and that he appeared distant and detached. The members said that although he was physically in the room, he often looked at the ceiling and sighed, moved his chair away from the circle, yawned, and sometimes even took a short nap. In short, they felt that he had no interest in them and that it was difficult for them to get close to him. Dan was surprised by this feedback and insisted that his behavior in the group was very different from his behavior in his outside life—that on the outside he felt close to people and was interested and involved. It seems unlikely that someone could be so different in the two areas, however, and the leader intervened with: "You may be different in here than you are on the outside. But would you be willing to monitor how people respond to you away from here and be open to noticing if any of the feedback given to you might indeed fit you?" The leader's response eliminated unnecessary argumentation and debates over who was right.

Don't Categorize Yourself   During the initial stage of a group, members often present themselves to the other clients in terms of a role, one that they dislike but at the same time appear to cling to. For instance, we've heard people introduce themselves as "the group mother," "the walled-off and impenetrable one," "the fragile person who can't stand confrontation," and "the one in this group whom nobody will like." There are times when a person who views him or herself as "walled off" would like to be different. What is important is for people not to fatalistically pin labels on themselves and for the group not to fulfill the expectations and thereby even further convince members that they are what they fear. It may be helpful for group leaders to remind themselves and the members of how certain participants can be pegged with labels such as "the monopolist," "the storyteller," "the intellectualizer," "the withdrawn one," "the obsessive/compulsive one," and so on. People may exhibit behaviors that characterize them in one way or another, and it is appropriate to confront them with these actions during the group. But this confronting can be done without cementing people into rigid molds that become very difficult to shatter.

Example: Roz presented herself to the group as withdrawn and fragile. When she was asked how she would like to be different, she said she would like to speak out more often and more forcefully. She was willing to make a contract that required her to speak out and at least act as if she were strong. In this way she was able to challenge an old image that she had clung to and was able to experiment with a different type of behavior.

Other Suggestions for Group Members   Some additional guidelines that we bring up early in a group as they seem appropriate are briefly listed below:

- Be willing to do work both before and after a group. Consider keeping a journal as a supplement to the group experience. Create homework assignments as a way of putting your group learning into practice in everyday living.
- Develop self-evaluation skills as a way of assessing your progress in the group. Examples of questions you might ask are "Am I contributing to the group?" "Am I satisfied with what is occurring in the sessions? If not, what am I doing about it?" "Am I using in my life what I'm learning in my group?"
- Spend time in clarifying your own goals by reviewing specific issues you want to explore during the sessions. This can best be done by thinking about specific changes you want to make in your life and by deciding what you are willing to do both in and out of the group to bring about these changes.

- Concentrate on making personal and direct statements to others in your group, as opposed to giving advice, making interpretations, and asking impersonal questions. Instead of telling others how they are, let them know how they are affecting you.
- Realize that the real work consists of what you actually do outside of your group. Consider the group a means to an end, and give some time to thinking about what you will do with what you are learning. Expect some setbacks, and be aware that change may be slow and subtle. Do not expect one group alone to renovate your entire life.

AVOID TOO MUCH TEACHING

Even though we've stressed the value of preparing members for how groups function, be aware that too much emphasis on teaching the group process can have a negative influence. All the spontaneous learning can be taken out of the group experience if members have been told too much of what to expect and have not been allowed to learn for themselves. Moreover, it is possible to foster a dependency on the structure and direction provided by the leader.

Our hope is that members will increasingly be able to function with less intervention from the leader as the group progresses. There is a delicate balance between providing too much structuring and failing to give enough structure and information, which results in confusion. Especially important, perhaps, is that the leader be aware of factors such as group cohesion, group norms, and group interactions at any given point. With this awareness the leader can decide when it is timely and useful to suggest a discussion of certain behavior that is occurring in the here and now.

We mentioned earlier that the stages in the life of a group are not rigidly defined but, rather, fluid and somewhat overlapping. What we teach and how we teach members about the group process have a lot to do with the level to which the group has evolved. Burlingame and Fuhriman (1990) have identified particular therapeutic characteristics that are primarily linked to the various stages of a group. During the beginning phase, the crucial factors are identification, universality, hope, and cohesion. During the middle phase, catharsis, cohesion, interpersonal learning, and insight are essential. As termination approaches, existential factors surface. Conceptualizing a group in this way provides an understanding of the group's dynamics and suggests appropriate strategies for intervention.

LEADER ISSUES AT THE INITIAL STAGE

Early in the history of a group it is especially important to think about the balance of responsibility between members and the leader (or co-leaders) as well as the degree of structuring that is optimal for the group. If you are working with a co-leader, discussing these issues is essential, for divergent views are bound to hurt the group. If you assume the majority of the responsibility for keeping the group moving, for example, and your co-leader assumes almost no responsibility on the ground that the members must decide for themselves what to do with group time, the members will sense this division and are bound to be confused by it. Similarly, if you function best with a high degree of structure in groups and your co-leader believes that any structuring should come from the members, this difference of opinion will have a detrimental effect on the group.

For these reasons, it is wise to select a co-leader who has a philosophy of leadership that is compatible with yours, though this does not mean that both of you need to have the same style of leading. You can have differences that complement each other.

DIVISION OF RESPONSIBILITY

A basic issue you will have to consider is responsibility for the direction and outcome of the group. If a group proves to be nonproductive, will this failure stem from your lack of leadership skills, or does the responsibility rest with the group members?

One way of conceptualizing the issue of responsibility is to think of it in terms of a continuum. At one end is the leader who assumes a great share of the responsibility for the direction and outcomes of the group. Such leaders tend to have the outlook that unless they are highly directive the group will flounder. They tend to see their role as that of the expert, and they actively intervene to keep the group moving in ways they deem productive. A disadvantage of this form of leadership is that it robs the members of the responsibility that is rightfully theirs; if members are perceived by the leader as not having the capacity to take care of themselves, they soon begin to live up to this expectation by being irresponsible, at least in the group.

Leaders who assume an inordinate degree of responsibility not only undermine members' independence but also burden themselves. If people leave unchanged, such leaders see it as their fault. If members remain separate, never forming a cohesive unit, these leaders view this outcome as a reflection of their lack of skill. If the group is disappointed, they feel disappointed and tend to blame themselves, believing that they didn't do enough to create a dynamic group. This style of leadership is draining, and leaders who use it may eventually lose the energy required to lead groups.

At the other end of the responsibility continuum is the leader who proclaims: "I am responsible for me, and you are responsible for you. If you want to leave this group with anything of value, it is strictly up to you. I can't do anything for you—make you feel something or take away any of your defenses—unless you allow me to." This extreme style absolves leaders of any responsibility for what takes place in their groups.

To be sure, leaders do have a significant role to play both in the process of a group and in the outcomes. By denying responsibility, leaders do not have to look at what they are doing to establish and maintain a climate that allows productive work to occur in the group.

Ideally, you will develop a leadership style that entails a balance between accepting your share of the responsibility and usurping the members' share. This issue is central, because your approach to other issues (such as structuring and self-disclosure) hinges on your approach to it.

DEGREE OF STRUCTURING

The issue is not *whether* a group leader should provide structure but, rather, *what degree* of structure. Like responsibility, structuring exists on a continuum. The leader's theoretical orientation, the type of group, and the membership population are some of the factors that determine the amount and type of structuring employed.

Balance at the Initial Stage   Providing therapeutic structuring is particularly important during the initial stage of a group, when members are typically unclear about what behavior is expected and are therefore anxious. Structure can be both useful and inhibiting in a group's development. Too little structure results in members' becoming unduly anxious, and although some anxiety is productive, too much can inhibit spontaneity.

Although you may be particularly active during the early phase of a group, it is important that you encourage members to assume an increasing role. Too much structuring and direction can foster leader-dependent attitudes and behavior. The members may wait for the leader to "make something happen" instead of acting themselves.

Yalom (1983, 1995) sees the basic task of the group leader as providing enough structure to give a general direction to the members yet avoiding the pitfalls of fostering dependency. His message for leaders is to structure the group in a fashion that facilitates each member's autonomous functioning. An example of fostering dependency on the leader would be encouraging members to speak only when they are invited to do so. Instead, the leader can encourage members to bring themselves into the interactions without being called on.

We do not subscribe to a passive style of group leadership; we do not simply wait and let the group take any direction it happens to go in. By providing some structure we give group members the opportunity to experiment with new levels of awareness and to build new forms of behavior from this awareness. During the initial stage our structure is aimed at helping members identify and express their fears, expectations, and personal goals. For example, we often use dyads, go-arounds, and open-ended questions as ways of making it easier for members to talk to one another about current issues in their lives. After talking to several people on a one-to-one basis, members find it easier to talk openly in the entire group. The leadership activity we provide is designed to help members focus on themselves and the issues they most want to explore in the group.

Many short-term psychoeducational groups are structured around a series of topics. In a group for learning effective parenting skills, for example, the sessions are guided by topics such as listening well, setting limits, learning to convey respect, and providing discipline without punishment. Group leaders sometimes rigidly adhere to a structured exercise or a discussion of a topic when another pressing matter demands attention. If there is conflict in the group, it is more important to suspend the topic or exercise until the conflict has been attended to. If the conflict is brushed aside, there is a greater likelihood that discussion of the topic will be superficial. At other times, members spontaneously bring up unrelated concerns, and leaders have difficulty keeping the group focused on the topic in a meaningful way. The leader and members of the group need to explore whether the shift in the topic is due to their discomfort with the issue or to the fact that a more relevant subject has surfaced. If the shift is an avoidance tactic, the facilitator might point out the dynamics of what is occurring.

We often supervise leaders who are facilitating structured interpersonal groups. These groups are focused on different themes for each session. Some of these topics are sex roles, body image, meaning and values, work and leisure, love and sexuality, loneliness, intimacy, and death and dying. We try to teach the group facilitators how to balance a discussion of group-process concerns (trust, confrontation, unfinished business, subgrouping) with an exploration of the particular topic. Process issues among members (such as clients' feeling isolated in the group) generally take precedence over dealing with the topic. It is not a matter of either focusing on a member's particular concern or dealing with a topic. The art consists of learning how to help members relate topics to themselves in significant ways so that group interaction and group learning can occur.

Research on Structuring   Research indicates the value of an initial structure that builds supportive group norms and highlights positive interactions among members. Leaders must carefully monitor this therapeutic structure throughout the life of a group, rather than limiting the evaluation process to the final stage. Structuring that offers a coherent framework for understanding the experiences of individuals and the group process will be of the most value. When goals are clear, when appropriate member behaviors are identified, and when the process provides a framework for change, members tend to engage in therapeutic work more quickly (Dies, 1983b). Moreover, leader direction during the early phase of a group tends to facilitate the development of cohesion and the willingness of members to take risks by making themselves known to others and by giving others feedback (Stockton & Morran, 1982).

Bednar, Melnick, and Kaul (1974) developed a group model that shows the value of structure for group process and outcome. In their formulation, as group cohesion increases, members gradually begin to feel safer in sharing themselves in meaningful ways, in giving feedback, and in providing support and challenge to others. Their general model specifies the following sequence: initial ambiguity and anxiety, increased structure through specific instructions, increased risk taking, increased group cohesion, and increased personal responsibility.

Research-Based Guidelines for Leaders   Here are some guidelines for providing therapeutic structure in your groups; they underscore many of the major points we have developed in this chapter and the previous one. What follows is an adaptation of some of the conclusions of research on short-term groups, as summarized by Dies (1983b):

- Be aware that direct instruction, or teaching, tends to facilitate a group's development during the early stages.
- Introduce an initial structure to build supportive group norms and foster the establishment of trust.
- Once the basic norms are established and the therapeutic potential of the group is developed, the degree of structure can be lessened. A less directive structure is appropriate during the later stages as the members assume increased direction of their group.
- Use more structured interventions with clients whose level of personal functioning restricts their capacity to interact in socially competent ways.
- Employ active leadership, yet at the same time use interventions that encourage members to assume increased responsibility.
- Develop and maintain a task-oriented focus by helping members develop and stick to clear goals.
- Help members understand the value of disclosing themselves, of providing feedback to one another, and of providing a balance between support and confrontation. You can do this by giving them a clear rationale for such group behaviors.
- Acknowledge what members do by providing positive reinforcement. Make statements to members more often than asking them questions. Provide concrete feedback that describes specific behavioral characteristics, and teach members to do the same.
- Model directness by speaking *to* members instead of talking *about* them.
- Structure initial sessions in a way that will help members acquire a clear framework for understanding experiences within the group.
- Use interpretations that help members generalize from how they behave in the here and now of the group situation to their problems in everyday living. Discuss with them the value of experimenting outside of the group with new interpersonal behaviors.

In summary, some degree of structuring exists in all groups. It is not possible to have an "unstructured" group, for even this is a form of structure. The art is to provide structuring that is not so tight that it robs the group members of the responsibility for finding their own structure.

OPENING AND CLOSING GROUP SESSIONS

The procedures leaders use in opening and closing group sessions are an important aspect of structuring. These skills are important throughout the group process, and we suggest that you return to this discussion as you read about subsequent stages. We discuss opening and closing group sessions here because you need to be aware of this essential aspect of group leadership from the very beginning. The interventions we describe here are not the only "right" ones. There are many effective ways to intervene, depending on your theoretical orientation or leadership style and also on the kind of group you are leading. We have found the following guidelines useful.

Guidelines for Opening Sessions   We have observed that many leader trainees do not pay attention to how they open group sessions. These leaders are all too ready to focus on the first person who speaks and stay with that person for an undue length of time because at least someone is speaking. There is often no attempt to link the coming session with the last session, and the leader does not check with each member to determine how the members want to use the time for this particular session. If a session begins abruptly, it may be difficult to involve many of the members in productive work for that session. Therefore, some kind of warm-up is essential before work on problems begins.

We've emphasized in our workshops the value of learning the skills necessary for introducing each session in an effective way. For groups that meet on a regular basis, such as once a week, we suggest some of the following procedures to open each session:

• We find it useful to have all the members briefly say what they want from the upcoming session. A quick go-around is all that is needed for the members to identify issues that they are interested in pursuing; in this way an agenda can be developed that is based on some common concerns. If several members say that they are having difficulties talking with their spouse, for example, you can then bring the group together to work on communication problems. If you do not check out what issues the members have brought to a particular session and if you stay with the first member who speaks, much important material is lost.

• Give members at least a brief opportunity to share what they have done in the way of practice outside of the group since the previous session. Some may want to talk about problems they are experiencing in transferring their learning from the group into everyday situations. This difficulty can then be the basis for work in that session.

• The participants may have unresolved feelings about the previous session, or they may have given thought to that session during the week. If members don't have a chance to mention these concerns, hidden agendas will probably develop and block effective work.

• As a leader, you may also have afterthoughts about the previous session. You can begin some sessions by letting the group know what you have been thinking during the week about how the group is progressing. This practice is especially appropriate when you see certain problems emerging or when you think the group is getting stuck. Your self-disclosure can lead the way for members to be open with their reactions to what is or is not going on in the sessions.

• In an open group (in which the membership changes somewhat from week to week), introduce any new members. Rather than putting the spotlight on the incoming member, you can ask some of the clients who have been a part of the group for a time to briefly reflect on what they have been learning about themselves in the group. You can point out that some members may be attending for only a few sessions and can also ask them how they expect to get the most from the brief time that they may have in the group. A question we sometimes ask is "If this were the only session you had, what would you most want to accomplish?"

Although we don't want to suggest that you memorize certain lines to open a session, we'd like to support some comments that convey the spirit of eliciting important material for leading into a session. Let these lines serve as catalysts that can be part of your own leadership style. At different times we've opened a session with remarks such as:

• "How is each of you feeling about being here today?"
• "Before we begin today's session, I'd like to ask each of you to take a few minutes to silently review your week and think about anything you want to tell us."
• "Are you here because you want to be?"
• "Did anyone have any afterthoughts about last week's session?"
• "As a way of beginning tonight, let's have a brief go-around. Each of you say what you'd most like to be able to say by the end of this session."
• "Could each of you briefly complete this sentence: 'Today I'd like to get actively involved by . . .' "
• "What are you willing to do to get what you say you want?"
• "What were you thinking and feeling before coming to the group?"
• "Whom are you most aware of in this room right now, and why?"

Guidelines for Closing Sessions   Just as important as how you open a session is the way in which you bring a meeting to closure. Too often a leader will simply announce that "time is up for today," with no attempt to summarize and integrate and with no encouragement for members to practice certain skills. Some time, if even only ten minutes, should be set aside to give participants an opportunity to reflect on what they liked or did not like about the session, to mention what they hope to do outside of the group during the week, and so forth. Attention to closing ensures that consolidation of learning will take place.

For groups that meet weekly, it is important to summarize what occurred in that session. At times, it is useful to stop the group halfway through the session and say: "I notice that we have about an hour left today, and I'd like to check out how each of you feels about what you've done so far today. Have you been as involved as you want to be? Are there some issues you'd like to explore before this session ends?" This does not need to be done routinely, but sometimes such an assessment during the session can help the members focus their attention on problem areas, especially if you sense that they are not doing and saying what they need to.

In closing a weekly group session, consider the following guidelines.

• It is good for clients to leave a session with some unanswered questions. We think it's a mistake to try to ensure that everyone leaves feeling comfortable. If clients leave feeling that everything is nicely closed, they will probably spend very little time during the week reflecting on matters raised in the group.

• Some statement from the members concerning their level of investment of energy is useful. If clients report feeling bored, you can ask them what they're willing to do to relieve their boredom: "Is your boredom all right, or is this something that you want to change?"

• You can ask members to tell the group briefly what they're learning about themselves through their relationships with other members. The participants can briefly indicate some ways in which they've changed their behavior in response to these insights. If participants find that they would like to change their behavior even more, they can be encouraged to develop specific plans or homework assignments to complete before the next session.

• Ask members whether there are any topics, questions, or problems they would like to explore in the next session. This request creates a link between one session and the next. Prompting the members to think about the upcoming session also indirectly encourages them to stick to their contracts during the week.

• You can ask members to give one another feedback. Especially helpful are members' positive reactions concerning what they have actually observed. For instance, if Doug's voice is a lot more secure, others may let him know that they perceive this change. Of course, feedback on what members are doing to block their strengths is also very helpful.

• If your group is one with changing membership, you need to be especially alert to reminding members a week before certain participants will be leaving the group. Not only do the terminating members need to talk about what they have learned from the group, but other members are also likely to want to share their feelings. It is essential that time be allotted for any unfinished business.

As we did for opening sessions, we present some comments for you to consider in closing a session. Of course, not all of them need to be asked at any one time.

- "What was it like for you to be in this group today?"
- "What affected you the most, and what did you learn?"
- "What would each of you be willing to do outside of the group this week to practice some of the new skills you are acquiring?"
- "I'd like a quick go-around to have everyone say a few words on how this group is progressing so far and make any suggestions for change."
- "Are you getting what you want from this group?"
- "If you are not satisfied with what is happening in this group, what do you see that you can do to change things?"
- "Before we close tonight, I'd like to share with you some of my reactions and observations of this session."

By developing skills in opening and closing sessions, you increase the possibility of continuity from meeting to meeting. Such continuity can help members transfer insights and new behaviors from the group into daily life and, along with encouragement and direction from your leadership, can facilitate the participants' ongoing assessment of their level of investment for each session.

If you work with a co-leader, the matter of how the sessions are opened and closed should be a topic for discussion. A few questions for exploration are: Who typically opens the sessions? Do the two of you agree on when and how to bring a session to closure? With five minutes left in the sessions, does one leader want to continue working, whereas the other wants to attempt some summary of the meeting? Do both of you pay attention to unfinished business that might be left toward the end of a session? Although we are not suggesting a mechanical division of time and functions when you begin and end sessions, we think it is worth noting who tends to assume this responsibility. If one leader typically opens the session, members may be likely to direct their talk to this person. In our groups, one of us may open the session while the other elaborates and makes additional remarks. In this way spontaneous give-and-take between co-leaders can replace an approach characterized by "Now it's your turn to make a remark."

INITIAL STAGE: SUMMARY

STAGE CHARACTERISTICS

The early phase of a group is a time for orientation and determining the structure of the group. At this stage:

- Participants test the atmosphere and get acquainted.
- Members learn what is expected, how the group functions, and how to participate in a group.
- Risk taking is relatively low, and exploration is tentative.
- Group cohesion and trust are gradually established if members are willing to express what they are thinking and feeling.
- Members are concerned with whether they are included or excluded, and they are beginning to define their place in the group.
- Negative reactions may surface as members test to determine if all feelings are acceptable.
- A central issue is trust versus mistrust.
- There are periods of silence and awkwardness; members may look for direction and wonder what the group is about.
- Members are deciding whom they can trust, how much they will disclose, how safe the group is, whom they like and dislike, and how much to get involved.
- Members are learning the basic attitudes of respect, empathy, acceptance, caring, and responding—all attitudes that facilitate building trust.

MEMBER FUNCTIONS AND POSSIBLE PROBLEMS

Early in the course of the group some specific member roles and tasks are critical to shaping the group:

- taking active steps to create a trusting climate
- learning to express one's feelings and thoughts, especially as they pertain to interactions in the group
- being willing to express fears, hopes, concerns, reservations, and expectations concerning the group
- being willing to make oneself known to the others in the group
- being involved in the creation of group norms
- establishing personal and specific goals that will govern group participation
- learning the basics of group process, especially how to be involved in group interactions

Some possible problems that can arise are:

- Members may wait passively for "something to happen."
- Members may keep to themselves feelings of distrust or fears pertaining to the group and thus entrench their own resistance.
- Members may keep themselves vague and unknown, making meaningful interaction difficult.
- Members may slip into a problem-solving and advice-giving stance with other members.

LEADER FUNCTIONS

The major tasks of group leaders during the orientation and exploration phase of a group are:

- teaching participants some general guidelines and ways to participate actively that will increase their chances of having a productive group
- developing ground rules and setting norms
- teaching the basics of group process
- assisting members in expressing their fears and expectations, and working toward the development of trust
- modeling the facilitative dimensions of therapeutic behavior
- being open with the members and being psychologically present for them
- clarifying the division of responsibility
- helping members establish concrete personal goals
- dealing openly with members' concerns and questions
- providing a degree of structuring that will neither increase members' dependence nor result in floundering
- assisting members to share what they are thinking and feeling about what is occurring within the group
- teaching members basic interpersonal skills such as active listening and responding
- assessing the needs of the group and leading in such a way that these needs are met

EXERCISES

1. Initial-Session Exercise.   For this exercise ten students volunteer to play group members at an initial group session, and two volunteer to play co-leaders. We suggest that the co-leaders begin by giving a brief orientation explaining the group's purpose, the role of the leader, the rights and responsibilities of the members, the ground rules, group-process procedures, and any other pertinent information they might actually give in the first session of a group. The members then express their expectations and fears, and the leaders try to deal with them. This lasts for approximately half an hour, and the class members then describe what they saw occurring in the group. The group members describe how they felt during the session and offer suggestions for the co-leaders. The co-leaders can discuss with each other the nature of their experience and how well they feel they did, either before any of the feedback or afterward.

2. Introducing-Yourself Exercise.   This exercise consists of telling the class what you would tell a group about yourself if you were the group leader. About four people volunteer, and each person is given five minutes. When this is completed, the four talk among themselves first, and then the class offers input regarding the impact made by each person.

3. Exercise for the Beginning Stage of a Group.   This exercise can be used to get group members acquainted with one another, but you can practice it in class to see how it works. The class breaks into dyads. Select a new partner every ten minutes, and each time you change partners, consider a new question or issue. The main purpose of the exercise is to get members to contact all the other members of the group and to begin to reveal themselves to others. We encourage you to add your own questions or statements to our list of issues:

- Discuss your reservations about the value of groups.
- What do you fear about groups?
- What do you most want from a group experience?
- Discuss how much trust you have in your group. Do you feel like getting involved? What are some things that contribute to your trust or mistrust?
- Decide which of the two of you is dominant. Does each of you feel satisfied with his or her position?
- Tell your partner how you imagine you would feel if you were to co-lead a group with him or her.

4. Exercise in Meeting with Your Co-Leader.   Select a person in your class with whom you might like to co-lead a group. Explore with your partner some of the following dimensions of a group during the initial stage:

- How would both of you assist the members in getting the most from this group? Would you be inclined to discuss any guidelines that would help them be active members?
- How would the two of you attempt to build trust during the initial phase of this group?
- How much structuring would each of you be inclined to do early in a group? Do both of you agree on the degree of structure that would help a group function effectively?
- Whose responsibility is it if the group flounders? What might you do if the group seemed to be lost at the first session?
- What are some specific procedures that each of you might use to help the members define what they want to get from their group?

5. Brainstorming about Ways of Creating Trust.   In small groups, explore as many ideas and ways you can think of that might facilitate the establishment of trust in your group. What factors do you think are likely to lead to trust? What would it take for *you* to feel a sense of trust in a group? What do you see as the major barriers to the development of trust?

CHAPTER 6

TRANSITION STAGE
OF A GROUP

FOCUS QUESTIONS

Introduction

Characteristics of the Transition Stage

Anxiety
Defensiveness and Resistance
The Struggle for Control
Conflict
Confrontation
Challenges to the Group Leader
The Leader's Reactions to Resistance

Problem Behaviors and Difficult Group Members

Silence and Lack of Participation
Monopolistic Behavior
Storytelling
Questioning
Giving Advice
Band-Aiding
Hostile Behavior
Dependency
Acting Superior
Socializing
Intellectualizing
Emotionalizing

**Interventions for Dealing
with Resistance Therapeutically**

**Interventions for Dealing with Resistance
by the Whole Group**

Dealing with Transference and Countertransference

How Members May View the Leader
Guidelines for Leaders

Effective Leadership: Research Findings

Support versus Confrontation
Guidelines for Creating Therapeutic Relationships
  with Members

Co-Leader Issues at the Transition Stage

Transition Stage: Summary

Stage Characteristics
Member Functions and Possible Problems
Leader Functions

Exercises

Self-Assessment Scale
Exercises and Questions for Exploration

FOCUS QUESTIONS

1. If your group consisted of members much like yourself, what do you imagine it would be like to lead it?

2. Sometimes cultural factors account for lack of verbal participation by a group member. How might you work with such a member? What other reasons can you think of for lack of participation by group members?

3. Have you been in a group with people who demand a lot of group time? What effect did they have on you? On the group?

4. What might you say or do (as a group leader) when one of the group members reminds you of a person in your life? What sources of potential countertransference might you have to deal with as a group leader?

5. What guidelines can you think of for effectively confronting others in a group? How can you challenge members in a caring way and not increase their defensiveness? What cultural dimensions will you need to consider with respect to confrontation?

6. What is the difference between giving advice and giving feedback?

7. How can you distinguish support that is helpful from support that is a form of defense?

8. How might you, as a leader, deal with a member's hostility?

9. What member behavior would you find most difficult to deal with as a leader? Why?

10. If you have been in a group before, did you experience any resistance in either yourself or others? How was it handled?

INTRODUCTION

Before groups progress to a working stage, they typically go through a transitional phase. During this phase, groups are generally characterized by anxiety, defensiveness, resistance, the struggle for control, member conflicts, challenges to or conflicts with the leader, and various patterns of problem behaviors. For a group to move to a working stage, these problems must be recognized and dealt with effectively. Some groups remain stuck at a transitional phase because resistance is bypassed or because conflict is smoothed over and left as an undercurrent that destroys open group interaction. What the members and leaders do during this transitional period often will determine whether a group will endure and whether it will be effective. At times, it seems as though the group is "stuck." Members need to be willing to say aloud some of what they are internally processing to get the group "unstuck." Because a group's ability to move forward is dependent on the ability and willingness of both members and leader to face and work with various forms of resistance, leaders must fully understand the dynamics of a group during the transition period. This chapter focuses on a discussion of typical characteristics of a group during the transition stage and intervention strategies for dealing with transitional group problems.

CHARACTERISTICS OF THE TRANSITION STAGE

ANXIETY

During the transition stage anxiety is high. The sources of this anxiety are found within individuals and within the group itself. For example, Christie's anxiety stems primarily from internal factors: "I'm really afraid to go any further for fear of what I'll find out about myself." But when Sunny says "I'm afraid to speak up in here because several people are so judgmental," her anxiety is due to external factors as well as internal ones; she is inhibited by what others in the group think of her and how they are liable to judge her.

Anxiety also relates to the fear of looking foolish, of losing control, of being misunderstood, of being rejected, and of not knowing what is expected. As participants come to more fully trust one another and the leader, they become increasingly able to share their concerns. This openness lessens the anxiety group members have about letting others see them as they are.

DEFENSIVENESS AND RESISTANCE

Group participants need to test the leader and other members before the group can move from the transition phase to the working phase. It is essential that the leader encourage openness so group members will express their hesitations and anxieties. Participants are torn between wanting to stay safe and wanting to risk getting involved. Often they are wise to show some resistance. It is foolish for a leader to think that a group will gather and effortlessly begin intensive work. Both leader and members must understand the meaning of resistance.

From a psychoanalytic perspective, resistance is defined as the individual's reluctance to bring into conscious awareness threatening material that has been previously repressed or denied. It can also be viewed as anything that prevents members from dealing with unconscious material. From a broader perspective, resistance can be viewed as behavior that keeps oneself or others from exploring personal problems or painful feelings.

Resistance needs to be respected, which means the leader does not chastise a reluctant member but explores the source of the reluctance.

Members often have realistic reasons for their reluctance or holding back. Take, for example, the woman who was typically quiet in group and who would speak only with considerable urging on the leader's part. Eventually she said that she felt embarrassed to speak because of her accent. She was convinced that she did not speak English well enough to be understood; this kept her silent. Although she wanted to bring up this subject, the thought of being the center of attention was so anxiety-provoking for her that she said as little as she could.

Members often struggle with their fears and rely on defenses they have long used when coping with uncomfortable situations. These resistive and problematic behaviors vary widely and are often quite creative. Resistive behavior is an inevitable phenomenon in groups, and unless it is recognized and explored it can block the progress of a group. It is useful to think of resistance as the very material that can be explored productively in a group. It is a normal process and should not be thought of as something that needs to be "gotten around quickly" or bypassed. A degree of defensive behavior is to be expected in a group situation, because fears are attached to change. This should not be seen as a failure in a group.

Resistive behaviors provide fruitful avenues for exploration that can reveal important clues about a member's interpersonal style outside of the group. Ormont (1988) associates resistance with a fear of intimacy. The defensive style may take various forms such as conflict, detachment, distrust, or diverting, but the underlying fear is of getting close and the vulnerability this implies. If group leaders demonstrate a willingness to explore and understand members' resistive behavior, the group is likely to progress.

Although dealing with difficult group members is sometimes painful, doing so is often the best way to establish a working relationship with members based on trust. By working through the fears associated with intimacy with others in the group, members become aware of some ways they keep others in their lives at a distance. They also move toward greater intimacy within the group. When members develop mature forms of intimacy as described by Ormont (1988):

- members make emotional connections with each other;
- talk is simple and direct;
- hidden agendas are not present in the group;
- members openly take risks with one another;
- feelings are acknowledged and expressed; and
- members are able to experience the present moment as the lingering remnants of their past hurts have been worked through successfully.

The best way for leaders to therapeutically deal with resistance is to simply describe to members what they are observing and let members know how they are affected by what they see and hear. This approach is an invitation for members to determine if what they are doing is working for them. If leaders do not respect the members' resistances, they are really not respecting the members themselves. For example, Betty reveals some painful material and then suddenly stops and says that she doesn't want to go on. In "going with" the resistance, the leader asks her what is stopping her. Betty indicates that she is afraid of losing people's respect. The issue now becomes her lack of trust in the group rather than a painful personal problem. If the leader proceeds in this manner, Betty is more likely to eventually talk openly about personal matters. If the leader ignores her initial resistance by pushing her to open up, she will probably become increasingly defensive and resistant.

Not every instance of a member's unwillingness to participate fully can be accurately labeled "resistance." Sometimes members' unwillingness to cooperate is the result of factors such as an unqualified leader, an aggressive and uncaring leadership style, or a failure to prepare members to participate in the group. One of the key tasks of leadership is for you to accurately appraise whether the source of resistance is members' fears or ineffective leadership. Simply labeling a member "resistant" is to entrench this resistance even more deeply. If you show a willingness to understand the context of members' resistive behavior, the likelihood of cooperation and risk taking is increased.

If group members keep their fears inside, all sorts of avoidances are bound to occur. Although you cannot pry open members and force them to discuss the fears that could inhibit their participation, you can sensitively invite them to recognize that they may be suffering from fears they share with others. Brief descriptions of common fears that manifest themselves during the transition stage are presented next, along with possible interventions you might make to help members.

The Fear of Making a Fool of Oneself   People often worry about looking foolish if they step out of roles that are familiar to them. Mike disclosed that he had held back from saying much because he did not want to take the chance of being seen as a fool. Therefore, he decided to enter in only when he was extremely sure of himself. At other times he found it safer to take the course of censoring and endlessly rehearsing his "performances." The leader asked Mike: "Next time you become aware of sitting here quietly rehearsing, would you be willing to do so out loud?" The leader was operating on the assumption that Mike's internal critic was far harsher on him than others in the room would be. As Mike rehearsed out loud, others had a better appreciation of the nature of his struggle.

The Fear of Rejection   We often hear participants say that they are reluctant to get involved with others in the group because of their fear of being rejected. Stephen repeatedly came back to his fears that people would not want anything to do with him. He frequently said that he had erected walls to protect himself from the pain of rejection, and he made the assumption that nobody in the group would like what they might discover about him. The leader asked: "Are you willing to look around the room and see if indeed you feel that every person in here would surely reject you?" Stephen took some time to look around the room and discovered that out of ten, he was convinced that four of them would reject him, and he was not sure of two of them. If Stephen agreed to continue working, he could be asked to "own" his projections by addressing those whom he had decided might reject him. He could do this by completing the sentence "I'm afraid that you will reject me by . . ." He could also talk to the people whom he saw as more accepting by letting them know what it was about him that they would accept. After Stephen did his work, others could react to him in a sensitive way. Some in the group might say that they were afraid of him and that they found it difficult to penetrate his walls. Through this exploration, Stephen could learn about his part in creating a sense of rejection.

The Fear of Emptiness   Members sometimes fear that if they do get involved and explore issues that they've kept tucked away, they'll discover that they are merely hollow and empty, that there is nothing in them that anyone could like or value. Janice expressed this fear, yet she continued in spite of her fears. She realized that even if she did find that she was empty, she could begin a process of creating a different kind of existence for herself. She chose not to let her fear prevent her from looking at her life.

The Fear of Losing Control   Debbie expressed her fear that she might open up some potentially painful areas and then be left without closure. She was anxious about "opening up Pandora's box," as she put it. She wondered: "Will I be able to stand the pain? Maybe it would be best if things were just left alone. If I started crying, I might never stop! Even though I might get support in the group, what will I do when I'm on my own if I'm stuck with this pain?" The leader responded: "I'm sure you've been alone and have found it painful. What do you normally do when this happens?" Debbie replied that "I lock myself in the room, I don't talk to anyone, and I just cry by myself and then get depressed." The leader asked her to pick two or three people in the room whom she thought would be most able to understand her pain and tell them about some of the distress in her life. As she did this, she would be likely to discover the difference between isolating herself with her pain and sharing it with others and experiencing their support. She could also come to the realization that she was not condemned to dealing with her pain in isolation, unless she chose to do so. She could be challenged to identify a few people in the group and in her outside life whom she could reach out to in time of need.

The Fear of Self-Disclosure   Members often fear self-disclosure, thinking that they will be pressured to open up too far as part of the "admission dues" for being in the group. It often helps to reinforce emphatically to members that they can make themselves known to others and at the same time retain their privacy. Consider this example: "I can't imagine myself talking about my parents in the negative ways that others are doing in here," Charlene said. "If I were to talk this way about my parents, I would be overcome with shame and disloyalty." Because the leader was aware of certain cultural values that Charlene held, he let her know that he respected her deep-seated injunctions. He did not push her to do something that she would later regret. But he did encourage her to think of ways in which she could participate in the group that would be meaningful to her. There is a delicate balance between reluctance because of cultural injunctions and resistance over moving into frightening territory. As we explained in Chapter 5, it is the choice of members to determine what and how much they share. When they recognize that they are responsible for what they tell others about themselves, participants tend to be less fearful of self-disclosure.

Some Other Fears   A variety of other fears are often expressed by members:

- "I'm afraid if I show others who I most deeply am, people won't like me."
- "I'm concerned about seeing these people out of group and what they will think of me."
- "The leaders and members intimidate me, making me want to retreat."
- "If I tell people about some of the things that I've done in the past, I worry about their judging me."
- "I'm afraid I'll get too dependent on the group and rely on others to solve my problems for me."
- "I'm afraid that if I let my anger out, I'll lose control and hurt somebody."
- "I'm uncomfortable with physical contact, and I'm afraid I'll be expected to touch and be touched even though I don't want to."
- "I'm worried that I'll take too much group time by talking about my problems, that I'll bore people, and that they'll just tune me out."
- "I'm afraid I'll get close to people in here and then I'll never see them again once the group ends."

Though it is not realistic to expect that all these fears can be eliminated, we do think that members can be encouraged to face their fears. Through what you model as a leader, you can help create a trusting climate in which members will feel free enough to test their fears and put the unrealistic ones to rest. If members decide to be open about the fears that are keeping them from talking about themselves and if this decision can be made relatively early in a group, a good foundation of trust is created that will enable them to deal constructively with other personal issues as the group evolves.

THE STRUGGLE FOR CONTROL

Struggles over control are common at the transition stage. Some characteristic group behaviors include competition, rivalry, jockeying for position, jealousies, challenges to the leadership (or lack of it), and discussions about the division of responsibility and decision-making procedures. Participants' main anxieties relate to having too much or too little responsibility. To deal constructively with these control issues, members must bring them to the surface and talk about them. If the here-and-now problems are ignored, the group will be inhibited by a hidden agenda. Below are some comments we have heard members make that illustrate control issues:

- "I don't want to talk just because you want me to talk. I learn just as much by listening and observing."
- "There are several people in here who always get the attention. No matter what I do, I just don't seem to get recognized, especially by the leaders."
- "You leaders should pay more attention to Paul. He's been crying several times, and you haven't been taking care of him."
- "How come when I cried you didn't hold me the way you're holding Harold right now."
- "No matter what I say, you leaders never seem to think I'm doing it right. Why can't I just do it my way?"

In response to any one of these members' statements, it is imperative that the leader not assume a defensive stance. The leader's task is to help members understand that their struggle for control may be a form of resistance. Assume that Brenda says: "No matter what I say, you leaders never seem to think I'm doing it right. Why can't I just do it my way?" The leader might respond with: "I'm not looking at what you're doing in terms of right or wrong. I'm more concerned that what you do in here will help you achieve the goals you set for yourself. I've noticed that you sometimes avoid talking about difficult areas in your life." Another intervention would be to ask Brenda, "What would your way be of using time in this group?" Or the leader could say, "Tell me more about what is helpful to you in this group and what is not helpful."

CONFLICT

Conflict often carries a negative connotation. People sometimes assume that it is a sign of something intrinsically wrong and should be avoided at all costs. When there are conflicts within a group, both the leader and the members often want to avoid them rather than spending the time necessary to work through them. However, because conflict is inevitable in all relationships, including groups, it is the avoidance of conflict that makes it destructive. Unexplored conflict is typically expressed in defensive behavior, hostility, indirectness, and a general lack of trust. In the transition stage it is crucial that conflict be managed effectively so that the level of trust will increase. Thus, a primary task of leaders is to teach members the value of working through conflicts in a constructive way.

Diane expressed a conflict within one group: "There are some people in here who never say anything." Jeff immediately replied, defensively, "Not everybody has to be as talkative as you." Sylvia joined in, sarcastically, "Well, Diane, you talk so much you don't give me a *chance* to participate!" Bert's contribution was: "I wish you would be nicer to one another and stop this arguing. This isn't getting us anywhere."

Unproductive interventions by the leader would have been: "I agree with you, Bert, and I wish people would knock it off!" Or "Diane, you're right. There are too many people in here who blend into the woodwork. I wish everyone would take as many risks as you do!" Such remarks increase the members' defensiveness and entrench resistance.

The emerging conflict was dealt with constructively when the leader took the approach of exploring the underlying dynamics of what had been said and what was *not* being said: "I agree with you, Bert, that right now we're not getting anywhere. But I don't want people to stop talking, because we need to get to the bottom of what all this means." Turning to Diane, the leader asked her: "How are you affected by all these reactions? Whom in particular do you want to hear from? What does it do to you when people don't say anything? What do you imagine that these people may be saying about you to themselves?"

Diane's original statement was a defensive and chastising remark to the group in general. The group reacted with appropriate defensiveness. The leader was refocusing on Diane's difficulty with the group and trying to get her to be more specific about how she was affected by people whom she saw as being silent. The conflict found resolution when she let people know that she was afraid that they were judging her when they said very little and that she was interested in how they perceived her. The chances are that this conflict would not have come about if Diane had made such statements to begin with. For example, she might have said to Sylvia: "I notice that you're quiet, and I often wonder what you think of me. I don't like it when you don't say much, because I'm really interested in what you have to say." Such a statement would have reflected more accurately what was going on inside Diane than did her punitive remark. It is important for the leader not to cut off the expression of conflict but to facilitate more direct expression of feeling and thinking among the members.

Cohesion within a group typically increases after conflict and anger are recognized and expressed, for venting such feelings is one way of testing the freedom and trustworthiness of the group. The participants soon discover whether this group is a safe place in which to disagree openly and whether they will be accepted in spite of the intensity of their feelings. When conflict is constructively dealt with, the participants learn that their relationships are strong enough to withstand an honest level of challenge.

CONFRONTATION

Our view of a therapeutic group includes both support and challenge. In Chapter 5 we noted that people sometimes see confrontation as a negative act with destructive potential. Because of this, they sometimes avoid confrontation at all costs. In contrast, we think that people cease being effective catalysts to others' growth if all they offer is support and rarely challenge one another. If people want to take a deeper and more honest look at themselves, it is necessary that they be willing to risk expressing what is on their minds, even though doing so may be difficult both to say and to hear. If confrontations are presented in a caring and respectful manner, these interventions often promote change.

We think leaders have a responsibility to teach members what confrontation is and what it is not and how to challenge others in constructive ways. Confrontation is *not* (1) tearing others down carelessly, (2) hitting others with negative feedback and then retreating, (3) committing an act of hostility aimed at hurting others, (4) telling others what is basically wrong with them, or (5) assaulting others' integrity. Ideally, we see confrontation as a form of corrective feedback—an invitation for participants to look at some aspect of their interpersonal style or their lives to determine if they want to make changes. Caring confrontation is designed to help members make an honest assessment of themselves or to speak more about their own reactions rather than talking about others.

In working with culturally diverse clients in groups, even caring confrontations need to be timed well and delivered in such a way that members are more likely to hear the feedback. For example, being indirect may be a cultural value for some group members. If confronted too quickly on their indirectness, or expected to change, these group members may perceive such confrontations as signs of rudeness. They may even feel a sense of embarrassment, which could result in their deciding not to return to the group. Respect for a diversity of values and behaviors is crucial; in making confrontations, timing and sensitivity to members' cultural backgrounds are key factors in determining whether confrontations will be effective.

Our approach to group practice entrails providing members with guidelines for appropriate and responsible confrontation:

- Members or leaders should know why they are confronting.
- Confrontations should not be dogmatic statements concerning who or what a person is.
- The person being confronted is likely to be less defensive if told what effect he or she has on others rather than simply being branded with a label or judgment.

- Confrontations are more effective if, instead of being global generalizations about a person, they focus on specific, observable behaviors.
- One of the purposes of confrontation is to develop a closer and more genuine relationship with others.
- Sensitivity is an important element of effective confrontation; it is useful for the person doing the confronting to imagine being the recipient of what is said.
- Confrontation should give others the opportunity to reflect on the feedback they receive before they are expected to respond or to act on this feedback.
- Those confronting would be wise to ask themselves if they are willing to do what they are asking others to do.

The quality of the confrontations that occur in a group is an index of how effective the group is. The more cohesive a group is, the more challenging and daring the members and leaders can be. Groups that disintegrate under challenge are based on a false sense of cohesion.

To make the issue of confrontation more concrete, we present the following examples. The first statement in each set illustrates an ineffective confrontation; this is followed by an effective confrontation statement.

- "You're always so judgmental, and you make me feel inadequate." This could be changed to: "I feel uncomfortable with you because I'm afraid of what you think of me. Your opinion is important to me. I don't like it that I often feel inadequate when I'm with you."
- "You're a phony! You're always smiling, and that's not real." An effective confrontation is: "I find it difficult to trust you, because often when you say you're angry, you're smiling. That makes it hard for me to get close to you."
- "You aren't getting anything from this group. All you ever do is sit and observe. We're just interesting cases for you." An effective challenge would be: "I'd like to get to know you. I'm interested in what you think and feel, and sometimes I worry that you see me as an interesting case. I'd like to change the way I feel around you."
- "If I were your husband, I'd leave you. You're full of venom, and you'll poison any relationship." A more effective statement is: "I find it hard to be open with you. Many of the things you say really hurt me, and I want to strike back. It would be difficult for me to be involved in an intimate relationship with you."
- "You do nothing but play games." A more concrete and effective statement is: "When you cry, I'm bothered, because it's not easy for me to feel compassionate. I'd like to talk to you more about this."

In each of the ineffective statements, the people being confronted are being told how they are, and in some way they are being discounted. In the effective statements the members doing the confronting are revealing their perceptions and feelings about the other members and how they are being affected by them.

CHALLENGES TO THE GROUP LEADER

Although leaders may be challenged throughout a group, they are more often confronted both personally and professionally during the transition stage. For example, several members may complain about not getting the "right" type of leadership, thereby challenging the leader's competence. It is a mistake for leaders to assume that every confrontation is an attack on their integrity. Instead, they need to nondefensively examine what is being said so they can differentiate between a *challenge* and an *attack*. How they respond to members' confrontations has a bearing on how trustingly the participants will approach them in the future.

If Art says to the leader "I'm bored in here, and I wish you'd do more to make this a better group," a nontherapeutic reply is "Do you think you could do it better yourself?" By contrast, therapeutic replies might include: "Tell me more about what you'd like from me or what you'd like me to do differently." "Say more about what's missing for you in this group." "What could you continue to do to make this a more meaningful group for you?" (By saying what he does, Art has already taken the first step in changing the situation for himself.) It is not necessary that the leader quickly comply with Art's demand to conduct the group differently. What is essential is that she listen nondefensively and promote a full expression of his dissatisfaction. The leader is not willing to assume total responsibility for his boredom. She explores with him their mutual responsibility to make this a meaningful and productive group, and she invites others to express their reactions to what she has said.

Though challenges may never be comfortable to the leader, it is important to recognize that these confrontations are often the members' significant first steps toward testing the leader and thus becoming less dependent on the leader's approval. The way the group leader responds to challenges such as Art's has a powerful effect on the members' willingness to continue to take risks and to trust. Leaders can be good role models if they respond openly and avoid becoming defensive.

THE LEADER'S REACTIONS TO RESISTANCE

As we have stressed, a central characteristic of the transition stage is resistance, which manifests itself in many forms of members' behavior. It is essential that you not only learn to recognize and deal with the members' resistance but also become aware of your own reactions to resistance. A mistake that we commonly observe when we supervise group leaders is their tendency to focus on "problem members" or difficult situations rather than on their own dynamics and how they are affected personally when they encounter a "resistant group." Typically, leaders have a range of feelings: being threatened by what they perceive as a challenge to their leadership role; anger over the members' lack of cooperation and enthusiasm; feelings of inadequacy to the point of wondering if they are qualified to lead groups; resentment toward several of the members, whom they label as some type of problem; and anxiety over the slow pace of the group, with a desire to stir things up so there is some action.

One of the most powerful ways to intervene when you are experiencing strong feelings over what you perceive to be resistance is to deal with your own feelings and possible defensive reactions to the situation. If you ignore your reactions, you are leaving yourself out of the interactions that occur in the group. Furthermore, by giving the members your reactions, you are modeling a direct style of dealing with conflict and resistance, rather than bypassing it. Your own thoughts, feelings, and observations can be the most powerful resource you have in dealing with defensive behavior. When you share what you are feeling and thinking about what is going on in the group—in such a way as not to blame and criticize the members for deficiencies—you are letting the members experience an honest and constructive interaction with you.

We hope that you will keep these thoughts in mind as you read the next section, which deals with problem behaviors and difficult group members. Although it is understandable that you will want to learn how to handle problem members and the disruption of the group that they can cause, the emphasis should be on actual *behaviors* rather than labels. It is helpful to consider problem behaviors as manifestations of resistance that most participants display at one time or another during the history of a group.

PROBLEM BEHAVIORS AND DIFFICULT GROUP MEMBERS

Sometimes members become problematic because of problematic behaviors on the part of group leaders. But even in groups with the most effective group leader interventions, certain members display problematic behaviors that are a source of difficulty to themselves, other members, and the leader. In working with difficult group members, leaders should be mindful of how their interventions can either decrease or escalate these problematic behaviors. Some common denominators characterize appropriate group leader interventions when dealing with difficult behaviors of group members (see Corey & Corey, 1993b). Effective group leaders:

- do not dismiss clients but demonstrate acceptance of the person of the client;
- express their annoyance and anger at a member without denigrating the character of the person;
- avoid responding to a sarcastic remark with sarcasm;
- educate the members about how the group works;

- are honest with members, rather than mystifying the process;
- encourage members to explore any form of resistance, rather than demanding they give up their resistance;
- avoid labeling and judging any member, and instead describe the behavior of the member;
- state observations and hunches in a tentative way, as opposed to being dogmatic;
- demonstrate sensitivity to a member's culture and avoid stereotyping the individual;
- let members who are difficult know how they are affecting them in a nonblaming way;
- avoid using their role and power to intimidate members;
- monitor their own countertransference reactions;
- challenge members in a caring and respectful way to do things that may be painful and difficult;
- confront in a caring manner;
- avoid retreating when conflict arises;
- provide a balance between support and challenge;
- do not take member reactions in an overly personal way, nor do they have a fragile ego;
- facilitate a more focused exploration of the problem, rather than giving simple solutions;
- do not meet their own needs at the expense of the clients;
- invite group members to state how they are personally affected by problematic behaviors of other members while blocking judgments, evaluations, and criticisms.

In working with difficult group members, Kottler (1994b) suggests that it is important for us to confront our own issues. We might ask questions such as: "What am I feeling as I'm working with this client? What is the source of my feelings? What am I doing to create or exacerbate the problems? Does the client remind me of anyone I know? What expectations do I have of this client?" He suggests that problematic behaviors are as much a matter of the leader's perception as of the actual behavior. Further, Kottler (1992) cautions therapists against calling clients names in the form of roles they exhibit (monopolizer, help-rejecter) or formal diagnostic labels (narcissistic, borderline personality disorder). When we reduce clients to labels we begin to think about them as enemies to be defeated rather than as people who are in pain and doing the best they know how to cope.

We agree with Kottler's contention that it is more helpful to put difficult behavior patterns into a context. We present member behaviors that are counterproductive to group functioning in the context of trying to understand the meaning these behaviors have for the individual member. People in a group are likely doing the best they know how, even if they become aware that what they are doing is not working well for them. It is useful for us to remind ourselves that the very reason people seek a group is to assist them in finding more effective ways of expressing themselves and dealing with others. For a further discussion of how group leaders can explore and understand members' problematic behavior, see Corey and Corey (1993b).

SILENCE AND LACK OF PARTICIPATION

Silence and withdrawal are two forms of behavior that most group leaders must eventually learn to deal with. Even though the silent and withdrawn member does not interfere verbally with group functioning, this behavior may constitute a problem for both the member and the group. The danger is that quiet or withdrawn members will go unnoticed and that their pattern of silence may indicate a problem.

Some silent group members may argue that their lack of verbal participation is not an index of their involvement. They may maintain that they are learning by listening and by identifying with others' problems. These members may say that "I don't feel like talking just to hear myself talk" or that when they have something important to contribute, they'll do so. Group leaders should encourage these members to discuss their silence in the group. There are many reasons for nonparticipating behavior, and these should be explored. Some of the reasons are:

- politeness and waiting to be called on by the leader
- the feeling that one doesn't have anything worthwhile to say
- the feeling that one shouldn't talk about oneself or that one should be seen and not heard
- the fear of looking foolish; not knowing the appropriate thing to say or do
- a fear of certain members in the group or of the authority of the group leader
- resistance, particularly if the person doesn't really want to be a member of the group
- uncertainty about how the group process works
- fear of being rejected or of being accepted
- lack of trust in the group; fear of leaks of confidentiality

It is important that members not be attacked for their silence but instead be invited to participate. Also, group leaders must be careful to avoid consistently calling on a silent person, for in this way the member is relieved of the responsibility of initiating interaction. A "game" can be made of drawing out the person, and this can lead to resentment on the part of both the rest of the group and the silent member and frustration on the part of the leader who perpetuates this behavior.

Silent members can be invited to explore what their silence means. For example, are they this way outside of the group as well? How does it feel for them to be in this group? Do they want to do anything about becoming verbally active participants? The rest of the group can participate in this discussion, for group members generally do have reactions to nonparticipating members. They may feel cheated that they know so little of that person, or they may resent that the person is observing them as they risk and reveal themselves. If there are several silent members in a group, the verbally active members may become less revealing because they don't trust those who aren't revealing also.

Silent members can be taught that others will not know of their involvement unless they express it in words. Furthermore, such members should know that others in the group are more likely to project onto them if they remain silent. The leader may ask such members to make a contract to speak at every session, sharing with the group at some point how they responded to the session that day. Another way for the leader to handle this behavior is to ask the relatively silent members at the end of a session whether they got from the session what they had wanted. If they indicate that there were some things they wanted to talk about but that time ran out before they got a chance, they can make a contract to be the first on the agenda at the next group meeting.

MONOPOLISTIC BEHAVIOR

At the other end of the participation continuum is the person who exhibits a high degree of self-centeredness by monopolizing the activities of the group. This member is continually "identifying with others"—that is, taking others' statements as openings for detailed stories about his or her own life. Because of a great need to talk, this person prevents others from getting their share of group time. People sometimes operate under the assumption that a good group member is one who talks a lot. Leaders need to help such members explore the possible dynamics of their behavior. They may be talking excessively out of anxiety, they may be accustomed to being ignored, or they may be attempting to keep control of the group.

During the beginning stage of a group, members as well as some leaders may be relieved that someone else is going first, and no one will intervene to stop the person from taking center stage. However, as time goes on, both leaders and members will tire of this behavior and will become increasingly frustrated. As meetings continue, the group generally becomes less tolerant of the person who monopolizes, and unless these feelings of annoyance are dealt with early, they may be bottled up and then released in an explosive way.

For both ethical and practical reasons it is essential that the monopolizing person be gently challenged to look at the effects of such behavior on the group. Ethical practice dictates that group leaders acquire intervention skills necessary to block rambling. The relevant ASGW (1989) guideline is: "Group counselors ensure equitable use of group time for each member by inviting silent members to become involved, acknowledging nonverbal attempts to communicate, and discouraging rambling and monopolizing of time by members" (8. c). It is desirable that the leader intervene before the members react out of frustration and make a hostile remark such as "Shut up!" Some possible leader interventions are:

- "Tanya, you talk often. I notice that you typically identify with most problems that are raised. You tell stories, and I get lost in the details. I'm confused about what you want to say. In one sentence, what do you most want me to hear?"
- "Tanya, you seem to have a lot to say. I wonder if you're willing to go around the room to different members and finish the following sentence: 'What I most want you to hear about me is . . .' "
- Other possible incomplete sentences that could lead to fruitful exploration are:
  "If I didn't talk . . ."
  "If I let others talk . . ."
  "I have a lot to say because . . ."
  "When people don't listen to me I feel . . ."
  "I want you to listen to me because . . ."

Tanya can be asked to make the rounds by addressing each person in the group through the process of completing any one of these sentences. It is important for her not to elaborate or explain but to say the first thing that comes to her mind. It is best to instruct members not to respond during the time that she is going around. Through such exercises we usually discover crucial information that helps everyone get a better sense of the function served by the monopolizing behavior.

Assume that another member, Vance, confronts Tanya in a hostile manner before the leader has said anything about her behavior. Vance asks Tanya: "Why don't you shut up for a change? Do you think you're the only one who has a right to speak in here?" An appropriate leader intervention could be: "Vance, I'd like you to say more to Tanya. Tell her how her talking gets in your way of understanding her. What all had you been feeling and thinking before it ended in your feeling this frustrated?"

We can dismiss Tanya's behavior as simply a nuisance, or we can see it as a defense and encourage her to explore the price she is paying for her defenses. Consider that she initially appeared to be a motivated member. She seemed to reveal personal aspects of herself, she readily made suggestions to others, she could identify with most who spoke, she became an "assistant therapist" by questioning and interpreting, she told detailed stories of her past, and most of her behavior was an expression of the message "Please notice me and like me." In her own mind she felt that she was doing what was expected of her and viewed herself as an eager participant. One of the issues that she had initially said she wanted to look at was her difficulty in getting close to people. She acknowledged that she had few friends and that people were typically annoyed with her, which she found perplexing. By confronting Tanya in an honest and sensitive manner, the leader can help her learn what she is doing that prevents her from getting what she says she wants in her relations with people. She may discover that during her childhood she was often ignored and not listened to. She had to fight to be heard by her family then, and she is still behaving in somewhat the same way. She may have decided that if she didn't talk a lot, she would be ignored. The fact is that her familiar behavior is not getting her what she wants, either inside or outside the group. The group experience offers her the possibility of behaving in other ways that can satisfy her wants.

You can approach difficult members like Tanya with a sense of interest and ask questions such as: "How is it that Tanya is working so hard at getting me to pay attention to her, yet I feel that I want to ignore her? How is it that she can get a whole group of people to be angry with her? How is she replicating, in this group, behavior that is problematic on the outside?" You cannot afford to stop at the tendency to remain annoyed with people like Tanya. Instead, you can explore the context of how this behavior makes sense in her life.

STORYTELLING

Self-disclosure is frequently misunderstood by some group members to mean a lengthy recitation about their life, past and present. If they are confronted about continually relating their detailed history, they sometimes express resentment, maintaining that they are risking disclosing themselves. In teaching group process, leaders need to differentiate between pseudodisclosure, which is merely talking about oneself or about others and life situations, and disclosure of what a person is thinking and feeling now. During the beginning stages of a group the leader may allow some storytelling, for people who are new to groups frequently need to hear facts about others or to share some of their own past. However, if storytelling behavior becomes a familiar style (either for the whole group or for one member), the leader should recognize this problem and deal with it. The following examples illustrate how storytelling can be handled.

Richard would, almost predictably, bring the group up to date each week on developments in his marriage. He focused on details of his wife's behavior during the week, but he rarely described his own feelings or behavior. Since Richard was the spouse who was in the group, the leader pointed out, it was him the group was interested in. As Richard and the group looked more at this behavior, it became obvious to him that this was his way of avoiding talking about himself. He thus made a contract to talk about his reactions and not to talk about his wife in the group each week.

Sandra typically told every detail of her earlier experiences, but even though the group knew a lot about the events in her past, they knew very little about how she felt about what she had experienced. Like Richard, she felt that she was open in sharing her private life with the group; and, like Richard's group, her group wanted to know more about how she responded to her life situations. The group leader told her that he was "losing Sandra" in all of the details. He let her know that he was indeed interested in knowing her but that the information she was offering was not helping him do so.

Storytelling can be any form of talking about out-of-group life that leaves the person telling the story unknown. Feedback from the group given directly, without judgment, can assist the person to speak in personal terms and keep the focus on feelings, thoughts, and reactions.

QUESTIONING

Another counterproductive form of behavior in the group is interrogation. Some members develop a style of relating that involves questioning others, and they intervene at inappropriate times, asking why a person feels a certain way. People who habitually ask questions should be helped to see that this behavior may be a way of hiding, of remaining safe and unknown in a group. And they should be taught that the people to whom the questions are addressed typically lose the intensity of any emotion they may have been experiencing; questions tend to direct people toward thinking and away from feeling.

If members can be made to understand that questions not only intrude on others but also keep the questioner's feelings about others disguised, there is a good chance that they will change. Practice for behavior change might consist of trying to make only direct statements. For example, Marie could be invited to say what had prompted her to ask a question. If she had asked another member why he was so quiet, the leader could encourage her to say what had been going on in her mind before she asked the question. She may tell the leader "I noticed that Jim hardly says anything in here, and I'm interested in him and would like to get to know him." In such a statement Marie discloses her investment in her question without putting Jim on the spot. Questions often arouse defensiveness, whereas personal statements are less likely to do so.

Because questions do not tell the entire story, we typically ask members who raise them to fill in the details. We might say: "What prompted you to ask . . .?" "How come you want to know?" "What are you aware of right now that makes you want to ask that question?" Or "Tell [the person] what led up to your question." Following are some examples of questions and the possible hidden messages they contain:

- "How old are you?" ("I'm much older than you, and I wonder if I'll be able to identify with you.")

- "Why did you make Shirley cry?" ("I don't trust you, and I would never open myself up to you the way she did.")
- "Why do you push people so hard?" ("I'm scared, and I don't know how far I want to go.")
- "Why are you laughing?" ("I'm irritated at you, and I don't think you take seriously what goes on in this group.")
- "What do you think of me?" ("I like and respect you, and your view of me matters.")
- "Why don't you leave your husband?" ("I care about you and the way you struggle, and I worry over how long you can keep going.")
- "Why do people in here always criticize their parents?" ("I'm a parent, and I wonder if my kids are that angry at me.")

GIVING ADVICE

A problem behavior that is related to questioning is giving advice. It is one thing to offer a perception or opinion to other members and quite another to tell people what they should feel or what they should or shouldn't do. The advice giving may be subtle: "You shouldn't feel guilty that your parents divorced, because that was their decision and not something you made them do." Although this is true, the point is that the young woman does feel guilty and believes that if it had not been for her, her parents might still be married. It does not serve the best interest of the woman to advise her not to feel guilty. She has to resolve this feeling for herself. The man who had a need to tell her that she shouldn't feel guilty could profit from examining his own motives for wanting to remove the guilt. What does this mean about him? At this point the focus might be shifted to the advice giver, and the meaning of his giving such advice might be explored.

Advice giving can be less subtle. Pam has been considering not only leaving her husband but also leaving her two teenage daughters with him. She is confused, and though she thinks she wants to live alone, she feels somewhat guilty. Robin intervenes: "Pam, you owe it to yourself to do what you want to do. Why should you be stuck with your kids? Why not let him take them? If I were you, I'd leave both my kids and my husband, get an apartment, and take that job as an investment counselor." This type of behavior raises a lot of questions about Robin. What are her values and possible unresolved problems? Why does she feel a need to straighten Pam out? Wouldn't it be better for Robin to talk about herself instead of trying to be helpful by deciding what is best for Pam? The group might now focus on Robin's need to provide others with a pat solution. Robin might learn about what she is getting from giving others advice.

Advice giving has the tendency to interrupt the expression of thoughts and feelings and to increase dependency. If Pam were given enough time to explore her conflict more fully, she would be better able to make her own decision. In essence, an abundance of advice tells her that she is not capable of finding her own way, and it conditions her to become more dependent on others for direction. In our opinion, this is not a positive outcome of a therapeutic group. Even if the advice given is helpful and sound, in the long run it does not teach Pam the process of finding her own solutions to new problems as they occur.

A related behavior is displayed by members who want to assist the leader. They ask questions, probe for information, freely give advice, and focus more on others in the group than on themselves. This issue must be dealt with, because it will create resentment among the other members as well as the leader. Recognizing this behavior as a possible defense, or form of resistance, the leader can sensitively block it by pointing out to such members that they are depriving themselves of maximum benefit from the group by paying more attention to others than to themselves.

BAND-AIDING

Related to the advice-giving style is the style of trying to soothe wounds, lessen pain, and keep people cheerful. This behavior is sometimes manifested by a person who complains of how negative the group is and who wants to focus more on the positive side. Here are two examples of "Band-Aiding":

> Jack was finally able to feel his sadness over the distance between his sons and himself, and he sobbed in the group as he talked about how much he wanted to be a better father. Before Jack could have a cathartic cry, Randy put his hands on Jack's shoulders and tried to reassure him that he wasn't such a bad father, because at least he lived with his kids. Randy might have wanted to make Jack feel better so that he himself would feel more comfortable.

> Jan revealed her memories of the loneliness, rejection, and fright she had felt when she had an abortion as an adolescent. She was reliving the emotions she had felt earlier. Louise moved across the room, held Jan, and tried her best to take Jan's lonely feelings away. What had Jan provoked in Louise? Why did Louise need to protect her from the intensity of her pain? Far too often, people fail to see the therapeutic value in the release of pain.

There is a real difference between behavior that is Band-Aiding and behavior that is genuine expression of care, concern, and empathy. When there is real caring, the interests of the people who are experiencing the pain are given paramount importance. Sometimes it is best to allow them to experience the depths of their pain; ultimately, they may be better off for having done so. They can be supported after they've had the chance to intensely experience their pain. Band-Aiding is pseudosupport, designed primarily to aid the one who is supporting. Finding it too difficult to witness another's pain, the supportive one attempts to distract the other. Like questioning and giving advice, Band-Aiding needs to be examined at some point for its meaning to the person who performs it.

We want to emphasize that we are not opposed to members' touching others who are experiencing pain. It is the motivation behind the touch that is crucial. Does the person want to communicate "I can't tolerate seeing you in pain, and I want you to stop"? Or is the person saying "I know how hard this is for you, and I want you to know that you don't have to cry alone"? It is surprising to us how often people who are in pain accurately pick up the message of the touch. An important lesson for those who are uncomfortable witnessing or experiencing pain is that the release of pain is often the first necessary step toward healing.

HOSTILE BEHAVIOR

Hostility is difficult to deal with in a group, because the person who is expressing it often works indirectly. Hostility can take the form of caustic remarks, jokes, sarcasm, and other "hit-and-run" tactics. Members can express it by missing group sessions, by coming late, by acting obviously bored and detached, by leaving the group, by being overly polite, and the like. Extremely hostile people are not generally good candidates for a group, because they are so defensive that they will not acknowledge their fears. In addition, extreme hostility can have a devastating effect on the group climate. People are not going to make themselves vulnerable if there is a good chance that they will be ridiculed or in some other way devalued.

One way to deal with the person who behaves in a hostile way is to request that he or she listen without responding while the group members tell how they are being affected by that individual. It is important that the members not be allowed to dump their own feelings of hostility, however. Instead, they can describe how they feel in the group with the hostile person and what they would like the person to do differently. Then it should be ascertained what the hostile individual wants from the group. Hostile behavior may be a manifestation of fear of getting intimate or of a limited capacity for vulnerability. If the fears underneath the hostility can be brought to the surface and dealt with, the hostility may decrease.

One notable manifestation of hostility is passive/aggressive behavior. This behavior characteristically involves the element of surprise: the person confronts and then quickly retreats. The confrontation has a sharp and cutting quality, and the person attacking withdraws, leaving the attacked person stunned.

For example, Karl, who has a good relationship in the group with Karen, suddenly calls her a "castrating female." Before she has a chance to express her surprise, hurt, and anger, he tells her that he sees his wife in her, and it isn't really her he is upset with. Karl has attempted to take back what he said, yet Karen is still stuck with her hurt feelings. On an intellectual level she may understand that he is transferring his reactions to her, but on an emotional level she is hurt and has become distrustful of him. Even though it makes sense on an intellectual level, she needs some time to recover emotionally. Eventually, Karl acknowledges that he indeed had some negative feelings toward her personally, not just as his symbolic wife. He quickly wanted to retreat when he saw that she had responded strongly.

DEPENDENCY

Group members who are excessively dependent typically look either to the group leader or to the other members to direct them and take care of them. Dependency is manifested in a variety of behaviors in the group, such as exclaiming that one couldn't live without one's wife (or husband, or parents, or children), presenting oneself as stupid so that others will provide one with answers, and playing helpless.

Consider Donald, 25 years old and living with his mother. He has been complaining that his mother constantly harasses him, treating him like a child, reminding him to take his vitamins, telling him to do his homework, admonishing him that he should not stay out too late, and on and on. The group members soon tire of listening to his litany of complaints, and the following exchanges occur:

Maria: "If things are as bad as you say, why do you stay at home? Wouldn't it be a good idea to leave?"

Donald: "Yes, but I don't have a job, and I'm broke."

Jim: "If you don't like the way your mother treats you, wouldn't it help to let her know?"

Donald: "I'm afraid that she would just disintegrate if I were to confront her."

The starting point for helping dependent people is to refuse to reinforce the helpless position by refusing to fill the dependency needs. At the same time, the leader should help such people realize the means they are using to keep themselves dependent.

In confronting Donald with his dependent behavior, the leader could work toward getting him to recognize the ways in which he is continuing his dependency. She might say: "Donald, I've noticed in several sessions now that you seem to provoke people into helping you. You complain that your mother is treating you like a child, but I wonder whether you solicit this kind of response from your mother also." As an alternative, she might say: "Do you really want to change, or do you think you're waiting for your mother to change? When will *you* begin to be different with your mother?" Or the leader could ask Donald to list all the possible reasons for being afraid of leaving home.

Leaders sometimes foster dependency in their clients. Some leaders have an exaggerated need to be wanted and needed, and they feel a sense of importance when participants rely on them. This is an example of the

leader's unmet psychological needs interfering with the therapeutic outcome of a group. There are many other reasons that leaders collude with
members to form a dependent alliance, some of which are:

- The leader may need the economic rewards from the members' attendance.
- The group may be filling the leader's unmet needs for a social life.
- Some leaders have a need to be parental in the sense of directing others' lives.
- Leaders may rely on their groups as the sole source of feeling appreciated and recognized.
- Leaders may feel useful when participants tell them how much they
need them.
- Leaders may attempt to work through their own unresolved conflicts
by using the group.

These examples show how the personality of the leader cannot be separated from what sometimes appears as problem behavior within the
group. The behaviors of leader and members have a reciprocal effect.

ACTING SUPERIOR

Some group members take on a superior attitude. They may be moralistic
and find ways to judge or criticize others for their behavior. Such people
are unable to identify any pressing problems in their lives. Their attitude
and behavior tend to have the same effect on a group as hostility.
Participants freeze up, for they are more hesitant to expose their weaknesses to someone who projects an image of being perfect. Take the example of Eliseo, who says: "My problems are nothing compared to yours. I
feel sorry that so many of you had such terrible childhoods, and I feel for-
tunate that my parents really loved me." Eliseo is likely to respond to
someone who is sharing a problem with "I used to have your problem, but
I don't anymore." He will antagonize others with comments such as "I
can identify with you, because at one time I was where you are." In his
condescending tone is the message "I really don't need anything for
myself, and there are no problems in my life; I'm perfectly content now."

One option is to ask group members to respond to Eliseo by letting
him know how his behavior is affecting them. However, it is important
that members speak about themselves and not judge Eliseo. It is also crucial to block a tendency to use Eliseo as a scapegoat.

You can challenge Eliseo's comments by asking him what he wants
from the group. A possible intervention is: "You're comparing your problems with those of others in here. You're saying that you feel pressured to
come up with problems so that you can be accepted. What is it that you'd
like to get from this group? How is it for you to be here? How are you
being affected personally by what you're hearing? How does it feel that

people are annoyed with you and don't believe that you're problem-free?" This intervention lessens the chances of pressuring Eliseo to come up with problems that he is likely to deny having. Instead, it gives him some room to talk and respond without having to defend a position of being without problems. Taking an argumentative stance generally leads to a fruitless and frustrating debate. Instead, your focus needs to be on the reasons Eliseo continues attending this group. However, if he insists that his primary reason for attending is to observe others and learn about how people function, you may have made a mistake in initially not screening him out. You may now be stuck with the difficult task of recommending that he leave, for the purpose of the group is not to learn by merely observing others.

SOCIALIZING

When members socialize outside of these sessions, group cohesion can be increased. They can extend what they are learning in their group to the informal gatherings. Such meetings can also be useful in challenging members to follow through with their plans and commitments. For some populations, such as an inpatient group for the elderly, this can be the only network of support.

Meetings outside the group can also be a form of resistance, however, and can therefore work against cohesion. This is especially true when participants talk about group matters but refuse to discuss these issues in the group. Other signs that indicate counterproductive socializing include forming cliques and excluding certain members from such gatherings, forming romantic involvements without a willingness to share them in the group, refusal to challenge one another in the group because of a fear of jeopardizing friendships, and an exclusive reliance on the group as the source of social life.

When socializing outside of the sessions hampers group progress, it is essential that the issue be openly examined by the group. You can ask the members if they are genuinely concerned about developing the kind of group that will function effectively. You can help them see that forming cliques and making pacts to keep information out of the regular sessions do not lead to a productive and cohesive group.

INTELLECTUALIZING

Some cognitive work is a necessary part of group process, but it should be integrated with members' feelings. When group members discuss, in a very detached way as though out of intellectual interest, topics that for most people are emotionally loaded, they can be said to be intellectualizing. One of our colleagues tells us that in his groups some men will claim that they are different from women and that they are not prone to look at feelings. They then want to discuss this topic in the abstract by focusing on society rather than by sharing the way they are affected by a social injunction.

Most of us rely on our intellect. Nothing is amiss in using our intellectual faculties, but when intellectualizing is used as a defense against experiencing feelings it may become problematic in a person's life and in his or her functioning in a group. Members should think about their concerns, but in a group situation it is helpful for them to talk about how these concerns pertain to their own lives.

People who intellectualize need to be made aware of what they're doing. A question you might raise with members who rely heavily on their intellect is: "Does what you are doing most of the time get you what you want? Is this something you want to change?" Some experiential techniques (borrowed from Gestalt therapy and psychodrama) can be useful in helping these group members more directly experience the emotions associated with the events they talk about. Clients can be directed to reexperience events, perhaps by role playing. You need to be alert, however, when dealing with intellectualizing. As with other counterproductive styles, a defensive purpose is being served. You ought to ask yourself whether you're competent to deal with what would be revealed should the defenses be given up. Avoid making quick judgments about members who do not readily display intense emotions and labeling them as "removed from their feelings" or "detached." This defensive strategy is often employed by individuals who have become overwhelmed by feelings at some point in the past.

EMOTIONALIZING

Although groups provide an opportunity for members to focus on expressing a range of their emotions, some individuals dwell on "getting in touch with their feelings" to the extent that it can be a resistance. Lori is triggered by everyone's emotions, and her responses manage to draw attention to herself. Perhaps she believes that the only way to be productive in the group is to be highly cathartic and, consequently, to be seen by the leader as a "good" member. She can be deceiving herself in thinking that she is "really working" when she cries so easily and frequently. This behavior can also serve as a defense, because others are likely to hesitate to confront her. In Lori's case it is not so much a matter of her being sad. Instead, her issues are wanting attention from people—wanting to be liked, accepted, and approved of. Her fear may be that if she does not display emotions most of the time, she will be ignored. In some ways, she may be clinging to her problems so she can keep being emotionally reactive. Her emotionalism is an indirect way of getting what she wants. You need to be sensitive in determining when catharsis is an expression of a genuine struggle and when it is a form of resistance and, therefore, counterproductive.

INTERVENTIONS FOR DEALING WITH RESISTANCE THERAPEUTICALLY

In addition to the descriptions we have given of ways to deal with various forms of resistive behavior, we also list interventions that can facilitate work *with* resistance, rather than against it. The statements below often help members get beyond their resistance. First we give examples of comments that illustrate resistance. These are followed by several simple responses that usually result in helping clients get unstuck. Of course, not all these responses are made simultaneously to each member comment.

Member: "I don't know."
Leader: "Pretend you knew." "And if you did know, what might you say?" "What *do* you know?" "What are you aware of as you look at me or others in the room?" "Say the first thing that comes to your mind."

Member (during a role play): "I don't know what to say to my father."
Leader: "That's a good place to start. Tell him that." "If this is the last chance you have to speak to him, what do you want to tell him?" "If you were your father, what would you want to say?" "If you were your father, what do you fear you would say?" "Tell your father what stops you from talking to him."

Member: "I try so hard to say things the right way."
Leader: "Say it the wrong way." "What I would say if I knew how to say it right would be . . ." "Rehearse out loud."

Member: "I don't want to be here."
Leader: "Where would you rather be?" "What or who made you come here?" "You *are* here, so how can you make the most of it?" "What makes it difficult for you to be here?" "How come you're here if you didn't want to come today?"

Member (after an intense piece of work): "I feel like withdrawing."
Leader: "What or whom do you want to get away from?" "Go to a few people and finish the sentence 'I want to get away from you because . . .'" "Say more about your feeling."

Member (to the leader, sarcastically): "You think you're so high and mighty!"
Leader: "What do you really want to say to me?" "Tell me all the ways I've put myself above you." "Tell me the ways you put yourself down."

Member: "I'm afraid to talk more about this."
Leader: "What's stopping you?" "What do you fear would happen if you said more?" "What do you imagine will happen if you don't talk about it?" "What would it take for you to feel safer in here?" "I hope you'll say more about your fears of talking."

Several Members: "It's far easier to talk in the coffee shop to other group members than it is to express ourselves here."

Leader:	"Form an inner circle. Imagine you're out having coffee. What are you saying?" "Say at least two things to several members about your difficulty in talking in here." (Some possibilities for incomplete sentences to be completed by a client are: "I find it hard to talk in here because . . ." "I'm afraid to talk in here because . . ." "When I stop myself from talking, I'm most aware of . . .")
Member:	"I'm very uncomfortable with the anger in here."
Leader:	"Tell those who are angry how you're affected by them." "What happens [happened] when people express [expressed] their anger in your life?" (Some possibilities for incomplete sentences to be completed by the client are: "I'm afraid to get angry like this because . . ." "When you're angry with me, I . . ." "I'm afraid of my anger because . . ." "When I witness anger, I want to . . .")
Member	(who typically engages in storytelling): "But you don't understand. I need to tell you all the details so that you'll understand me."
Leader:	"Give me the topic of your story." "I get lost in your words. In one sentence, what do you most want me to hear?" "What's it like not to feel understood in here?" "What's it like to discover that people don't want to hear your stories?" "How does this story relate to the way you're struggling now in your life?" "What makes it important that I listen to your story?"
Member:	"I feel that my problems are insignificant."
Leader:	"Whose problems in here are more important?" "If you didn't compare your problems with those of others, what could you tell us about yourself?" "How are you affected by hearing all these problems?" "Tell us about one of your insignificant problems."
Member	(who has been feeling close to others in the group): "I'm afraid of this closeness, because I'm sure it won't last."
Leader:	"What did you do to get close to people?" "Tell a few people what scares you about remaining close to them." "Tell us how you can get close in here but not in your life." "What will it be like for you if people don't stop feeling close to you?" "What is one thing that keeps you from maintaining the closeness you felt?" "If nothing changed for you, how might this be?" "Tell us all the advantages of isolating yourself."
Member	(who is typically silent): "I don't think I need to be talking all the time. I learn a lot by observing."
Leader:	"So, tell us some things you've been observing but keeping to yourself." "Are you satisfied with the way you are in this group, or would you like to change?" "What are some of the things that make it difficult to speak out more?" "Would you be willing to select two people you've been observing and tell them how they have affected you?" "Does this behavior get you what you want, both in here and on the outside?" "I'm interested in knowing what you have to say, and I'd like to hear more from you." "When you observe me and quietly make assumptions about me, I feel uncom-

fortable. I'd like to be included in the conclusions you're drawing about me. I hope you'll check out your assumptions with me." "If you don't talk about yourself, people are likely to project onto you, and there's a good chance you'll be misunderstood."

Member   (who tends to give people advice): "I think you should stop criticizing yourself, because you're a wonderful person."

Leader: "For several weeks now, you've observed people in this room. Give each person an important piece of advice." "What advice would you like to give to yourself?" "When you give advice, do you sound like anyone you know?" "How is it for you when others reject your advice?" "How are you affected by the person you're ready to give advice to?" "How do people in your life respond to you when you give them advice?"

Most of these suggestions for responses by the leader provide encouragement for members to say more rather than stopping at the point of initial resistance. The questions are open-ended and are presented in an invitational manner. The interventions all grow out of clues provided by members, and they are designed to offer directions that clients might pursue in becoming unstuck.

INTERVENTIONS FOR DEALING WITH RESISTANCE BY THE WHOLE GROUP

We have been focusing on ways of dealing therapeutically with the resistive behaviors of individuals. At times an entire group colludes and presents a profile of resistance. In this section we describe one of our experiences when this was the case. In the interest of maintaining the anonymity of a particular group, we are changing some of the details, and we are including themes that have been characteristic of a number of groups that we have co-led. Our main purpose is to demonstrate how group resistance affects us as co-leaders and how we deal with the phenomenon of group resistance. We also describe some of the ways in which this group resistance affects the members as individuals and the group as a whole.

At one of our weeklong residential training workshops for group counselors, it was not possible to individually screen candidates. In lieu of screening, we provided all who were interested with a detailed letter describing the workshop and outlining our expectations of participants. We repeated this information at the first session, and participants had an opportunity to raise questions. It was especially crucial to us that they understand that they were to become personally involved and would function both as members and as co-leaders during different sessions. The full group was divided into two groups of eight. Each two-hour period

was co-led by two different trainees so that they all had an equal opportunity to function both as members and leaders. As supervisors, we
changed groups each two-hour session. This change presented problems
for some of the trainees, who said they were inhibited because the same
supervisor was not continually in their group.

One of the groups (Group 1) was formed by people who got up and
actively chose to be with one another. By contrast, the other group (Group
2) was largely formed by one member who remained seated and said: "I'm
staying here. Anyone who wants to join my group can come over here."
As the week progressed, some interesting differences arose between the
two groups. Group 2 was characterized by a series of resistive moves on
the part of most members. Many of them complained that they had not
understood that they were to become personally invested in the group
process. They said they had expected to learn about groups by observing
us do the work, rather than by getting actively involved. Although a few
of the members disclosed readily, others refused to share and did very
little interacting, which eventually led to an increased sense of withholding on the part of all members.

The participants in Group 2 were apparently feeling many things that
they refused to express. Some of them said that they were enjoying the
group time, yet they spoke little and appeared bored. There was considerable subgrouping. During the breaks the members talked about difficulties they were experiencing in the sessions, yet they did not bring this
information back to their group. Two members ended a session with an
unresolved conflict and decided to clear the air during the break, but they
did not inform the group of the outcome. During a subsequent session,
one of us observed that the group seemed to have a hard time interacting
and wondered if there was anything that was not being said. At first, the
entire group accused the supervisor of being "too picky" and asserted that
everything was "just fine." Only after some probing by the supervisor did
the members eventually acknowledge that they were preoccupied and
concerned about the two people who had had the conflict. The supervisor attempted to teach again how subgrouping can be deleterious to a
group's attaining its purpose.

Several women in Group 2 often confronted one of the male members
in a harsh manner. When a supervisor asked how he was affected by the
confrontations, he quickly insisted that he was not fazed in the least.
After several sessions, however, he blew up at everyone in the group
(including the supervisor) and let them know how angry he was. He
declared that he was ready to leave. The group mood was again one of
hesitancy, and members very tentatively interacted.

During one of the sessions a cat wandered into the group room and
defecated in a corner. Although the odor was undeniably strong, people
attempted to ignore the obvious. Finally, one of the supervisors (Jerry)
exclaimed "There's cat shit in this room, and I find it distracting to go on
as though nothing has happened!" Symbolically, this pattern expressed

this group's tendency to deny interpersonal conflict and to pretend that all was well. As a group, it preferred to ignore dealing directly with uncomfortable situations.

Another pattern that emerged was a tendency of Group 2 to judge itself against the performance of the other group. The members compared themselves unfavorably to those in Group 1 at those times when the two groups joined to discuss the day's progress. At a later point, people in Group 2 revealed the jealousy they had felt over the intensity and closeness that seemed to characterize the other group.

On the next to last day, Group 2's level of trust continued at a low ebb. The members showed great reluctance to be personal and to interact with one another. One of the supervisors (Jerry) told them before the lunch break: "I hope each one of you will spend some time in determining if you are getting what you wanted. This workshop is almost over. If today were the end, how would that be for you? If you aren't satisfied, what do you see that you can do to change the situation?"

The members of Group 2 decided to have lunch together for the first time. The group sessions were scheduled to resume promptly at 1 o'clock. What follows are the comments of the supervisor (Marianne) about what occurred:

"I arrived at the group I was to supervise shortly before 1:00, and at 1:20 I was still waiting impatiently in a hot and stuffy room with empty chairs. At 1:25 the group members finally sauntered into the room laughing and joking, telling me what a 'wonderful, intimate lunch' they had had. As they sat down, they let me know that they had felt much more comfortable and cohesive than they did in the group room. Even though I suspected what was occurring with them as a group, I would not have felt very honest if I had not let them know of my annoyance over their being late and not acknowledging this fact.

"Once I had taken care of my feelings with them, I was able to explore the dynamics of what was occurring. I confronted them by saying: 'You say that talking at lunch was very easy and that you felt close to one another. You also say that when you come into this room, you feel stifled. What do you think is different?' Of course, the most obvious variable was the presence of the supervisor. As they began to open up, they initially lashed out at both supervisors. They perceived us as demanding too much, expecting them to be personal and academic at the same time, wanting them to perform, and demanding that they have problems (even if they didn't). They insisted that we had been unclear with them about our expectations. I listened to their grievances, attempting not to be defensive, which was not easy with the degree of hostility that was directed toward me. I did acknowledge that it was a difficult workshop and that indeed much was demanded of them, but I was not apologetic about my standards.

"Finally, as a group, they admitted their envy over the intimacy the other group seemed to have, and they said they had tried to replicate this closeness at lunch. It was then that I challenged them again, as had Jerry before lunch, to reflect and begin to verbalize what they were rehearsing internally and what they were keeping from one another. Furthermore, I told them that I had a difficult time in trusting the sincerity of the intimacy they supposedly had had at lunch if they could not be more direct with one another in the session a few minutes later."

The next session took place the following morning, which also was the last full day of the workshop. At that session the members finally displayed more honesty. They had taken our challenges seriously and had given thought during the night to their behavior during the workshop. They were willing to take personal responsibility for their actions in the group, and there was no blaming. They achieved more closeness in this final session because of their willingness to say what was on their minds. They learned in an experiential way that what they had not expressed during much of the week had kept them from having genuine cohesiveness. They also learned that they could not have the true intimacy that they envied in Group 1 because of their decision to interact at a relatively superficial level. Yet neither they nor we thought that their group had been a failure, because they realized how their behavior had thwarted their progress as a group. Most of them were able to see some of the ways in which their low level of risking had inhibited the flow of their group. They all agreed that they were sorry that the group was ending, for they were just beginning to establish the trust necessary to significantly encounter one another. Since they were willing to talk in honest ways about their group, they learned some important lessons about themselves as persons as well as about the group process.

When the two of us conferred privately, we made some comparisons between the two groups. Our comparisons did not focus on labeling one group as a success and the other as a failure. Rather, we were acutely aware of the different dynamics that had characterized each group. Supervising and facilitating each group was demanding work, yet the main difference was Group 1's willingness to at least talk about its difficulties, whereas Group 2 continually withheld important reactions. In the follow-up papers the participants wrote, our hunches were confirmed, for many members of Group 2 wrote about many of their reactions during the week that they had never mentioned in the sessions. Had they chosen to express them at the time, we are quite certain that their experience as a group and their individual experience would have been greatly different.

As supervisors, we felt that we had worked diligently with both groups, yet at times we had wondered what the participants in Group 2 were really gaining from the workshop. We experienced how draining it can be to work with a group that has a number of hidden agendas. Not only did Group 2 display resistance, but there were times when we also felt discouraged and resistant. It was necessary to remind ourselves that this was not the first time we had worked with a difficult group. Our experience has taught us the importance of making a commitment to face what is going on, to bring to the surface the hidden agendas, and to refuse to give up. In spite of our belief in the natural process of a group, our patience was tested. It often seemed that we were doing most of the work. As has been true with other groups, our patience paid off, for the members of this group eventually developed the trust necessary to explore the ways in which they had become stuck and learned what was necessary to move forward. Even though this group did not become cohesive, the members did learn important lessons about what had held them back as individuals and how this impasse at the transition stage had stalled their efforts to become a working group.

DEALING WITH TRANSFERENCE AND COUNTERTRANSFERENCE

As we've emphasized, it is essential when leading groups to recognize how your unresolved personal issues can feed into problematic behaviors in members. This interplay involves transference and countertransference. *Transference* consists of the feelings clients project onto the counselor. These feelings usually have to do with relationships the clients have experienced in the past. When such feelings are attributed to the group leader, the intensity of the feelings have more to do with unfinished elements in a member's life than to the current situation. *Countertransference* refers to the feelings aroused in the counselor by clients, feelings that, again, have more to do with unresolved conflict from other past or present relationships than with any feature of the therapeutic relationship.

A group context has the potential for multiple transferences. Members may project not only onto the leaders but also onto other members in the group. Depending on the kind of group being conducted, members may identify people who elicit feelings in them that are reminiscent of feelings they have for significant people in their lives, past or present. Again, depending on the purpose of the group, these feelings can be productively explored so members become aware of how they are keeping these old patterns functional in present relationships. The group itself provides an ideal place to become aware of certain patterns of psychological vulnerability. Members can gain insight into the ways in which their unresolved conflicts create certain patterns of dysfunctional behavior. By focusing on what is going on within a group session, the group provides a dynamic understanding of how people function in out-of-group situations.

When clients appear to work very hard at getting the counselor to push them away, it can be therapeutically useful to explore what they are getting from this self-defeating behavior. And the transference reactions members develop toward the group leader and other members can bring out resistance in those who are the target of this transference. Handled properly in the therapeutic setting, members can experience and express feelings toward others in the group and discover how they are projecting outside situations onto the group. When these feelings are productively explored in the group, members often become better able to express their feelings appropriately.

Your own supervision is a central factor in learning how to deal effectively with both transference and countertransference reactions. Your blind spots can easily hamper your ability to deal with difficult members or with your old wounds that surface as you work with the members' pain. Ongoing supervision will enable you to accept responsibility for your reactions and at the same time prevent you from taking full responsibility for directions that specific members take. Meeting with your co-leader to talk about how you are affected by certain members is an excellent way to get another's perspective on difficult situations. Self-knowledge is the basic tool in dealing effectively with transference and countertransference.

HOW MEMBERS MAY VIEW THE LEADER

Regardless of the value you may place on exploring transferences, you should be aware of the expectations that members are likely to have of you as their group leader. Unless their feelings about you are dealt with in the group, meaningful work may never occur. Participants have an image of the group leader, and sometimes they harbor unrealistic notions. We'll now describe some of the more common ways in which clients may initially perceive you in your leadership role.

The Expert   Some members enter a group because they are seeking direction and help. They hope that the answers to their problems rest with the therapist, who is empowered to show them how they should live. They want to increase their self-confidence, to know themselves better, to become more assertive, to feel more intensely, to lose their fears, and to gain courage. If they don't move in this direction, they may resent you for not doing your job.

Some clients, because of their cultural conditioning, will perceive of and react to you as the expert. Indeed, they often present their problems and then expect you as an expert in human relations to provide them with advice, direction, and solutions. At least initially, these clients are unaware that counseling is a collaborative effort. Their perceptions of you may not be a transference reaction but more of a response to their cultural conditioning. For both clients from mainstream society and clients from a minority group, you need to sensitively explain the role that you will each play in the group process.

The Authority Figure   It is not uncommon for members, during the transition phase of a group, to feel embarrassed about disclosing that they feel awkward and self-conscious in your presence. They say that they feel judged, that they feel inferior and insignificant, and that they don't see themselves as able to measure up to your standards. These people may be psychologically bringing their parents (or other significant authority figures) with them into the group; how they feel toward you is much the way they've felt toward the significant people in their lives. By elevating you to a superior place, they discount their own worth. They cannot really enjoy, like, or respect you as a person, for they are too intimidated. It is often said that those who are placed on a pedestal can go only one way: down.

In culturally diverse groups, some clients may treat counselors as authority figures because they have been encouraged and taught to show respect and deference for all types of authority. We are reminded of a group member who made it a point never to sit next to either of us. To our surprise, we found out from him that indeed he was deliberately avoiding sitting next to us. From his cultural perspective, doing so would have been a sign of disrespect for us. He also had trouble respecting Jerry and questioned his level of expertise because of his use of humor. Our client was not sure that he could take Jerry as a serious professional.

The Superperson   Clients often view the group leader as infallible. It is inconceivable to them that leaders may feel inadequate at times, that their marriage may not be perfect, or that they do not have all the answers to human suffering. These clients are amazed if they discover that you are not a perfectly adjusted, self-actualizing being. Perhaps they need to believe that you have actually reached perfection and that, therefore, they can also hope to do so. One danger is that you will actually believe these grandiose perceptions of some of your clients. You may engage in self-deception and convince yourself that you do have the superpowers that some clients attribute to you.

The Friend   Some clients resent the professional aspects of a client/therapist relationship. Others feel jealous over having to share "their" therapist. Some say that the office structure—appointments, fees, waiting room, and so on—interferes with the spontaneity they would like. It is not realistic for members to expect you, as their therapist, to be their friend, the kind with whom they would have a social relationship. If clients rely too heavily on this therapeutic relationship for friendship, they may fail to develop friendships on the outside. The dynamics of making you their friend are similar to the dynamics of reacting to you as one or both of their parents. Clients hope that you will care for them in a special way, that you will approve of and even love them unconditionally, and that you will see them as desirable. From an ethical perspective, you are cautioned to avoid dual relationships: "Group counselors do not misuse their professional role and power as group leader to advance personal or social contacts with members throughout the duration of the group" (ASGW, 1989, 9.a).

GUIDELINES FOR LEADERS

It is essential for group leaders to consider their countertransference as a possible source of difficulties that develop in a group. Some leaders project their own problems and unfinished business onto difficult members as these members pose a threat to the group leader. If leaders are not willing to deal with their own issues, how can they expect members to take the risks necessary for them to change? As you reflect on ways you may be emotionally triggered in groups you lead, examine your response to members that you perceive as being difficult. Remember, it is generally not useful to assume that your clients merely want to annoy you. Ask yourself these questions: "How do I respond to the different forms of transference exhibited by members?" "What kind of transference tends to elicit my countertransference?" "Do I take the resistance of members in a personal way?" "Do I blame myself for not being skillful enough?" "Do I become combative with clients I view as problematic?"

As a group leader, you must deal with the transference reactions members develop toward you, but the solution is often complex and depends on the circumstances under which the relationship develops. Here are some general guidelines to follow.

Do not quickly discount members' reactions to you as transference. Be willing to explore the possibility that members have genuine reactions to the way you have dealt with them. It takes courage on your part to acknowledge that you may have been insensitive to a client and are now receiving warranted reactions. Often, however, members will treat you as if you were a significant figure in their lives. This is especially likely to be true if members have intense feelings toward you when they have had very little contact with you.

Even if you strongly suspect transference feelings, you would be discounting the person if you said: "You are having a transference reaction toward me. This is not my problem, it's your problem." A less defensive response is "Tell me more about how you see me." This intervention elicits additional information about how the client developed a set of reactions to you. After both you and the client express your reactions, you could acknowledge that the client does have some real perceptions of your behavior by saying: "I think you have a point. I was preoccupied, and I didn't notice that you wanted to talk to me." Or you might say: "I'm surprised at the reactions you're having to me. I wonder if I remind you of anyone for whom you have similar feelings?"

When clients identify you as an object of transference, there is the potential for rich therapeutic work. You can take on a symbolic role and allow the client to talk to you and work through unfinished business.

Additionally, you and the client can engage in role reversal as a way to explore feelings and to gain insight. Assume that a member, Mark, becomes aware that he is behaving around you much as he does with his father. During a role play, in which he is talking to you as his father, he says: "I don't feel important in your life. You're too busy and never have time for me. No matter what I do, it's never enough for you. I just don't know how to go about getting your approval." Because you don't know how Mark's father relates to him, you could ask him to take on the role of his father by responding as he imagines that his father would respond. After Mark has several interchanges in which he is both himself and his father, you will have a clearer sense of how he struggles with his father. Armed with this information, you can help him work through his unresolved issues with both his father and with you. Through the process of his therapeutic work, he may be able to see you as the person who you are, rather than as the father with whom he is struggling.

These are but a few illustrations of how transference problems can be worked out. The important elements are that (1) the feelings be recognized and expressed and that (2) the feelings then be dealt with therapeutically.

A more delicate issue is how the leader can best deal with feelings toward a group member. Even in the Freudian tradition, which dictates that therapists spend years in analysis to understand and resolve blocked areas, countertransference is a potential problem. So it can be a big problem for the beginning group leader. Some people are attracted to this profession because, on some level, they imagine that as a helper they will be respected, needed, admired, looked to as an expert, and even loved. Perhaps they have never experienced the acceptance and self-confidence in their ordinary lives that they feel while helping others. Such leaders are using groups to fulfill needs that would otherwise go unmet.

The issue of power is germane here, for as group members elevate the leader to the level of expert, perfect person, or demanding parent, they also give away most of their power. A self-aware therapist who is interested primarily in the client's welfare will not encourage the member to remain in an inferior position. The insecure leader who depends on clients' subordinate position for a sense of adequacy and power will tend to keep the group members powerless.

We do not want to convey the impression that it is inappropriate for you to meet your needs through your work. Nor are we suggesting that you should not feel powerful. In fact, we think that if you are not meeting your needs through your work, you are in danger of losing your enthusiasm. What is crucial is that you do not exploit the members as a way of fulfilling yourself. The problem occurs when you put your own needs first or fail to be sensitive to the needs of group members.

Countertransference feelings are likely to develop in the romantic/sexual realm, particularly when an attractive group member indicates an interest in a group leader. Group leaders may never have felt desirable before assuming their professional role. Now that they do, there is the danger that they will depend on group members for this feedback.

Dealing with countertransference openly can compound the complexities of the group process by generating critical feelings and reactions toward the leader. Nevertheless, you may at times have to do so. One of the advantages of working with a co-leader is that the partner can offer valuable feedback from an objective viewpoint and can help the other partner see things that he or she had been blocking from awareness.

Through your training, you may have the opportunity to explore with a supervisor feelings of attraction or repulsion toward certain members. If you are conducting groups independently and become aware of a pattern that indicates possible countertransference problems, you should seek consultation with another therapist or become a member of a group to work through these problems.

Three additional points need to be emphasized:

1.   Don't be gullible and believe uncritically whatever group members tell you, particularly initially. It's easy to become enamored with feedback that tells you how helpful, wise, perceptive, attractive, powerful, and dynamic you are; don't be swept away by the unrealistic attributions of group members.

2.   Don't be overly critical and thus discount genuine positive feedback. All members who see a leader as helpful or wise are not suffering from "transference disorders." Members can feel genuine affection and respect for group leaders. By the same token, just because participants become angry with you does not mean that they are transferring anger toward their parents onto you. Clients can feel genuine anger and have negative reactions toward you personally. It may be true that certain leaders radiate a distant, know-it-all manner, manipulate the group toward their own ends, or are seductive with certain members. In short, all feelings that members direct toward the group leader should not be "analyzed" as transference to be "worked through" for the client's good. A useful rule of thumb that we apply to ourselves is that if we hear a consistent pattern of feedback, it is imperative that we seriously examine what is being told to us. If we see validity in this feedback, we are likely to make some changes in our behavior.

3.   Recognize that not all of your feelings toward members can be classified as countertransference. You may be operating under the misconception that you should remain objective and care for all members equally. One of your unrealistic beliefs could be your expectation that you should be superhuman and be all things to all members. Countertransference is indicated by exaggerated and persistent feelings that tend to recur with various clients in various groups. You can expect to enjoy some members more than others, yet all the members of your group deserve a chance to be liked by you. What is important is that you recognize your own feelings for what they are and that you avoid emotional entanglements that are countertherapeutic.

EFFECTIVE LEADERSHIP:
RESEARCH FINDINGS

Research has yielded considerable evidence of the importance of a positive therapist/client relationship. A consistent empirical finding in the psychotherapy literature is the role of a favorable therapeutic relationship as a contributing factor to positive change in clients (Burlingame & Fuhriman, 1990). The group leader plays a significant role in fostering an interpersonal climate among the members that encourages intermember feedback and participation as key group norms. Indeed, such a climate is often viewed as the basic therapeutic factor of group treatment. A high degree of intermember interaction is thought to foster establishment and maintenance of cohesion and group identity, reality testing, and development of coping skills (Burlingame & Fuhriman, 1990).

In addition to facilitating a high level of client interaction, the group leader's relationship with members is also seen as a crucial determinant of the process and outcome of a group. The leader's interpersonal skills, genuineness, empathy, and warmth are significant variables associated with effective group work. Some of the literature focuses on the therapist's contributions to the therapeutic enterprise and specifies personality characteristics of successful group leaders. These include empathy, competence, responsiveness and attentiveness, presence, and engagement. The therapist's personal development and awareness of personal style are influential aspects of the therapeutic relationship (Fuhriman & Burlingame, 1990). The therapist's style is a significant factor, but awareness of how the therapist's behavior may influence the group is also crucial. Group leaders are responsible for activating the therapeutic factors within the group. Identifying the key therapeutic factors for a particular group is the first step.

As we discussed in Chapter 3, however, these relationship variables and other personal characteristics by themselves are not sufficient for effective group outcomes. Simply because group leaders possess desirable personal attributes does not necessarily mean that they will be successful. It is generally accepted that a good working relationship (or a positive therapeutic relationship) is necessary but not sufficient to produce client change. Certainly it is essential that leaders possess the knowledge of how groups best function and the skills to intervene in timely and effective ways. As we have mentioned, one of the leader's tasks is to promote good working relationships among the members and to teach them how to work productively in a group. Dies (1983b) maintains that the quality of interpersonal relationships among group members is more important for therapeutic change than is the leader's relationship to individual members. The leader's central task is to create interpersonal norms such as openness, directness, respect, and concern for one another that will lead to therapeutic interactions among members.

SUPPORT VERSUS CONFRONTATION

Forging an effective group requires achieving an appropriate balance between support and challenge. In our opinion, groups having either explicit or implicit norms limiting group interactions to supportive ones do not have the power to help people challenge themselves to take significant risks. We further think that those groups that stress confrontation as a requisite for peeling away the defensive maneuvers of members are characterized by hostile and increasingly defensive interactions. The reviews of research that describe negative outcomes in groups consistently cite aggressive confrontation as the leadership style with the highest risks (Lieberman, Yalom, & Miles, 1973; Yalom, 1995). Based on research findings, Dies (1983b) suggests that leaders should not engage in highly confrontational interventions until they have earned that right by building a trusting relationship with the members. Once the foundation of interpersonal trust is established, group members tend to be more open to challenge. Dies recommends that because it takes time to create a supportive atmosphere, confrontational interactions are probably most appropriate at a later stage of a group's development.

We agree that there are dangers in confronting too soon and that leaders must earn the right to challenge. Attacking defenses can lead to an entrenchment of resistance and may breed hostility and mistrust within the group. But we think confrontation is appropriate even during the initial stages of a group if it is done with sensitivity and respect. In fact, the foundations of trust are often solidified by caring confrontations on the leader's part. Beginning with the early phase of the group, the leader needs to model ways of providing appropriate support and challenge. To avoid challenging a group in its early phase, when this is what the group needs, is to treat the group members as though they were fragile. How leaders deal with conflict, resistance, anxiety, and defensiveness does much to set the tone of the group. In our view, members have a tendency to follow the leader's manner of confronting.

GUIDELINES FOR CREATING THERAPEUTIC RELATIONSHIPS WITH MEMBERS

In this section we present an adaptation of further guidelines for group leadership practice based on research summaries done by Dies (1983b), Fuhriman and Burlingame (1990), Burlingame and Fuhriman (1990), Stockton and Morran (1982), and Bednar and Kaul (1978):

- Strive for positive involvement in the group through genuine, empathic, and caring interactions with the members. Impersonal detached, and judgmental leadership styles can create resistance and can thwart the development of trust and cohesion.

- Develop a reasonably open therapeutic style characterized by appropriate and facilitative self-disclosure, but do not make it a practice to use the group you lead as a therapy group for yourself. Be willing to share your own reactions and emotional experiences, especially as they relate to events and relationships within the group.
- Keep in mind that leader self-disclosure can have either a constructive or a detrimental effect on the group process and outcome, depending on specific factors such as the type of group, the stage of its development, and the content and manner of the disclosure.
- Help members make maximum use of effective role models, especially those members who demonstrate desirable behavior. Members can be encouraged to learn from one another. If you have a co-leader, model openness with your partner.
- Provide opportunities for all members to make maximum use of the resources within the group by teaching them skills of active participation in the group process.
- Demonstrate your caring by being willing to confront members when that is called for, but do so in a manner that provides the members with good modeling of ways to confront decently.
- Intervene when a member is preventing others from using the group's resources by engaging in nonconstructive confrontations, hostility, and indirect exchanges. Help members deal with one another in direct and constructive ways.

We want to underscore our belief that you can do much to encourage members to give up some of their defensiveness by reacting to them with directness, honesty, and respect. Members are more likely to develop a stance of openness in a group that they perceive as being safe for them, and your modeling has a lot to do with creating this therapeutic atmosphere.

CO-LEADER ISSUES AT THE TRANSITION STAGE

As you can see, the transition stage is a critical period in the history of the group. Depending on how conflict and resistance are handled, the group can take a turn for the better or for the worse. If you are working with a co-leader, you can efficiently use the time you have for meeting before and after sessions to focus on your own reactions to what is occurring in the group. Here are a few problems that can develop between leaders at this time.

Negative Reactions toward One Leader   If members direct a challenge or express negative reactions toward your co-leader, it is important to avoid either taking sides with your colleagues in attacking clients or siding with the members in ganging up against the co-leader. Instead, nondefensively (and as objectively as possible) continue your leadership by facilitating a constructive exploration of the situation.

Challenges to Both Leaders   Assume that several members direct criticism to both you and your co-leader, saying: "You leaders expect us to be personal in here, but we don't know anything about you that's personal. You should be willing to talk about your problems if that's what you expect us to do." In such a case, difficulties can develop if one of you responds defensively while the other is willing to deal with this confrontation from the members. Ideally, both leaders should talk about the confrontation objectively. If not, this disagreement would surely be a vital topic to discuss in the co-leaders' meeting outside of the group or during a supervision session. We don't want to convey the impression that all difficulties should be reserved for a private discussion between the co-leaders. As much as possible, matters that pertain to what is happening during sessions should be discussed with the entire group. The failure to do so can easily lead to a you-versus-them split within the group.

Dealing with Problem Behaviors   We have discussed a variety of difficult members that you and your co-leader might have to confront. We want to caution against the tendency of co-leaders to chronically discuss what such members are doing or not doing and never to explore how such behavior affects them as leaders. It is a mistake to dwell almost exclusively on strategies for "curing" problem members while ignoring your own personal reactions to such problematic behaviors.

Dealing with Countertransference   It is not realistic to expect a leader to work equally effectively with every member. At times, ineffectiveness results from countertransference reactions on the part of one of the leaders. For example, a male leader could have strong and irrational negative reactions to one of the women in the group. It may be that he is seeing his ex-wife in this member and responding to her in nontherapeutic ways because of his own unresolved issues over the divorce. When this situation occurs, the co-leader can be therapeutic for both the member and the leader who is not being helpful. The colleague can intervene during the session itself as well as exploring these countertransference reactions with the other leader outside the session. Co-leaders who are willing to be objective and honest with each other can have a positive impact through this process of mutual confrontation.

TRANSITION STAGE: SUMMARY

STAGE CHARACTERISTICS

The transitional phase of a group's development is marked by feelings of anxiety and defenses in the form of various resistances. At this time members are:

- concerned about what they will think of themselves if they increase their self-awareness, and are concerned about others' acceptance or rejection of them.
- testing the leader and other members to determine how safe the environment is.
- struggling between wanting to play it safe and wanting to risk getting involved.
- experiencing some struggle for control and power and some conflict with other members or the leader.
- observing the leader to determine if he or she is trustworthy.
- learning how to express themselves so that others will listen to them.

MEMBER FUNCTIONS AND POSSIBLE PROBLEMS

A central role of members at this time is to recognize and deal with the many forms of resistance. Tasks include:

- recognizing and expressing any negative reactions.
- respecting one's own resistances but working with them.
- moving from dependence to independence.
- learning how to confront others in a constructive manner.
- being willing to face and deal with reactions toward what is occurring in the group.
- being willing to work through conflicts, rather than avoiding them.

Some of the problems that can arise with members at this time are:

- Members may be categorized according to "problem types," or they may limit themselves with some self-imposed label.
- Members may refuse to express persistent negative feelings, thus contributing to the climate of distrust.
- If confrontations are poorly handled, members may retreat into defensive postures, and issues will remain hidden.
- Members may form subgroups and cliques, expressing negative reactions outside of the group but remaining silent in the group.

LEADER FUNCTIONS

The major challenge facing leaders during the transition period is the need to intervene in the group in a sensitive and timely manner. The major task is to provide the encouragement and the challenge necessary for members to face and resolve conflicts and negative reactions that exist within the group and the resistances that stem from their defenses against anxiety. Groups need to move from a stage of conflict and confrontation to an effective level of relating. To meet this challenge, leaders have the following tasks:

- teaching members the value of recognizing and dealing fully with conflict situations
- assisting members to recognize their own patterns of defensiveness
- teaching members to respect resistance and to work constructively with the many forms it takes
- providing a model for members by dealing directly and tactfully with any challenges, either personal or professional
- avoiding labeling members but learning how to understand certain problem behaviors
- assisting members to become interdependent and independent
- encouraging members to express reactions that pertain to here-and-now happenings in the sessions

EXERCISES

SELF-ASSESSMENT SCALE

Use the following scale to determine your strengths and weaknesses as a group member. Rate yourself as you see yourself at this time. This inventory assumes that you have had some type of group experience. If you have not, you might rate yourself in terms of your behavior in the class you're now in. This exercise can help you determine the degree to which you may be either a resistive or a productive member in a group. If you identify specific problem areas, you can decide to work on them in your group.

After everyone has completed the inventory, the class should break into small groups, each person trying to join the people he or she knows best. Members of the groups should then assess one another's self-ratings.

Rate yourself from 1 to 5 on each of the following self-descriptions, using these extremes:

1 = This is almost never true of me.
5 = This is almost always true of me.

_____   1. I'm readily able to trust others in a group.
_____   2. Others tend to trust me in a group situation.
_____   3. I disclose personal and meaningful material.
_____   4. I'm willing to formulate specific goals and contracts.
_____   5. I'm generally an active participant, as opposed to an observer.
_____   6. I'm willing to openly express my feelings about and reactions to what is occurring within a group.
_____   7. I listen attentively to what others are saying, and I'm able to discern more than the mere content of what is said.
_____   8. I don't give in to group pressure by doing or saying things that don't seem right to me.
_____   9. I'm able to give direct and honest feedback to others, and I'm open to receiving feedback about my behavior from others.
_____   10. I prepare myself for a given group by thinking of what I want from that experience and what I'm willing to do to achieve my goals.
_____   11. I avoid monopolizing the group time.
_____   12. I avoid storytelling by describing what I'm experiencing now.
_____   13. I avoid questioning other group members and instead make direct statements to them.
_____   14. I'm able to be supportive of others when it is appropriate without giving pseudosupport.
_____   15. I'm able to confront others in a direct and caring manner by letting them know how I'm affected by them.

EXERCISES AND QUESTIONS FOR EXPLORATION

Many of the following exercises are ideally suited for small-group inter-action and discussion. Explore these questions from the vantage point of a group leader.

1.   Assume that various members make these statements:

- "I'm afraid of looking like a fool in the group."
- "My greatest fear is that the other members will reject me."
- "I'm afraid to look at myself, because if I do, I might discover that I'm empty."
- "I'm reluctant to let others know who I really am, because I've never done it before."

With each of these statements, what might you say or do? Can you think of ways to work with members who express these fears?

2.   Imagine that you are leading a group that does not seem to want to get beyond the stage of "playing it safe." Members' disclosures are super-ficial, their risk taking is minimal, and they display a variety of resis-

tances. What might you do in such a situation? How do you imagine you'd feel if you were leading such a group?

3. Assume that there is a good deal of conflict in a group you are leading. When you point this discord out to members and encourage them to deal with it, most of them tell you that they don't see any point in talking about the conflicts because "things won't change." What might be your response? How would you deal with a group that seemed to want to avoid facing and working with conflicts?

4. In a group that you are co-leading, several members attack your competence. In essence, they give you the message that you are not working professionally and that they favor the other leader. How do you imagine you'd feel in such a situation? What do you think you'd do or say?

5. In one of your groups there is a member, Betty, who rarely speaks, even if encouraged to do so. What are your reactions to the following leader interventions? (a) Ignore her. (b) Ask others in the group how they react to her silence. (c) Remind her of her contract detailing her responsibility to participate. (d) Ask her what is keeping her from contributing. (e) Frequently attempt to draw her out. What are some interventions you would be likely to make?

6. Larry has a style of asking many questions of fellow group members. You notice that his questioning has the effect of distracting members and interfering with their expression of feelings. What are some things you might say to him?

7. Jill has a habit of going into great detail in telling stories when she speaks. She typically focuses on details about others in her life, saying little about how she is affected by them. Eventually, another member says to her: "I'm really having trouble staying with you. I get bored and impatient with you when you go into such detail about others. I want to hear more about you and less about others." Jill responds: "That really upsets me. I feel I've been risking a lot by telling you about problems in my life. Now I feel like not saying any more!" What interventions would you make at this point?

8. From what you know of yourself, in what areas are you most likely to experience countertransference? If you found your objectivity seriously hampered in a group because of your own personal issues, what might you do?

FOCUS QUESTIONS

1. What are the major differences between a working and a nonworking group? between a working and a nonworking member?

2. How can a client who has gained insight into the reasons for a problem be helped to act on this awareness?

3. What is your position on the values and limitations of catharsis in groups?

4. As a group leader, what do you think you can do to assist participants in making constructive choices about their behavior in the group?

5. What is your position on the use of techniques and exercises to facilitate communication and interaction?

6. What is your view of the "ideal" group member?

7. What are three major factors that you think bring about change in clients?

8. What specific guidelines can you come up with to determine whether self-disclosure would be appropriate and facilitative for you as a leader?

9. What would you want to teach members during the working stage about giving and receiving feedback?

10. What factors prevent a group from reaching a working stage?

INTRODUCTION

There are no arbitrary dividing lines between the phases of a group. In actual practice there is a considerable overlapping of the stages. This is especially true of movement from the transition stage to the working stage. The line between expressing conflicts and resistance, so characteristic of the transition stage, and working them through to move the group into a more advanced stage of development is thin indeed.

Many groups never evolve to a true working level. However, significant work takes place at all stages of a group, not just during the working stage. Even when groups are stuck, or are embroiled in conflict, or members are extremely anxious and hesitant, many lessons can be learned. Some open groups with rapidly changing memberships may not reach the working stage because members lack the opportunity to develop trust, cohesion, and continuity. Closed groups that fail to master the major tasks of conflict management and dealing with resistance do not establish enough trust to allow members to reach a level of what they (or the leader) consider productive work. However, individuals may still benefit from a group even if it does not reach a working stage.

Being in a working stage as a group does not imply that all members are able to function optimally. Indeed, some members may be on the fringe, some may be highly resistant, and some may not feel they are an integral part of the group. Conversely, a highly resistive group might well have one or more members who are very willing to engage in productive work. All members are not at the same level of readiness, nor are they developmentally the same. Some members may be more motivated than others; some may be more resistant or less willing to take risks. Individual differences among members are characteristic of all group stages.

As we discussed earlier, conflict, resistance, and feelings of mistrust must be expressed and a commitment made to face and work through barriers that interfere with a group's progress. In this chapter we examine the following questions:

- What are the characteristics of the working stage of groups?
- How does a leader facilitate a group's movement from the transition stage to the working stage?
- What are some of the therapeutic factors that operate in the working stage? What are some of the factors that influence change within an individual and a group, and how are these changes brought about?
- How does cohesion foster a spirit of productivity among the members?
- How are leader and member self-disclosures particularly important during the working stage?
- What kind of feedback is especially valuable to members during a working stage? What are some guidelines for giving and receiving feedback?
- What are some co-leader issues to consider at this stage?

PROGRESSING FROM THE TRANSITION STAGE TO THE WORKING STAGE

In Chapter 6 we described the characteristics of a group in its transition stage. With a few examples, we now show how a leader's intervention can assist a group in transition to become a working group.

EXAMPLE 1

Frank and Judy complain that not enough is happening in the group and that they are getting impatient. They are likely to back off if the leader responds defensively. Therapeutic interventions could be any of the following statements:

- "What would you like to see happening?"
- "I suggest that you tell each person one thing you would like him or her to do to improve this group."

- "You might have some reactions to the way I'm leading. Is there anything you need to say to me?"

These interventions can help Frank and Judy go beyond complaining, explore the source of their dissatisfaction, and express what they would like to see happen. When Joe, another member, makes a hostile remark ("If you don't like it, leave the group"), the leader can bring it into this interaction. This could be accomplished by asking Joe to make some direct statements to Frank and Judy instead of dismissing them. As Joe talks about his own reaction to Judy and Frank, he might well get involved in the work in a deeply personal way. Joe's reaction to others in the group could open up some unresolved business he has with others in his life. By engaging Judy and Frank, Joe opens up possibilities for identifying with them. If the leader does not address Joe's hostile remarks, they may have a negative impact on the group.

EXAMPLE 2

Sunny says that she is afraid of talking about herself in the group. This is another opportunity for productive work. A good place to begin is with her admission that she feels judged. The leader can further Sunny's work by intervening in any of these ways:

- "Would you be willing to talk to one person in here who you think would judge you the most harshly? Tell that person all the things you imagine he or she would think about you?"
- "Go around the group and finish this sentence: 'If I let you know me, I'm afraid you would judge me by . . .' "
- "Would you be willing to close your eyes and imagine all the judgments that people in here could possibly make about you? You don't need to verbalize what you imagine, but do let yourself feel what it is like to be judged by everyone in the group."

Each of these interventions has the potential for leading to further exploration, which can assist Sunny in learning how she allows herself to be inhibited by her fear of others' judgments. If she follows any of these leader suggestions, she has a basis for actually working through her fears.

EXAMPLE 3

Jennifer says that she never gets any attention in her group and that the leader gives everyone else priority over her. The leader does not waste time trying to persuade her that she is indeed important to him; rather, he listens to her perceptions and feelings. He then asks her to talk directly to the members whom she sees as getting more of his attention. She talks about her feelings about being pushed aside. The leader intervenes with:

"I wonder if the feelings you are having in this group are familiar to you in your life outside of group?" This intervention can encourage Jennifer to work in greater depth on connecting her past and present outside life with reactions she is having in the here-and-now context of her group.

If Jennifer acknowledges that she often feels ignored and pushed aside in her family of origin, especially by her father, the leader can give her an opportunity to continue her work by helping her explore some of the ways she might be identifying the leader with her father. Once Jennifer recognizes that she is polluting the relationship with the leader with feelings she has toward her father, she is free to discover that the leader is quite different from her father. She finds out that she is often overly sensitive to the ways older male authority figures interact with her. She reads into these interactions much more than is warranted. Where she sees rejection, the reality could be a busy leader who is attending to many members.

Jennifer's declaration that she does not get proper attention in the group is a typical reaction during the transition stage. As the leader works with this feeling, Jennifer ends up having new insight regarding how she is making the group leader (and others) into her father. Jennifer's insights and behavior changes are indicative of productive activity in the working stage. The leader's intervention did not entrench her resistance further but resulted in some significant work on her part. In addition, she might well experience intense emotions over her feelings about her father, and she is likely to express and explore such painful feelings in the group. As a result of her work in the group, Jennifer now pays attention to how she feels when she is with her father and tries out new ways of responding to him. Because she is aware of her tendency to attribute certain qualities to some men, she is now in a position to react differently around them.

WORKING WITH A MEMBER'S FEAR

To illustrate the progression of one member's work from the initial to working stage of a group, let's examine how one member's fear was addressed at each group stage. For the sake of the discussion, assume that Joan, a member of an ongoing group, says "I'm afraid people in here will think I'm foolish." Members often express a range of similar apprehensions, fearing that others will see them as stupid, egocentric, weird, evil, crazy, and the like. The techniques we describe in working with Joan's particular fear of looking foolish can easily be applied to these other fears. The way we work with her differs according to the depth of the relationship we have established with her.

INTERVENTIONS AT THE INITIAL STAGE

During the initial phase, our interventions are aimed at providing encouragement for Joan to say more about her fear of being seen as foolish and to talk about how this fear is affecting what she is doing in the group. We facilitate a deeper exploration of her concern in any of the following ways:

- We encourage other members to talk about any fears they have, especially their concerns over how others perceive them. If Susan also says that she fears others' reactions, we can ask her to talk directly to Joan about her fears. (Here we are teaching member-to-member interaction.)
- After the exchange between Susan and Joan we ask "Do any of the rest of you have similar feelings?" (Our aim is to involve others in this interaction by stating ways in which they identify with Susan and Joan.)
- Members who have fears that they would like to explore are invited to form a small inner group. We leave the structure open-ended, so they can talk about whatever fears they are experiencing. (In a nonthreatening way we link Joan's work with that of others, and both trust and cohesion are being established.)

INTERVENTIONS AT THE TRANSITION STAGE

If during the transition stage Joan makes the statement "I'm afraid people in here will think I'm foolish," we are likely to encourage her to identify ways in which she has already inhibited herself because of her fear. She can be asked to say *how* she experiences her particular fear in this group. Such an intervention demands more of her than our interventions at the initial stage. We ask her questions such as "When you have that fear, whom in this room are you the most aware of?" "What are your fears about?" "How have your fears stopped you in this group?" "What are some of the things you've been thinking and feeling but haven't expressed?" "What do you fear would happen if people perceived you as being foolish?" We also suggest to Joan that she speak to the people whom she feels most foolish around and tell them what she imagines they are thinking and feeling about her. In this way we get her to acknowledge her possible projections and to learn how to check out her assumptions. We are also gathering data that can be useful for exploration later in the group.

We can bring group members into this interaction by inviting them to give their reactions to what Joan has just said. The interchange between her and other members can lead to further exploration. She has probably created some distance between herself and others in the group by avoiding them out of fear of their negative reactions. By talking about her reactions to others, she is taking responsibility for the distance she has partially created. She can work out a new stance with those whom she has been avoiding.

The work that we have just described could be done during any stage. What makes this scenario characteristic of the transition stage is the fact that members are beginning to express reaction and perceptions that they have been aware of but have kept to themselves.

INTERVENTIONS AT THE WORKING STAGE

If Joan discloses her fear during the working stage, we look for ways to involve the entire group in her work. Members may acknowledge how they feel put off by her, how they feel judged by her, or how they harbor angry feelings toward her. By expressing feelings that they have kept to themselves, they are moving out of the transition stage and into the working stage. They acknowledge reactions and perceptions, clear up projections and misunderstandings, and work through conflict. The group can get stuck in the transition stage if people do not go further and express reactions that have undermined their level of trust. What moves the group into the working stage is the members' commitment to work through an impasse.

We can use other techniques to help Joan attain a deeper level of self-exploration. One is to ask her to identify people in her life with whom she has felt foolish, allowing her to connect her past struggles to her present ones. We may then ask her to tell some members how she has felt toward significant people in her life. She may even let others in the group "become" these significant figures and may say things to them that she has kept to herself. Of course, doing this may well serve as a catalyst for getting others to talk about their unfinished business with important figures in their life.

Other strategies we might use include:

- Joan can be invited to simply talk more about what it is like for her to be in this group with these fears: "How have your fears been affecting you in here? What have you wanted to say or do that you were afraid to say or do? If you didn't have the fear of looking foolish, how might you be different in this group?"
- Joan can role-play with a member who reminds her of her mother, who often cautioned her about making a fool of herself.
- Joan can write an uncensored letter to her mother, which she does not mail.
- By using role reversal, Joan can "become" her mother and then go around to each person in the room, telling them how they are foolish.

- She can monitor her own behavior between group sessions, taking special note of those situations in daily life in which she stops herself because of her fear of looking foolish.
- Using cognitive procedures, Joan can pay more attention to her self-talk and eventually learn to give herself new messages. Instead of accepting self-defeating messages, she can begin to say constructive things to herself. She can change her negative beliefs and expectancies to positive ones.
- She can make decisions to try new behavior during the group, giving herself full permission to be foolish.
- Both in the group and in daily life, Joan can make a contract to forge ahead with what she wants to say or do in spite of fears she may have about being seen as foolish.

As can be seen, our interventions in working with Joan's fear are geared to the level of trust that has been established in the group, the quality of our relationship with her, and the stage of the group's development. In the later stage of a group we are inclined to emphasize the importance of her reviewing what she has learned, how she acquired these insights, and how she can continue to translate her insights into behavioral changes outside of the group. We hope Joan has learned the value of checking out her assumptions with others before deciding that they are true. We challenge her to continue acting in new ways, even if this means putting herself in places where she runs the risk of looking foolish. By now Joan may have developed the personal strength to challenge her fears rather than allowing herself to be controlled by them.

CHARACTERISTICS OF THE WORKING STAGE

After the tentativeness of the initial stage and the expression of feelings and difficulties in the transition stage, the working stage is characterized by the commitment of members to explore significant problems they bring to the sessions and their attention to the dynamics within the group. At this time in a group's evolution, we find that our degree of structuring and intervention is lower than during the initial and transition stages. By the working stage, participants have learned how to involve themselves in group interactions, rather than waiting to be invited into an interaction. In a sense there is a sharing of the group-leadership functions, for the members are able to assume greater responsibility for the work that occurs. This does not mean that the members become co-leaders. It does imply that they initiate work more readily, bring themselves into the work of others without waiting for the leader to call on them, and offer personal feedback to others.

GROUP NORMS AND BEHAVIOR

During the working stage there is a further development and solidifica-tion of group norms that were formed in the earlier stages. Members are more aware of facilitative behaviors, and unspoken norms become more explicit. At this time the following group behaviors tend to be manifested:

- Members are provided with both support and challenge; they are re-inforced for making behavioral changes both inside and outside of the sessions.
- The leader employs a variety of therapeutic interventions, designed to further self-exploration, that lead to experimentation with new be-havior.
- Members increasingly interact with one another in more direct ways; there is less dependence on the leader for direction and less eye con-tact directed toward the leader as the members talk.
- Control issues, power struggles, and interpersonal conflicts within the group are frequently the basis of discussion and tend to be explored on a deeper level. Members learn about how they deal with conflict in everyday situations by paying attention to how they inter-act with one another in the group.
- A healing capacity develops within the group as members increas-ingly experience acceptance of who they are. There is less need to put up facades, for members are learning that they are respected for show-ing deeper facets of themselves.

Group cohesion, a primary characteristic of a well-functioning group, actually fosters action-oriented behaviors such as self-disclosure, giving and receiving feedback, discussion of here-and-now interactions, con-frontation, and translating insight into action.

Though cohesion is necessary for effective group work, it is not suffi-cient. Some groups make an implicit decision to stop at the level of com-fort and security and do not push ahead to new levels. Groups can reach a plateau unless members are willing to confront one another. In an effec-tive group the cohesion that has developed marks the beginning of a lengthy working process.

In the next section, we provide a further discussion of the factors that differentiate a working group from a nonworking one.

CONTRASTS BETWEEN A WORKING GROUP AND A NONWORKING GROUP

The following lists represent our view of some basic differences between productive and nonproductive groups. As you study the lists, think of any other factors you could add. If you are or have been in a group, think about how these characteristics apply to your group experience.

Working Group

Members trust other members and the leaders, or at least they openly express any lack of trust. There is a willingness to take risks by sharing meaningful here-and-now reactions.

Goals are clear and specific and are determined jointly by the members and the leader. There is a willingness to direct group behavior toward realizing these goals.

Most members feel a sense of inclusion, and excluded members are invited to become more active. Communication among most members is open and involves accurate expression of what is being experienced.

There is a focus on the here and now, and participants talk directly to one another about what they're experiencing.

The leadership functions are shared by the group; people feel free to initiate activities or to suggest exploring particular areas.

There is a willingness to risk disclosing threatening material; people become known.

Cohesion is high; there is a close emotional bond among people based on sharing universal human experiences. Members identify with one another. People are willing to risk experimental behavior because of the closeness and support for new ways of being.

Conflict among members or with the leader is recognized, discussed, and often resolved.

Nonworking Group

Mistrust is evidenced by an undercurrent of unexpressed hostility. Members withhold themselves, refusing to express feelings and thoughts.

Goals are fuzzy, abstract, and general. Members have unclear personal goals or no goals at all.

Many members feel excluded or cannot identify with other members. Cliques are formed that tend to lead to fragmentation. There is fear of expressing feelings of being left out.

People tend to focus on others and not on themselves, and storytelling is typical. There is a resistance to dealing with reactions to one another.

Members lean on the leaders for all direction. There are power conflicts among members as well as between members and the leader.

Participants hold back, and disclosure is at a minimum.

Fragmentation exists; people feel distant from one another. There is a lack of caring or empathy. Members don't encourage one another to engage in new and risky behavior, so familiar ways of being are rigidly maintained.

Conflicts or negative feelings are ignored, denied, or avoided.

Working Group

Members accept the responsibility for deciding what action they will take to solve their problems.

Feedback is given freely and accepted without defensiveness. There is a willingness to seriously reflect on the accuracy of the feedback.

Members feel hopeful; they feel that constructive change is possible—that people can become what they want to become.

Confrontation occurs in such a way that the confronter shares his or her reactions to the person being confronted. Confrontation is accepted as a challenge to examine one's behavior and not as an uncaring attack.

Communication is clear and direct.

Group members use one another as a resource and show interest in one another.

Members feel powerful and share this power *with* one another.

There is an awareness of group process, and members know what makes the group productive or nonproductive.

Diversity is encouraged, and there is a respect for individual and cultural differences.

Group norms are developed cooperatively by the members and the leader. Norms are clear and are designed to help the members attain their goals.

There is an emphasis on combining the feeling and thinking functions. Catharsis and expression of feeling occur, but so does thinking about the mening of various emotional experiences.

Nonworking Group

Members blame others for their personal difficulties and aren't willing to take action to change.

What little feedback is given is rejected defensively. Feedback is given without care or compassion.

Members feel despairing, helpless, trapped, and victimized.

Confrontation is done in a hostile, attacking way; the confronted one feels judged and rejected. At times the members gang up on a member, using this person as a scapegoat.

Communication is unclear and indirect.

Members are interested only in themselves.

Members or leaders use power and control *over* others.

There is an indifference or lack of awareness of what is going on within the group, and group dynamics are rarely discussed.

Conformity is prized, and individual and cultural differences are devalued.

Norms are merely imposed by the leader. They may not be clear.

The group relies heavily on cathartic experiences but makes little or no effort to understand them.

Working Group	**Nonworking Group**
Group members use out-of-group time to work on problems raised in the group.	Group members think about group activity very little when they're outside the group.

THE NONWORKING GROUP MEMBER

Having described the characteristics of a working and nonworking group in general, we now move to specifics. In the previous chapter we examined a variety of problem behaviors, and what follows is a composite picture of a nonworking group member.

Barney has joined a weekly ongoing group because his wife thinks he needs such an experience. Although he agreed to sign up for the group, he had many doubts that it would help him. He was convinced that groups do more harm than good.

Barney keeps all his reservations to himself. For several group sessions he either says nothing or reacts in a hostile manner to many of the women. When several of them let him know that they are feeling distant and are having difficulties with him, he reacts sarcastically and defensively by saying: "Well, aren't you supposed to be honest in here? What's wrong with my saying that you girls are all alike?"

At one point, tears come to Barney's eyes, and he looks very scared. When the leader checks with him about what he is feeling, he replies: "Stop pushing me, and leave me alone. All you ever do is make people cry." After that he storms out of the room.

Barney often talks about his wife, blaming her for most of his misery. When the leader suggests a role-playing exercise in which he could talk directly to his "wife" in this room, Barney refuses by saying: "That's silly. I can't talk to Bertha [a group member], because she's not my wife." At times he comes late to sessions or misses a session, either having a "good" excuse or simply not giving any reason.

Several times, toward the end of a session, Barney begins what could become some meaningful work. The leader lets him know of her concern that time is running out and makes the observation that his waiting until the end seems to be a pattern. He brusquely responds: "You don't care about me the way you do about the rest of the people. I can't program my feelings."

Although in some sessions Barney says almost nothing and expects to be drawn out, at other times he interrupts others' work by giving them unsolicited advice and solutions to their problems. He then rambles on with stories about himself. When confronted on his behavior, Barney replies, aggressively, "When I don't talk, you criticize me, and when I do talk, you want to shut me up!" He makes no attempt to listen to any constructive feedback given to him, and he is always quick to take a defensive stance.

When conflict arises in the group, Barney is quick to note: "See, I was right. All groups ever do is tear people down." He is very able to stir up conflict in his group, yet he quickly retreats in a hit-and-run fashion. At one point he admits that he feels isolated in this group, as well as in his outside life. But he is unable to see how his behavior contributes to his feelings of isolation.

In considering Barney's case, how might you deal with him? Which of his behaviors would cause you the most difficulty? Would you have let him into the group to begin with? On what basis would you have included or excluded him at the outset? Would you have excluded him later, after he had joined the group? If so, how would you go about doing this?

THE WORKING GROUP MEMBER

Now we describe the combination of traits that we think makes for a working and productive group member. We encourage you to create your own profile of the ideal group participant. Our ideal member is a woman we'll call Sandy.

Sandy wants to participate in a weekly, ongoing counseling group. She wants to take a good look at herself, her marriage, her career goals, and her relationship with her son, and she wants to discover more ways of feeling alive. She has sought group counseling voluntarily. She is motivated to work, as evidenced by her willingness to spend time thinking about what she wants from her group sessions. She eventually forms a contract that guides her work in the group. She is specific about what she wants, and she is willing to explore her problems with the group.

Sandy is sometimes scared by her feelings, and she expresses these fears. For example, she sometimes doubts that she wants to stay with her husband, and she's willing to face this issue squarely.

Sandy says what she feels, not what others in her group (including the therapist) might expect of her. She confronts both leader and members when she feels that something needs to be challenged, and she does so by bringing her own reactions into the confrontation. She avoids labeling or judging and instead speaks of how she is affected by what others are doing in the group. Sandy gives feedback when she has something to offer and gives support or affection when she genuinely feels this toward another member. She resists participating in activities that don't seem right for her, and she is not pressured into doing or saying something to please anyone but herself. During the group sessions she listens undefensively to what others tell her, and when she is given feedback, she doesn't try to rationalize her behavior. Instead, she considers the feedback seriously. Then she decides for herself how accurate others' perceptions of her are and what she will do with this information.

Sandy devotes time between sessions to reflecting on her involvement in the group, and she eventually makes decisions to change her behavior. She not only tries out new behavior in her group but also risks applying what she has learned in the group to her daily affairs. In between sessions she reads books dealing with areas of struggle for her and keeps a daily journal. She brings into therapy any insights she has about herself or about the group. She commits herself to doing things actively outside her group, yet at times she doesn't live up to these contracts. If she feels that she's backsliding, she mentions this in her sessions. At this point she evaluates her contract and determines how realistic her expectations are. Sandy realizes that she's not perfect, yet she accepts herself.

GROUP PROCESS DURING THE WORKING STAGE

Even if groups reach a high level of productivity during the working stage, this achievement does not imply that the group will always remain at that level. The group may stay on a plateau for a time and then regress to an earlier developmental phase characterized by issues faced during the initial and transition stages. For example, trust can become an issue again, and it may need to be reestablished. Some members may have the tendency to close off and withdraw. The reasons for this lack of trust may be that intensive work threatens them, that they have doubts about the validity of what they have experienced, that they have second thoughts about how involved they want to remain, that they are frightened by the display of anger between members or the expression of painful experiences, or that they are anticipating the eventual ending of the group and are prematurely winding down.

As is the case with personal relationships in daily life, groups ebb and flow. Periods of stagnation can be expected, but if they are recognized, they can be challenged. Because groups are not static entities, both the leader and the members have the task of accurately assessing a group's ever-changing character, as well as its effectiveness.

The reality of the changing character of trust within a group is illustrated in the following example of an adolescent group. Members had done some productive work, both with individuals outside of the group and with one another during the sessions. At one previous meeting, several members experienced intense emotional catharsis. Felix, who had initially identified his worst fear as "breaking down and crying in front of everyone," did cry and released some stored-up pain over being denied his father's acceptance. In role playing with his "father," Felix became angry and told him how hurt he felt because of his seeming indifference. Later in this scenario, he cried and told his "father" that he really loved him. Before he left the session, Felix said that he felt relieved.

The particular session just described was characterized by a high level of trust, risk taking, caring, and cohesion. At the subsequent session, however, the group leader was surprised at how difficult it was to draw people out. Members were hesitant to speak. Felix, other than saying

"Hello," said little else. The leader described what she saw in the room and asked the members why it seemed so hard to talk, especially in light of the fact that the previous session had gone so well. At first, several members expressed annoyance by making comments such as: "Do we always have to bring up problems in here?" "Can't we talk about something other than problems?" "Do we need to cry to show that we're good members?" "I think you're pushing people too hard." Felix finally admitted that he had felt very embarrassed over "breaking down" and that during the week he had convinced himself that others saw him as weak and foolish. Some others admitted that although they saw value in what Felix had done, they would not want to go through what he had out of fear of what others might think of them. Again, the task of this group was to deal with the lack of trust that members had in one another ("I'm afraid what others will think of me"). Several of the members' statements implied a lack of trust in the leader, which made it imperative that she encourage the members to discuss this dynamic.

In retrospect, what could the leader have done differently? It is possible that Felix might have felt less embarrassed had the leader remembered his original fear and dealt with it. She might have said: "Felix, I remember that one of your fears was crying in the presence of others. You just did. How was it for you to have done this?" She could also have invited others to tell him how they had been affected by his work. Assume that Felix had said "I feel good, and I got a lot from what I did." Then, she might have replied: "Imagine two days from now, when you think about what you did this morning. Could it be possible that you might regret what you've done or that you might be critical of yourself?" If Felix had replied with a smile, saying "You may be right," she could have suggested that if he caught himself discounting his work, it would be helpful to remember the support he had felt from everyone in the room and how they had acknowledged his courage.

On the other hand, assume that Felix had responded to the leader's inquiry by saying "I feel embarrassed" and looking down at the floor. She might have replied: "I know how hard it was for you to express yourself in this way. I really hope you won't run away. Look at different people in this room, especially the ones whom you feel most embarrassed with. What do you imagine they're saying about you right now?" After Felix told others what he imagined they were thinking of him, they could be invited to give their honest reactions. Typically, members do not have disparaging remarks after someone has done significant work.

As this example shows, it is not uncommon for the issue of trust to resurface in an intense and productive session. After times like this, members may be frightened and may have a tendency to retreat. Leaders who are aware of this tendency can take some preventive measures, as we have described. When a group does appear to regress, the most critical intervention is for the leader to describe what is happening and to get members to express what they are thinking and feeling.

CHOICES TO BE MADE DURING THE WORKING STAGE

In discussing the initial stages of a group's evolution, we described several critical issues, such as trust versus mistrust, the struggle for power, and self-focus versus focus on others. During the more intensive working period of a group, certain other key issues are at stake, and again the group as a whole must resolve the issues for better or worse. We now discuss each of the choices a group must make at this stage. Remember that a group's identity is shaped by the way its members resolve these critical issues.

Disclosure versus Anonymity   Clients can decide to disclose themselves in a significant and appropriate way, or they can choose to remain hidden out of fear that if they were to reveal themselves to others, they would be rejected. People may protect themselves through anonymity, yet the very reason that many become involved in a therapeutic group is that they want to make themselves known to others and to come to know others in a deeper way. If the group process is to work effectively, the participants must be willing to reveal themselves, for it is through self-disclosure that they begin to learn about themselves.

Honesty versus Game Playing   Some people believe that to survive in the real world they must sacrifice their honesty and substitute deceit, game playing, and manipulation. They may say that to get ahead they have to suppress what they really think and feel, figure out what others expect from them, and then meet those expectations.

It is fundamental to the success of a therapeutic group that honesty prevail and that a person not have to be dishonest to win acceptance. If these conditions hold, participants can both be themselves and learn to accept the true selves of others. If they don't, group interaction can deteriorate into another form of game playing. However, honesty does not mean saying anything and everything to another person (or about oneself). Saying "I hate the sight of you" is not honest, it is cruel. As one of our colleagues says, "Honesty without caring is cruelty."

Spontaneity versus Control   We hope that group participants will make the choice to relinquish some of their controlled and rehearsed ways and allow themselves to respond more spontaneously to events of the moment. We encourage spontaneity indirectly, by making clients feel that it's all right to say and do many of the things they've been preventing themselves from saying or doing. This does not mean that members "do their own thing" at the expense of others. Members sometimes stifle themselves by rehearsing endlessly everything they say. As a result, they often sit quietly and rehearse internally. We generally make contracts with clients like this. We get them to agree to rehearse out loud and to speak more freely, even at the risk of not making sense.

Acceptance versus Rejection   Throughout the course of a group the members frequently deal with the acceptance/rejection polarity. We sometimes hear a member say "I'd like to reveal more of myself, but I'm afraid that if I'm me in here, I'll be rejected." The basis of this fear can be explored, which often results in challenging unrealistic fears. Members are likely to find that they reject themselves more often than others reject them. These members may also discover that they are frightened about the prospects of being accepted, as well as of being rejected. Although they do not enjoy rejection, it has often become a familiar feeling. Therefore, feelings of acceptance can be unsettling. It's as though some say "If you accept me or love me or care for me, I won't know how to respond."

The group setting offers people opportunities to learn some of these ways in which they are setting themselves up to be rejected by behaving in certain ways. We hope that group members will recognize their own role and responsibility in the creation of an accepting climate and come to understand that by contributing to a climate either of acceptance or of rejection, they can help determine whether they as individuals will be accepted or rejected.

Cohesion versus Fragmentation   Our conviction is that cohesion is largely the result of the group's choice to work actively at developing unifying bonds. Members do this mainly by choosing to make themselves known to others, by sharing their pain, by allowing caring to develop, by initiating meaningful work, and by giving honest feedback to others.

If a group chooses to remain comfortable or to stick with superficial interactions, there will be little group togetherness. There are times when members choose not to express their fears, suspicions, disappointments, and doubts. When they do bury their reactions, fragmentation typically results. Cohesion comes from working with meaningful, painful problems as well as from intimately sharing humorous and joyous moments.

Responsibility versus Blaming   In any form of therapy, clients must accept responsibility for their behavior if any significant behavior changes are to take place. Thus, group members must stop viewing themselves as victims of external factors.

At some point in group work, clients typically focus their anger on others, whom they blame for their unhappiness. But during the more intensive phases of a group, clients generally come to accept the fact that a blaming style will get them nowhere. What they need to realize is that they can change only themselves. If they do succeed in changing, others may change in response. When members stop blaming others, they find that they are in control and are more able to make changes in their lives.

Consider a mother, Christie, who complains endlessly about her husband and her children taking advantage of her. She often exclaims "If only they were different, my life would be so much better!" She could be challenged to consider the reality that her family is not likely to change. If she focuses on blaming others and getting them to be different, she will keep herself in a powerless position. Christie is the one who will have to be different. She will need to say no, set firm limits, follow through with consequences, and learn to live with the fact that she may not always be liked by her family.

THERAPEUTIC FACTORS THAT OPERATE IN GROUPS

In this section we give attention to the special forces within groups that produce constructive changes. We've come to believe that a variety of forces within groups can be healing, or therapeutic, and that these forces are interrelated. We came up with the therapeutic factors listed below by reflecting on our experiences in leading groups and by reading the reports of hundreds of people who have participated in our groups. (We've always had the participants in our groups write follow-up reaction papers telling what factors they think were related to their changes in attitudes and behavior.) We are also indebted to other writers in the field of group work, especially Yalom (1983, 1995).

SELF-DISCLOSURE

The willingness to make oneself known to others is part of each stage of a group, but at the working stage self-disclosure is more frequent and more personal. Although disclosure is not an end in itself, it is the means by which open communication occurs within the group. Through this process, the participants experience a healing force and gain new insights that often lead to desired life changes. If disclosures are limited to safe topics, the group does not progress beyond a superficial level.

SELF-DISCLOSURE AND THE GROUP MEMBER

Group members are able to deepen their self-knowledge through disclosing themselves to others. They develop a richer and more integrated picture of who they are, and they are better able to recognize the impact they have on others.

We tell the members of our groups that it is essential to let others know about them. Otherwise, they are likely to be misunderstood, because people tend to project their own feelings onto members who are mysterious. For example, Andrea thinks that Hal is very critical and judgmental of her. When Hal finally talks, he discloses that he is both attracted to and fearful of Andrea. Self-disclosure entails revealing current struggles with unresolved personal issues; goals and aspirations; fears and expectations; hopes, pains, and joys; strengths and weaknesses; and personal experiences. If members keep themselves anonymous and say little about themselves that is personal, it is difficult for others to care for them, because genuine concern implies knowledge of the person. This disclosure is not limited to revealing personal concerns; it is equally important to disclose ongoing persistent reactions toward other members and the leader.

What Disclosure Is Not   We've found that group participants frequently misunderstand what it means to be a self-disclosing person, equating disclosure with "letting it all hang out" without any discrimination. They may believe that the more they can dig up hidden secrets and display them in the group, the more they are being disclosing. Below are some observations on what self-disclosure is *not*.

- Self-disclosure is not merely telling stories about one's past in a rehearsed and mechanical manner. It is not a mere reporting of there-and-then events. A client needs to ask the question "How is what I reveal related to my present conflicts?"
- In the name of being open and honest and as a result of the pressure of other group members, people often say more than is necessary for others to understand them. They confuse being self-disclosing with being open to the extent that nothing remains private, and as a result they may feel exposed in front of others.
- Dumping every fleeting feeling or reaction on others is not to be confused with self-disclosure. Judgment is needed in deciding how appropriate it is to share certain reactions. However, persistent reactions are generally best shared. People can be honest without being tactless and insensitive.

Guidelines for Appropriate Member Self-Disclosure   In our groups we suggest the following five guidelines as a way of assisting participants in determining *what* and *when* self-disclosure is both appropriate and facilitative.

1. Disclosure needs to be related to the purposes and goals of the group.
2. If members have persistent reactions to certain people in the group, we encourage them to bring them out into the open, especially if these reactions are inhibiting their level of participation.
3. Members must determine what and how much they want others to know about them. They also have to decide what they are willing to risk and how far they are willing to go.

4. Reasonable risks can be expected to accompany self-disclosure. If groups are limited by overly safe disclosures, the interactions become boring.

5. The stage of group development has some bearing on the appropriateness of self-disclosure. Certain disclosures may be too deep for an initial session but quite appropriate during the working stage.

Related to the issue of member self-disclosure is the role of self-disclosures by the leader. We now turn to some guidelines designed to assist leaders in thinking about what disclosures can have a facilitative effect on a group.

SELF-DISCLOSURE AND THE GROUP LEADER

The key question is not whether leaders should disclose themselves to the group but, rather, how much and when. What are the effects of leaders' disclosures on the group? What are the effects on the leader?

Some group leaders keep themselves mysterious. They're careful not to make themselves personally known to the group, and they strive to keep their personal involvement in the group to a minimum. Some do this because of a theoretical preference. They view their role as one of a "transference figure" on whom their "patients" can project feelings that they've experienced toward parents and other "authority figures." By remaining anonymous, the leader tends to limit the reactions of group members to projections. Through this re-creation of an earlier relationship, unresolved conflicts can be exposed and worked through.

Other reasons some group leaders don't reveal themselves personally are that they don't want to incur the risk of losing their "professional" image and that they don't want to be uncomfortable. They may also operate on the assumption that personal disclosure would contaminate the therapeutic relationship. Some leaders, in addition to keeping their personal lives a secret, disclose very little about how they feel in the group or how they feel toward different members. Instead of sharing these reactions, they intervene, making interpretations and suggestions, clarifying issues, acting as a moderator or coordinator, evaluating, and imposing structured exercises to keep the group moving. Admittedly, all of these functions are necessary at various times, but it is both possible and desirable for leaders to get involved in these activities by revealing what they are experiencing in this process.

What about the leaders at the other end of the continuum, whose ethic is the more disclosure, the better? Inexperienced group leaders tend to make the mistake of trying too hard to prove that they're just as human as the members. They freely disclose details of their personal lives and explore their current problems in the groups they lead. There are several rationales for such an approach. These leaders may have submitted to group pressure to stop acting like a leader and become more of a group member. They may also feel that it is unfair to expect members to disclose and risk unless they are also willing to do so. Although this reasoning has merit, it is important that group leaders not fall into the trap of pretending that there are no differences between the roles and functions of leaders and members. Even though group leaders can function as participants at times, their primary reason for being in the group is to initiate, facilitate, direct, and evaluate the process of interaction among members. If leaders are uncomfortable in this role, perhaps this is an indication that they should be participating in a group as a full-fledged member.

Following are four guidelines for your consideration in determining your own position on the issue of leader self-disclosure.

1. If you determine that you have problems you wish to explore, consider finding your own therapeutic group. This would allow you to be a fully participating member without the concern of how your personal work would affect the group. You have a demanding job and shouldn't make it even more difficult by confusing your role with that of the participants.

2. Ask yourself why you're disclosing certain personal material. Is it to be seen as a "regular person," no different from the members? Is it to model disclosing behavior for others? Is it because you genuinely want to show private dimensions to the members? It may be therapeutic for group members to know you and your struggles, but they don't need to know in elaborate detail. For instance, if a member is exploring her fear of not being loved unless she is perfect, you might reveal in a few words that you also wrestle with this fear, if indeed you do. Your sharing makes it possible for your client to feel a sense of identification with you. At another time it may be appropriate for you to talk at greater length about how this fear is manifested in the way you lead groups, particularly if it is revealed in your feeling pressured to be a good therapist and feeling afraid of not being loved if you do not help the group. Again, the timing is crucial, as is being true to yourself and doing what is compatible with your personal therapeutic style. Although this disclosure may be appropriate in the advanced stages of a group, sharing it initially may burden the participants with the feeling that they should help you or should take your pain away.

3. Disclosure that is related to what is going on in the group is the most productive. For instance, any persistent feelings you have about a member or about what is happening (or not happening) is generally best revealed. If you feel annoyed at a member's behavior, it is usually advisable to let the member know your reaction. If you sense a general resistance in the group, it is best to talk openly about the resistance and about how it feels to experience it. Disclosure related to how you feel in the group is generally more appropriate than disclosure of personal material that is not relevant to the ongoing interaction of the group.

4. Ask yourself how much you want to reveal about your private life to the many people with whom you will come into contact. In our workshops, other groups, and classes we want to feel the freedom to function

openly as people, but at the same time we want to preserve a measure of our privacy. Moreover, if we made it a pattern to give detailed accounts about ourselves, we would lose spontaneity, for it would probably be impossible with this kind of repetition to maintain a fresh and unrehearsed style. Having said this, we hasten to add that we see ourselves as generally being personal in our groups. We are not overly concerned when people in our groups come to know about us as individuals and as a couple. We also usually decide to disclose worries or preoccupations we have that could interfere with our ability to be present and to listen effectively to the members.

CONFRONTATION

As was discussed in both Chapters 5 and 6, constructive confrontation is a basic part of a productive group. A lack of confrontation results in stagnation. It is through acts of caring confrontation that members are invited to examine discrepancies between what they say and do, to become aware of potentials that are dormant, and to find ways of putting their insights into action. Done with sensitivity, confrontation by others ultimately assists members to develop the capacity for the self-confrontation they will need in applying what they have learned to the problems they face in their daily lives.

Example: Rich complained of feeling tired and drained. He asserted that everyone in his life was too demanding. In the group, his style of interacting involved being a helper. He was attentive to what others needed, yet he rarely asked anything for himself. In one session he finally admitted that he was not getting what he wanted from the group and that he did not feel like returning again. The leader confronted Rich with: "I have seen you do many times in this group what you say you typically do with people in your life. I see you as being very helpful, yet you rarely ask for anything for yourself. I'm not surprised about your resistance over coming back to this group. You've created the same environment in here as the one at home. I'm glad you're finally talking about this, and I hope you'll continue talking."

FEEDBACK

One of the most important ways by which learning takes place in a group is through the willingness of members to give and to receive feedback. If feedback is given honestly and with sensitivity, members are able to understand the impact they have on others and decide what, if anything, they want to change about their interpersonal style. The process of interpersonal feedback teaches members that they are responsible for creating favorable and unfavorable outcomes and for changing the style in which they relate to others (Rothke, 1986).

Although feedback as a process in groups is given further consideration in the next chapter, we want to discuss some guidelines for effective feedback during the working stage. Below are some ideas that are modified from Rothke's (1986) article on the role of interpersonal feedback in group psychotherapy, as well as some of the key points we emphasize in teaching members how to give and receive feedback:

- Concise feedback given in a clear and straightforward manner is more helpful than statements with qualifiers. For instance, Brenda is being quite clear and direct with Brian when she tells him: "I feel uncomfortable when I'm sharing very personal things about myself and I see you smiling. It makes me wonder if you're taking me seriously."
- Give others feedback throughout the course of a group. In doing so, share with them how they affect you, rather than giving them advice or judging them. In the example above, Brenda is speaking about her own discomfort and how she is affected by Brian's smiling, rather than telling Brian how he is.
- Avoid giving global feedback, for it is of little value. Feedback that relates to specific behavior exhibited in the group provides members with helpful information that they can consider using. Feedback that is particularly helpful deals with immediate events in the group. With this kind of here-and-now feedback, others in the group can confirm the message that is being sent, or they can offer a different perception.
- Feedback must be timed well and given in a nonjudgmental way, or else the person receiving it is likely to become defensive and reject it. In Brenda's case, her feedback to Brian is focused on her feelings, and it represents a risky self-disclosure. She is not judging Brian, which increases the chance that he will be able to consider what she is telling him.
- The most meaningful kind of feedback deals with the relationship between the sender and the receiver. For instance, in giving feedback to Brian, Brenda might add: "I really do want your acceptance, and I'd like to feel closer to you. But I'm aware that I'm careful what I say when I'm around you, because I'm afraid that you might be judging me. When you look away and either smile or frown when I talk, I'm left wondering how what I'm saying affects you. I'd like not to feel so cautious around you, and this is why I'm telling you this." With this kind of statement, Brenda is talking about her feelings of fear and uncertainty, but she is also letting Brian know that she would like a different kind of relationship with him.
- In giving feedback, concentrate on what you like about a person and on the person's strengths as well as the difficulties you might be experiencing with this person. This is not to imply that you should sugarcoat your message, but it is also a good idea to focus on strengths and how people might be blocking them.

Examples: Members sometimes make a sweeping declaration such as Florian's comment: "I'd like to know what you think of me, and I'd like some feedback!" His spontaneous request puts people in the group on the spot. He has hit the ball into their court. If we were to hear this, we would probably say to the group "Before any of you give Florian feedback, we'd like him to say more about what prompted him to ask for your reactions." This intervention puts the ball back into Florian's court, for he will be making significant disclosures about himself rather than insisting that others disclose themselves to him first. Members are more likely to respond to him when they know more about his needs for their feedback. Behind his question may well be any of these statements: "I'm afraid in here, and I don't know if I'm liked." "I'm afraid people in here are judging me." "I don't have many friends in my life, and it's important that people like me." If Florian has said very little about himself, it is difficult to give him many reactions. To find out how others perceive him, it is necessary that he let himself be known. After he has explored his need for feedback, the group leader can ask members if they want to react to him. However, the leader should not pressure everyone in the group to give him their comments. When people do offer their reactions, the leader can ask Florian to listen nondefensively, to hear what others have to say to him, and to consider what, if anything, he may want to do with this information. As the group progresses to a working stage, we typically see a willingness of members to freely give one another their reactions. Feedback is at its best when members spontaneously let others know how they are affected by them and their work. The norm of asking for, receiving, and giving feedback is one that needs to be established early in a group. Furthermore, it is the leader's task to teach members how to give useful feedback, which can be done by giving examples of both appropriate and inappropriate feedback.

Joseph's situation is an example of how feedback can be helpful in teaching a member about specific behaviors that others are reacting to negatively. Joseph joined a group because he found himself isolated from people. Soon he found that he felt isolated in the group also. He was sarcastic with everyone in his group, a trait that quickly alienated others. Because the members were willing to tell him in a caring way that they felt put off and distanced by his sarcastic style, he was able to examine and eventually assume responsibility for creating the distance and lack of intimacy he typically experienced. With the encouragement of his group, he sought out his son, toward whom he felt much anger. He found that when he let go of his sarcasm and talked honestly with his son, his son was willing to listen and they felt closer to each other.

COHESION AND UNIVERSALITY

A central characteristic of the working stage is group cohesion, which results from members' willingness to let others know them in meaningful ways. If they have faced the conflicts of the earlier stages, the deep level of trust they have developed allows for a working-through process.

At the working stage the members are able to see commonalities, and they are struck by the universality of their life issues. For example, our growth groups are composed of a very wide mixture of people. The clients come from all walks of life, their age range is from 18 to 65 years, they represent various social and cultural backgrounds, and they have a variety of careers. Although in the earlier stages members are likely to be aware of their differences and at times feel separated, as the group achieves increased cohesion, these differences recede into the background. Members comment more on how they are alike than on how they are different. A woman in her early 50s discovers that she is still striving for parental approval, just as is a man in his early 20s. A man learns that his struggles with masculinity are not that different from a woman's concern about her femininity.

The circumstances leading to hurt and disappointment may be very different from person to person or from culture to culture. But the resulting emotions have a universal quality. Although we may not speak the same language or come from the same society, we are connected through our feelings of joy and pain. It is when group members no longer get lost in the details of daily experiences and instead share their deeper struggles with these universal human themes that a group is most cohesive. The leader can help the group achieve this level of cohesion by focusing on the underlying issues, feelings, and needs that the members seem to share.

This bonding provides the group with the impetus to move forward, for participants gain courage by discovering that they are not alone in their feelings. A woman experiences a great sense of relief when she discovers, through statements by other women, that she is not strange for feeling resentment over the many demands her family makes on her. Men find that they can share their tears and affection with other men without being robbed of their masculinity. Other common themes evolving in this stage that lead to increased cohesion and trust are members' fears of rejection, feelings of loneliness and abandonment, feelings of inferiority and failure to live up to others' expectations, painful memories, guilt and remorse over what they have and have not done, discovery that their worst enemy lives within them, need for and fear of intimacy, feelings about sexual identity and sexual performance, and unfinished business with their parents. This list is not exhaustive but merely a sample of the universal human issues that participants recognize and explore with one another as the group progresses. Earlier we discussed group cohesion as an achievement of the initial stage of a group. The cohesion that is characteristic of the working stage is a deeper intimacy that develops with time and commitment. This bonding is a form of affection and genuine caring that often results from sharing the expression of painful experiences.

Example: A couple of women, both of whom immigrated to this country, express the pain they feel over having left their own countries.

Until this time, they had felt rather isolated from other group members. Sharing their struggle touched just about everyone in the group. Members could identify with their pain and loss even though they did not share the same experiences. Not only was the work of these two women productive for them but it stimulated other members to talk about times in their lives when they felt deep loss. During closure of the session, as members made comments about how they were affected by the meeting, they talked about how close they felt and the bond of trust that had developed. Despite having different backgrounds, these group members were brought together by a deeply personal sharing of common themes and feelings.

HOPE

Hope is the belief that change is possible—that one is not a victim of the past and can make new decisions. Hope is therapeutic in itself, for it gives members confidence that they have the power to choose to be different. Some people approach a group convinced that they are victims of external circumstances over which they have no control. At times members who are mandated to attend group may feel extremely hopeless and be convinced that nothing will really change. In the group, however, they may encounter others who have struggled and found ways to assume effective control over their lives. Seeing and being associated with such people can inspire a new sense of optimism that their lives can be different. It is imperative that leaders approach their groups with a conviction that change and a better outcome are possible.

Example: Pete, who was left paralyzed as a result of a motorcycle accident, spent most of his energies thinking about all that he could no longer do. With the encouragement of his physician, Pete joined a rehabilitation group where he met several people who had at one time felt as he was feeling. By listening to their struggles and how they had effectively coped with their disabilities, Pete found hope that he, too, could discover more effective ways of living his life.

WILLINGNESS TO RISK AND TRUST

Risking involves opening oneself to others, being vulnerable, and actively doing in a group what is necessary for change. Taking risks involves letting go of what is known and secure and moving toward uncertain terrain. If members are primarily motivated to remain comfortable, or if they are unwilling to risk challenging themselves and others, they stand to gain very little from the group. Members' willingness to reveal themselves is largely a function of how much they trust the other group members and the leader. The higher the level of trust in a group, the more likely members are to push themselves beyond their own comfort level. From the outset, members can be invited to risk by talking about their feelings of being in the group. As a few members engage in even minor risk taking, others will follow suit. By taking risks in disclosing here-and-now observations and reactions, members are actively creating trust and making it possible to engage in deeper self-exploration. Trust is therapeutic; it allows people to show the many facets of themselves, encourages experimental behavior, and allows people to look at themselves in new ways.

Example: Jane expressed considerable resentment and hostility to the men in her group. Eventually, she took the risk of disclosing that as a child she had been sexually exploited by her stepfather. As she explored ways in which she had generalized her distrust of getting close to men in everyday life and in her group, she began to see how she was keeping men at a distance so they would never again have the chance to exploit her. Finally, she made a new decision that all men would not necessarily hurt her if she allowed herself to get close to them. Had she been unwilling to risk making the disclosure in her group, it is unlikely that she would have made this attitudinal and behavioral change.

CARING AND ACCEPTANCE

Caring is demonstrated by listening and involvement. It can be expressed by tenderness, compassion, support, and even confrontation. One way that caring is demonstrated is by staying present with someone who has received some corrective feedback that was difficult to hear. If members sense a lack of caring, either from other members or from the leader, their willingness to drop their masks will be reduced. Members are able to risk being vulnerable if they sense that their concerns are important to others and that they are valued as people.

Caring implies acceptance, a genuine support from others that says, in effect: "We will accept all of your feelings. You do count here. It's acceptable to be yourself—you don't have to strive to please everyone." Acceptance involves affirming each person's right to have and express feelings and values.

Caring and acceptance develop into empathy, a deep understanding of another's struggles. Commonalities emerge in groups that unite the members. The realization that certain problems are universal—loneliness, the need for acceptance, the fear of rejection, the fear of intimacy, hurt over past experiences—lessens the feelings that we are alone. Moreover, through identification with others we are able to see ourselves more clearly.

Example: Bobby, who was in a group for children of divorce, finally began to talk about his sadness over not having his father at home anymore. Other children were very attentive. When Bobby said that he was embarrassed by his crying, two other boys told him that they also cried. This sharing of loneliness and hurt bonded the children, who learned that what they were feeling was normal.

POWER

A feeling of power emerges from the recognition that one has untapped internal reserves of spontaneity, creativity, courage, and strength. This strength is not a power over others; rather, it is the sense that one has the resources necessary to direct the course of one's life. In groups, personal power can be experienced in ways that were formerly denied, and people can discover ways in which they are blocking their strengths. Some people enter groups feeling victimized, and they cannot see any power to choose their destiny. Indeed, some of them *were* victimized by people in their lives, yet they may live with the untested assumption that the rest of the world is bent on bringing them harm. They become empowered when they realize that they can take certain steps in their current situation to make life more rewarding.

Examples: As a child, Ethyl usually got hit by her parents if she made herself visible. She made an early decision to keep a low profile to avoid being abused physically and psychologically. Through her participation in a group she discovered that she was still behaving as if everyone was out to get her, even though her defensive ways were no longer warranted. Because she chose not to make her presence known in her group, people saw her as distant, cold, and aloof. Ethyl gradually discovered that she was no longer a helpless child who could not protect herself in a cruel adult world. By challenging her assumptions and by taking risks with people in her group, she also assumed more power over how she felt about herself and how she allowed herself to be treated by others.

Another case shows how a person can learn skills that will lead to empowerment. Carl, a recovering alcoholic, admitted that he felt powerful only when he drank. In addition to his Alcoholics Anonymous group he joined an assertion-training group, where he learned social skills that helped him deal effectively with situations in which he had felt powerless. He found the courage to ask people directly for what he wanted from them, and he learned how to nonaggressively deny unreasonable requests made of him.

CATHARSIS

The expression of pent-up emotions can be therapeutic, because clients release energy that has been tied up in withholding threatening feelings. These unexpressed feelings often result in physical symptoms such as chronic headaches, stomach pains, muscle tension, and high blood pressure. At times we hear group members say that they don't want to remember painful feelings, not understanding that the body is carrying the pain and giving expression to it with various physical symptoms. When people finally do express their stored-up pain and other unexpressed feelings, they typically report a tremendous physical and emotional release.

For instance, Cheryl reported that all of her chronic neck pains were gone after she expressed some very painful feelings.

While members often report that their cathartic experiences feel good, it is unrealistic to encourage people to give vent to their pent-up emotions in everyday life. If these emotions are expressed when they have been submerged, they can be overwhelming to both the recipient and the giver. It is critical to help members learn how to monitor their emotions and express them in ways that are appropriate to the context of their encounters.

Emotional release plays an important part in many kinds of groups, and the expression of feeling can facilitate trust and cohesion. However, both group leaders and members sometimes make the mistake of concluding that only experiencing catharsis implies "real work." Members who do not have an emotional release may become convinced that they are not really getting involved. Although it is often healing, catharsis by itself is limited in terms of producing long-lasting changes. Members need to learn how to make sense of their emotional experiences, and one way of doing so is by putting words to their intense emotions and attempting to understand them.

Example: Susan learned that she could experience both love and hate toward her mother. For years she had buried her resentment over what she saw as her mother's continual attempts to control her life. In one session Susan allowed herself to feel and to fully express her resentment to her mother in a symbolic way. The group leader assisted her in telling her mother, in role playing, many of the things that had contributed to her feelings of resentment. She felt a great sense of relief after having expressed these pent-up emotions. The leader cautioned her about the dangers of repeating in real life everything that she had just said in the therapy session. It would not be necessary to harshly confront her mother and to expose the full range of her pain and anger. Instead, Susan learned that it was important to understand how her resentment toward her mother was continuing to affect her now, both in her present dealings with her mother and in her relationship to others. It was essential that Susan become clear about what she really wanted with her mother and what was still keeping her from getting closer to her. Susan can choose what she wants to tell her mother, and she can also deal with her in more direct and honest ways than she has in the past. She can be aware of and sensitive to her mother and at the same time can behave differently with her.

THE COGNITIVE COMPONENT

Members who simply *experience* feelings often have difficulty integrating what they learn from these experiences. After catharsis has occurred, it is extremely important to work through the feelings that emerged, to gain some understanding of the meaning of the experience, and also to formulate new decisions based on their understanding. Some conceptualization of the meaning of the intense feelings associated with certain experiences is essential to further deeper exploration of one's struggles. The cognitive component includes explaining, clarifying, interpreting, formulating ideas, and providing the cognitive framework for creating a new perspective on problems. Yalom (1983, 1995) cites substantial research evidence demonstrating that to profit from a group experience the members require a cognitive framework that will allow them to put their here-and-now experiencing into perspective.

Example: Earlier we described the case of Felix, an adolescent who expressed pent-up hurt. As you recall, he initially felt better after an outburst of crying, but he soon discounted the experience. Felix needed to put into words the meaning of his emotional interchange. He may have learned any of the following: that he was storing up feelings of anger toward his father, that he had a mixture of resentment and love for his father, that he had made a decision that his father would never change, that there were many things he could say to his father, or that there were numerous ways that he could act differently with his father. It was therapeutically important for him to release his bottled-up emotions. It was also essential that he clarify his insights and discover ways to use them to improve his relationship with his father.

COMMITMENT TO CHANGE

The commitment to change involves members' being willing to make use of the tools offered by group process to explore ways of modifying their behavior. If group members are motivated to become active participants, the groundwork has been laid for change to occur. But participants need to formulate action plans and strategies to employ in their day-to-day existence to implement change. Members need to learn how to evaluate the effectiveness of their plans, and the group affords them the opportunity to plan realistically and responsibly through contact with both the other members and the group leader. It is crucial for members to commit themselves to following through on their plans, and the group itself can help members develop the motivation to follow through with their commitments. If members find that carrying out some of their plans is difficult or if they do not do what they had planned, it is essential that they talk about their difficulties in group sessions.

Example: Pearl discovered her tendency to wait until the session was almost over to bring up her concerns. She described many situations in her life when she did not get what she wanted. She insisted that she wanted to make some changes and behave differently. The leader issued the following challenge: "Pearl, would you be willing to be the first to speak at the next group session? I'd like you to also think of at least one situation this week in which your needs are not being met because you are holding yourself back. What could you do to bring about a more positive outcome for yourself?" Thus, the leader provided Pearl with alternatives for taking the initiative to try new ways of acting, both in real life and in the group sessions. If she continued to sabotage meeting her needs by not doing what she said she would do, the leader would certainly need to confront her with her lack of commitment.

FREEDOM TO EXPERIMENT

The group situation provides a safe place for experimentation with new behavior. Members are able to show facets of themselves that they often keep hidden in everyday situations. In the accepting environment of a group, a shy member can exhibit spontaneous behavior and be outgoing. A person who typically is very quiet may experiment with being more verbal. After trying new behaviors, members can gauge how much they want to change their existing behavior.

Example: Myrtle said she was tired of being so shy all the time and would like to let people know her better. The leader responded "Myrtle, would you be willing to pick out a person in this group who is the opposite of you?" Myrtle identified Patti. After getting Patti's approval, the leader suggested to Myrtle: "Go around to each person in the room, and act in a way that you have seen Patti behave. Assume her body posture, her gestures, and her tone of voice. Then, tell each person something that you would want them to know about you." As a variation, Myrtle could have been asked to share with all of the members her observations and reactions to them. Yet another variation would have included asking Patti to be Myrtle's coach and assist her in carrying out this task. It can be surprising how outgoing members are when they pretend to be in someone else's skin. What Myrtle gained from this experiment was the recognition that she did possess the capacity to be outgoing and that she could practice being different by being herself.

HUMOR

Not everything that goes on in group has to be heavy and serious. Effective feedback can sometimes be given in a humorous way. Laughing at oneself can be extremely therapeutic. This requires seeing one's problems in a new perspective. Laughter and humor can draw everyone in the group closer. Humor often puts problems in a new light, and it sets a tone in a group indicating that work can occur in a context of fun. The power of humor as a therapeutic tool is often underrated. Vergeer (1995) suggests that humor can assist in coping with stress, promote honesty by facilitating self-disclosure, and provide an outlet for frustration and anger. Vergeer states that humor can be useful in both the assessment and the treatment process. It often balances the relationship between the client and the counselor, it can empower clients, and it establishes an environment that is maximally therapeutic to the client. Humor is a coping strategy that allows clients to find the absurd or ironic aspects in their situations. It also has a transformational character in that it allows clients to gain a sense of perspective and control over situations not under their direct control.

Spontaneity seems to be the key to using humor effectively, for "planned humor" can certainly fall flat. A level of trust must be established before taking too many liberties with humor. This brand of humor is not laughing *at* people, but laughing *with* them, out of a sense of affection and caring. Perhaps most important of all, humor allows clients to laugh at themselves.

Example: Abe was a serious person who tended to sit back quietly and observe others in the group. When the leader challenged Abe on his observational stance, he said that he could write a comedy about this group. The leader knew that he was a creative writer, and hoping to get him involved in verbal ways, asked him to write in his journal a comical account of what he saw taking place in the group. When he later read parts of what he had written in his journal about this group, just about everyone in the group laughed. In the process Abe also shared many of his own reactions to others in the group through his humor. Clearly he was not laughing at them, yet he was able to capture some of the humorous dimensions of what was taking place. By getting active through humor he was able to give a number of members some very insightful feedback, which they would have been denied had he continued sitting silently and observing others. In his account he was able to capture some very funny sides of his own behavior, which gave others a completely different picture of him.

RESEARCH IMPLICATIONS FOR
THE WORKING STAGE

In their comparative analysis of research into individual and group psychotherapy, Fuhriman and Burlingame (1990) conclude that the two forms of treatment share many therapeutic factors. Some of the common factors they identify are insight, catharsis, reality testing, hope for change, disclosure, and identification.

- **Insight** is thought to be a central therapeutic factor in fostering clients' improvement. There appears to be unanimity concerning the importance of insight for both forms of treatment.
- **Catharsis,** or emotional ventilation, is valued as a therapeutic process of both individual and group therapy from a conceptual perspective. However, empirical reviews of individual therapy do not show a consensus supporting the relationship between catharsis and clients' improvement.

- **Reality testing** is provided in a group by both the leader and the members through feedback. There is a great deal of conceptual support for the importance of this therapeutic factor for both individual and group therapy.
- **Hope for change,** or the expectation of improvement, has both conceptual and empirical support in both individual and group therapy and has been shown to be related to clients' improvement.
- **Disclosure** can be divided into two categories: therapist self-disclosure and client self-disclosure. In group therapy, there is a considerable amount of evidence suggesting that client disclosure facilitates the development of other therapeutic factors.
- **Identification** is the process by which a client can relate to others. The group-therapy literature suggests that clients who identify with both the therapist and with other group members tend to improve more than those who do not. The group process affords opportunities for members to form multiple identifications.

In addition to this brief review of findings about therapeutic factors, we will consider in more detail research into three group-process variables as they are related to the working stage. We have selected *cohesion, self-disclosure,* and *feedback* because these factors have a central role in determining group productivity.

RESEARCH INTO COHESION

Perhaps no other construct in group counseling has received as much extensive and intensive study as has cohesion. Nevertheless, it is difficult to demonstrate a clear relationship between cohesion and the outcomes of a group because cohesion is a multidimensional, interactive construct that can be studied from various perspectives (Fuhriman & Burlingame, 1990). Although cohesion has been defined in a variety of ways, phrases commonly used include: a climate of support, bonding, attractiveness, sharing of experiences, mutuality within a group, the togetherness that unites members, a sense of belonging, warmth and closeness, and caring and acceptance. A group characterized by a high degree of cohesion provides a climate in which members feel free enough to do meaningful work. Cohesiveness seems to be a critical factor in the successful outcomes of a group, with members more likely to express what they feel and think, engage in significant self-exploration, and relate more deeply to others (Bednar & Kaul, 1978).

If members experience little sense of belongingness or attraction to the group, there is little likelihood that they will benefit from a group experience, and they may well experience negative outcomes (Lieberman et al., 1973). Yalom (1995) maintains that research evidence shows cohesion to be a strong determinant of positive group outcome. He has summarized research that shows that highly cohesive groups tend to be characterized by better attendance and less turnover. The evidence indicates that this stability increases cohesiveness and leads to inceased self-disclosure, risk taking, and the constructive expression of conflicts in the group. Furthermore, group cohesiveness has consequences for other factors contributing to the success of a group. Cohesion operates as a therapeutic factor at first by enhancing group support and acceptance, but later it plays a crucial role in interpersonal learning. Yalom points out that members of a cohesive group, in contrast to members of a noncohesive group, tend to:

- be more interested in influencing other group members,
- be more open to influence from others in the group,
- be more willing to listen to others and be accepting of others,
- experience more safety within the group,
- participate more freely and actively in sessions,
- self-disclose to a greater extent,
- protect group norms and exert more pressure on members who are not supporting these norms, and
- be less susceptible to disruption as a group when a member terminates membership.

Although members of a cohesive group show greater acceptance, intimacy, and understanding, Yalom claims there is evidence that cohesion also allows members to recognize and work through conflicts. Members feel free to express anger and deal with conflict if they feel a sense of commitment to the group and if they perceive the group as a safe place.

How, then, is group cohesion developed? If a group is to be cohesive, its members must perceive it as a means to helping them achieve their personal goals. According to Yalom (1983, 1995), groups with a here-and-now focus are almost invariably vital and cohesive. By contrast, groups in which members engage in much "talking about" with a there-and-then focus rarely develop much cohesiveness.

Although cohesion is thought to be one of the crucial factors related to positive group process and outcomes, despite the vast amount of research on it the literature provides some conflicting conclusions. Rather than being a stable factor, group cohesion is a complex process (Bednar & Kaul, 1994; Kaul & Bednar, 1986; Stockton & Hulse, 1981), and systematic research is needed. In summarizing the current status of research into cohesion, Bednar and Kaul (1994) conclude that the field is about where it was in 1985; there is no consensus about the definition or composition of the cohesion construct. They compare cohesion to the concept of dignity—a concept everyone is able to recognize but apparently no one is able to describe let alone measure accurately.

RESEARCH INTO SELF-DISCLOSURE

Like cohesion, self-disclosure cannot be studied and discussed in a simple way. The empirical base for self-disclosure in group counseling is somewhat limited, but it suggests a complex, multidimensional interaction between frequency of disclosure and other factors such as type of group and population, level of disclosure, and timing (Morran, 1982; Stockton & Morran, 1982).

Robison, Stockton, and Morran (1990) found that providing more structure during the early phase of a group increased the frequency of intermember communications such as self-disclosure, feedback, and confrontation. However, members who are not inclined to take risks in a group tend to remain concerned about the undesired consequences of engaging in self-disclosure and giving feedback. When members are provided with an opportunity to discuss and evaluate their concerns about the undesired consequences associated with self-disclosure, their negative attitudes about disclosure tend to be reduced and they will disclose more readily.

Although research and clinical evidence clearly point toward the desirability of encouraging the norm of member self-disclosure, these findings do not imply that more disclosure is always better. There is a curvilinear relationship between self-disclosure and optimal group functioning, with either too much or too little disclosure being counterproductive. Although self-disclosure should be encouraged, a balance must be maintained so that a single member does not lead the others by too great a gap in terms of frequency and depth of disclosure (Yalom, 1995).

After surveying the literature on leader self-disclosure, Dies (1983b) suggests that this behavior may have either a constructive or a detrimental effect on group process and outcome, depending on specific factors such as the type of group, the stage of group development, and the content of disclosure. Dies concludes that therapist self-disclosure is less appropriate with client populations that are psychologically impaired. Group leaders who are willing to be open about their own reactions to what is going on within the group are more likely to foster development of positive interpersonal relationships. But Dies adds the cautionary note that clients tend to expect the group leader to possess confidence and competence and to provide some initial structuring and direction. Clients may not want leaders to be too revealing of their feelings, experiences, or conflicts early in the course of a group.

Leaders can facilitate interaction within the group by disclosing some of their personal reactions related to the here and now, because this type of information generally pertains directly to member opportunities for interpersonal learning (Morran, 1982). But leaders who disclose to meet their own needs rather than the needs of the members may cause members to question their leadership capabilities. Yalom (1983, 1995) stresses that leader self-disclosure must be instrumental in helping the *members* attain their goals. He calls for selective therapist disclosure that provides members with acceptance, support, and encouragement. For Yalom, group leaders who disclose here-and-now reactions, rather than detailed personal events from their past facilitate the movement of the group.

Jourard (1968) suggests that the group leader is a strong determiner of how open and trusting the client will become. He maintains that the therapist is the leader in the therapeutic dance and that the client follows the leader. Jourard's studies (1971a, 1971b) led him to conclude that therapist self-disclosure begets client self-disclosure and that therapist manipulation begets counter-manipulation on the client's part.

RESEARCH INTO FEEDBACK

Interpersonal feedback is one of the major therapeutic factors in group therapy. The exchange of feedback among group members is widely considered to be a key element in promoting interpersonal learning (Morran, Stockton, & Bond, 1991). One study found that incorporating structured feedback exercises into a group contributed to the attainment of members' goals (Rohde & Stockton, 1992). For members to benefit from feedback, it is critical that they be willing to listen to the reactions others offer. Members are more likely to consider feedback that may be difficult to hear if there is a balance between "positive" feedback and "corrective" feedback (sometimes referred to as "negative" feedback).

Kaul and Bednar (1986) suggest that feedback can be considered along a number of dimensions, including its *valence* (the positive or negative nature of the message), *content* (either behavioral, which describes another member's behavior, or emotional, which describes the feelings of the person giving the feedback), *source* (public or anonymous), *form of delivery* (written or spoken), and *time reference* (here and now or there and then). Some research findings on these specific dimensions of feedback are listed below:

- Positive feedback is almost invariably rated as being more desirable, having greater impact, and leading to greater intention to change than negative (or corrective) feedback (Dies, 1983b; Morran, Robison, & Stockton, 1985; Morran & Stockton, 1980).
- Group members tend to be more accepting of positive feedback than of corrective (or negative) feedback. Corrective feedback is more readily accepted when it follows, rather than precedes, the exchange of positive feedback (Stockton, Morran, & Harris, 1991).
- Feedback that describes specific behaviors is rated by group members as more effective than interpretive or mixed feedback (Stockton & Morran, 1980).
- Corrective feedback seems to be more credible and helpful if it comes at a later phase of the group (Stockton & Morran, 1981).

- Group members are more reluctant to give corrective feedback than positive feedback, which may be due to fears of rejection for engaging in therapeutic confrontations and fear of harming the recipient. It is a good practice for group leaders to guide the members toward exploring these fears and teach them how to give and receive feedback (Morran et al., 1991).
- Leader feedback is generally of higher quality than member feedback, but it is not more readily accepted; feedback tends to be of higher quality and to be more accepted in later sessions than in earlier ones (Morran et al., 1985).
- The feedback leaders give may elicit strong reactions from group members. Thus, leaders should carefully evaluate a member's readiness before giving feedback. It is also important to allow adequate time for processing corrective feedback (Stockton et al., 1991).
- The feedback offered by both members and the leader is useful in reality testing. A group offers opportunities for members to check out some of their assumptions underlying their behaivor, and feedback can add realistic and objective perspectives (Fuhriman & Burlingame, 1990).
- One of the main goals of feedback is to provide individuals with information to correct their distortions and past errors. When reality testing is considered in this light, research shows a relationship between feedback and other therapeutic factors in groups, such as cohesion (Kaul & Bednar, 1986).
- In small groups, structured feedback contributes to helping members attain their goals (Rohde & Stockton, 1992).
- The impact of the feedback being offered in a group is a reflection of the progress the group has made (Rothke, 1986). If the feedback being given is honest, personal, risky, and deals with interpersonal relationships within the group, this in itself is a sign that cohesion and trust have been established. Feedback that may be difficult to hear must be presented in a timely way and given in a nonjudgmental manner. Otherwise, the person receiving it will probably become defensive and reject it. The quality of feedback exchanged is one of the indicators that the group is moving toward a working stage.

In summarizing the research findings, Morran, Robison, and Stockton (1985) identify conditions associated with effective feedback. Feedback is most readily accepted when it focuses on observable behaviors, is unqualified, refers to specific and concrete situations, is delivered after trust has developed, and describes the giver's reactions, rather than being evaluative or judgmental. Also, a consistent finding is that feedback is more effective when positive comments are given before negative ones (Stockton & Morran, 1981).

CO-LEADER ISSUES DURING
THE WORKING STAGE

When we co-lead groups or intensive workshops, we become energized if the group is motivated to work. In effective groups the members do the bulk of the work, for they bring up subjects they want to talk about and demonstrate a willingness to be known. Between group sessions we devote time to discussing our reactions to group members, to thinking of ways of involving the various members in transactions with one another, and to exploring possible ways of helping participants understand their behavior in the group and resolve some of their conflicts. We also look critically at what we are doing as leaders and examine the impact of our behavior on the group. Toward this end we reflect on the patterns of feedback we have received from the members about how our behavior has affected them. We also talk about the process and dynamics of the group. If we find that we have differing perceptions of the group process, we discuss our differences.

TOPICS FOR CO-LEADER MEETINGS

We cannot overemphasize the importance of meeting with one's co-leader throughout the duration of the group. Much of what we have suggested in earlier chapters as issues for discussion at these meetings also applies to the working stage. We will briefly consider a few other issues that are particularly relevant to the working stage.

Ongoing Evaluation of the Group   Co-leaders can make it a practice to devote some time to appraising the direction the group is taking and its level of productivity. If the group is a closed one with a predetermined termination date (say, 20 weeks), co-leaders would do well to evaluate the group's progress around the 10th week. This evaluation can be a topic of discussion both privately and in the group itself. If both leaders agree that the group seems to be bogging down and that members are losing interest, for example, they should surely bring these perceptions into the group so that the members can look at their degree of satisfaction with their direction and progress.

Discussion of Techniques   It is useful to discuss techniques and leadership styles with a co-leader. One of the leaders might be hesitant to try any technique because of a fear of making a mistake, because of not knowing where to go next, or because of passively waiting for permission from the co-leader to introduce techniques. Such issues, along with any stylistic differences between leaders, are topics for exploration.

Theoretical Orientations   As we've mentioned earlier, it is not essential that co-leaders share the same theory of group work, for sometimes differing theoretical preferences can blend nicely. You can learn a lot from discussing theory as it applies to practice. Therefore, we encourage you to read, attend workshops and special seminars, and then discuss with your co-leader what you are learning. Doing so can result in bringing to the group sessions some new and interesting variations.

Self-Disclosure Issues   Co-leaders should explore their sense of appropriate and therapeutic self-disclosure. For example, if you are willing to share with members your reactions that pertain to group issues yet are reserved in disclosing personal outside issues, whereas your co-leader freely and fully talks about her marital situation, members may perceive you as holding back. This issue, too, can be discussed both in the group and privately with your co-leader.

Confrontation Issues   What we have just said about self-disclosure also applies to confrontation. You can imagine the problems that could ensue from your co-leader's practice of harsh and unrelenting confrontations to get members to open up, if you believe in providing support to the exclusion of any confrontation. You might easily be labeled as the "good guy" and your co-leader as the "bad guy." If such differences in style exist, the two of you surely need to talk about them at length if the group is not to suffer.

WORKING STAGE: SUMMARY

STAGE CHARACTERISTICS

When a group reaches the working stage, its central characteristics include the following:

- The level of trust and cohesion is high.
- Communication within the group is open and involves an accurate expression of what is being experienced.
- Leadership functions are likely to be shared by the group, in that members interact with one another freely and directly.
- There is a willingness to risk threatening material and to make oneself known to others; members bring to the group personal topics they want to discuss and understand better.
- Conflict among members is recognized and dealt with directly and effectively.
- Feedback is given freely and accepted and considered nondefensively.

- Confrontation occurs in a way in which those doing the challenging avoid slapping judgmental labels on others.
- Members are willing to work outside the group to achieve behavioral changes.
- Participants feel supported in their attempts to change and are willing to risk new behavior.
- Members feel hopeful that they can change if they are willing to take action; they do not feel helpless.

MEMBER FUNCTIONS AND POSSIBLE PROBLEMS

The working stage is characterized by the exploration of personally meaningful material. To reach this stage, members have certain tasks and roles, which include:

- bringing into group sessions issues they are willing to discuss
- offering feedback and being open to feedback from others
- assuming some leadership functions, especially by sharing their personal reactions of how they are affected by others' presence and work in the group
- being willing to practice new skills and behaviors in daily life and to bring the results to the sessions
- offering both challenge and support to others and engaging in self-confrontation
- continually assessing their level of satisfaction with the group and actively taking steps to change their level of involvement in the sessions if necessary

Some problems that can arise with members at this time are:

- Members may form a collusion to relax and enjoy the comfort of familiar relationships and avoid challenging one another.
- Members may gain insights in the sessions but not see the necessity of action outside of the group to bring about change.
- Members may withdraw because of anxiety over others' intensity.

LEADER FUNCTIONS

Some of the central leadership functions at this stage are:

- continuing to model appropriate behavior, especially caring confrontation, and disclosing ongoing reactions to the group
- providing a balance between support and confrontation
- supporting the members' willingness to take risks and assisting them in carrying this into their daily living

- interpreting the meaning of behavior patterns at appropriate times so that members will be able to engage in a deeper level of self-exploration and consider alternative behaviors
- assisting members to pay attention to and ask clearly for what they want from the group
- exploring common themes that provide for some universality and linking one or more members' work with that of others in the group
- focusing on the importance of translating insight into action; encouraging members to practice new skills
- promoting those behaviors that will increase the level of cohesion
- paying attention to the intensification and further development of group norms
- being aware of the therapeutic factors that operate to produce change and intervening in such a way as to help members make desired changes in thoughts, feelings, and actions

EXERCISES

1. What signs do you look for to determine whether a group has attained the working stage? Identify specific characteristics you see as especially related to this stage.

2. Assume that you are leading a group with a changing membership. Although there is a core of members who attend consistently, clients eventually terminate, and new members join the group. What obstacles will the members have to deal with if this group is to reach a working stage? What are your ideas on ways in which to increase cohesion in this type of group? How would you handle the reality of members' terminating and new members' being assimilated into the group?

3. What guidelines would you offer to members on appropriate self-disclosure? How might you respond to the following statement made by a member, Carol? "I don't see why there is so much emphasis on telling others what I think and feel. I've always been a private person, and all this personal talk makes me feel uncomfortable." How might you deal with Carol if she were in a voluntary group? an involuntary group?

4. There are important differences between effective and ineffective confrontation. How would you explain this difference to group members? Think about how you might respond to a person who had been in your group for some time and who said: "I don't see why we focus so much on problems and on confronting people with negative feelings. All this makes me want to retreat. I'm afraid to say much, because I'd rather hear positive feedback."

CHAPTER 8

ENDING A GROUP

FOCUS QUESTIONS

Introduction

Tasks of the Final Stage: Consolidation of Learning

Termination of the Group Experience

Dealing with Feelings of Separation
Dealing with Unfinished Business
Reviewing the Group Experience
Practice for Behavioral Change
Giving and Receiving Feedback
Ways of Carrying Learning Further
The Use of a Contract
Guidelines for Applying Group Learning to Life
Some Final Considerations

Evaluation of the Group Experience

Co-Leader Issues as the Group Ends

Final Stage: Summary

Stage Characteristics
Member Functions and Possible Problems
Leader Functions

Follow-Up

Postgroup Sessions
Individual Follow-Up Interviews

Postgroup Stage: Summary

Member Functions and Possible Problems
Leader Functions

Exercises

FOCUS QUESTIONS

1. If a member wants to leave a closed group before its termination, how should the leader handle the situation?
2. What activities are important during the closing phase of a group?
3. What questions might you as a leader ask members to determine how the group had affected them?
4. How might you deal with members' requests to continue a time-limited group that is approaching termination?
5. How important do you think it is to hold some type of follow-up session? What might you want the group to discuss at such a session?
6. How might you handle an individual's leaving an open group? How would you work a new member into the group?
7. What personal characteristics of yours could get in the way of helping members in your groups deal fully with separation and termination issues?
8. What specific methods and procedures would you use to help members review the group experience and make plans for using what they had learned in the group in everyday life?
9. What assessment techniques might you use at both the beginning and the end of a group? How can you build evaluation research into your group design? What are your attitudes about combining research and practice in group work?
10. What issues might you explore with your co-leader after a group terminates?

INTRODUCTION

The initial phase of a group's development is crucial—participants are getting acquainted, basic trust is being established, norms are being determined that will govern later intensive work, and a unique group identity is taking shape. The final stages of group evolution are also vital, for members have an opportunity to clarify the meaning of their experiences in the group, consolidate the gains they've made, and decide what newly acquired behaviors they want to transfer to their everyday lives.

In this chapter we discuss ways of terminating the group experience. We show how you can help those who participate in your groups evaluate the meaning of their behavior in the group. Questions we explore are these: How can the members be encouraged to evaluate the degree of their satisfaction with each session? How can a group complete its unfinished business? How can the members best be prepared for leaving the group and continuing to carry their learning into the real world? What are the difficulties in saying good-bye, and are they avoidable? How can you help members prepare to cope with their tendencies to regress to old ways or to discount the meaning of their experiences in the face of the outside world's pressures and skepticism? Are follow-ups necessary? If so, how should they be designed? How can leaders get participants to actively prepare themselves for a follow-up session? How can members and leaders evaluate the group experience?

We describe many tasks that need to be accomplished in the final stage of a group's history. It is difficult to offer one general guideline that covers all kinds of groups. Many variables must be considered in deciding how much time to allow for closure. For example, the number of sessions devoted to reviewing and integrating the group experience is dependent on how long the group has been in existence. A group that has been meeting weekly for two years will need more time for closure than one that has met for only ten weeks. Whatever the type of group, adequate time should be set aside for integrating and evaluating the experience. There is a danger of attempting to cover too much in one final meeting, which can have the effect of fragmenting the group instead of leading to closure.

TASKS OF THE FINAL STAGE: CONSOLIDATION OF LEARNING

During the final stage of a group, members need to be asked certain questions: "What has this experience meant to you?" "Where can you go from here?"

The final phase in the life of a group is critical, for this is when members must consolidate their learning. It is a difficult time, because the members are aware that their community is about to dissolve, and they are mourning the loss of it in advance. Sometimes the intensity of work tapers off during the final sessions, because participants are reluctant to bring up new business to explore. It is important that you focus on the feelings of loss that may permeate the atmosphere. These feelings need to be identified and explored, although they probably cannot be alleviated. Members must face the reality of termination and learn how to say goodbye. If the group has been truly therapeutic, they will be able to extend and continue their learning outside, even though they may well experience a sense of sadness and loss.

As members realize that their group is ending, there is a danger that they will begin to distance themselves from the group experience and thus fail to closely examine the ways their learning in the group might affect their out-of-group behavior. For this reason you need to learn to help members put what has occurred in the group in a meaningful perspective. Typically, this is the phase of group work that leaders handle most ineptly, partly owing to their lack of training and partly because of their own resistance to termination. Avoiding acknowledgment of a group's termination may reflect discomfort on the leader's part in dealing with endings and separations. Therapists may unconsciously resist ending their treatment of clients who provide much gratification for them, particularly if they do not have meaningful lives themselves (Kramer, 1990). When termination is not dealt with, the group misses an opportunity to explore concerns that may affect many members, and the clients' therapy is jeopardized. Kramer nicely captures the main tasks of termination:

> The termination stage is characterized by a mixture of feelings, among them sadness, confusion, and joy. The tasks are numerous and difficult. They include understanding endings as a psychological experience, recapitulating the treatment experience, obtaining closure and letting go, and finally, the ultimate freedom of experiencing new beginnings. No other stage in treatment or in life, for that matter, challenges us more. (p. 25)

The potential for learning permanent lessons is likely to be lost if the leader does not provide a structure that helps members review and integrate what they have learned. In a closed group, leaders can help the members review their individual work and the evolving patterns from the first to the final session. Of particular value is having the members give one another feedback on specific changes they have made. The task to be accomplished with a person who is terminating membership in an open group include:

- announcing in advance the person's intended departure to ensure that any potential unfinished business is cleared up
- allowing time for the person to prepare for termination
- giving an opportunity to others to say good-bye and to share their own reactions and give feedback
- assisting the member who is leaving to review what has been learned in the group and, specifically, what to do with this learning
- making referrals, when appropriate, such as couple therapy, family therapy, individual therapy, or another type of group therapy or a support group

This discussion on the consolidation and termination phase applies to both closed groups (those with the same membership for the group's history) and open groups (those with a turnover of members).

At times, members may want to leave a group prematurely. As you will recall from Chapter 2, there are ethical guidelines for dealing with matters such as leaving a group, exerting pressure for members to remain in a group, and ways of dealing with premature termination. We find that members rarely leave a group prematurely when they are encouraged in a nonthreatening way to fully explore their reasons for wanting to leave. Yet there are times when it is wise that clients discontinue membership. When it becomes clear that the needs of a member cannot be met within a particular group, there is an ethical responsibility to suggest appropriate referrals (ASGW, 1989, 15). It is essential that group counselors know about local community resources for further professional assistance.

TERMINATION OF THE GROUP EXPERIENCE

DEALING WITH FEELINGS OF SEPARATION

In discussing the initial phase of a group, we commented on the importance of leaders' encouraging members to express their fears and expectations so that trust would not be inhibited. As members approach the ending of the group, it is equally essential that they be encouraged to express their reactions. They may have fears or concerns about separating; leaving the group may be as threatening for some as entering it. Some members are likely to be convinced that the trust they now feel in the group will not be replicated outside. A central task of the leader at this time is to remind the participants that the cohesion they now have is the result of active steps they took. They need to be reminded that close relationships don't happen by accident; rather, they are the product of considerable struggle and commitment to work through personal conflicts.

Even if the participants realize that they can create meaningful relationships and build a support system outside the group, they still may experience a sense of loss and sadness over the ending of this particular community. The members are likely to need encouragement in facing the fact that their group is terminating, and some mourning over this separation can be expected if the group has become a cohesive one. If this mourning is avoided, the members are deprived of a valuable experience in learning how to cope with feelings of grief and loss. To facilitate members' expressions of their feelings over separation, it is important for you, as the facilitator, to recognize and be able to deal with your own feelings about the ending of the group. If you avoid dealing with feelings of sadness, the members will probably follow this example.

In many of the groups we lead, we typically ask members at the first session to spend a few minutes looking around the room quietly. We say: "As you are looking at different people, be aware of your reactions. Are you already drawn to certain people more than others? Are there some in here whom you already feel intimidated by? Are you catching yourself making judgments about people?" After a few minutes of this silent scanning of the room, we tell them to refrain from sharing anything that they have just thought or felt. Generally, we let the members know that we'll ask them to repeat this exercise at the final group session. When this time arrives, we tell them: "Check out the room again, being aware of each person in here. Do you remember the reactions you had at that first meeting? How have your reactions changed toward group members, if at all? How does it feel to be in here now compared with what it was like for you when the group began?" A main task for members during the final session is to put into words what has transpired from the first to the final session and what they have learned about others and themselves. If the group appears different at this final meeting than it did initially, they are asked to think about how this change came about. We point out to them that this transformation was not magic, nor was it something we did to the group. It largely stemmed from their commitment to hard work.

DEALING WITH UNFINISHED BUSINESS

During the final phase of a group, time needs to be allotted for expressing and working through any unfinished business relating to transactions between members or to the group process and goals. Some members may not get their issues fully resolved, but they should be encouraged to discuss them. For example, Edward may have unfinished business with another member (or members) or with the leader. It may well be his responsibility for having waited too long to bring up such matters, and he can be assisted in looking at some of the ways in which he got into the situation. Members like Edward may need help in bringing some closure to deeply personal issues they have raised and explored.

It is not realistic to assume that all the issues that were explored will have been worked through. If members are given this reminder a few sessions before the final meeting, they can be motivated to use the remaining time to complete their own personal agenda. We often ask the question "If this were the last session of this group, how would you feel about what you have done, and what would you wish you had done differently?" In addition, the group may point out many areas on which people could productively focus once they leave the group. In this way members can be prepared to continue working with these issues in further groups or in individual counseling. One index of a successful group is that members do not get disillusioned by the experience and would consider seeking this kind of help (or another avenue of personal growth) at other phases in their development.

REVIEWING THE GROUP EXPERIENCE

At the final stage of a group we again review what members have learned throughout the sessions and how they learned these lessons. For example, Ralph learned that keeping his anger inside had contributed to his feelings of depression and to many psychosomatic ailments. In the sessions he practiced expressing his anger, instead of smiling and denying those feelings, and he acquired important skills. It is helpful for Ralph to recall what he actually did to get others to take him seriously, for he could easily forget these hard-earned lessons.

Part of our practice for ending groups involves setting aside time for all the participants to discuss matters such as what they've learned in the group, turning points for them, what they liked and did not like about the group, ways that the sessions could have had a greater impact, and the entire history of the group seen in some perspective. To make this evaluation meaningful, we encourage participants to be concrete. When members make global statements such as "This group has been fantastic, and I grew a lot from it" or "I don't think I'll ever forget all the things I learned in here," we assist them in being more specific. We might ask some of these questions: "How has this group been important for you?" "In what ways has it been fantastic?" "What are a few of the things you've learned that you'd most want to remember?" "When you say that you've grown a lot, what are some of the changes you've seen in yourself?"

One way to help members review concrete highlights of their experience is to ask them to take a few minutes to spontaneously recall moments they shared together. Members can be helped to briefly relive their initial reactions to being in the group and to recall specific events. Each member can take several turns in completing the sentence "I remember the time when . . ." Recalling incidents of conflict and pain in the group as well as moments of closeness, warmth, humor, and joy can contribute to putting the group experience into perspective. Such turning points can provide a conceptual framework needed to make sense of what has taken place. We frequently emphasize to members the importance of putting what they have learned into specific language and stating the ways in which they have translated their insights into action.

PRACTICE FOR BEHAVIORAL CHANGE

In groups that meet weekly there are many opportunities for practicing new behaviors during each group session. It is good to encourage members to think of ways in which they can continue such work between the sessions. They can carry out homework assignments and give a report in the next week's session on how well they succeeded with trying new ways of behaving in various situations. In this way the transfer of learning is maximized.

During the final stage of a group, we re-emphasize the value of such actual practice (both in group situations and in outside life) as a way of solidifying and consolidating one's learning. We rely heavily on role-playing situations and rehearsals for anticipated interactions, teaching participants specific skills that will help them make their desired behavioral changes. We encourage them to continue to take action and try out new behavioral patterns with selected others outside the group.

We ask members to look at themselves and the ways in which they want to continue changing, rather than considering how they can change others. If Carol would like her husband to show more interest in the family and be more accepting of her changes, we encourage her to tell her husband about *her* changes and about herself. We caution her about the dangers of demanding that her husband be different. In rehearsals and role-playing situations we typically ask members to state briefly the essence of what they want to say to the significant people in their lives so that they do not lose the message they'd most want to convey. For example, a man rehearses telling his father that he loves him and would like closer contact with him.

Feedback from others in the group is especially helpful as the members practice for the behavioral changes they expect to make in their everyday situations. If Carol appears apologetic, for example, members may comment on ways in which she might be more assertive. If in role playing she lectures her husband on all the ways he is deficient, people can share with her how they would be affected if they were her husband. This preparation for dealing with others outside the group is essential if members are to maximize the effects of what they've learned. They can benefit by practicing new interpersonal skills, by getting feedback, by discussing this feedback, and by modifying certain behaviors so that they are more likely to bring about the desired changes once they leave the group.

GIVING AND RECEIVING FEEDBACK

Throughout the history of a group the members have been giving and receiving feedback, which has helped them assess the impact of their behavioral experiments on others. During the closing sessions, however, we like to emphasize a more focused type of feedback for each person. We generally begin by asking members for a brief report on how they've perceived themselves in the group, what the group has meant to them, what conflicts have become clearer, and what (if any) decisions they've made. Then the rest of the members give feedback concerning how they've perceived and felt about that person.

Here we want to point to a potential problem: too often people give only positive feedback at this time, particularly if they feel a closeness with the others and some misgivings about the termination of the group. Favorable comments may give a person a temporary lift, but we also like members to express doubts or concerns, in ways such as the following:

- My greatest fear for you is . . .
- My hope for you is . . .
- I hope that you will seriously consider . . .
- I see you blocking your strengths by . . .
- Some things I hope you will think about doing for yourself are . . .
- Some ways I hope you'd be different with others are . . .

We caution against global feedback that will be of little use to members in remembering how others saw them. Examples of feedback that are not too helpful are "I really like you." "I feel close to you." "You are a super person." "I will always remember you." In contrast, feedback that members can remember and can think about is most useful in making changes. Following are examples of this specific type of feedback:

- "I hope you remember that the reason you and I felt distant from each other is that we were scared of each other. What brought us closer is that we talked about our fears and our assumptions."
- "I like your ability to be direct and honest in giving feedback and at the same time to treat people with dignity."
- "Remember that people liked you much better when you stopped being sarcastic."
- "The times you gave advice, people tended to reject it. They responded more favorably to you when you shared your own struggles, rather than giving them solutions."
- "I hope you will remember how easy it was for me to respond to you when you stopped bombarding me with questions and instead started to tell me about yourself."
- "My fear for you is that you will forget that more often than not you are judging yourself more harshly than others do."
- "Remember that when you started expressing your annoyances toward others in this group, you became much less hostile."
- "I hope that you remember that your isolation not only keeps others away from you but also keeps you lonely."
- "My hope for you is that when you criticize yourself and tell yourself that you are not enough, you will listen to the other voice that tells you that you are lovable."

The feedback at the end of a group needs to be constructive and to be stated in such a manner that the individual is given an opportunity for closure. It is inappropriate for members to now unload stored-up negative reactions, for the member being confronted does not have a fair opportunity to work through this feedback.

During this feedback session we emphasize that participants can make some specific contracts to explore further areas after the group ends. We suggest some type of group follow-up session at a later date, which gives the members added incentive to think about ways to keep some of their new decisions alive.

WAYS OF CARRYING LEARNING FURTHER

Assisting members to carry their learning into action is one of the most important functions of leaders. It is our practice to routinely discuss with participants various ways in which they can use what they've learned in the group in other situations. For many members a group is merely the beginning of personal change. At the end of a member's first group experience she might say: "One of the most valuable things I'm taking from this group is that I need to do more work on how I tend to invite people to walk all over me. Before this group I wasn't even aware of how passive

I was. I let myself listen to what others in the group had to say about how I had affected them, and I really saw how I was backing away from any possible conflict."

If a group has been successful, the ending stage is a *commencement*; members now have some new directions to follow in dealing with problems as they arise. Furthermore, members acquire some needed tools and resources for continuing the process of personal growth. For this reason, discussing available programs and making referrals is especially timely as a group is ending. In this way the end of a group, at least for some members, leads to new beginnings.

THE USE OF A CONTRACT

One useful way to assist members in continuing the new beginnings established during the group is to devote time during one of the final sessions to writing contracts. These contracts outline steps the members agree to take to increase their chances of successfully meeting their goals once the group ends. It is essential that the members themselves develop their own contract and that the plan is not so ambitious that they are setting themselves up for failure. If the participants choose to, they can read their contracts aloud, so others can give specific suggestions for carrying them out. It is also of value to ask members to select at least one person in the group to whom they can report on their progress toward their goals, especially now when they are about to lose the support of their weekly group. This arrangement is useful not only for encouraging accountability but also for teaching people the value of establishing a support system as a way to cope with possible setbacks and discouragement.

Here are a few illustrations of contracts members have made during final group sessions:

- Robert has worked on speaking up more frequently in his classes. He contracts to continue his verbal participation in class and to call at least two members at the end of the semester to let them know about his progress.
- Miriam contracts to call Kathy when she feels misunderstood by her husband and wants to shut him out.
- Paul has explored his tendency to isolate himself from people and has made some gains in reaching out to others, both in and out of group. He says that he feels better about himself, and he contracts with Josephine and Margaret to call them once a month to simply talk to them.
- Larry became aware of his bias against people who think and act differently from him. In his group he has challenged himself to approach members that he might shy away from because of such differences, which resulted in favorable outcomes. He wants to continue this new

behavior once he leaves the group. He contracts to call several of the group members that he initially backed away from to inform them of his progress.

GUIDELINES FOR APPLYING GROUP LEARNING TO LIFE

Certain behaviors and attitudes increase the chances that meaningful self-exploration will occur in a group. At this time we suggest that you refer to the section in Chapter 5 that deals with guidelines on getting the most from a group experience. As members are entering a group during the early phase, we teach them how to actively involve themselves. This teaching continues throughout the life of the group. At the final phase we reinforce some teaching points to help members consolidate what they have learned and apply their learning to daily life. Toward the end of a group, the participants are likely to be receptive to considering how they can extend what they have learned.

Realize that the Group Is a Means to an End   Unfortunately, there are those who consider a group experience an end in itself. For them, the main pay-offs are the social interaction with the group setting and the temporary excitement and emotional closeness they feel during the sessions. Although feeling close may be pleasant, the purpose of a group is to enable participants to make decisions about how they will change their outside lives. Groups that are therapeutic encourage people to look at themselves, to decide whether they like what they see, and to make plans for change.

As a group approaches termination, it is your task to help members reflect on *what* they have learned, *how* they have learned it, and *what* they intend to continue doing with their insights. Members are then in a position to decide what they are willing to do about what they have learned about themselves.

Example: Marnie came to the group as a frightened, tough, isolated, hurt, and skeptical person. To survive her hurts, she had learned to suppress her need for others, and she prided herself on her independence. During the course of the group she demonstrated great courage by letting others become important to her. She allowed herself to be needy and to trust people and, finally, made a decision to at least share the pain of her isolation and loneliness. The point is that after the group she acted on what she had learned: that some people can be trusted. She allowed herself to be loved by a few people outside the group. She discovered that although she could still make it alone, life was more fulfilling if she allowed herself to care for others and others to care for her.

Realize that Change May Be Slow and Subtle   People sometimes expect change to come about automatically, and once they do make changes, they may expect them to be permanent. This expectation can lead to discouragement when temporary setbacks occur. Ideally, members will bring these setbacks back to their group. This realization that the process of change is slow can make superb material for exploration in a group.

Example: In her group-therapy sessions Barbara decided that she would no longer allow herself to be controlled by her husband and children. She engaged in rehearsing and role playing, saw that she had become what she thought her husband expected, and eventually made a contract to change those behaviors that had resulted in her feeling powerless. Later she reported to her group that she had regressed—that she seemed to be even more susceptible to being controlled. She didn't fulfill her contract, and she began losing hope that she would really change. It would have been helpful if she had realized that setbacks are a part of the growth process, that entrenched habits cannot be changed quickly, and that she had, in fact, made many strides that she was not giving herself full credit for. Her expectations of overnight changes are directional shifts in attitudes and behavior, for these subtle beginnings may be significant in the redecision and relearning processes.

Don't Expect One Group Alone to Renovate Your Life   Those who seek a therapeutic group sometimes cling to unrealistic expectations. They expect rapid, dramatic change. Members need to be reminded that a single therapeutic experience, as potent as it may be in itself as a catalyst for significant change, is not sufficient to sustain their decisions. People spend many years creating a unique personality, with its masks and defenses. It takes time to establish constructive alternatives. People do not easily relinquish familiar defenses, for even though the defenses may entail some pain, they do work. The change process is just that—a process, not a product. Unfortunately, many group members see the group experience as a convenient shortcut to becoming their ideal "finished product."

Example: Betty, a very busy university professor, joined a weeklong group and said at the initial session: "I really think I need to clean up some personal problems that are interfering with my research, writing, and teaching. So I've set aside this week to get myself in psychological shape." She seriously thought that in a week she could see what her problems were, work through them, and be able to resume her work without the annoying distractions of personal conflicts. The leaders of the group reminded Betty that personal growth can't be made to proceed according to a schedule. They told her they hoped her expectations would change so that she wouldn't wind up disappointed.

Decide What to Do with What You've Learned   At its best, a group will provide moments of truth during which clients can see who they are and how they present themselves to others. Ultimately, it is up to the members to do something with the glimpses of truth they gain.

Example: Linda became aware that she (not her husband) was primarily responsible for her misery and depression. Before her participation in the group she had blamed other people for her unhappiness. If only they would change, she thought, I would have what I want. In the group she came to accept that if she waited for others to make her feel worthwhile, she might indeed be condemned to a hopeless existence. By accepting that only she could change things, she opened up options for redecisions. Regardless of what she decided to do, she now knew that she was not helpless. The realization that we do have choices and that we're responsible for how we live and what we experience through our decisions may well be the most valuable outcome of participation in a group.

Think for Yourself   Many people seek therapy because they've lost the ability to find their own way and have become dependent on others to direct their lives and take responsibility for their decisions. When such people enter a group, they adopt a new standard (that of the group) as their own. Although they may shed some of their inhibitions, they are still not deciding on their own direction. They expect the group to decide for them, or they are sensitively attuned to being what the group expects them to be.

Example: Very soon after disclosing her unhappiness with her marriage, Shirley decided to leave her husband. This decision was reached toward the end of her membership in a personal-growth group. Some participants had felt that because she had said she didn't love her husband anymore, for her own good she should file for divorce. Shirley might ultimately have reached this decision anyway, but she appeared to act in haste and somewhat under the influence of what other members felt.

SOME FINAL CONSIDERATIONS

As our groups are coming to an end, we take the opportunity to remind participants of a few concerns:

• We again comment on the importance of keeping confidentiality, even after the group has ended. We caution that confidences are often divulged unintentionally by members enthusiastically wanting to share with others the details of their group experience. We provide examples of how they can talk about the group without breaking confidences. A suggestion we offer is that members can tell others *what* they learned but should be careful about describing the details of *how* they learned something. It is when members discuss the "how" of their experience that they are inclined to inappropriately refer to other members. Also, we encourage participants to talk about themselves and not about the problems of other participants.

• We have observed that even enthusiastic group members are not beyond forgetting and discounting what they have learned soon after the termination of their group. This is especially true if they leave a supportive group and go out into an environment that is not supportive or speaks disparagingly about the value of groups. For example, Dennis learned the value of being open and direct with people in the group. Later he tried this same approach with certain people at work, only to meet with resistance and hostility. Before the group ends, we ask members such as Dennis to imagine how they might discount the value of the lessons they have learned when they are faced with people who do not appreciate their changes. In the case of Dennis we might have said: "So talk out loud now about how honesty doesn't really work in everyday life. How might you convince yourself that the only place you can be direct and honest with people is in this group?" If people are able to foresee how they might minimize their hard-earned lessons, they are less likely to do so.

• Some type of rating scale can be devised to give the leader a good sense of how each member experienced and evaluated the group. Standardized instruments can also tap individual changes in attitudes and values. Such practical evaluation instruments can help the members make a personal assessment of the group and can also help the leader know what interventions were helpful and what aspects of the group were least helpful. A willingness to build evaluation into the structure of the group is bound to result in improving the design of future groups.

EVALUATION OF THE GROUP EXPERIENCE

After a group ends, we have at times sent out a questionnaire to the members. The responses tell us whether we succeeded in our therapeutic efforts. The following is a sample questionnaire:

1. What general effect, if any, has your group experience had on your life?
2. What were some specific things you became aware of about your lifestyle, attitudes, and relationships with others? What are some changes you've made in your life that you can attribute at least partially to your group experience?
3. Which of the techniques used by the group leaders had the most impact on you? What perceptions do you have of the group leaders and their styles?
4. What problems did you encounter on leaving the group and following up on your decisions to change?
5. Did the group experience have any negative effects on you?
6. What effects do you think your participation in the group had on the significant people in your life?
7. Have there been any crises in your life since the termination of the group? How did you handle them?

8. How might your life be different now had you not experienced the group?
9. Since the group, have you encouraged others to become involved in a group or in some other kind of growth experience?
10. Do you have anything else to say about yourself and your experience either during or since the group?

We use the following measures to evaluate the effectiveness of our groups:

- We conduct individual follow-up interviews with members or keep in contact with members; letters and telephone conversations have been substituted when person-to-person interviews were not feasible.
- We hold one or more postgroup meetings, which will be described in a later section.
- We ask members to complete brief questionnaires, such as the one above, to assess what they found most and least valuable in their group experience.
- We ask or require (depending on the type of group) that members keep process notes in a journal. On the basis of their journal notes, which are private, they write several reaction papers describing their subjective experience in the group as well as what they are doing outside the group. These reaction papers are given to us both during the life of the group and after the group has terminated.

We have found that asking the members to write about their group experience has been very useful in evaluating our groups. And members have continued to report to us that they found the writing they did both during and after the group extremely valuable to them in consolidating what they learned. By writing, members are able to focus on relevant trends and the key things they are discovering about themselves. Through the use of journals, they have a chance to privately clarify what they are experiencing and to rehearse what they want to say to significant people. Their writing also gives them a chance to recall turning points in the group for them, helps them evaluate the impact of the group in retrospect, and gives them a basis for putting this experience into meaningful perspective.

CO-LEADER ISSUES AS THE GROUP ENDS

It is critical that co-leaders agree on termination. They need to be in tune with each other about not bringing up new material that can't be dealt with adequately before the end of the group. Members sometimes save up topics until the very end, almost hoping that there will be no time to explore them. It could be tempting to one of the co-leaders to initiate new work with such a member; the other co-leader may be ready to bring the group to an end.

There are some other specific areas that you and your co-leader can talk about during the final stage to ensure that you are working together:

- Is either of you concerned about any members? Are there any things you might want to say to certain members?
- Are there perceptions and reactions either of you has about the group that would be useful to share with the members before the final session?
- Are both of you able to deal with your own feelings of separation and ending? If not, you may collude with the members by avoiding talking about feelings pertaining to the termination of the group.
- Have both of you given thought to how you can best help members review what they've learned from the group and translate this learning to everyday situations?
- Do you have some plan to help the members evaluate the group experience before the end of the group or at a follow-up session?

Once the group ends, we encourage co-leaders to meet to discuss their experience in leading with each other and to put the entire history of the group in perspective. What follows are some ideas that you might want to explore with your co-leader as a way to integrate your experiences and learning:

- Discuss the balance of responsibility between the co-leaders. Did one co-leader assume primary responsibility for directing while the other followed? Did one leader overshadow the other?
- Was one co-leader overly supportive and the other overly confrontational?
- How did your styles of leadership blend, and what effect did this have on the group?
- Did you agree on basic matters such as evaluation of the group's direction and what was needed to keep the group progressing?
- You can each talk about what you liked and did not like about leading with each other. You can benefit by a frank discussion of what each of you learned from the other personally and professionally, including weaknesses and strengths, skills, and styles of leading.
- It would be helpful to evaluate each other in addition to evaluating yourselves. Comparing your self-evaluation as a leader with your co-leader's evaluation of you can be of great value. What is especially useful is to be aware of certain areas needing further work; in this way each of you can grow in your capacity to lead effectively.
- You both can learn much from reviewing the turning points in the group. How did the group begin? How did it end? What happened in the group to account for its success or failure? This type of global assessment helps in understanding the group process, which can be essential information in leading future groups.

FINAL STAGE: SUMMARY

STAGE CHARACTERISTICS

During the final phase of a group the following characteristics are typically evident:

- There may be some sadness and anxiety over the reality of separation.
- Members are likely to pull back and participate in less intense ways in anticipation of the ending of the group.
- Members are deciding what courses of action they are likely to take.
- There may be some fears of separation as well as fears about being able to carry over into daily life some of what was experienced in the group.
- Members may express their fears, hopes, and concerns for one another.
- Group sessions may be devoted partly to preparing members to meet significant others in everyday life. Role playing and behavioral rehearsal for relating to others more effectively are common.
- Members may be involved in evaluation of the group experience.
- There may be some talk about follow-up meetings or some plan for accountability so that members will be encouraged to carry out their plans for change.

MEMBER FUNCTIONS AND POSSIBLE PROBLEMS

The major task facing members during the final stage of a group is consolidating their learning and transferring it to the outside environment. This is the time for them to review and put into some cognitive framework the meaning of the group experience. Some tasks for members at this time are:

- dealing with their feelings about separation and termination
- preparing for generalizing their learning to everyday life
- offering feedback that will give others a better picture of how they are perceived
- completing any unfinished business, either issues they have brought into the group or issues that pertain to people in the group
- evaluating the impact of the group
- making decisions and plans concerning what changes they want to make and how they will go about making them

Some possible problems that can occur at this time are:

- Members may avoid reviewing their experience and fail to put it into some cognitive framework, thus limiting the generalization of their learning.

- Due to separation anxiety, members may distance themselves.
- Members may consider the group an end in itself and not use it as a way of continuing to grow.

LEADER FUNCTIONS

The group leader's central goals in the consolidation phase are to provide a structure that allows participants to clarify the meaning of their experiences in the group and to assist members in generalizing their learning from the group to everyday life. Group leader tasks at this period include:

- assisting members in dealing with any feelings they might have about termination
- providing members an opportunity to express and deal with any unfinished business within the group
- reinforcing changes that members have made and ensuring that members have information about resources to enable them to make further progress
- assisting members in determining how they will apply specific skills in a variety of situations in daily life
- working with members to develop specific contracts and homework assignments as practical ways of making changes
- assisting participants to develop a conceptual framework that will help them understand, integrate, consolidate, and remember what they have learned in the group
- providing opportunities for members to give one another constructive feedback
- reemphasizing the importance of maintaining confidentiality after the group is over
- administering some type of end-of-group assessment instrument to evaluate the nature of individual changes and to evaluate the strengths and weaknesses of the group

FOLLOW-UP

POSTGROUP SESSIONS

A follow-up group session three to six months after the termination of a group can be an invaluable accountability measure. Because the members know that they will come together to evaluate their progress toward their stated goals, they are likely to be motivated to take steps to make changes. Participants can develop contracts at the final sessions that involve action between the termination and the follow-up session. Members often use one another as a support system. If they experience difficulties in following through on their commitments after the group, they can discuss these difficulties. It is a matter not so much of relying on one another for advice as of using the resources of the group for support.

At follow-up sessions the participants can share difficulties they have encountered since leaving the group, talk about the specific steps they have taken to keep themselves open for change, and remember some of the most positive experiences during the group itself. Follow-ups also give members a chance to express and possibly work through any afterthoughts or feelings connected with the group experience. The members report on whether and how they are using their expanded self-awareness in their relationships in the outside world. A member may have met with resistance or hostility from other people, and the group can reinforce the member's new style of behavior at a time when his or her will to change may be weakening.

We ask members at the follow-up session whether they are continuing to reach out for what they want. Are they taking more risks? What results are they getting from their new behavior? People frequently report: "The outside world isn't like this group. I've been honest with some people out there, and they don't know how to take me!" At this point we usually remind them again that people do need to be selective about whom to be completely honest with, because many people will resist directness and openness or will not desire intimacy. The follow-up can thus help the members become more realistic about their expectations.

A follow-up session offers us one more opportunity to remind people that they are responsible for what they become and that they must take risks in order to grow. We have found that some members make decisions at the follow-up session to seek further ways of challenging themselves. Some may decide to enter individual or group therapy, some will take a drama class, some will make the choice to return to college, some will get motivated to start a self-directed program to change certain behavior patterns, and so forth. Thus, the follow-up session provides a timely opportunity to discuss other avenues for continued personal growth.

If you administered any pretests to assess beliefs, values, attitudes, and levels of personal adjustment, the postgroup meeting is an ideal time to administer some of these same instruments for comparison purposes. We support the practice of developing an assessment instrument that can be given before members join a group (or at the initial session), again at one of the final sessions, and finally at some time after termination. If you meet with the members on an individual basis to review how well they have accomplished their personal goals, these assessment devices can be of value in discussing specific changes in attitudes and behaviors.

Of course, follow-up group sessions are not always practical or possible. Alternatives can be developed, such as sending a brief questionnaire to assess members' perceptions about the group and its impact on their lives. Members can also be contacted for individual follow-up sessions.

Both members and leaders benefit from follow-up meetings. Follow-up sessions give leaders access to valuable information that can help them evaluate the effectiveness of the groups they lead. As a result of our many follow-up meetings, we have revised some of the ways in which we facilitate our groups. For instance, we pay much more attention to finding ways to teach members to implement their group learnings in everyday living situations. Because of members' feedback, we now do not assume that all members know how to participate and get the most from a group. Thus, we provide more structuring and information during the early phases of a group to help members maximize their involvement. Although follow-up meetings may seem impractical and be time consuming, we are convinced that the merits of this practice are worth our efforts.

INDIVIDUAL FOLLOW-UP INTERVIEWS

If group follow-up sessions are impractical, an alternative is one-to-one sessions with as many members as would like such a meeting. Though ideally it is a good practice to meet with each member, even if the session lasts only 15 minutes, we realize the practical problems in arranging these sessions. If you are working in private practice, in a school setting, or in an institution and if you see the members on a fairly regular basis, then such follow-up interviews may be realistic. In other cases, the members may never be seen again.

The individual screening interview at the pregroup stage is partly devoted to ascertaining why people would like to join a group, helping them identify some personal goals, and discussing their expectations. The postgroup interview can be used to determine the degree to which members have accomplished their stated goals and met their expectations. Participants can also discuss what the group meant to them in retrospect. In addition, this one-to-one interview provides an ideal opportunity to discuss referral resources, should they be indicated. In our opinion this practice is one of the best ways for a leader to evaluate the effectiveness of a group.

The individual follow-up sessions can be very informal, or they can be structured with a common set of questions the leader asks of each member. Of course, members should be given latitude to say whatever they want and not merely answer questions. The questionnaire to evaluate a group experience that we presented earlier can apply to individual follow-up meetings as well. You can adapt your questions to the population of your group. The data from these individual sessions, especially when combined with a follow-up group session, provide valuable information you can use to decide how future groups could be improved.

In open groups it is not feasible to arrange for group follow-up sessions, because the membership changes over a period of time. However, it is an excellent practice to schedule an individual follow-up session about a month after a member terminates. This gives both the member and the leader an opportunity to review significant turning points in the group as well as the ways in which the group experience has influenced the member's behavior.

POSTGROUP STAGE: SUMMARY

MEMBER FUNCTIONS AND POSSIBLE PROBLEMS

After their group is terminated, the members' main functions are applying in-group learning to an action program in their daily lives, evaluating the group, and attending some type of follow-up session (if practical). Some key tasks of the postgroup stage for members include:

- finding ways of reinforcing themselves without the support of the group
- keeping some record of their changes, including progress and problems, so that they can determine the long-term effects of their group experience
- finding ways of continuing with new behaviors through some kind of self-directed program for change
- attending an individual session, if it is scheduled, to discuss how well their goals were met, or attending a follow-up group session to share with fellow members what they have done with their group experience after termination

Some possible problems that can occur at this time are:

- If members have difficulty applying what they learned in the group to everyday situations, they might become discouraged and discount the value of the group.
- Members may have problems in continuing with new behaviors without the supportive environment of the group.
- Members may forget that change demands time, effort, work, and practice, and thus they may not use what they've learned.

LEADER FUNCTIONS

Leaders have the following tasks after a group ends:

- offering private consultations if any member should need this service, at least on a limited basis to discuss a members' reactions to the group experience
- if applicable, providing for a follow-up group session or follow-up individual interviews, to assess the impact of the group

- finding out about specific referral resources for members who want or need further consultation

- encouraging members to find some avenues of continued support and challenge so that the ending of the group can mark the beginning of a search for self-understanding

- assisting members to develop contracts that will enable them to make use of support systems among the group members and outside the group

- if applicable, meeting with the co-leader to assess the overall effectiveness of the group

- administering some type of postgroup assessment to determine the long-range impact of the group

EXERCISES

Here are a few exercises appropriate to the final stage of a group. Again, most of the exerJ274
cises we suggest are suitable both for a classroom and for a counseling group.

1. **Discounting Exercise.** After a group the participants may find ways of discounting that experience, or old patterns may erupt and block establishment of new behavior. When she left her group, Jane felt close to many people and decided that it was worth it to risk getting close. She tried this at work, was rebuffed, and began telling herself that what she had experienced in the group was not real. In this exercise you are asked to imagine all the things you might say to yourself to sabotage your plans for change. The idea is to openly acknowledge tendencies you have that will interfere with establishing new behavior.

2. **Group-Termination Exercise.** Students take turns pretending that they are leaders and that the class is a group about to terminate. The idea is for students to consider how to prepare members for leaving a group.

3. **Termination-Interview Exercise.** A person in the class volunteers to become a group leader and to conduct an interview with a group member (also a volunteer) as though they had just completed a group experience together. For about ten minutes the group leader interviews the client regarding the nature of his or her group experience. After the exercise the client reacts to the interview.

4. **Future-Projection Exercise.** During the last session, members can be asked to imagine that it is one year (or five years or ten years) in the future, and the group is meeting in reunion. What would they most hope to be able to say to the group about their lives, the changes they have

made, and the influence the group had on them? What fears might they have concerning this reunion?

5.   Remembering Exercise. It is helpful to simply share memories and turning points during the group's history. Members could be given the task of recalling events and happenings that most stand out for them.

6.   Working on Specific Contracts. During the final sessions, members might formulate contracts that state specific actions they are willing to take to enhance the changes they have begun. These contracts can be written down and then read to the group. Others can give each member feedback and alternative ways of completing the contract.

7.   Reviewing the Class Experience. A useful exercise is to form small groups and discuss what you have learned about yourself up to this point that you think would either contribute to or detract from your effectiveness as a group leader. How willing have you been to take risks in this class? What have you learned about how groups best function (or what gets in the way of an effective group) through your experience in the class?

REFERENCES AND SUGGESTED READINGS FOR PARTS ONE & TWO

Alonso, A., & Rutan, J. S. (1988). The experience of shame and the restoration of self-respect in group psychotherapy. *International Journal of Group Psychotherapy, 38*(1), 3–14.

American Association for Marriage and Family Therapy. (1991). *AAMFT code of ethics.* Washington, DC: Author

American Counseling Association. (1995). *Code of ethics and standards of practice.* Alexandria, VA: Author.

American Psychological Association. (1992). Ethical principles of psychologists and code of conduct. *American Psychologist, 47*(12), 1597–1611.

American Psychological Association. (1993). Guidelines for providers of psychological services to ethnic, linguistic, and culturally diverse populations. *American Psychologist. 48*(1), 45–48.

Arredondo, P., Toporek, R., Brown, S. P., Jones, J., Locke, D. C., Sanchez, J., & Stadler, H. (1996). Operationalization of the multicultural counseling competencies. *Journal of Multicultural Counseling and Development, 24*(1), 42–78.

Association for Specialists in Group Work. (1989). *Ethical guidelines for group counselors.* Alexandria, VA: Author.

Association for Specialists in Group Work. (1991). Professional standards for the training of group workers. *Together: Association for Specialists in Group Work Newsletter, 20*(1), 9–14.

*Atkinson, D. R., Morten, G., & Sue, D. W. (1993). *Counseling American minorities: A cross-cultural perspective.* (4th ed.). Madison, WI: Brown & Benchmark.

Aubrey, M., & Dougher, M. J. (1990). Ethical issues in outpatient group therapy with sex offenders. *Journal for Specialists in Group Work, 15*(2), 75–82.

Austin, K. M., Moline, M. E., & Williams, G. T. (1990). *Confronting malpractice: Legal and ethical dilemmas in psychotherapy.* Newbury Park, CA: Sage.

Banawi, R., & Stockton, R. (1993). Islamic values relevant to group work, with practical applications for the group leader. *Journal for Specialists in Group Work, 18*(3), 151–160.

Bednar, R. L., Corey, G., Evans, N. J., Gazda, G. M., Pistole, M. C., Stockton, R., & Robison, F. F. (1987). Overcoming obstacles to the future development of research on group work. *Journal for Specialists in Group Work, 12*(3), 98–111.

Bednar, R. L., & Kaul, T. J. (1978). Experiential group research: Current perspectives. In S. L. Garfield & A. E. Bergin (Eds.), *Handbook of psychotherapy and*

*Entries marked with an asterisk are recommended for further study.

behavior changes: An empirical analysis (2nd ed.) (pp. 769–815). New York: Wiley.

Bednar, R. L., & Kaul, T. J. (1979). Experiential group research: What never happened. *Journal of Applied Behavioral Science, 11,* 311–319.

*Bednar, R. L., & Kaul, T. J. (1994). Experiential group research: Can the cannon fire? In A. E. Bergin & S. L. Garfield (Eds.), *Handbook of psychotherapy and behavior change* (pp. 631–663). New York: Wiley.

Bednar, R. L., & Lawlis, F. (1971). Empirical research in group psychotherapy. In A. E. Bergin & S. L. Garfield (Eds.), *Handbook for psychotherapy and behavior change* (pp. 812–838). New York: Wiley.

Bednar, R. L., Melnick, J., & Kaul, T. J. (1974). Risk, responsibility, and structure: A conceptual framework for initiating group counseling and psychotherapy. *Journal of Counseling Psychology, 21,* 31–37.

Bennett, B. E., Bryant, B. K., VandenBos, G. R., & Greenwood, A. (1990). *Professional liability and risk management.* Washington, DC: American Psychological Association.

Borgers, S. B., & Tyndall, L. W. (1982). Setting expectations for groups. *Journal for Specialists in Group Work, 7*(2), 109–111.

Bowman, V. E., & DeLucia, J. L. (1993). Preparation for group therapy: The effects of preparer and modality on group process and individual functioning. *The Journal for Specialists in Group Work, 18*(2), 67–79.

Brabender, V., & Fallon, A. (1993). *Models of inpatient group psychotherapy.* Washington, DC: American Psychological Association.

*Burlingame, G. M., & Fuhriman, A. (1990). Time-limited group therapy. *The Counseling Psychologist, 18*(1), 93–118.

Burlingame, G. M., & Fuhriman, A. (1994). Methodological considerations in group psychotherapy research: Past, present, and future practices. In A. Fuhriman & G. M. Burlingame (Eds.), *Handbook of group psychotherapy: An empirical and clinical synthesis* (pp. 41–80). New York: Wiley.

CACREP. (1994, January). *CACREP accreditation standards and procedures manual.* Alexandria, VA: Council for Accreditation of Counseling and Related Educational Programs.

Chu, J., & Sue, S. (1984). Asian/Pacific-Americans and group practice. In L. E. Davis (Ed.), *Ethnicity in social group work practice* (pp. 23–35). New York: Haworth.

*Comas-Diaz, L. (1992). The future of psychotherapy with ethnic minorities. *Psychotherapy, 29*(1), 88–94.

Conyne, R. K., Wilson, R. F., Kline, W. B., Morran, D. K., & Ward, D. E. (1993). Training group workers: Implications of the new ASGW training standards for training and practice. *Journal for Specialists in Group Work, 18*(1), 11–23.

*Corey, G. (1995). *Theory and practice of group counseling* (4th ed.) and *Manual.* Pacific Grove, CA: Brooks/Cole.

Corey, G. (1996a). *Case approach to counseling and psychotherapy* (4th ed.). Pacific Grove, CA: Brooks/Cole.

Corey, G. (1996b). *Theory and practice of counseling and psychotherapy* (5th ed.) and *Manual.* Pacific Grove, CA: Brooks/Cole.

Corey, G., & Corey, M. (1997). *I never knew I had a choice* (6th ed.). Pacific Grove, CA: Brooks/Cole.

Corey, G., Corey, M., & Callanan, P. (1990). Role of group leader's values in group counseling. *Journal for Specialists in Group Work, 15*(2), 68–74.

Corey, G., Corey, M., & Callanan, P. (1993). *Issues and ethics in the helping professions* (4th ed.). Pacific Grove, CA: Brooks/Cole.

*Corey, G., Corey, M., Callanan, P., & Russell, J. M. (1992). *Group techniques* (2nd ed.). Pacific Grove, CA: Brooks/Cole.

Corey, M., & Corey, G. (1986). Experiential/didactic training and supervision workshop for group leaders. *Journal of Counseling and Human Service Professions, 1*(1), 18–26.

Corey, M., & Corey, G. (1993a). *Becoming a helper* (2nd ed.). Pacific Grove, CA: Brooks/Cole.

*Corey, M., & Corey, G. (1993b). Difficult group members—Difficult group leaders. *The New York State Journal for Counseling and Development, 8*(2), 9–12.

*Corey, G., Williams, G. T., & Moline, M. E. (1995). Ethical and legal issues in group counseling. *Ethics and Behavior, 5*(2), 161–183.

D'Andrea, M., Daniels, J., & Heck, R. (1991). Evaluating the impact of multicultural counseling training. *Journal of Counseling and Development, 70,* 143–150.

*DeLucia, J. L., Coleman, V. D., & Jensen-Scott, R. L. (1992). Cultural diversity in group counseling. *Journal for Specialists in Group Work, 17*(4), 194–195.

Dies, R. R. (1983a). Bridging the gap between research and practice in group psychotherapy. In R. R. Dies & R. MacKenzie (Eds.), *Advances in group psychotherapy: Integrating research and practice* (American Group Psychotherapy Association Monograph Series) (pp. 1–26). New York: International Universities Press.

Dies, R. R. (1983b). Clinical implications of research on leadership in short-term group psychotherapy. In R. R. Dies & R. MacKenzie (Eds.), *Advances in group psychotherapy: Integrating research and practice* (American Group Psychotherapy Association Monograph Series) (pp. 27–28). New York: International Universities Press.

*Dies, R. R. (1992). The future of group therapy. *Psychotherapy, 29*(1), 58–64.

Dies, R. R. (1993). Research on group psychotherapy: Overview and clinical applications. In A. Alonso & H. I. Swiller (Eds.), *Group therapy in clinical practice* (pp. 473–518). Washington, DC: American Psychiatric Press.

*Donigian, J. (1993). Duality: The issue that won't go away. *Journal for Specialists in Group Work, 18*(3), 137–140.

Donigian, J., & Malnati, R. (1987). *Critical incidents in group therapy.* Pacific Grove, CA: Brooks/Cole.

*Dufrene, P. M., & Coleman, V. D. (1992). Counseling Native Americans: Guidelines for group process. *Journal for Specialists in Group Work, 17*(4), 229–234.

Forester-Miller, H., & Duncan, J. A. (1990). The ethics of dual relationships in the training of group counselors. *Journal for Specialists in Group Work, 15*(2), 88–93.

Fuhriman, A., & Burlingame, G. M. (1990). Consistency of matter: A comparative analysis of individual and group process variables. *The Counseling Psychologist, 18*(1), 6–63.

Fuhriman, A., & Burlingame, G. M. (1994). Group psychotherapy: Research and practice. In A. Fuhriman & G. M. Burlingame (Eds.), *Handbook of group psychotherapy: An empirical and clinical synthesis* (pp. 3–40). New York: Wiley.

Fukuyama, M. A., & Coleman, N. C. (1992). A model for bicultural assertion training with Asian-Pacific American college students: A pilot study. *Journal for
Specialists in Group Work, 17*(4), 210–217.

Gainor, K. A. (1992). Internalized oppression as a barrier to effective group work
with black women. *Journal for Specialists in Group Work, 17*(4), 235–242.

Gazda, G. M. (1989). *Group counseling: A developmental approach* (4th ed.).
Boston: Allyn & Bacon.

*Greeley, A. T., Garcia, V. L., Kessler, B. L., & Gilchrest, G. (1992). Training effective
multicultural group counselors: Issues for a group training course. *Journal for
Specialists in Group Work, 17*(4), 196–209.

Gumaer, J., & Forrest, A. (1995). Avoiding conflict in group therapy: Ethical and
legal issues in group training and practice. *Directions in Mental Health
Counseling, 5*(5), 1–16.

*Gumaer, J., & Martin, D. (1990). Group ethics: A multimodal model for training
knowledge and skill competencies. *Journal for Specialists in Group Work,
15*(2), 94–103.

Herlihy, B., & Corey, G. (1992). *Dual relationships in counseling*. Alexandria, VA:
American Counseling Association.

*Herlihy, B., & Corey, G. (1996). *ACA ethical standards casebook* (5th ed.).
Alexandria, VA: American Counseling Association.

Ho, M. K. (1984). Social group work with Asian/Pacific Americans. In L. E. Davis
(Ed.), *Ethnicity in social group work practice* (pp. 49–61). New York: Haworth.

Hopkins, B. R., & Anderson, B. W. (1990). *The counselor and the law* (3rd ed.).
Alexandria, VA: American Association for Counseling and Development.

*Hulse-Killacky, D. (1993). Personal and professional endings. *Journal of Hu-
manistic Education and Development, 32*(2), 92–94.

*Hunter, G. C. (1994). Who's the expert anyway? *The Person-Centered Periodical,
1*(1), 3–6.

Jacobs, E. F., Harvill, R. L., & Masson, R. L. (1994). *Group counseling: Strategies
and skills* (2nd ed.). Pacific Grove, CA: Brooks/Cole.

Johnson, I. H., Santos Torres, J., Coleman, V. D., & Smith, M. C. (1995). Issues and
strategies in leading culturally diverse counseling groups. *Journal for
Specialists in Group Work, 20*(3), 143–150.

Jourard, S. M. (1968). *Disclosing man to himself*. New York: Van Nostrand
Reinhold.

Jourard, S. M. (1971a). *Self-disclosure: An experimental analysis of the transparent self*. New York: Wiley.

Jourard, S. M. (1971b). *The transparent self* (rev. ed.). New York: Van Nostrand
Reinhold.

Kane, C. M. (1995). Fishbowl training in group process. *Journal for Specialists in
Group Work, 20*(3), 183–188.

Kaul, T. J., & Bednar, R. L. (1978). Conceptualizing group research: A preliminary
analysis. *Small Group Behavior, 9,* 173–191.

*Kaul, T. J., & Bednar, R. L. (1986). Experiential group research: Results, questions,
and suggestions. In S. L. Garfield & A. E. Bergin (Eds.), *Handbook for psychotherapy and behavior change* (3rd ed.) (pp. 671–714). New York: Wiley.

*Kottler, J. A. (1992). *Compassionate therapy: Working with difficult clients*. San
Francisco: Jossey-Bass.

*Kottler, J. A. (1994a). *Advanced group leadership.* Pacific Grove, CA: Brooks/Cole.

*Kottler, J. A. (1994b). Working with difficult group members. *Journal for Specialists in Group Work, 19*(1), 3–10.

Kramer, S. A. (1990). *Positive endings in psychotherapy: Bringing meaningful closure to therapeutic relationships.* San Francisco: Jossey-Bass.

LeCluyse, E. E. (1983). Pretherapy preparation for group members. *Journal for Specialists in Group Work, 9*(4), 170–174.

Lee, P. C., Juan, G., & Hom, A. B. (1984). Group work practice with Asian clients: A sociocultural approach. In L. E. Davis (Ed.), *Ethnicity in social group work practice* (pp. 37–47). New York: Haworth.

*Leong, F. T. L. (1992). Guidelines for minimizing premature termination among Asian American clients in group counseling. *Journal for Specialists in Group Work, 17*(4), 218–228.

*Lieberman, M., Yalom, I., & Miles, M. (1973). *Encounter groups: First facts.* New York: Basic Books.

Meadow, D. (1981). The preparatory interview: A client-focused approach with children of holocaust survivors. *Social Work with Groups, 4*(3 & 4), 135–144.

Meadow, D. (1988). Preparation of individuals for participation in a treatment group: Development and empirical testing of a model. *International Journal of Group Psychotherapy, 38*(3), 367–385.

*Merta, R. J. (1995). Group work: Multicultural perspectives. In J. G. Ponterotto, J. M. Casas, L. A. Suzuki, & C. M. Alexander (Eds.), *Handbook of multicultural counseling* (pp. 567–585). Newbury Park, CA: Sage.

Merta, R. J., Johnson, P., & McNeil, K. (1995). Updated research on group work: Educators, course work, theory, and teaching methods. *Journal for Specialists in Group Work, 20*(3), 132–142.

*Merta, R. J., & Sisson, J. A. (1991). The experiential group: An ethical and professional dilemma. *Journal for Specialists in Group Work, 16*(4), 236–245.

*Merta, R. J., Wolfgang, L., & McNeil, K. (1993). Five models for using the experiential group in the preparation of group counselors. *Journal for Specialists in Group Work, 18*(4), 200–207.

Morran, D. K. (1982). Leader and member self-disclosing behavior in counseling groups. *Journal for Specialists in Group Work, 7*(4), 218–223.

Morran, D. K., Robison, F. F., & Stockton, R. (1985). Feedback exchange in counseling groups: An analysis of message content and receiver acceptance as a function of leader versus member delivery, session, and valence. *Journal of Counseling Psychology, 32*, 57–67.

Morran, D. K., & Stockton, R. (1980). Effect of self-concept on group member reception of positive and negative feedback. *Journal of Counseling Psychology, 27*, 260–267.

Morran, D. K., & Stockton, R. (1985). Perspectives on group research programs. *Journal for Specialists in Group Work, 10*(4), 186–191.

Morran, D. K., Stockton, R., & Bond, L. (1991). Delivery of positive and corrective feedback in counseling groups. *Journal of Counseling Psychology, 38*(4), 410–414.

National Association of Social Workers. (1990). *Code of ethics.* Silver Spring, MD: Author.

Ormont, L. R. (1988). The leader's role in resolving resistances to intimacy in the group setting. *International Journal of Group Psychotherapy, 38*(1), 29–46.

Paradise, L. V., & Kirby, P. C. (1990). Some perspectives on the legal liability of group counseling in private practice. *Journal for Specialists in Group Work, 15*(2), 114–118.

Pedersen, P. (1989). Developing multicultural ethical guidelines for psychology. *International Journal of Psychology, 24,* 643–652.

Pedersen, P. (1990). The multicultural perspective as a fourth force in counseling. *Journal of Mental Health Counselors, 12*(1), 93–94.

*Pedersen, P. (1994). *A handbook for developing multicultural awareness* (2nd ed.). Alexandria, VA: American Counseling Association.

Pedersen, P., Draguns, J., Lonner, W., & Trimble, J. (Eds.). (1989). *Counseling across cultures* (3rd ed.). Honolulu: University Press of Hawaii.

Pierce, K. A., & Baldwin, C. (1990). Participation versus privacy in the training of group counselors. *The Journal for Specialists in Group Work, 15*(3), 149–158.

*Piper, W. E., & Perrault, E. L. (1989). Pretherapy preparation for group members. *International Journal of Group Psychotherapy, 39*(1), 17–34.

Pope, K. S., Sonne, J. L., & Holroyd, J. (1993). *Sexual feelings in psychotherapy: Explorations for therapists and therapists-in-training.* Washington, DC: American Psychological Association.

Remley, T. (1992). A model for teaching a graduate course in group counseling. *Together: Association for Specialists in Group Work Newsletter, 20*(2), 10–11.

*Ridley, C. R. (1995). *Overcoming unintentional racism in counseling and therapy: A practitioner's guide to intentional intervention.* Newbury Park, CA: Sage.

Robison, F. F., Stockton, R., & Morran, D. K. (1990). Anticipated consequences of self-disclosure during early therapeutic group development. *Journal of Group Psychotherapy, Psychodrama, and Sociometry, 43*(1), 3–18.

Robison, F. F., & Ward, D. (1990). Research activities and attitudes among ASGW members. *Journal for Specialists in Group Work, 19*(4), 215–224.

Rogers, C. R. (1970). *Carl Rogers on encounter groups.* New York: Harper & Row.

Rohde, R., & Stockton, R. (1992). The effect of structured feedback on goal attainment, attraction to the group, and satisfaction with the group in small group counseling. *Journal of Group Psychotherapy, Psychodrama, and Sociometry, 44*(4),172–180.

Rollock, D. A., Westman, J. S., & Johnson, C. (1992). A black student support group on a predominantly white university campus: Issues for counselors and therapists. *Journal for Specialists in Group Work, 17*(4), 243–252.

Rosenbaum, M., Lakin, M., & Roback, H. B. (1992). Psychotherapy in groups. In D. K. Freedheim (Ed.), *History of psychotherapy: A century of change* (pp. 695–724). Washington, DC: American Psychological Association.

Rothke, S. (1986). The role of interpersonal feedback in group psychotherapy. *International Journal of Group Psychotherapy, 36*(2), 225–240.

Sklare, G., Keener, R., & Mas, C. (1990). Preparing members for here-and-now group counseling. *The Journal for Specialists in Group Work, 15*(3), 141–148.

Sklare, G., Petrosko, J., & Howell, S. (1993). The effect of pregroup training on members' level of anxiety. *The Journal for Specialists in Group Work, 18*(3), 109–114.

Sleek, S. (1995). Group therapy: Tapping the power of teamwork. *The APA Monitor, 26*(7), 1, 38–39.

Stockton, R., & Hulse, D. (1981). Developing cohesion in small groups: Theory and research. *Journal for Specialists in Group Work, 6*(4), 188–194.

Stockton, R., & Morran, D. K. (1980). The use of verbal feedback in counseling groups: Toward an effective system. *Journal for Specialists in Group Work, 5*(1), 10–14.

Stockton, R., & Morran, D. K. (1981). Feedback exchange in personal growth groups: Receiver acceptance as a function of valence, session, and order of delivery. *Journal of Counseling Psychology, 28,* 490–497.

Stockton, R., & Morran, D. K. (1982). Review and perspective of critical dimensions in therapeutic small group research. In G. M. Gazda (Ed.), *Basic approaches to group psychotherapy and group counseling* (3rd ed.) (pp. 37–85). Springfield, IL: Charles C Thomas.

Stockton, R., Morran, D. K., Harris, M. (1991). Factors influencing group member acceptance of corrective feedback. *Journal for Specialists in Group Work, 16*(4), 246–254.

Sue, D., & Sue, D. W. (1993). Ethnic identity: Cultural factors in the psychological development of Asians in America. In D. R. Atkinson, G. Morten, & D. W. Sue (Eds.), *Counseling American minorities: A cross-cultural perspective* (pp. 199–210). Madison, WI: Brown & Benchmark.

Sue, D. W. (1990). Culture-specific strategies in counseling: A conceptual framework. *Professional Psychology: Research and Practice, 21*(6), 424–433.

Sue, D. W. (1992). The challenge of multiculturalism: The road less traveled. *American Counselor, 1*(1), 6–14.

Sue, D. W., Arredondo, P., & McDavis, R. J. (1992). Multicultural counseling competencies and standards: A call to the profession. *Journal of Counseling and Development, 70*(4), 477–486.

*Sue, D. W., Ivey, A. E., & Pedersen, P. (1996). *Multicultural counseling and therapy.* Pacific Grove, CA: Brooks/Cole.

*Sue, D. W., & Sue, D. (1990). *Counseling the culturally different: Theory and practice* (2nd ed.). New York: Wiley.

Vergeer, G. W. (1995). Therapeutic applications of humor. *Directions in Mental Health Counseling, 5*(3), 1–11.

Williams, G. T. (1990). Ethical dilemmas in teaching a group leadership course. *Journal for Specialists in Group Work, 15*(2), 104–113.

Woody, R. H. (1988). *Protecting your mental health practice: How to minimize legal and financial risk.* San Francisco: Jossey-Bass.

Woody, R. H. (1989). *Business success in mental health practice.* San Francisco: Jossey-Bass.

Woody, R. H., & Associates. (1984). *The law and the practice of human services.* San Francisco: Jossey-Bass.

Wrenn, C. G. (1985). Afterward: The culturally encapsulated counselor revisited. In P. Pedersen (Ed.), *Handbook of cross-cultural counseling and therapy* (pp. 323–329). Westport, CT: Greenwood Press.

*Yalom, I. D. (1980). *Existential psychotherapy.* New York: Basic Books.

*Yalom, I. D. (1983). *Inpatient group psychotherapy.* New York: Basic Books.

*Yalom, I. D. (1995). *The theory and practice of group psychotherapy* (4th ed.). New York: Basic Books.

*Yu, A., & Gregg, C. H. (1993). Asians in groups: More than a matter of cultural awareness. *The Journal for Specialists in Group Work, 18*(2), 86–93.

GROUP PRACTICE
Some Specific Groups

In Part Two our focus was on describing the group process at various stages of a group's history. In Part Three we describe how to apply these concepts and practices to groups geared to the particular needs of clients at various ages. We also discuss the special responsibilities of group leaders who work with children, adolescents, adults, and the elderly. We describe how we set up these specialized groups and share with you approaches that we hope will be useful to you as you design your own groups.

Students in counseling and related programs must often complete an internship involving work with a variety of people: children or adolescents, the elderly, clients with substance-abuse problems, hospital patients, and outpatients in a community agency. On your job as a mental-health worker, you may be asked to set up and lead a variety of groups. If you work with children, you may have a group of children of divorce, a group of acting-out children, or a group of terminally ill children. For adolescents, you may be asked to organize a group program for alcohol and drug rehabilitation, a growth group to meet normal developmental needs, or a group for young people who are the victims of some tragedy. For adults, there are groups for single parents, for middle-aged people doing career planning, and for the physically handicapped. With the elderly population, you may find yourself leading a preretirement group or a theme-oriented personal-growth group. The types of groups available for each of the four age levels are as many as there are special problems and needs. Of course, not all of them can be described in this book, but a sample of programs can give you ideas to apply in creating a group that especially appeals to you.

Our intention is to stimulate you to think creatively about how to design groups to effectively meet the needs of diverse clients. We think that the ideas presented here can be adapted to your own groups with these populations. We encourage you to adapt these practices to suit your personal style, your settings, and the populations with which you work.

CHAPTER 9

GROUPS FOR CHILDREN

Introduction: Special Needs and Problems of Children

**Guidelines for Group Work with
Children and Adolescents**

Developing a Sound Proposal
Legal Considerations
Practical Considerations
Tactics in the Group
Personal and Professional Qualifications
Be Aware of Your Own Limitations

A School Counseling Program

The Initial Phase
Evolution of the Group
Special Problems Requiring Out-of-Group Attention
Working Outside the Group

Children's Groups in Community Agencies

A Group for Children of Divorce

Preliminary Considerations in Forming the Group
Highlights of the Group Sessions
The Role of Teachers and Parents in the Group Program
Outcomes, Follow-Up, and a Personal Perspective

Where to Go from Here

References and Suggested Readings

INTRODUCTION: SPECIAL NEEDS
AND PROBLEMS OF CHILDREN

In this chapter we describe children's groups that were led by one of us (Marianne) or by colleagues. The general group format described here can be applied in various other settings, including private practice and public and private clinics. You can also use many of the ideas in this chapter for groups dealing with a variety of special needs, including those of abused children, children of alcoholic families, and children with learning and behavioral disorders. Creating groups to meet the needs of these children is challenging. A few of the problems for which children are sent to group counseling include:

- low self-esteem
- inability to get along with peers
- excessive fighting
- feelings of failure
- loss and grief
- physical and sexual abuse
- feeling isolated and lonely
- struggling with living between two cultures
- frequent hurting of other children
- violation of school rules
- poor attitude toward school
- depression and anxiety
- violent or angry outbursts at home or school
- children without a home
- excessive truancy
- substance abuse
- dealing with divorce

This chapter alone will not provide you with enough information to conduct your own groups with children. We hope, however, that it will stimulate you to do further reading, attend specialized workshops, and arrange for supervised field experience.

GUIDELINES FOR GROUP WORK
WITH CHILDREN AND ADOLESCENTS

This section consists of some practical guidelines for counselors who are considering setting up groups for minors. These guidelines apply to groups for adolescents, which we consider in the next chapter, as well as to children's groups.

DEVELOPING A SOUND PROPOSAL

In designing your proposal, make sure you describe your goals and purposes clearly. Avoid arousing suspicion with global language or loaded words such as *sensitivity group* or *group therapy*. Develop a clearly stated rationale for your proposed group. State your aims, the procedures to be used, the evaluation devices you will use, and the reasons a group approach has particular merit. Too many potential groups fail to materialize because the leader has impulsively decided to lead a group but has put little serious thought into planning an effective design. Refer to Chapter 4 for more information on developing a group proposal.

The support of administrators in both schools and agencies is essential, and if your design for a group is well organized, you will probably receive support and constructive suggestions from them. It may be necessary to make certain compromises in your proposal, so keep an open mind. Remember that the school principal or the agency head—not you—will probably be the target of criticism if your counseling group is ineffectively run or compromises the integrity of the institution. The administrator will be the one who, if you've overlooked the need to get parental permission (where required), fields the calls from parents who want to know what right the school has to probe into the personal lives of their children. One practitioner reported that she had encountered resistance from her school principal when she suggested a "divorce group" for children. She formally proposed a "loss group," which satisfied the principal but confused the children. They reported to the office saying "We're the *lost* group; we're here to be found."

LEGAL CONSIDERATIONS

Be aware of your state's laws regarding children. Know the rules and regulations as they specifically apply to your agency or institution, as well as its ethical principles. For example, don't tell the children that you can keep everything they discuss confidential and then be put in the position of having to disclose information about them to your agency or school administrator. Be clear about what you can and cannot promise in the way of privacy. Be aware of your legal responsibility to report abuse or suspected abuse of minors. In this situation, confidentiality *must* be broken, because the law requires you to take action by notifying the appropriate authorities. For other ethical considerations in setting up groups for minors, review the discussion of such standards in Chapter 2.

For some groups, written parental permission may not be a legal requirement. It is usually a good idea to secure the written consent of the parents or guardians of any person under 18 who wishes to participate in group counseling.

PRACTICAL CONSIDERATIONS

The size and duration of a group depend on the age of the members. As a rule of thumb, the younger the children, the smaller the group and the shorter the duration of the sessions. Take into account the fact that the attention span of a child aged 4 to 6 is quite different from that of a child who is 10 or 12. Another consideration in forming a group is the severity of the children's problems. For example, a group of hyperactive 12-year-olds might have to be as small as a group of preschoolers. You must also consider your own attention span and tolerance for dealing with children who will test your limits. Resist getting impatient at each session, thus becoming more of a disciplinarian than a counselor.

The Setting   Consider the meeting place in terms of its effectiveness for the work you want to do with your young clients. Will they be able to roam around freely and not have to be continually asked to talk softly so as not to disturb others in an adjacent room? Will the site for group meetings provide privacy and freedom from interruptions? Is there anything in the room that could easily be damaged by the children or that is obviously unsafe for them?

Communicate Your Expectations   Be able to tell the children or adolescents in a simple way about the purpose of your group, what you expect of them, and what they can expect from you. Make sure that they understand the basic, nonnegotiable ground rules and, as much as is realistic, attempt to involve them in the establishment and reinforcement of the rules that will govern their group. In setting certain rules, it is essential to follow through with firmness (without an autocratic tone and style). For example, you may have the policy of not allowing members who have left a session to return. Be careful not to give in to their demands for a "second chance." Young people will quickly learn that you mean what you say. They may not always like what you do at the time, but your chances for earning their respect are increased.

Preparation   Prepare adequately for each session. In fact, you may need to structure sessions even more carefully than you would for some adult groups. However, be flexible enough to adjust your format and topics for a given session to respond to spontaneous situations. Avoid insisting on "covering your agenda" no matter what; be creative but not careless.

Involvement of Parents   As with the young people, explain to their parents your expectations and purposes in such a way that they can understand and not become suspicious. You reduce the chances of encountering resistant and defensive parents by approaching them with an attitude of "How can you help me in my work with your child, and how can we work as a team for a common purpose?" Rather than communicating to them in subtle ways that they are incompetent and that you are the expert who can remedy the situation, be sincerely interested in their reactions to your program. You might spend an evening presenting your program in a group meeting of parents, or you might send them a letter briefly describing your groups. This letter can be sent with the parental-consent form.

TACTICS IN THE GROUP

Use Judgment   Consider the purposes and goals of your group in deciding how much to encourage self-disclosure, especially in matters relating to family life. It is difficult to say what is the right degree of disclosure. The counselor needs to be careful because children may not keep confidentiality and may talk to other children about disclosures made in the group. It is more difficult to maintain confidentiality in a school setting than in private practice, where the children may have no contact outside of the group. Should you encourage an open discussion of personal matters? For example, in a group in an elementary school, you may not want to let a child go into detail about a parental fight. An important intervention is directing this child to express how he or she was affected by the incident. In any case, the focus of disclosure should be the child, not the parent.

Don't Take Sides   Avoid siding with children or adolescents against their parents or a particular institution. They may like and admire you for your patience and understanding and complain about missing these traits in parents or teachers. Deal with this complaint realistically, keeping in mind that you are spending an hour each week with them as opposed to living with them every day. Try to get the young people to understand the other side, through role playing, for example.

Use Appropriate Exercises and Techniques   If you use interaction exercises, you can explain their purpose in a general way without diminishing their impact. Realize, too, that young people should be granted the right not to participate in some activities. Although their unwillingness to take part often stems from a lack of understanding, children or adolescents will sometimes be resistant because they see such exercises as inappropriate. For example, it may be appropriate to ask 6-year-olds of the opposite sex to hold hands, but you are likely to meet with resistance if you ask 12-year-olds to do the same.

Listen and Be Open   Learn to listen to young people; let them say what they need to say in their own words. Let them lead the way, and follow their clues. Listen to their words, and also pay attention to the possible meanings of their behavior. For example, if a child is acting out, is she telling you "Please stop me, because I can't stop myself"? If a child is continually screaming, he might be saying "Notice me! Nobody else does."

Remaining open to what children are trying to tell you about themselves is difficult if you cling to preconceived labels and diagnoses. The children you work with are often categorized and labeled. Be careful not to limit their ability to change by responding to them in terms of rigid categories.

Prepare for Termination Children are quick to form attachments with adults who display a concerned and caring attitude toward them. Well before your group ends—for example, 3 sessions before the end of a 12-session group—you must let the children know that the termination point is not far off. This notice allows the children to express their sadness, and it allows you to share your sadness with them. Avoid promising them that you will keep in contact with them, if that is not possible. If you don't deal with these issues, they may see you as running out on them and consider you as one more adult they cannot trust. (At this point it is a good idea to review the guidelines for the final stage of a group, described in Chapter 8.)

Know Your Limitations Be realistic and realize that you cannot work effectively with every child or provide all the needed services. It is essential that you know the boundaries of your competence. You should also make it a practice to know referral resources and be willing to make use of these resources when it is in the child's best interest.

PERSONAL AND PROFESSIONAL QUALIFICATIONS

Some of the *personal* characteristics that we see as important in working with children are patience, caring, playfulness, a good sense of humor, the ability to tune in to and remember one's own childhood and adolescent experiences, firmness without punitiveness, flexibility, the ability to express anger without sarcasm, great concern for and interest in children, and the other characteristics of group leaders that were described in Chapter 3.

Five of the *professional* qualifications that we believe are especially important for those leading groups with children are:

- a thorough understanding of the developmental tasks and stages of the particular age group
- a good understanding of counseling skills, especially as they pertain to group work
- knowledge and skills necessary to work effectively with children from culturally diverse populations
- supervised training in working with minors in groups before leading a group alone
- knowledge of the literature and significant research pertaining to counseling children and adolescents

In addition to these qualifications, other specific competencies and skills are essential to effectively lead groups of children or adolescents. For a listing, refer to Chapter 3 and review the *Professional Standards for Training of Group Workers* of the Association for Specialists in Group Work.

BE AWARE OF YOUR OWN LIMITATIONS

It is easy to overextend yourself when working with children and adolescents whose problems are pressing and severe. Working with youngsters who are abused and neglected, you might find it difficult to separate yourself from their life situations. If you are consistently preoccupied with their problems, you may discover that this is affecting your life and your relationships negatively. It is a personal matter for you to discover how much you are capable of giving, as well as how much and what you need to do to replenish yourself to stay excited and creative in your work.

A SCHOOL COUNSELING PROGRAM*

I designed a group for children ranging in age from 6 to 11 at an elementary school. The program was federally funded, and its continuation was constantly threatened by financial cutbacks. This is a reality many counselors have to deal with, since so many programs depend on external sources of funding.

Ten to 15 children made up my caseload; I was to see each child once a week for about an hour for a total of 24 visits. The children were referred to me by the principal, the teacher, or the school nurse, and had a host of problems similar to those listed in the introduction to this chapter. It was up to me to design a program that would improve the children's behavior in class. My goal was to deal with the problems underlying the children's behavior, which tended to alleviate the children's school difficulties and prevented development of more serious problems.

THE INITIAL PHASE

Contact with School Personnel Being fully aware that counselors are often mistrusted in schools, I set out to earn the trust of the teachers and administrators. First, I met with them to determine what they hoped the project would accomplish. I told them that I wanted to work closely with them, providing feedback about the children, making

*This section is written from the perspective of Marianne Corey.

specific recommendations, and getting their suggestions. I let them know that I intended to work with the children individually and in groups and to involve the parents in the treatment process as much as possible.

Accordingly, I developed a program in which I was in continuous contact with the children's teachers, principal, and parents. The teachers and the principal were very cooperative about meeting with me. I also spoke frequently with the school psychologist, the school nurse, and the school secretaries about particular children, gathering as much information as I could. This information turned out to be most helpful.

The Setting   The setting for my work with the children was not ideal. The school was short on space (a new school was being built), and I was continually looking for a place to meet with the children. When the weather allowed, we often met on the school lawn, because I needed a place where they could explore, touch, talk loudly, shout if they were angry, or give vent to any other emotions they were experiencing. If I took them off campus or did anything special with them, I first obtained written permission from the parents and the school authorities. Although I never had an ideal place to work, this did not keep me from working effectively with the children, as we often improvised together. The children were very adaptive.

Because the same private office was not available to me on a regular basis, I had to pick up the children from their classrooms, something that concerned me. How would the children react to being singled out? Would my special attention to them amid their peers affect them negatively? Fortunately, I found the contrary to be true. The children responded very positively to my coming to pick them up and were always ready to come with me, even during recess time. Frequently, their classmates would ask whether they could come see me too.

Initial Contact with the Parents   After meeting with the school staff, who identified which children I would be working with, I contacted the parents of each child. The parents knew before I visited them about my intended involvement with their child, because I had asked the principal and the child's teacher to contact them. During my initial contact, I explained that their child had been referred to me by the teacher, who had become concerned about the student's behavior in class. This interview gave the parents a chance to get to know me and to ask questions, and it gave me the chance to get the parents' permission to work with their child. At this time I gathered information regarding any difficulties the parents were having with the child and collected the data I needed to complete numerous forms. If parents became anxious over my probing or over the fact that *their* child had been singled out for counseling, I explained to them that because teachers have to deal with so many children, they can't always provide all the attention a child needs. It would be my job, I said, to provide this extra attention.

Although the school's policy stipulated obtaining parental permissions for children to become participants in a group, this is not a required policy in all school districts. State laws regarding parental permission to counsel minors also vary. As a general rule, I think it is best to get the parents' permission and to work with them as allies, rather than risking their disapproval by counseling their children without their knowledge and consent. There are exceptions, however. When counselors are not legally required to secure the consent of parents and when notifying them could be detrimental to the minor client, the welfare of these children should always take priority.

I had previously counseled only people who had requested my services. It was a new experience to be confronted by the suspicions of parents who had been informed that their child needed my services. But for the most part parents were willing to cooperate and gave their consent. In response to my question about any difficulties they might be experiencing with their child at home, which I asked to get clues to the child's behavior in school, the parents were guarded at first. They became much more open with time and frequent contacts. My aim was not to communicate in any way that they were "bad" parents, as this would certainly have aroused their defensiveness. Their children were experiencing difficulties, and I wanted to solicit their help in assisting the students to work through these problems. By going into the child's home, I was able to get much more information relating to the problems the child was exhibiting that would otherwise have been difficult, if not impossible, to obtain.

I told the parents that their children would be discussing with me problems related to school, home, and peers. I explained that I wished to keep as confidential as possible what the child and I would be exploring in our sessions. Therefore, I explained, I would let them know in a general way how I was proceeding with the child but would not reveal any of the specifics, unless I was required to do so by law. The parents were agreeable. I also told them that I hoped to see them sometimes together with their children. However, it was difficult to see some parents again after my initial contact because every one of them was employed. I was able to make at least some additional contact with most parents, and I spoke with others on the telephone.

Initial Contact with the Children   The children were reluctant to initiate a conversation, being accustomed only to answering questions. They needed some structure and some guidelines for expressing themselves and an acknowledgment that it was difficult for them.

I introduced myself to them, saying that I was a special type of teacher called a counselor. I explained that their teacher was concerned about their behavior in class and that they would be talking with me several times a week—individually, as a group, and in their homes. I told them that we would be discussing problems they had in school, at home, or with fellow pupils.

I let the children know that I would be talking about them with their parents and teachers and that I would tell them when I made such contacts. Although I said I did consider much of what we would talk about in the group to be confidential, I told them I would discuss with their parents and teachers anything that would be important in helping them work through any of their difficulties. I felt strongly that it was just as important for a 6-year-old to know that what he or she told me would be treated with confidentiality as it would be for a 60-year-old. Children's rights are too often violated, and their need for privacy is too often ignored. At this time I also let them know that they were not to talk to others about what fellow group members revealed. This was one of the rules we discussed again in the group sessions. I told them that they could talk about matters that concerned them, including their fears and their hurts. Additionally, I let them know that I could not keep everything confidential, especially if it concerned their safety. In language that they could understand, I explained the purpose of confidentiality and its limitations. They were also informed that they would not be allowed to hurt other children, either physically or verbally, or to destroy any property. Other rules were established, and I made the children aware of their responsibility. To be part of the group, they had to agree to follow these rules.

There turned out to be little problem with maintaining confidentiality. When others in the children's classes asked them what they did in their sessions, I heard them say that they played games and talked about feelings.

EVOLUTION OF THE GROUP

Working with the Children in a Group   My goal was to pinpoint some of the children's maladaptive behaviors, teach them how to express emotions without hurting themselves or others, and provide a climate in which they would feel free to express a range of feelings. I wanted to convey to the youngsters that feelings such as anger did not get them into trouble; it is certain ways of acting on these feelings that can lead to problems. In an effort to teach them ways of safely expressing the full gambit of their feelings, I involved them in a variety of activities, including role playing, play therapy, acting out special situations, painting, finishing stories that I began, putting on puppet shows, playing music, and dancing.

The groups that were easiest to work with and most productive were composed of three to five children of the same age and same sex. In larger groups I found myself (1) unable to relate intensely to individuals, (2) slipping into the role of disciplinarian to counteract the increased distractions, (3) feeling frustrated at the number of children competing for my attention, and (4) not having enough time left over to pay attention to underlying dynamics. In addition, children between the ages of 6 and 11 tend to become impatient if they have to wait very long for their turn to speak.

I took care to combine withdrawn children with more outgoing ones, but I also felt that it was important for the children to be with others who were experiencing similar conflicts. For example, I put in the same group two boys who felt much anger, hurt, grief, and frustration over their parents' divorces and subsequent remarriages. They slowly learned how to express their feelings about not having much contact with the parent they didn't live with. At first, the boys could only express their feelings symbolically, through play; later, they learned to put words to their emotions and to talk about their feelings.

As I had planned, I provided some time for each child during which he or she could have my attention alone. I noticed that in the group all the children became less jealous of one another about me and trusted me more once I had begun to provide this individual time. Alone, the children were more cooperative and less competitive. They felt less need to show off. Having an adult spend time with them individually gave them a sense of importance. With the teacher's consent I also visited the children who were in my group frequently in their classrooms and on the playground, sometimes just observing and sometimes making a brief contact through touch or words. While this was time consuming, it proved to be productive in the long run.

Our scheduled group and individual sessions took place twice a week and lasted from half an hour to an hour. It would have been a mistake for me to insist that sessions always last a certain length of time, because the children's patience varied from session to session. When they wanted to leave a group session, I would say in a friendly manner that they were free to leave, but I wished they would stay until the session was over. They usually elected to stay. If they chose to leave, I would not have them come back to that session. Most of the time the children enjoyed the sessions. It was a good practice to let them know in advance that a session was coming to an end and then to be firm about having them leave and not give in to their demands that the group continue.

My groups were open, in that new members could join. The children already in the group handled this situation very well. They knew the newcomer from school and didn't meet the child with any negative reactions or resistance.

During the sessions, I let the children lead the way and listened to what they had to say, directly or through various symbolic means. Playing with puppets turned out to be an excellent means of revealing a variety of emotions and dramatizing situations that produce conflict. I made puppets available to the first- and second-grade children but found that even the fourth- and fifth-grade students were able to use them to vent their pent-up emotions.

The groups offered the children the opportunity to act out situations that aroused conflicting feelings. Sometimes I would suggest a problem situation, and at other times the children would select a problem to act out. The children would take the role of teacher, friend, principal, parent, brother, sister, or whoever else was involved. In this way they were able to release their emotions without hurting others.

Several sessions might pass before a child would speak freely. I sat close to the children during the sessions, often maintaining physical contact, which seemed to have a calming effect by itself. I listened to them attentively, often reflecting for them what they were saying but, more importantly, communicating to them, usually nonverbally, that I was with them, what they were saying was important, and that I cared about what they had to say. I insisted that other members in the group listen and reassured all of them that each would have a time to speak. This is a very difficult concept to get across, especially to a 6- or 7-year-old who is still very self-centered and learning to share.

Sometimes, after a session that I thought had been unproductive, I was surprised to hear a teacher comment on a child's changed behavior. After one such session a boy who had previously been very destructive and disobedient became cooperative and able to relate to his peers. Pounding a lump of clay, which could be interpreted as nonproductive, turned out to have been very important to him. It had relieved much of his anger and so reduced his need to strike out at others.

At times I questioned whether my work with the children was doing any good. Changes in their behavior were slow in coming and sometimes temporary. Some children gave the appearance of improving one week, yet the next week their behavior would again be very negative. My firm belief that a child can change if afforded the opportunity to change was challenged again and again.

However, most children made definite changes, as observed by the teacher, the principal, the parents, and me. Truants began to come to school more regularly. A boy who was in the habit of stealing and giving his loot to other children so they would like him learned that his behavior was one of the reasons others disliked him in the first place, and he began to get their attention through more positive actions. A girl who had been conditioned not to trust learned to make friends and to reach out first, doing what at one time she had most feared.

These changes, though encouraging, needed to be reinforced at home. Although most parents welcomed many of their child's new behaviors, some found the new behavior threatening. For instance, one girl caused her mother some anxiety by beginning to ask probing questions about her absent father. I encouraged this mother—and other parents facing similar problems—to try to listen to the child nondefensively.

It was disconcerting to know that some of the children frequently faced difficult circumstances at home, and yet I realized that I did not have control over that domain. Rather than allowing myself to get too discouraged over the fact that I could not change their situation at home, I had to remind myself that I could provide them with a positive experience at school that would have a constructive impact on them. As counselors we need to remind ourselves to focus on what we can do and not become overwhelmed by all that we cannot do.

Termination of the Group   When I began to work with the children, I told them that the sessions would go on for only a limited time during the school year. Several sessions before termination, I reminded them that the group and individual sessions would be ending soon, and we discussed the imminent termination of our meetings.

Although I had been affectionate with the children during our time together, I hadn't deceived them by becoming a substitute mother or by establishing myself as a permanent fixture who would totally satisfy all their needs. I was aware of establishing appropriate boundaries in carrying out the primary purpose of the group experience. By being realistic about the limits of my job from the beginning, I was able to prevent termination from being a catastrophic experience for the children.

Teacher Evaluation of the Counseling Program   Like the parents, the teachers provided me with ongoing information regarding the children's progress. I was able to use this information in deciding how long to see a particular child or what problem area to focus on. In addition, the teachers prepared written evaluations for my program director, and they shared these evaluations with me.

Why the Group Format Is Effective   My clients, aged 6 to 11, were at a stage of growth in which they were leaving parents and home part of the day, expanding their relationships to include other adults, exploring and testing out-of-home environments, and developing peer relationships. Since most of my referrals were children who had deficiencies in relating to others, the group was an excellent means for them to learn and practice relational skills.

In addition, using the group format allowed me to spend more time with each child than would have been possible had I used only individual sessions. However, since individual sessions are valuable for their own reasons, I preferred having both types of contact with each child. The groups also allowed me to experience the child as the teacher did, thus giving me another perspective to assess interactions with peers. I could witness interactions firsthand, and I could give immediate feedback. This process maximized the chances that learning would take place. By its very nature, the group encouraged the children to discuss problems they had in common. After directly expressing emotions that had been bottled up, the children had less need to express these feelings indirectly by withdrawing, fighting, or getting sick.

SPECIAL PROBLEMS REQUIRING OUT-OF-GROUP ATTENTION

Children have a multitude of developmental problems, and there are many avenues of help for these problems. In working effectively with children, counselors must be willing to involve as many resources and people as possible. There is much room for creativity in developing a variety of programs to meet the diverse needs and the diverse cultural backgrounds of children. It is important to let the parents know about these programs and resources so that they, too, are involved in the helping process.

The children referred to me were, almost without exception, identified as having learning problems. Often these learning disabilities were a reflection of their emotional conflicts. Because I was unable to provide the necessary tutorial assistance, I contacted a nearby university and recruited five graduate students to tutor the children for credit in their child psychology course. In addition to providing tutorial services, they gave the children additional positive individual attention. This tutoring proved very successful for both the children and the university students.

When I detected health problems I referred the child to the school nurse. When I suspected neglect or abuse, I took the appropriate action. Counselors who work with minors need to be aware of the reporting laws for suspected abuse in their state as well as their work setting. They must know the specific steps to be taken in making the required reports. It is always helpful to communicate with Child Protective Services to obtain information on assessing and reporting suspected child abuse.

WORKING OUTSIDE THE GROUP

Working with Families   I've already stressed that I contacted the parents as often as I could to involve them in their child's counseling. On several occasions I was able to arrange for family sessions, not only discussing the child's problems but also inquiring into the child's behavior within the context of the family. I felt enthusiastic about working with entire families, yet it was hard to arrange such sessions, for reasons of time and scheduling. I found that stopping by a child's home just to visit or to show movies and pictures of the child that I had taken during a trip to the mountains or at a swimming party was just as valuable as "work" sessions. It seemed especially meaningful to show the movies of the children to the families, because this made the children feel special and proud. These visits increased the parents' trust in what I was doing and their willingness to cooperate with me.

Working with Teachers   It helps to work with an enthusiastic and caring teaching staff. We combined our efforts to come up with ways of improving the children's overall school experience. The teachers instituted classroom procedures that were extensions and continuations of the work I was doing. For instance, a teacher might give a few moments of individual positive attention when he or she saw that the child was about to ask for attention in a negative way. In addition to meeting with the teachers, I also made frequent contacts with the principal, the school nurse, the school secretaries, the school psychologist, and the school librarian to solicit additional information about the children and feedback about what I was doing.

Tapping Outside Resources   Because a counselor works with the total child, he or she needs to know what services, agencies, associations, companies, and individuals can be contacted for help when counseling is not enough. Many children are undernourished, underclothed, and in need of medical assistance, recreational opportunities, or supervision after school. Counseling is more likely to have an effect if the child's basic needs are being met. The counselor may have to do much of the legwork required to obtain food, clothing, money, or special services for the children and their families. Some families resisted turning to outside agencies because of pride or fear that strings would be attached or simply out of ignorance about where to go for help. When a family did want help with emotional, economic, or medical problems, I referred them to one of the appropriate agencies. However, I often made the contacts with the agencies and did the paperwork they required. More often than not, counselors do not have time to make the contacts I've described. But they can sometimes be creative in finding ways to delegate these tasks to others.

Probably the most important (and most often overlooked) method of obtaining services for children and their families is asking. Private companies, concerned citizens, and the school staff are all potential resources, both for material goods and for suggestions about where else to go for help. I can't stress enough that the total needs of the child must be considered if his or her emotional needs are to be met.

CHILDREN'S GROUPS IN COMMUNITY AGENCIES*

One of our colleagues, Randy Alle-Corliss, who has worked as a clinical social worker in several community mental health agencies and now works in a department of psychiatry in a large health maintenance organization (HMO), has designed groups for children with much the same basic structure and format as the one just described. In the following section, Randy describes his way of organizing and leading children's groups.

---

* This section is written from the perspective of Randy Alle-Corliss. If you would like more information about this group for children, you can contact Randy Alle-Corliss at his private practice: 440 W. Baseline Road, Claremont, CA 91711; telephone (909) 920-1850.

I originally got the idea to organize groups for children as a result of working with parents who came to my agency complaining about the behavioral problems of their children. I also had observed and participated as a co-leader in a number of childrens' groups within a community agency. When I began my first group I sought out other therapists on the staff as referral sources, giving them information that would help them determine what kind of children might benefit from the group. Conversely, the themes of my groups are often determined by the needs of the referral sources. I also typically obtain additional information by consulting with teachers, parents, and therapists who have any involvement with the children to be placed in the group.

I screen and orient the children, as well as educate and orient parents about the nature of the group. I meet with the child individually to talk about the group and to answer any questions. This is an excellent way to establish a trusting relationship. I also see the parents without the child, and then I see the parents and the child together to get a sense of the family situation. Selecting the group membership is an extremely important issue. I purposely screen to balance the qualities in a group—for example, mixing acting-out children with passive and withdrawn children. It is also important to balance the group by gender. The age of the children is another factor. The age range among the members should not be too wide, or it is difficult to provide for a commonality of developmental issues and concerns of the children.

I prefer to work with a female co-leader. This provides adult modeling and allows for parental transference issues to be explored in the sessions. The groups are limited to nine months, with some changing membership. They meet once a week for an hour. During the first 20 minutes, the co-leaders talk with the children about their current concerns. The next 20 minutes is devoted to various play activities. The children draw pictures, use sand trays, and engage in both structured and spontaneous play. The leaders are involved in the play, either by observing or by actually participating in the activities. The final 20 minutes is set aside to discuss what happened during the play session, which often serves as a catalyst for brief role playing. Common topics and themes explored in these sessions are: family conflicts; school problems; peer relationships; abandonment, loss, and death; dealing with frustration, aggression, and anger; and dealing with reactions to others in the group.

The primary goals of this group are learning that all feelings are acceptable; learning how to express feelings constructively; identifying with others and feeling less alone with one's problems; learning to change those attitudes, beliefs, feelings, and behaviors that they have the power to change; and accepting the things they can't change, such as the reality of their parents' divorce.

The outcomes include improved peer relations and social skills, cohesion within the group, increased ability to express feelings appropriately, and a decrease of target behaviors such as aggression or withdrawal.

My co-leader and I deal with the eventual termination of the group by alerting the children four weeks in advance. Children thus prepared for the ending of their group are given opportunities to express their feelings about separation, loss, and death. We do this by encouraging the children to review the highlights of the group's history by reminiscing. We facilitate the children's discussion of gains they felt they made. If they could not recall certain significant events, we reminded them about what they actually did in a particular session. We took special care to positively reinforce any gains they had made during the life of the group. Many times there is food and a party at the final session as a way of celebrating the end of a meaningful experience.

A GROUP FOR CHILDREN OF DIVORCE*

It is not uncommon for many children in any elementary school to come from divorced homes. These pupils face a number of personal and social problems, which include being lonely, feeling responsible for the divorce, experiencing divided loyalties, not knowing how to deal with parental conflicts, and facing the loss of family stability. Schools and community agencies are addressing the needs of these children by offering groups structured around these themes. This section describes counseling groups designed for children from divorced families.

PRELIMINARY CONSIDERATIONS IN FORMING THE GROUP

Before actually getting a group going, a great deal of careful preliminary work needs to be done. This preparation includes conducting a needs survey, announcing the group to children and teachers, obtaining parental permission, orienting the children to the rules for participating in a group, and presenting my goals in a clear way to the children, parents, teachers, and administrators. If adequate attention is not given to these preliminary details, the group may never materialize.

Beginning with a Survey of Children's Needs   It is very helpful to assess the needs of children before deciding on a program. I do this by making an initial classroom visit to discuss with both the teachers and the children how small-group counseling can be beneficial. I explain the topical focus of these groups or, as I later refer to them, "clubs." These topics include divorce, stepfamilies, death, stress, and friendship. I run these groups from kindergarten through the fifth grade. The family club is

*The material in this section is written from the perspective of Karen Kram Laudenslager. For more information on these groups, you can contact Karen at: Allentown School District, 31 S. Penn Street, Box 328, Allentown, PA 18105; telephone (610) 820-2128.

geared for grades two through five. I explain that a specific day and time have been scheduled for club meetings at each grade level and that all clubs run for 30 minutes once a week for six sessions.

The needs survey is then handed out, and I ask all students to think about the issues and react truthfully. I explain that these surveys are private and will be read only by the classroom teacher and me. The selection of students is based on comments by both students and teachers.

This survey allows students to have a direct role in determining areas of concern that they are open to and willing to deal with. At the end of the survey, space is provided for students to write in detail about specific feelings or situations they would like me to know about.

Obtaining Parental Permission   A letter, which is reproduced here, is sent home with every child who has agreed to participate in the group. This letter outlines the issues and topics to be discussed and requests parental permission. It also encourages parental support and involvement as well as opening up lines for communication.

Sample Parental-Consent Letter

Dear Parents,

During my time as guidance counselor at _____ Elementary School, I have found that many children have questions and concerns about family situations.

Research has shown that it is helpful for children to share their concerns and feelings with others in a small group. Through this interaction with others who have similar feelings, the child learns to accept and deal with family situations in a positive way.

During the next few months, I will be meeting with children who have experienced a family separation, divorce, remarriage, or loss of a loved one. Some of the topics we will be discussing are feelings, divorce and separation, skills for coping with problems, and building identity and self-esteem.

The groups will be made up of approximately six students from your child's school and will meet for six weeks.

If you have any questions about the group or would like to speak to me about your child, please call me at _____.

Please return the permission form below by _____ to let me know if your child will be participating in the program.

Sincerely,

Karen Laudenslager

. . . .

I acknowledge and support my son's/daughter's participation in the above program and hereby give my written consent.

_____   _____
Parent's signature   Date

Group Rules   All students voluntarily agree to be members of the club. I encourage children who are shy or slightly reluctant to give it a try. Anyone who wishes to discontinue the group is free to do so, but to date I have never had a student drop out.

Children always have the right to remain silent. I reinforce the importance of listening and learning from one another. Some students feel more comfortable knowing that they will never be forced to share or discuss any issue that they feel is private. Other rules are: anyone who wants to can have a turn, everyone is listened to, no laughing or making fun of what anyone says, honesty is required, and confidentiality is respected.

The students, with my guidance, make up the rules during the first session. They usually come up with all of the above on their own. If the group does not identify some critical norms, I will add them to our list of rules. I explain the reasons for the rules, which increases the chances that the children will abide by them. Finally, we all sign our names, making a commitment and agreement to follow the rules.

What Children Need to Know   Following is a list of what I have found through my research, reading, and direct contact with children to be important messages for them to hear. I continually discuss, explain, and reinforce these statements throughout the six-week sessions:

- You are special.
- You can get through this difficult time.
- You have people who care about you.
- It [the divorce or separation] is not your fault.
- You are not to blame.
- It is not your divorce, and no one is divorcing you. Mom and Dad are divorcing each other.
- You did not cause the problems between your parents, and you can't fix them.
- You can help each other.

What I Hope to Accomplish   I have a number of objectives in these groups, some of which are:

- to give support when needed
- to let children know they are not alone
- to teach coping skills
- to reinforce students' need to talk and deal with feelings
- to help them deal with emotional and behavioral concerns so they can reach their potential
- to offer resources to students and parents such as bibliotherapy and outside private counseling when needed
- to help children open lines of communication with other students, teachers, and parents

HIGHLIGHTS OF THE GROUP SESSIONS

The focus of these clubs is developmental rather than therapeutic. The groups are designed to provide support, teach coping skills, and help children of changing families explore ways to express and deal with their feelings. When more involved counseling is needed, the parents are always contacted, and an outside referral is made.

Sessions of 30 minutes each, once a week for six weeks, work well. This schedule allows me time to run more groups and see more children. With so many students experiencing family changes, I try to help as many as possible. This time structure interferes only minimally with classroom learning. I try to be sensitive to the reactions of both students and teachers to interrupting the learning process. Too much time out of class for extended periods can cause additional stress, and we are all concerned with supporting and enhancing the learning process, not disrupting it. At times, these clubs meet at lunch.

The Initial Meeting   The first session is clearly structured by focusing on a discussion of the purpose of the club, on my role as a group facilitator, and on helping the children identify why they are in the group. We play a "name game," in which the children introduce themselves by selecting an adjective describing them that starts with the first letter of their first name (such as Wonderful Wanda or Nice Nick). The only guideline is that the adjective must be a positive one. We define *family*, and each child introduces himself or herself by answering the question "Who am I, and who lives at my house?" We discuss how many different places we live and with whom. I encourage them to describe how it is for them to be in their family. At this session the ground rules are established and written on chart paper for use as a reminder at all subsequent sessions. My goal for this first meeting is to help the children find out that they are not alone in their situation. If time allows, I encourage them to see similarities and differences in their family situations. I may ask "Who would like to share how your family is the same as or different from others in this group?"

The Next Four Sessions   I have found that my groups differ somewhat. Depending on the themes that are brought out at the initial session, I use selected exercises as a focus for interaction. The middle four sessions are structured in accordance with the needs of those who are in the group. Here are a few of the activities that are often part of these sessions:

•   We play the "feeling game." Students brainstorm feelings, and we write them down. The children then select three feelings that describe how they feel about their family situation, and we discuss them.
•   The children identify three wishes they have for their family. One overwhelming wish that generally emerges is that their mother and father

will get back together. They also wish to spend more time with the non-custodial parent. These children often express how difficult it is for them to be placed in the middle of a struggle, and they wish for peace. They would like this harmony at any cost, and they are willing to do anything to bring it about.

• The children decide "what I want each of my parents to know." (Stepparents and stepbrothers and stepsisters may also be included, if appropriate.) I often find that the children are hesitant to reveal some differences they might have with their new stepmother or stepfather. They frequently want their parents to understand their feelings about being in a new family. Sometimes children feel forced to make an adjustment before they are ready, and they often have uncomfortable feelings that have not been discussed.

• We discuss what children can control and what they cannot. For example, they can control their own behavior. We also talk about ways they can control certain feelings. However, they cannot control the decisions that their parents make about the divorce or current living situations. I also talk with the children about the fact that this is not *their* divorce. In other words, Mom and Dad are divorcing each other, not the children. What I hope to get across to the group members is that they did not cause the divorce and cannot "fix" the situation. Much of the group time is devoted to exploring and brainstorming alternatives for the children to change themselves in their situations at home.

• We discuss the issue of change. The children identify what they consider to be positive and negative changes in their lives as a result of the new family situation.

• A question box is available during all sessions. Students can anonymously write questions or concerns that they might not feel comfortable sharing in group and drop them in the question box. These issues are discussed at the next session.

• We read and discuss the following books, depending on relevance and interest:

> *Dinosaurs Divorce: A Guide for Changing Families* (Brown & Brown, 1986).
>
> *Now I Have a Step Parent and It's Kind of Confusing* (Stenson, 1979).
>
> *Divorce Is a Grown-up Problem* (Sinberg, 1978).
>
> *The Divorce Workbook: A Guide for Kids and Families* (Ives, Fassler, & Lash, 1985).

The Last Session   As is true of the initial session, the final meeting is fairly structured, this time around the tasks of termination. The children typically discuss feelings about the club ending and identify what they have learned from these sessions. There is also some time for a special celebration with cupcake treats. Each student receives a recognition certificate, which says: *The Counselor Said I Am Special!*

THE ROLE OF TEACHERS AND PARENTS IN THE GROUP PROGRAM

Any counselor who works in an elementary school can testify to the importance of getting feedback and support from teachers and parents. I have found that it is critical to involve parents, teachers, and administrators in these group programs, so that they become allies of the children and the counselor. Their support of the program goes a long way toward ensuring its success; their resistance can thwart its progress.

Comments from Teachers   Teachers' feedback is critical, because they see the student daily and can monitor changes in behavior. I make an effort to talk with each classroom teacher as often as possible, yet time often works against me. I hope to develop a teacher checklist and rating scale to document and facilitate this interaction. I have found that most teachers are concerned about the emotional and behavioral blocks that interfere with learning. They can tell counselors about pupils' self-esteem, self-confidence, interaction with their peers, and homework completion. They can also share comments and reactions that students make in class, both orally and in their written work. All of this information helps me monitor the student's emotional and social progress.

Parental Support   I always send the letter seeking parental permission home with the student and encourage each child to discuss the group with both parents. However, I realize that this does not always happen. I attempt to be sensitive to each individual family situation. Yet I am convinced of the value of involving both parents whenever possible.

OUTCOMES, FOLLOW-UP, AND A PERSONAL PERSPECTIVE

Student Perceptions   Students report feeling more comfortable with themselves and with their family situations when they belong to the club and realize that they are not alone. They need to identify with other children who are experiencing similar concerns and feelings. Together, group members can begin to understand the stages that everyone goes through and can learn skills to help themselves feel better. They help one another, through the group process, let go of what they cannot control and take responsibility for what they can control.

Teachers' and Administrators' Perceptions   Teachers report that students in the groups often concentrate better in class. Johanna Price, a second-grade teacher, said that "as teachers strive to adjust the learning environment to meet each child's needs, they may find that the many demands of the school day allow little opportunity to offer the child the kind of individual attention and interaction that is provided during the club sessions." Julie Zager, a fourth-grade teacher, commented: "The days are full and classes are large. Teachers provide personal attention, but it is not always possible to give as much encouragement and support to an individual student as might be needed. Small-group clubs led by a caring and sensitive counselor can provide feedback to help the teacher raise self-esteem, which in turn can increase student achievement." According to Dennis Blankowitsch, a school principal, "The school family now becomes the most consistent, predictable support for children adjusting to changing families."

Parent Perceptions   Parents report that their children enjoy the club meetings and often come home and share what was discussed. Their children gain a better understanding of divorce by learning how others adjust. Parents are often in so much pain and conflict themselves during the separation or divorce that they are relieved and happy that someone else is there supporting their children.

Parents show an interest in what their children are doing in the group, and parents often read some of the recommended books with their children. Many parents have expressed a need for more information on how they can help their children. I have offered evening workshops and parenting classes. I would like to develop an ongoing parent support group to meet the needs of adults. I have also thought it might be helpful to facilitate one or two sessions with both parents and children together.

Follow-Up   My follow-up consists of checking with teachers on the students' progress and checking with the students themselves by classroom visits, by seeing them individually, and by encouraging self-referrals. I also hold club "reunions" the following year to see how things have been going.

Personal Sources of Frustration   The biggest frustration for me is ending the clubs. The children always resist terminating and bargain or plead to continue with more sessions. I find it extremely difficult to end when I know how much these children need to talk and learn. I am unable to directly solve some of the children's problems, and that adds to my level of frustration. These complex problems include:

- infrequent visitations with a parent as a result of the parent's emotional problems
- dislocations because a child is "interfering" with a parent's relationships
- frequent court testimony in sexual abuse cases
- violence in the family

- parental neglect
- conflicts over being asked by parents to choose sides
- parents' extramarital affairs
- alcohol and drug abuse
- spousal abuse
- physical or emotional abuse
- custody battles
- financial concerns

Another source of frustration is time. There never seems to be enough time to see all the students who need help. Nor is there enough time to meet with all the parents to discuss the progress of each child. I do, however, refer families for outside counseling if during the club sessions I see a need for more in-depth therapy.

Concluding Comments   I have found the group experience to be very effective and instrumental in supporting students with changes and family issues. Students are able to connect with each other and offer support, encouragement, suggestions, and hope. In the group, they can help each other to understand feelings and learn how to handle difficult situations in a safe place. It has been my experience that this small group structure is extremely beneficial. I strongly recommend that counselors provide this kind of counseling service for students.

WHERE TO GO FROM HERE

Two useful resources by Paperbacks for Educators that contain a wide variety of books for children and adolescents are *School Counselor Catalog, K-5,* and *Bibliotherapy for Children Catalog,* both 1995 editions. These catalogs consist of an annotated list of books dealing with a wide range of topics, from abuse and neglect through values/decision-making and wellness. These catalogs can be obtained by contacting Paperbacks for Educators, 426 West Front Street, Washington, MO 63090; telephone (800) 227-2591.

A resource for videos is *Guidance Club for Kids,* a catalog of videos on a wide range of topics in areas of self-esteem, school success, drug education, and life skills. Also available is *Guidance Club for Teens,* which contains a video series for grades 7 to 12. For further information contact Ready Reference Press, P. O. Box 5249, Santa Monica, CA 90409; telephone (800) 424-5627.

Two useful books for those who counsel children in groups are *Skills for Living: Group Counseling Activities for Elementary Students* (Morganett-Smead, 1994) and *Skills and Techniques for Group Work with Children and Adolescents* (Smead, 1995). The first book provides practical suggestions for getting children's groups started and for developing group agendas. Some of the themes addressed in this book include: building self-esteem, getting along with others, coping with stress in divorce, grieving and growing, dealing with anger, and learning responsibility. The second book is a "how to" manual that describes how, why, and when to use 24 specific skills and techniques.

Other books that contain chapters of specific interest to those conducting groups with children include:

- *Windows to Our Children: A Gestalt Approach to Children and Adolescents* (Oaklander, 1978). This how-to book describes Oaklander's work with children in a very sensitive and straightforward manner and points out cautions and pitfalls to the counselor.
- *Working with Children and Adolescents in Groups* (Rose & Edleson, 1987). This excellent book presents a specific guide for the multimethod approach to treating children in groups, with many examples covering children in all age groups from kindergarten through adolescence. Separate chapters deal with specific topics for each stage of a group.

REFERENCES AND SUGGESTED READINGS*

Axline, V. M. (1976). *Dibs: In search of self.* New York: Ballantine.

Brown, L. K., & Brown, M. (1986). *Dinosaurs divorce: A guide for changing families.* Boston: Little, Brown.

Gladding, S. (1992). *Counseling as an art: Creative arts in counseling.* Alexandria, VA: American Counseling Association.

Guidance club for kids. (1994). Santa Monica, CA: Ready Reference Press.

Guidance club for teens. (1994). Santa Monica, CA: Ready Reference Press.

Ives, S. B., Fassler, D., & Lash, M. (1985). *The divorce workbook: A guide for kids and families.* Burlington, VT: Waterfront Books.

*Morganett, R. S. (1990). *Skills for living: Group counseling activities for young adolescents.* Champaign, IL: Research Press.

*Morganett-Smead, R. S. (1994). *Skills for living: Group counseling activities for elementary students.* Champaign, IL: Research Press.

*Oaklander, V. (1978). *Windows to our children: A Gestalt approach to children and adolescents.* Moab, UT: Real People Press.

*Paperbacks for educators. (1995). *Bibliotherapy for children catalog.* Washington, MO: Paperbacks for Educators.

*Paperbacks for educators. (1995). *School counselor catalog, K-5.* Washington, MO: Paperbacks for Educators.

Rose, S. D., & Edleson, J. L. (1987). *Working with children and adolescents in groups: A multimethod approach.* San Francisco: Jossey-Bass.

*Rudman, M. K., Gagne, K. D., & Bernstein, J. E. (Eds.). (1994). *Books to help children cope with separation and loss: An annotated bibliography.* New Providence, NJ: R. R. Bowker.

Sinberg, J. (1978). *Divorce is a grown-up problem.* New York: Avon.

*Entries marked with an asterisk are recommended for further reading.

*Smead, R. (1995). *Skills and techniques for group work with children and adolescents*. Champaign, IL: Research Press.

Stenson, J. S. (1979). *Now I have a stepparent and it's kind of confusing*. New York: Avon.

*Thompson, C. L., & Rudolph, L. B. (1996). *Counseling children* (4th ed.). Pacific Grove, CA: Brooks/Cole.

Vernon, A. (1993). *Counseling children and adolescents*. Denver, CO: Love Publishing.

CHAPTER 10

GROUPS FOR ADOLESCENTS

**Introduction: Special Needs and Problems
  of Adolescents**

Sample Proposal for an Adolescent Group

Rationale
Type of Group
Goals and Objectives
Basic Information
Basic Ground Rules
Topics for Possible Group Exploration
Evaluation Methods

**Organizing the Group Experience
  for Adolescents**

Description of an Adolescent Group

Establishing Trust and Dealing with Resistance
Working with Involuntary and Resistant Adolescents
The Influence of the Leader's Personality
Keeping the Sessions Moving
Action-Oriented Techniques of Role Playing
Getting Group Members to Participate and Initiate
The Use of Peer Counselors

Involving Parents

Parent-Consultation Groups
Groups of Parents and Adolescents

Children of Alcoholics

A High School Group for Children of Alcoholics

Practical Considerations
Group Goals

INTRODUCTION: SPECIAL NEEDS AND
PROBLEMS OF ADOLESCENTS

A detailed description of the unique needs and problems of adolescents is beyond the scope of this book. For group leaders who work with adolescents, good courses in the psychology of adolescence are essential. Reading and reflecting on one's own adolescent experiences and perhaps reliving some of these experiences are also valuable means of preparing oneself to counsel adolescents. Those who wish to review the field of the psychology of adolescence can refer to the suggested readings at the end of this chapter.

The adolescent period is a time of searching for an identity and developing a system of values that will influence the course of one's life. One of the most important needs of this period is to experience successes that will lead to a sense of self-confidence and self-respect. Adolescents need to recognize and accept the wide range of their feelings, and they need to learn how to communicate with significant others in such a way that they can make their wants, feelings, thoughts, and beliefs known.

The adolescent years can be extremely lonely ones; it is not unusual for adolescents to feel that they are alone in their conflicts and self-doubt. It is a period of life when people feel a desperate need for universal approval yet must learn to distinguish between living for others' approval and earning their own. During these years, the dependence/independence struggle becomes central. While part of the teenager yearns for independence from parents, another part longs for security. Adolescents must cope with decisions, such as vocational and educational choices, that will influence their future. To make these choices wisely, they must have information both about their abilities and interests and about such realities as job opportunities and college entrance requirements.

Sexual conflicts are also part of this period; adolescents not only need to establish a meaningful guide for their sexual behavior but also must wrestle with the problem of their sex-role identification. Teenagers may have real difficulty clarifying what it means to be a man or a woman and what kind of man or woman they want to become.

Adolescents are pressured to succeed; they are expected to perform, frequently up to others' standards. They need to be trusted and given the freedom to make some significant decisions, and they need the faith and support of caring adults. But they also need guidelines and limits.

Adolescence is a time for continually testing limits, for this period is characterized by an urge to break away from control or dependent ties that restrict freedom. Although adolescents are often frightened of the freedom they do experience, they tend to mask their fears with rebellion and cover up their dependency needs by exaggerating their newly felt autonomy. They are often moody, negativistic, and rebellious. The rebellion of adolescents can be understood as an attempt to determine the course of their own lives and to assert that they are who and what they want to be, rather than what others expect of them.

A central part of the adolescent experience is peer-group pressure, a potent force that pulls at the person to conform to the standards of friends. Because of adolescents' exaggerated need for approval, there is a danger that they will sell themselves out and increasingly look to others to tell them who and what they should be. The need for acceptance by one's peer group is often stronger than the need for self-respect. This can lead to a range of behaviors that cause problems for adolescents such as dependence on drugs or alcohol in order to feel anything or to escape from painful feelings.

Adolescents tend to be more aware of what the world does to them than of what they do to the world. Thus, they can be highly critical and fault finding. At times they may want to drop out of society, yet at other times they may idealistically strive to reform society. Adolescents confront dilemmas similar to those faced by the elderly in our society: finding meaning in life and wrestling with feelings of uselessness. Older people are often forced to retire before they feel ready to do so, and the young have not yet completed their education or acquired the skills essential for many lines of work. Thus, adolescents are continually preparing for the future, which is often marked by uncertainty.

In sum, for most people adolescence is a difficult period, characterized by paradoxes: they strive for closeness, yet they also fear intimacy and often avoid it; they rebel against control, yet they want direction and structure; although they push and test limits imposed on them, they see some limits as a sign of caring; they are not given complete autonomy, yet they are often expected to act as though they were mature adults; they are typically highly self-centered, self-conscious, and preoccupied with their own world, yet they are expected to cope with societal demands to go outside themselves by expanding their horizons; they are asked to face and accept reality, and at the same time they are tempted by many avenues of escape; and they are exhorted to think of the future, yet they have strong urges to live for the moment and to enjoy life. With all these polarities it is easy to understand that adolescence is typically a turbulent and fast-moving time, one that can accentuate loneliness and isolation. Group experiences can be very useful in helping teenagers deal with these feelings of isolation and make constructive choices for a satisfying life.

This brief sketch of the main currents of adolescent life highlights the need for developmental counseling in this population. Group counseling is especially suitable because adolescents can identify and experience their conflicting feelings, discover that they're not unique in their struggles, openly question those values they decide to modify, learn to communicate with peers and adults, learn from the modeling provided by the leader, and learn how to accept what others offer and to give of themselves in return. Adolescents often need to learn to label and verbalize their feelings. Groups provide a place where they can safely experiment with reality and test their limits. A unique value of group counseling is that it lets adolescents be instrumental in one another's growth; group members help one another in the struggle for self-understanding. Most important, a group gives adolescents a chance to express themselves and to be heard and to interact with their peers.

Groups for adolescents can combine personal themes with psycho-educational goals. In working with adolescents, it is a good practice to have clearly defined goals, relevant themes, and a structure that will enable members to develop trust in the group. Aronson and Scheidlinger (1994) state that adolescents tend to function best in homogeneous groups with explicit limits and clear ground rules. They address the importance of considering the age of members in structuring an adolescent group, making these points:

• Between the ages of 10 and 14, young people are prone to denial and externalization, tend to be more concrete in their thinking, are more self-conscious, and may not show great interest in the process of self-awareness. They function better in either all-male or all-female groups.
• Between the ages of 15 and 18, adolescents are generally able to tolerate more anxiety, and it is critical that older adolescents learn how to interact in a group with both sexes.

Shorter-term groups are growing in popularity in schools, clinics, and community agencies. And the number of specialized groups has increased, including groups for sexually abused adolescents, teenagers from alcoholic families, and youths with chronic medical conditions (Aronson & Scheidlinger, 1994). But not all adolescents belong in a group or benefit from one. For instance, individual counseling may be more appropriate for adolescents who are acting out their hostility. Many times agencies and schools put young people into a group primarily because it is cost-effective or because there are not enough counselors to meet the demand for services. Adolescents should be carefully selected for a particular group.

SAMPLE PROPOSAL FOR
AN ADOLESCENT GROUP

We have worked with adolescents in groups using a developmental model, with a focus on the normal life concerns they face. The following proposal for a group could be modified to fit many special-interest adolescent groups and some children's groups as well. It could be adapted to various settings such as mental-health clinics, community centers, public schools, residential facilities, and family-service agencies.

RATIONALE

Adolescence is a time of paradox, in that conflicts often lead to considerable anxiety and feelings of separateness. Adolescents can benefit from having a place to openly explore a range of their developmental concerns at this juncture in life. Young people need to learn how to cope with increasing freedom and the responsibilities that accompany it. A group can provide the opportunity to share common problems and to find ways of making responsible choices.

TYPE OF GROUP

This will be a personal-growth and self-exploration group for clients between the ages of 15 and 18. The group is not designed to treat personality and behavioral problems. Instead, it is aimed at prevention. This time-limited group will consist of ten members and the two co-leaders. The group will meet for two hours each week, from 7 to 9 P.M., for 15 weeks, and there will be one all-day session around the fifth week. Membership is voluntary. A prerequisite for joining this group is attendance at an individual screening and orientation meeting. Once all the members have been selected, there will be a preliminary session designed to get acquainted with one another and to prepare the participants for a productive group experience. After this pregroup meeting, those members who decide to participate in the group will be asked to make a commitment to remain for its duration.

GOALS AND OBJECTIVES

The group will be a place for self-exploration and for sharing ideas and feelings. Participants will be invited to examine their values, behaviors, and relationships with others and to look at the direction of their lives to determine what changes they want to make. It is the members' responsibility to decide for themselves the nature and extent of these changes. The members will decide when to share personal issues and how much to share. Participants are expected to be active in the sessions, at least to the degree of sharing their reactions to the here-and-now events within the group.

Although each member will be assisted in developing specific, concrete, and personal goals early in the group, the following general goals will provide direction:

- to grow in self-acceptance and self-respect
- to become tolerant of others, to respect others' differences, and to develop a genuine caring for others
- to become sensitive to the needs of others
- to clarify values and examine one's philosophy of life

- to learn how to live with struggles and how to make one's own decisions and accept the consequences of these choices
- to explore conflicts and look for one's own answers
- to develop sufficient trust within the group to allow for an honest sharing of attitudes and feelings
- to learn ways of applying what is learned in the group to everyday situations

BASIC INFORMATION

The proposal gives the names, qualifications, and experience of the co-leaders. It provides pertinent information concerning the fees (if any), dates, and how to sign up for a screening interview.

BASIC GROUND RULES

The group will operate under these rules:

- Members are expected to attend all the sessions and to participate by disclosing themselves and giving feedback to others.
- Members are asked to make a commitment to remain in the group for its entire 15-week life span.
- Members must maintain the confidential nature of others' disclosures.
- It is the participants' responsibility to decide on specific personal goals. This choice will be made within the first few sessions by developing a contract that clearly states what members want to change and how they will go about it.
- Members will not come to the group meeting under the influence of drugs or alcohol.
- Smoking is not allowed during the sessions.
- Members must have the written consent of their parents to participate in the group.

TOPICS FOR POSSIBLE GROUP EXPLORATION

The initial session is typically devoted to teaching the participants how to get the maximum benefit from a group experience, orienting them to the ground rules, and working toward the establishment of trust. Subsequent sessions can be designed jointly by the members and the leaders. Collectively, they can decide on certain common themes and personal issues to provide some structuring to the group. Some examples of theme-oriented sessions are the following:

- dealing with alcohol and drug abuse
- learning how to cope with feelings (of depression, guilt, anxiety, anger, rejection, hostility, loneliness)

- discussing the differences between being alone and being lonely
- exploring conflicts related to school
- dealing with racism and prejudice
- exploring issues of sexual orientation
- discussing careers and post–high school plans
- dealing with violence in the home
- discussing love, sex, intimacy, and gender roles
- dealing with bicultural concerns
- exploring the quality and meaning of one's life
- exploring identity issues ("Who am I?")
- considering separation-individuation concerns
- discussing conflicts over dependency and independence
- discussing conflicts with parents; learning how to live with and appreciate them

Other topics of concern to group participants can be developed as the sessions progress.

EVALUATION METHODS

A follow-up meeting will be held about six weeks after the group ends to assess the impact the group has had on clients. The meeting can provide reinforcement to members, especially to those who have had setbacks since termination of the group. Referrals will be made to other sources to help members continue building on the gains they made in the group.

ORGANIZING THE GROUP EXPERIENCE FOR ADOLESCENTS

Once the proposal for a group for adolescents has been designed, the next major task is dealing with all the preliminary details involved in forming a group. We suggest that you refer to the discussion of procedures for forming groups in Chapter 4 and also review the guidelines for group work with children and adolescents in Chapter 9.

Much of the tedious work of getting a group into operation begins well before the initial meeting. In her very useful manual, *Skills for Living: Group Counseling Activities for Young Adolescents,* Morganett (1990) describes the following ten steps in forming and conducting a structured counseling group for young people:

1. **Conduct a needs assessment.** This process will help you focus your efforts on critical group services needed by specific clients in a particular setting. The assessment can be one of the instruments used

as part of the accountability process. (Morganett provides a sample assessment in an appendix of her book.)

2. **Develop a written proposal.** A written proposal consists of a general description and rationale, objectives, logistics, procedures, and evaluation methods.

3. **Advertise the group.** As a way of letting potential participants know about a group, educate referral sources such as administrators, teachers, and counselors.

4. **Obtain informed consent from the parents or guardians.** Informed consent involves giving specific information about a group so that both the participant and the parent or guardian can make an intelligent decision about whether to participate. (Morganett also provides a sample parent/guardian consent form.)

5. **Conduct pregroup interviews.** In addition to giving a general orientation to the group experience, the purposes of this interview are to ask for the student's commitment and to obtain information that will be useful in making decisions about whom to admit.

6. **Select the group members.** Selections will be largely determined by the purpose of the group. It is the leader's responsibility to choose members who have a good chance of having a positive experience and to screen out those applicants who may not be appropriate for a particular group.

7. **Administer a pretest.** The practice of giving pretests and posttests can provide a framework for assessing the degree to which an individual or the group as a whole has benefited from the experience. (Morganett provides examples of pretests and posttests.)

8. **Conduct the group sessions.** The length of the group can be determined by the group's topic or theme. In most school settings, 8 to 12 sessions are optimum. Morganett provides detailed descriptions of ways to organize group agendas around the following themes:
   - dealing with a divorce
   - meeting, making, and keeping friends
   - learning to communicate assertively
   - developing self-esteem
   - learning stress-management skills
   - learning anger-management skills
   - surviving and succeeding in school
   - coping with grief and loss

9. **Administer a posttest.** After the termination of a group (or at the final group session), it is a good practice to administer the pretest as a posttest instrument.

10. **Conduct a postgroup follow-up and evaluation.** One to two months after the final group session, schedule a follow-up meeting. This will allow members to share their accomplishments and relate the impact the group has had on them. This is a good time to offer

encouragement and provide referrals for further growth experiences. The follow-up meeting is also an excellent source for evaluating the outcomes of a group.

DESCRIPTION OF AN ADOLESCENT GROUP

In this section we discuss ways of motivating the adolescent to become an active group participant and guidelines for conducting the sessions and keeping the meetings moving in a meaningful direction. We address dealing with resistance, facilitating action, using role playing, sustaining the interest of the group, and involving as many members as possible.

We use as an example our experiences as co-leaders of a weekly counseling group for adolescents. Our group consisted of students from a local high school. This was an experimental 15-week program, offered free to the school district and to the participating members. The members were expected to attend all the sessions, which were on Wednesday evenings from 7 to 9 for one semester. In addition to these 15 meetings we held one all-day ten-hour marathon. The group consisted of ten members, all of whom were there by choice. Most of the participants were functioning relatively well, so the focus of the group was developmental and preventive rather than remedial. In many respects the group became a personal-growth group. Members were encouraged to initiate discussions of matters important to them at that time in their lives.

During the initial sessions we talked to the members about the need to specify group goals as well as individual ones. We devoted the beginning sessions to encouraging participants to formulate their personal goals as concretely as possible. Contracts were useful in this respect. Some of the personal goals members set were "to feel less self-conscious and more comfortable around members of the opposite sex," "to decide what to do after high school," "to learn to like myself better and to feel more self-confident," "to learn how to get along with my parents," "to learn ways of expressing anger without getting into trouble," "to feel less lonely and different," "to learn how to communicate what I really feel," "to learn how to be part of a group and to be accepted by others," and "to figure out what my values really are." Most adolescents are struggling with these concerns, although they may state them in different words. One of our functions was to help members translate their goals into behaviors that they could practice inside and outside the group.

ESTABLISHING TRUST AND DEALING WITH RESISTANCE

At a point early in an adolescent group's history we might say something like: "We hope you will come to feel free enough to say in the group what you think and feel, without censoring or rehearsing. It is especially important that you talk about any fears you are having about being in this group. What do you imagine it would be like for you to talk about personal struggles with the people in this room? We hope this will become a place where you can reveal personal concerns and find, with the help of others, a way of recognizing, understanding, and perhaps resolving certain problems. Our aim is to create a climate in which you can feel that what you say is important and that you're respected for who you are. The value of the sessions depends on your level of commitment. If you merely show up and listen, you are likely to leave disappointed. We'd like you to think about what you want from each session. These sessions are aimed at exploring any topics that you bring to the group. There may be times when you will be uncomfortable in here, and we encourage you to take the risk of talking about your discomfort. You are likely to discover that the atmosphere in this group differs from many other social settings. It is our expectation that you will be honest with yourself and with others in this group."

As part of the discussion in an initial session, we also make sure to cover issues such as confidentiality, group norms, ground rules, ways to get involved in the group, how to give and receive feedback, and suggestions for applications outside of the group. (For other topics that we typically explore during the early phase of a group as a way of generating trust, refer to the discussion in Chapter 5 on the initial stage.)

Remember that many of the freedoms a group offers typically do not exist for adolescents in their daily lives. Their teachers may not be interested in their personal views or concerns, the atmosphere of their school may be one of oppression and control, and they may be victims of racist attitudes. Their parents may not hear what they say or appreciate them as young adults. We've found that adolescents will test us to determine whether we mean what we've told them about the group. How we respond to their testing tells the members how much they can trust us as group leaders. If we accept their testing in a nonjudgmental and nondefensive way and resist giving lectures about how they should be, we progress a long way toward gaining their acceptance. We've found that adolescents are quick to detect phoniness (and sincerity) and that practicing what we preach is the surest way to earn their respect and to generate an atmosphere of trust in the group.

WORKING WITH INVOLUNTARY AND RESISTANT ADOLESCENTS

Although the group we have described consisted of voluntary members, many groups are composed of court-referred or school-referred clients. In working with adolescents who are reluctant to participate, we have found some of the following interventions helpful, and we suggest that you consider how these ideas could be applied to some groups you may lead or co-lead.

First of all, much of the resistance of adolescents to participating in a group can be effectively explored by meeting first with them individually. At this meeting you can find out about their reservations, give them specific information about the group, and in a nondefensive way explore their negative attitudes and provide them an opportunity to express their reactions to being "forced" into the group. You can also point out to them that they *did* make a choice to come to the group. They could have refused and then taken the consequences of not complying with the directive. During the individual pregroup meeting it is helpful to explore any of the adolescent's past experiences with therapy. You can do a lot to demystify the process by providing accurate information about the goals of a group, your role as a group leader, and other considerations that we discussed in Chapters 2, 3, and 4.

Another way to work with uncooperative adolescents is to go *with* resistance, rather than fighting *against* it, and to attempt to work out alternatives to a group. One example of such an option is to continue seeing these adolescents individually for a number of sessions to establish a relationship with them before putting them in a group. You might also invite them to join the group for three sessions and to make a sincere effort to participate. Then if they are still reluctant, allow them to leave. The rationale for this strategy is that these adolescents will have some basis for a decision after they have been to a few group sessions. Even though they were directed to "get counseling," this is one way to provide some increased element of choice. Because forced therapy would only entrench negative attitudes, the leader may genuinely be able to help them find another solution.

Another alternative is to invite a skeptical adolescent to attend the group for a session or so without any pressure to participate. It is important to let the other members know that this person is an observer, there to determine if he or she wants to continue. They are less likely to resent the nonparticipant, and they can let this person know whether they themselves have overcome resistance to being in the group.

Adolescents who attend a session involuntarily often show their resistance through sarcasm and silence. It is important to respond not with defensiveness but with honesty, firmness, and caring confrontations. Assume that Darren says "I don't want to be here!" Examples of unhelpful responses are: "Look, I don't want to be here either." "Well, if you don't like being here, leave." "I don't care what you want. You're here, and I expect you to participate." "Life is tough. We don't always get what we want." Obviously, these leader responses are very defensive and do not invite an exploration of resistance; nor do they encourage the will to participate. What follows are some other interactions between Darren and the leader.

Leader   (in a nondefensive tone): "How come you don't want to be here?"
Darren: "They sent me, and I don't need this group."

Leader: "I know it's difficult doing something you don't want to do. I don't like it when people tell me what to do either. So tell me a bit more what it's like for you to be here."

Rather than responding too quickly in a defensive manner, the leader asks for more information in order to understand Darren's resistance. Instead of getting into a debate over whether he needs the group, the leader accepts his immediate feelings and makes them the focus of discussion. There are many appropriate responses to his reluctance, a few of which are:

- "How about if you come to the group twice to see what this is about and then decide if you want to continue?"
- "A lot of the members in the group felt the same way you do. Maybe they could tell you what it was like for them."
- "Do you know anything about counseling? Have you ever participated in a group before?"
- "Why do you think you were sent here?"
- "I understand that you don't want to be here. Are there consequences if you choose not to attend?"

It is essential to follow the adolescent's lead and go with the resistance, instead of fighting it or taking it personally. If you were a leader who was the recipient of this resistance, you might feel personally rejected. But it is essential not to get bogged down in feeling useless and unappreciated. You cannot afford the luxury of feeling vulnerable to rejection. Taking as a personal affront all the abrasiveness and defensiveness that some adolescents display is a quick route to burnout.

We are not suggesting that you give resistant adolescents permission to verbally abuse you. It is possible to stand up for yourself in a direct and nondefensive way. If an involuntary client taunts you with "You're a phony, and you're only in it for the money," it is not helpful to lash out and then proceed to defend your altruistic bent and your dedication to helping others. Doing this can easily lead to becoming entangled in countertransference. An alternative response could be: "I don't like being called a phony by you. We've just met, and you don't have enough information about me to make that judgment. I'd like to have a chance with you before you dismiss me." This is an example of speaking for oneself and keeping the lines of communication open.

One of our colleagues, Paul Jacobson, works with imprisoned young gang members who are ordered into counseling by the court. Paul has conducted a variety of groups for this involuntary population, including emancipation groups, groups for youthful sex offenders, drug-education groups, groups for teenage fathers, groups for those who chronically fail to conform to the rules of the residential facility, and groups for both perpetrators and victims of abuse. After he read about our high school group, he commented about how foreign our experience sounded compared with his experience with his adolescent population. He finds that his clients lack both insight and sophistication in expressing their thoughts and feelings. Another striking contrast is that their motivation for self-exploration is very low. His involuntary clients typically approach counseling with skepticism, doubt, and hostility. They do not believe that what occurs in a group can be applied to themselves and their life situation. In working with this difficult population, Paul has formulated some useful suggestions:

- Modify your expectations. Understand the client's world, which may be foreign to your life experience.
- Learn to accept subtle behavioral changes.
- Don't be blocked or put off by the client's abrasive language, especially if the client is cooperating behaviorally.
- Be aware of setting limits and establishing boundaries that may differ from individual to individual.
- Earn trust by being honest and direct in your reactions to clients personally.
- Find ways of supporting the expression of clients' feelings without necessarily approving of destructive actions.
- Be aware of your own motivations for choosing to work with a difficult population.
- Realize that the rewards may not be dramatic and that you may not often have the satisfaction of knowing that you have made a difference in a person's life.

In working with highly resistant adolescents, Paul continually reevaluates his goals and reflects on these issues. He knows that it is essential to pay attention to the impact that his work has on him personally and to take preventive measures against the ever-present threat of burnout.

THE INFLUENCE OF THE LEADER'S PERSONALITY

Our experience with adolescents continues to teach us how great an influence the personality of the group leader has on the evolution of the group. We find that adolescents respond well to a willingness to share oneself with the group, a caring attitude, enthusiasm and vitality, openness, and directness. Counselors are likely to learn that the respect they expect because of their title or position may not be forthcoming. Instead of relying on professional accomplishments or techniques, effective counselors know the value of using themselves as a therapeutic instrument.

Adolescents learn from watching the behavior that you model, but your behavior doesn't have to be perfect for them to benefit. In fact, adolescents will generally relate well to you if you appropriately reveal your personal experiences or concerns. If you genuinely respect and enjoy adolescents, you will typically be rewarded with a reciprocal respect.

Adolescents will also be aware if you have never fully experienced your adolescence or if you have some major unfinished business from those years that gets in your way as a leader. For example, an adult who has never faced or resolved certain adolescent fears related to sexuality or lovability may find these fears resurfacing as he or she leads an adolescent group. For this reason, it is crucial that those who lead adolescent groups be willing and courageous enough to explore, and perhaps relive, much of their own adolescent experience so it will not interfere with their work with adolescents or so they won't become enmeshed in countertransference.

In addition, adolescents may be psychologically threatening to adults, for they are full of energy, are often free from major responsibilities, have the capacity to have fun and experience joy, and are able to feel intensely. Leaders may feel that they have lost some of these lively qualities. They may be faced for the first time with the facts of their aging and their loss of the capacity to savor life. Such leaders can prevent the growth of resentment by first accepting the fact of their aging and then looking for new meaning and excitement in their lives.

We think it is wise to avoid trying to become "one of the gang." Because you want to win their approval, for instance, you might imitate the slang and manner of speaking of adolescents. Young people will be quick to detect your insincerity if you use expressions to impress them and to give the appearance of being "with it." Because of trying too hard to become accepted, you may have difficulty gaining the adolescents' trust and respect. You would do well to remember that you hold a different position from theirs and that they usually expect you to act differently. If you are powerful but don't use your power to control and stifle members, the chances are that they will treat you with respect.

Finally, our experience with adolescents has taught us that we have the most influence on them when we are attempting to be in our life what we are encouraging them to become. This does not mean that to be effective we must be ideal people whom the members can imitate. Rather, it means that we are most effective when the members feel that we practice what we preach.

KEEPING THE SESSIONS MOVING

In our weekly adolescent group a valuable skill was keeping the sessions going, which we accomplished mainly by helping the members speak for themselves in concrete terms. This was not an easy task, primarily because it was a challenge to get the participants to focus on themselves in the here and now. Especially in a beginning adolescent group, members have a tendency to tell stories endlessly, going into every detail yet going nowhere. When we listen to a member who is losing our attention because of wordiness, we may say something like: "I'd like to understand you, but I'm getting lost with all the details. Why is your story important at this moment in this group?" It is sometimes useful to say to a member after a long-winded story "If I allowed you only one sentence to express what you have just said, what would it be?" A detailed story that bores others could be simply stated as "I sometimes resent my girlfriend for the way she treats me!" Our task is to teach members to express themselves in personal and concrete ways and to steer them away from telling irrelevant stories.

Using Personal Statements   We have asked members to try to say how they were affected by a situation rather than how other people acted toward them. For instance, Carol began by talking about how she felt misunderstood by her mother. She started to tell stories about her mother, blaming her for her unhappiness, and focused on her mother's feelings. One of us remarked: "You seem to be talking more about your mother right now than about yourself. Tell us how *you* feel."

Another dynamic that commonly keeps a group from reaching a productive level is one member bombarding another with questions instead of making a personal statement. When such questioning occurs, it is appropriate for the group leader to make a comment such as "Marco, instead of questioning Charlene, tell her what it was that provoked you to ask the question." Unless the questioning is stopped in this way, the intensity of Charlene's emotional experience may soon be dissipated. The leader can try to prevent this from happening by stressing that it is far better for members to say how they are affected by someone's emotional experience and in what ways they're identifying with the person than to distract the member with questions.

Teaching members how to share themselves through statements rather than questioning is more effective when it's done in a timely, appropriate, and sensitive manner as certain behaviors or interactions are occurring in the session. For example, instead of asking, "Why are you so quiet?" a leader can intervene with "Would you be willing to let her know how you're being affected by her silence?"

Structuring Sessions   We favor active intervention and structuring for adolescent groups, particularly during the initial stage. Some structuring can provide the direction needed to keep the sessions moving. It might involve specifying a theme or topic for the group to deal with. Such topics should be related to the interests and needs of the adolescents and not merely be issues the leader feels are important, such as "How can you improve your study habits?" "What can be done to reduce the absentee rate in classrooms?" "How can you learn to respect your teachers?" The group may well have little interest in these topics, and the sessions are bound to bog down.

In our adolescent group we developed themes with the participants during the sessions. We didn't say "Since this is your group, what do you want to talk about?" Instead, we structured by limiting the choices somewhat, saying: "In working with groups like this, we have found that certain themes are of concern to most young people. A few of these are

'What do I want from my life, and what is stopping me from getting it?' 'Can I be who I am and be sincerely accepted by my parents?' 'How can I better understand my feelings of loneliness?' 'How can I deal with others more effectively?' These are only a few of the topics that we might consider. Every group moves in its own direction. What, in particular, would each of you like to see us focus on in this group?"

A general agenda for the next session can be decided on at the end of each meeting. Flexibility should be built into the structuring, though, for members will often spontaneously bring up pressing problems that are not related to the scheduled theme, and this deviation from the plan can be very fruitful. A theme, like an interaction exercise, is only a means to the end of involving the members in meaningful group work. It is important that topics or techniques not become ends in themselves. Our adolescent group once planned, at the end of a session, to deal with a certain theme the next week. However, a classmate of the group members committed suicide the night before the next session, and the group was preoccupied with him. The session was devoted to exploring the effect that this tragedy was having on each group member, and the topic of death was explored in a very personal way.

ACTION-ORIENTED TECHNIQUES OF ROLE PLAYING

In our adolescent groups we usually rely heavily on action-oriented methods, especially role playing. We find that role playing is an excellent way to keep the interest level high, to involve a lot of the members, and to give a here-and-now flavor to the work being done. Role playing fosters creative problem solving, encourages spontaneity, usually intensifies feelings, and gets people to identify with others. By role playing, participants can learn how to express themselves more effectively. They can test reality and practice new behavior.

If members are well prepared for action-oriented techniques, Gestalt and psychodramatic methods can bring vitality to the sessions. For instance, if Scott is complaining about how his girlfriend, Dawn, treats him, he can be asked to imagine that she is sitting in an empty chair and to tell her how he feels. If appropriate, another member can "sit in" for Dawn and carry on a dialogue with Scott. Scott might "become Dawn" and tell everyone in the group what she thinks of Scott; this could be useful in helping him stand in her shoes. Through such action-oriented techniques, more feelings are elicited, and boring stories are minimized. Members also get a chance to say out loud things that they have kept inside. Through role reversal, they can gain empathy for others in their lives.

We've found that it helps members become comfortable with role playing more quickly if we participate at first. For instance, if a girl has been describing how she views her parents and how frustrated she feels when she tries to talk with them, we might take the part of her mother and father. That will allow her to deal directly, albeit symbolically, with her parents and feel her frustration intensely. We can then stop the action and ask her: "What are you experiencing now? What would you most like to do now? If you could reach us, make us really hear you, what would you most want to say?" The role playing may be brief. When it's over, the person should discuss the experience and plan how to handle this situation when it arises in the future.

Adolescents are often self-conscious about getting involved in role playing. It is useful to provide a general orientation to the techniques you employ, which could be done at a pregroup session. Both the timing and manner of introducing techniques are directly related to whether adolescents are likely to cooperate. When an adolescent says he or she would feel silly in role playing, you might respond with "I know it seems silly and a bit awkward, but how about trying it anyway and seeing what you might learn about yourself?" Or you could say "I know it seems silly, but who says we always have to be serious?" Generally, if we approach role playing in this light and gentle way, the resistance dissipates, and before the participant knows it, he or she is playing a role with gusto. We check frequently to see whether a person wants to explore a particular problem and is willing to use role playing to do so. One of us might say: "You seem to be unclear about how your mother really affects you and how you should deal with her. Are you willing to try something?"

There are many variations of role-playing techniques. To illustrate, we'll use the example of Sally, who discloses that she feels she can never please her father and that this hurts her. She says that she and her father are not close and that she would like to change that. She is afraid of her father, for she sees him as critical of her, and she feels that unless she is perfect, she cannot win his approval. Several role-playing situations are possible:

- Sally can play her father, to provide a picture of how she perceives him. We can ask her to give Sally a long lecture and tell her all the things that she must become before she is worthwhile in his eyes. Speaking as her father, Sally might say something like: "I know you have a lot more ability than you show. Why didn't you get all As? Yes, I'm proud of you for getting five As, but I must confess I'm let down by that one B. If you really put your mind to it, I know you could do better." We would encourage her to stay in her father's role for a time and say things that she imagines he is thinking but not expressing.
- A group member who identifies with Sally can play her while Sally continues playing her father. From the dialogue that ensues, Sally can get an idea of how her father feels with her. A group member with a similar conflict can benefit from involvement in the situation.
- A member who feels that he or she can identify with the father can play that role. If nobody in the group jumps at this opportunity, the leader can take the parent role. This situation allows Sally to

intensify her feelings and to demonstrate how she deals with her father. As the role playing continues, she may achieve insight into herself that will help her make some changes.

- Sally can play both herself and her father. She can be directed to say (as her father) what she wishes he would say to her. This is a future projection, and it taps the person's hopes.
- Sally can present a soliloquy, talking aloud as her father, saying what she imagines her father might say about her. She can also use the soliloquy approach when she is in her own role, after she finishes an exchange with her father. She can express many of the thoughts and feelings she generally keeps locked within herself when she talks with her father.
- Several other group members can sit in for Sally and show how they would deal with her father. This may suggest to her options she hadn't thought of.
- Other members who role-played Sally's father can provide helpful feedback to her by telling her what they felt as they were listening to her. She may be less defensive in hearing from her peers about how they were put off by her abrasive style than if an adult provided his feedback.

Because it is important for members to process these dramas, the leader should ask them to think about the implications of what they observed in themselves in the role-playing situations. At this time feedback from other members and interpretations from the leader can enable the members to see with more clarity their own part in their conflicts with others and what they can do to make life better for themselves. If you are interested in a more in-depth discussion of role-playing techniques in groups, refer to Chapter 8 ("Psychodrama") and Chapter 11 ("Gestalt Therapy") in G. Corey (1995).

GETTING GROUP MEMBERS TO PARTICIPATE AND INITIATE

During the sessions we look for ways of bringing uninvolved group members into the interactions. After Sally's role playing, for example, we might encourage other members to tell what they experienced as she was working with her father. We might ask: "Can any of you give Sally feedback? What did you see her doing? Did she spark any feelings in you?" Adolescents are usually most eager to become personally involved when other members touch vulnerable spots in them. As we've mentioned, one real advantage of group counseling is that the members can be of service to their peers by giving their perceptions, revealing similar problems, suggesting alternatives, supporting them in times of despair, reflecting what they hear them saying, and confronting their inconsistencies.

Therefore, we try to involve as many members as possible in the group process. In addition, we try to shape the group so that we will be less and less required to give direction. One of the signs of an effective group is that members gradually assume an increasing share of the leadership functions. For instance, if a group that usually functions effectively begins to stray aimlessly, a member will probably point this out. If a group member gets bogged down in storytelling and intellectualizing, we expect members to react. In short, one of our aims is to teach adolescents to monitor themselves in their group and become less dependent on us for direction.

THE USE OF PEER COUNSELORS

Peer counselors can be used both in the classroom in human-relations courses and as part of the outreach program of the school's counseling and guidance program. Given proper training and supervision, peers can often be as effective in reaching fellow students as counselors or teachers.

An important consideration in using peer counselors is teaching them the boundaries of their competence. There is a strong possibility that peer counselors will become deeply involved in others' lives. They can play a supportive role, they can challenge fellow students to evaluate their behavior honestly, and they can share their own life experiences and learning with others. But they are not qualified to render psychotherapy. Thus, it is critical that peer counselors learn how to function as liaisons so that students who need professional assistance can get it.

For instance, a counselor we know commented that her groups explored the issue of adolescent suicide. Many of her counselees experience depression and alienation, and some are suicide-prone. A number use drugs and alcohol heavily, to the point that this abuse has interfered with their lives. It is essential for peer counselors to know the agencies to which to refer students who need further professional assistance. A valuable skill is being able to present information to young people in such a manner that they are likely to accept a referral in those situations that call for it.

Finally, in working with adolescents in personal areas, it is important for both counselors and their peer counselors to learn how to set personal limits so that they do not become burned out. Adolescents can easily become dependent on an adult or a peer counselor whom they respect and have affection for. Counselors who make it a practice to say "here is my phone number, and don't hesitate to call whenever you'd like" are likely to find themselves swamped by demands and not able to live up to what they promised. To remain effective in working with young people, the counselor must recognize personal limitations and take care to ensure that resentment does not build up over constantly being asked to help others in crisis situations.

INVOLVING PARENTS

PARENT-CONSULTATION GROUPS

A consultation group can give parents a chance to express some of their frustration and ambivalence. A good group leader can sensitize parents to the dynamics of adolescence and widen their perspectives, and parents can raise questions and bring up problems that they would like to discuss with other parents and the leader.

Most parents care about their children. Yet most parents go through a period when they would like to "divorce" their adolescent, for the possibility of any real communication seems remote. Like their adolescent children, parents need some assistance. They need more than general information about parent/adolescent relationships or methods of control. They need to talk about their feelings of inadequacy, guilt, resentment, and rejection. Many parents feel deeply unappreciated and feel that no matter how sincerely they try to improve relations at home things won't get better. Parents who feel defensive over being perceived as inadequate mothers or fathers may feel anxious about the group, but they often experience relief in learning that other parents share their feelings and difficulties.

Programs can also be designed for those willing to invest time and energy in becoming better parents. Many group leaders offer parent-effectiveness-training groups. Such groups can be held at the local high school or at one of the parents' homes one evening a week. For example, one of our colleagues, Deborah King, conducts active parenting workshops in the school district where she works as a counselor. She meets with parents for 12 evening sessions to explore topics such as: communication skills aimed at cooperation, keys to self-esteem, effective discipline methods, teaching young people responsibility, drawbacks of reward and punishment, and dealing with anger. Parents in such groups are encouraged to read books and to discuss them in the group. (See the suggested readings at the end of this chapter.) Role playing gives parents a chance to examine their relationships with their children and experiment with new, more effective behaviors.

GROUPS OF PARENTS AND ADOLESCENTS*

Groups of adolescents and their parents, or multiple-family groups, are usually conducted in psychiatric hospitals, residential treatment centers, or community clinics. They are primarily adjuncts to other methods of

*This section is written from the perspective of Paul Jacobson, a licensed marriage and family therapist with experience in leading multiple-family groups in several different agencies. For further information you can contact him at P. O. Box 2352, Idyllwild, CA 92549; telephone (909) 659-4484.

treatment in which the adolescent is usually the identified patient. I find this format exciting because of its possibilities for creatively combining family therapy with more traditional group work. Some of my groups have as few as two families (with four parents and four children), and others have as many as five different families (with a total of about 15 individuals). My groups typically meet weekly for 90 minutes. The groups are open, with membership changing periodically.

Theoretically, such groups can be thought of in three ways: as composed of discrete family units; as two subgroups, one of adolescents and another of parents; or as a group of individuals. All are occurring simultaneously and are developing throughout the various stages of the group. The facilitator needs to be aware of these different subgroups and the impact of them on the unfolding of group interactions. For example, members of the adolescent subgroup may have contact with one another outside the group (such as in the hospital or residential facility) and may consequently be more familiar, comfortable, and less guarded with one another than the parent subgroup, which may meet only infrequently. A minimal level of trust needs to be developed within the parental subgroup, whereas some basis for trust may already exist with the adolescents.

This process of differential rates of building trust is probably also reflected within each family. Parents are usually more reticent in discussing their own difficulties than they are in talking about the problems of their children. By initially focusing on parent/child difficulties, the leader can largely bypass parental resistance and defensiveness. Eventually, many parents become more willing to accept some of the responsibility for the problems between their children and themselves. Because the parents are not the focus of treatment, however, the main goal is improving skills in communication, problem solving, and parenting.

This type of group also enhances the treatment of adolescent populations that are not usually amenable to traditional counseling. The majority of adolescent problems involve parent/child conflicts, inappropriate conduct, or other behavioral difficulties. These adolescents frequently do not feel the need for relief through counseling, and they tend to resist this process. If skillfully conducted, these groups can lead to a family discussion of issues that are usually avoided. Furthermore, groups can be instrumental in modifying underlying tensions, attitudes, and motivations for acting-out behaviors.

Many adolescents present an entirely different demeanor to others than they do to their parents. This tendency can be used in a group for therapeutic gain. For example:

- If parents tolerate extreme rudeness from their daughter but observe her being polite to other adults in the group, they may then alter their own expectations.
- If parents view their son at home in highly negative ways, they could be looking for data to support their negativity. But if they observe

their child being helpful or supportive within the group, they may alter their perceptions.

- If an adolescent girl can communicate in an adult manner with other parents in the group, she can generalize this skill to avoid the explosive temper she displays with her own parents.
- If an adolescent boy uses passive/avoidance silence, his parents can view how others respond to this style and develop new options for relating to him.

Another advantage of combining families is that the leader can teach parenting skills. Unlike the traditional lecture approach to parent education, which usually falls on deaf ears, the group format can provide lessons in how to deal more effectively with problems by discussing them with others. At these times, the parents are more receptive to assistance and can be guided toward practicing new skills within the group and then trying them at home. In traditional parent education, the focus is often on learning techniques that may not take the underlying problems into full consideration. A group process that involves all parties, in contrast, can bring about significant learning that changes styles of interaction.

It takes considerable skill and sensitivity to keep group meetings that involve parents and adolescents from degenerating into gripe sessions. The leader needs to focus on both parents and teenagers learning how to listen with understanding. The group can be kept small, especially if the leader has not led such a group before. Before facilitating multiple-family groups, it is necessary to gain some education, training, and supervision in family therapy. Groups of parents and adolescents have the potential for improving relationships at home, especially if contracts are formed that include both parents' and adolescents' taking specific steps toward agreed-on changes.

CHILDREN OF ALCOHOLICS

Children raised in alcoholic families enter adolescence with strategies for survival that worked to some degree in their childhood years. But at this time in their lives, these coping strategies may be costly in terms of their psychological health and well-being. Over the years they have refined certain behaviors, such as being super responsible, adjusting, or placating as well as not talking, not trusting, and not feeling. When they grow up, most adult children of alcoholics (sometimes referred to as ACAs) continue to struggle with problems related to trust, dependency, control, identification, and expression of feelings.

In her research and therapeutic work, Black (1987) has found that these adults often act out the same three roles they played as children. First is the role of being super responsible. Children who miss out on their childhood by having to mature early often take on household and parenting responsibilities for other siblings. When structure and consistency are not provided, these children provide it for themselves. They rely completely on themselves, for they have learned many times over that they cannot count on their parents. Second is the role of the adjuster, who makes an early decision that "because I can't do anything about the family situation, I'll adjust to it." As children, adjusters become detached; as adults, they have no sense of self, they are not autonomous, and they typically feel that they have few choices. Third is the role of the placater, who has become skilled at listening and providing empathy. Placaters have a difficult time dealing with their own feelings. For example, if they cry, they tend to cry alone.

It is best not to treat people according to any label, including labels such as "ACAs" or "codependents," as well as "responsible ones," "adjusters," or "placaters." Instead of thinking of rigid categories that box people in, it is better to consider certain general patterns of learned behavior. These roles evolve from childhood and follow one into adulthood. As children, for example, placaters busy themselves by taking care of others; as adults, they often become professional helpers, carrying the pain of others. Yet if they don't attend to their own needs and feelings, they eventually burn out. They have a difficult time asking for what they need for themselves, and in their personal relationships they tend to seek out others who are takers.

In *It Will Never Happen to Me!* Black (1987) vividly portrays the life histories of adult children of alcoholics. We have adapted much of the material in this section from her book. She discusses three central familial injunctions that she detects over and over in her work with these clients: "Don't talk," "Don't trust," and "Don't feel."

In the "Don't talk" message, children are conditioned not to discuss real issues in the family but to ignore these problems in the hope that the hurt will go away. They learn not to rock the boat. The key dynamic is denial of the family secret of alcoholism. Of course, this injunction is challenged by the very nature of the group format. It can be therapeutic for these young people simply to share the secret that they have been burdened with for so long. Because the entire group is composed of people who are struggling with the same pain of denial and not talking, the group atmosphere can represent a significant turning point.

In the case of the "Don't trust" message, adult children of alcoholics learn always to be on guard, to rely on themselves, and not to trust others with their feelings. In alcoholic homes children learn that their parents are not consistently available and cannot be relied on for safety. Unfortunately, they carry this pattern of not trusting into their adulthood. Again, the group affords opportunities for taking the risk of trusting both peers and an adult leader. They can potentially learn that their family's lack of trustworthiness does not necessarily imply that the rest of the world is not to be trusted.

In the "Don't feel" message, children develop a denial system to numb their feelings. To bring stability and consistency to their lives, they acquire coping mechanisms. They learn not to share what they feel, because they are convinced that their feelings will not be validated within their family. Gradually, they build walls for protecting themselves from a feared world. They learn to deny and discount their feelings, they hide their pain, and they do not express what is inside of them. This process of denial is interfering with their emotional and social lives as adolescents, and the pattern will most likely continue into adulthood unless there is a therapeutic intervention. A group can encourage these young people to at least begin talking about the fortress they have built around themselves. The group also provides them with a place to share their pain of isolation instead of continuing to hide it. Through the support and encouragement within the group, they learn that they *can* feel and that they are not alone.

A HIGH SCHOOL GROUP FOR CHILDREN OF ALCOHOLICS*

The following section describes a counseling group designed for high school students living with a family member who has a problem with alcohol or other drugs. Deborah Lambert is a coordinator of a student assistance program at North Allegheny Senior High School in Pennsylvania. She works with Nancy Ceraso English, an education specialist with expertise in chemical dependency, to provide weekly support to students from dysfunctional families.

PRACTICAL CONSIDERATIONS

The groups are limited to ten students and are offered to students aged 16 to 18. This curriculum has also been used with students of 14 to 16 at North Allegheny Intermediate School. The length of the weekly sessions is one class period, typically 40 minutes. Two facilitators work together to provide a blend of academic and mental-health expertise. The co-leaders explain that the groups do not offer counseling per se but that therapeutic gains can occur. They also emphasize the importance of going to Al-Anon, Al-Ateen, Alcoholics Anonymous (AA), Narcotics Anonymous (NA), or other community groups that will provide the students with

*This section is written from the perspective of Deborah Lambert and Nancy Ceraso English. For further information contact them at North Allegheny High School, 10375 Perry Highway, Wexford, PA 15090; telephone (412) 934-7260. Or contact Nancy English at 6932 Bishop Street, Pittsburgh, PA 15206-1128.

additional tools and opportunities to practice sharing. The ground rules for confidentiality are presented and clarified. No one is permitted to share any information outside of the group. The only exceptions pertain to suspected child abuse or suicidal ideation.

Letters are sent home letting the parents know what the school is offering. There is typically a lot of secrecy associated with addicted families, and the co-leaders do not want to perpetuate the cycle of concealment. Before letters are sent, one of the counselors sits down with students who have been recruited to join and clarifies the group's purpose. Students see a copy of the letter so they know that the co-leaders are encouraging open communication. The letter would not be sent home if a student were anxious about the outcome.

GROUP GOALS

The aims of the group are to:

- learn how chemical dependency affects *all* family members
- learn alternatives to chemical use
- talk about our feelings and how they can help or hurt us
- meet with others who have had similar experiences
- have a safe place where confidential matters can be shared
- learn about codependent behaviors
- learn about the addiction process
- learn about community resources

Following is a typical format for meeting these goals in the group:

Session 1: Group Introduction

- Members introduce themselves and participate in establishing group rules—for example, everyone is expected to participate, students are expected to make up missed class work and assignments, it is good to speak for oneself, members should strive to be honest about their thoughts and feelings, and confidentiality is observed.
- Members explore the purpose of the group.
- Members identify the problem of addiction in their lives.

Session 2: The Impact of Addiction on the Family

- Members share how a family member's addiction has affected their lives.
- On an easel board, the members list all possible consequences when a family member is addicted.

Session 3: Introducing Addiction

- The co-facilitators discuss the progressive disease of addiction.

- Members draw a picture of a time when they were sick.
- After members share their pictures, the co-leaders introduce more facts about the disease of addiction as it parallels or differs from their pictures.

Session 4: "My Feelings about Addiction"

- Members share their feelings as they relate to a family member's addiction.
- Members think up as many "feeling words" as they can, and the co-leader puts these words on the easel board.
- Members are asked the question "What does it feel like when someone in the family is addicted?"

Session 5: The Addicted Parent

- Members talk about the behaviors that accompany addiction.
- Members draw a picture of the worst thing that has happened because of a family member's addiction.

Session 6: The Addicted Parent (continued)

- Members view a film or a television show depicting an alcoholic parent.
- At various points in the film or video it is turned off to allow for discussing the reality of the situation.
- Time is allotted for open dialogue and sharing of the members' situations.

Session 7: The Recovering Parent

- The co-facilitators explain the process of recovery and the dynamics of relapse.
- Members complete a handout and discuss the internal and external factors contributing to a relapse of their loved ones into addiction.

Session 8: Codependency

- Members are sensitized to the nonaddictive parent's predicament.
- The group lists behaviors typically associated with codependency.
- Members make a collage representing their own codependent tendencies.

Session 9: Roles

- The co-facilitators discuss the roles that generally characterize children of alcoholics.
- Members fill out a handout on how they've assumed these roles at different stages in their lives.

Session 10: Coping and Hoping

- Members select a card from a special deck, the "Problems Pack," and either talk about or role-play how they would feel and what they would do in each problem situation. Examples are as follows:

    a. It is very late, and your parent is not home from the bar.
    b. You need help with your homework, but your parent tells you, "Sorry, I have to go to an AA meeting."
    c. You are in a car with a drunken driver.

- Each member receives an updated listing of community resources and a schedule of the various support group meetings.
- Students are encouraged to go alone, with a friend, or with the group to an Al-Ateen or Al-Anon meeting.

Session 11: Self-Affirmations

- Students learn to avoid negative self-talk and to make statements about themselves that increase their self-esteem.
- In small groups, each member shares one or two self-criticisms and changes them into affirmations.

Session 12: Good Thoughts, Good Feelings, and Good-Byes

- The members talk about what the group has meant.
- One member sits in the center and receives positive feedback on his or her contributions.
- Each student gets an index card for listing phone numbers from the group.
- Students are asked to fill out a two-page questionnaire on the group process. This activity is optional.

OUTCOMES OF THE GROUP

Written and verbal responses from members consistently reflect positive feelings, attitudes, and experiences. The four areas of praise highlighted in all the evaluations are peer support; validation of thoughts, feelings, and experiences; exchange of practical and timely suggestions; and the opportunity to experience trust and intimacy. Some recommendations for changes include longer and more frequent sessions and additional specialty groups, such as ones dealing with divorce, family violence, and sexual abuse.

Parents of participating members have given their support. The teachers of participating members have routinely provided updates on the members' academic progress. Teachers have tended to be positive in backing the group. Administrators have offered continuing support, which has promoted effective outcomes.

REWARDS AND FRUSTRATIONS

Some of the rewards for the co-leaders are:

- participating in and witnessing students' personal growth
- sharing in the relief that accompanies personal disclosures
- observing members gain insight into their codependent behaviors and their attempts to correct them
- helping members establish and maintain contact with one another
- fostering and restoring playfulness in members

Some of the frustrations the co-leaders have experienced are:

- facing members' hesitancy to seek out community supports such as Al-Ateen and Al-Anon
- seeing the consequences of family dysfunction continue after members leave the group

AFTERCARE: A GROUP FOR STUDENTS FOLLOWING DRUG REHABILITATION*

In addition to the groups just described, Deborah Lambert and Nancy Ceraso English also offer a support group for students who are coming out of drug rehabilitation.

GROUP OVERVIEW

Because drug rehabilitation is a lifelong process, the school offers a continuing support group. The leaders meet with the students weekly and design rules and review the goals of the group. They try to obtain releases of information from the treatment facility so they can complement the student's already prescribed aftercare plan.

Counselors, teachers, students, and administrators all refer high school students to the group. The leaders also advertise in the school newspaper so everyone is aware that support groups are available to students. (See Chapter 4 for a description of the procedures used to identify and recruit group members.) They strongly urge students to continue with their AA, NA, therapy, or other aftercare groups.

The goals of the group are for the members to:

- learn about chemical dependency, relapse, and recovery
- focus on school-related issues

*This section, too, is written from the perspective of Deborah Lambert and Nancy Ceraso English.

- talk about successes and problems associated with recovery
- practice sharing in a safe place
- learn about healthy alternatives to chemicals
- communicate with other students and community groups
- enjoy fellowship with others having similar experiences

A FORMAT FOR AFTERCARE

The groups are run for one period a week for the entire school year. Here are samples of the sessions.

Session 1: Group Introduction

- Members introduce themselves and brainstorm to create a list of appropriate group rules and guidelines.
- The co-facilitators describe the purpose of the group.

Session 2: Their Own Addiction

- Students review the rules and the issue of confidentiality.
- Members provide a chronology of their abuse of drugs.
- Students share with the group some of their background of addiction.

Session 3: Safeguards for Special Events

- The co-leaders discuss issues and hazards associated with holidays and school-sponsored events such as dances and football games.
- Student compile a list of "relapse signals."

Session 5: Review of Recovery

- Students review their academic behavior and their attendance at AA or NA.
- Students discuss their worries and fears.

Session 10: Relapse

- Discussion focuses on a student's admission of a relapse. The group talks about relapse signals, which are typically ignored.
- Each student has the opportunity to say something positive and supportive.

Session 30: Final Group

- The final session lasts all day. A young recovering addict from a nearby college can provide a lead. The group can meet at a nearby park for a picnic.
- Students have the chance to ask questions and share their own experiences.

- The lead speaker also talks about ways to protect sobriety during the summer vacation.
- Members have the chance to say their good-byes to one another.

SUGGESTIONS FOR DESIGNING AFTERCARE GROUPS

Based on our experiences in designing and co-leading these aftercare groups, here are some pointers that may help others in setting up similar groups:

- Have a designated room and time. The time is best rotated at mid-semester or within each grading period, as opposed to more frequently.
- Have an established curriculum. Make it flexible to accommodate crises and special concerns of members.
- Prepare members for upcoming school functions and holidays that threaten sobriety.
- Have members give brief weekly updates on their sobriety, their attendance at AA or NA, and their aftercare agency in the community. Reinforce the effectiveness of AA, NA, and community aftercare groups.

A GROUP FOR UNWED TEENAGE FATHERS*

Wayne Huey, a former counselor at Gordon High School in Decatur, Georgia, designed a group called MALE (Maximizing a Life Experience). It included eight students, aged 14 to 18, who were already fathers or expectant fathers. He created this group after one of his school-board members commented on his school's counseling program for pregnant girls and wondered what help was available for the teenage fathers. After reviewing the literature, Huey concluded that counseling programs for unwed teenage fathers were practically nonexistent, especially in the schools. The remainder of this section describes the steps taken in setting up and evaluating this creative program.

INITIAL STEPS

The pregnant girls in the school were contacted, but it was found that none of them was pregnant by a student at the high school. Huey then contacted counselors, teachers, administrators, and coaches, and eight names of boys were eventually secured. The program was outlined to each of them, and they were asked if they wanted to make a commitment

*For further information on these groups, contact Wayne Huey, Ph.D., at Lakeside High School, 3801 Briarcliff Rd., N.E., Atlanta, GA 30345; telephone (404) 634-4412.

to participate in the group. Parental consent was required to join. All eight identified youths got parental consent, all made the commitment, and all completed the nine-session group.

GOALS AND OBJECTIVES

The MALE group had the general goal of offering assistance in a non-judgmental way. The initial plan focused on three Rs: rights, responsibilities, and resources. The specific objectives were for the participants (1) to learn more about themselves and their feelings in relation to their situation, (2) to understand their legal and emotional rights and responsibilities, (3) to identify and explore present and future options, (4) to learn to make sound decisions, (5) to realize what resources were available to them, (6) to accept that pregnancy is not an accident, and (7) to obtain information about contraception.

STRUCTURE OF THE GROUP SESSIONS

The nine sessions were held for an hour each week. They were held during the school day on a rotating schedule, so that no class was missed more than once or twice. The members were to make up all missed assignments. The nine sessions were structured as follows:

Session 1. An overview of the program was explained, as were general group goals and ground rules. Members got to know one another and developed their own personal goals.

Session 2. The group viewed and discussed the film *Teenage Father.*

Session 3. The group viewed and discussed the filmstrip *His Baby, Too: Problems of Teenage Pregnancy* (available from Sunburst Communications, 39 Washington Avenue, Room KT7, Pleasantville, NY 10570). The members also prepared questions on legal issues.

Session 4. The group explored legal issues, with a focus on the rights and responsibilities of unwed teenage fathers in Georgia. A guest speaker from the Legal Aid Society was heard.

Session 5. The reproductive system and contraception were discussed. A guest speaker from Planned Parenthood appeared.

Session 6. There was a field trip to Planned Parenthood, which included a tour of the facility and an overview of services provided for both girls and boys. There was also a presentation on sexually transmitted diseases.

Session 7. A session on problem solving and decision making was held, including models and practice activities.

Session 8. Problem-solving and decision-making models were used with actual personal situations.

Session 9. At the final session members summarized what they had learned about their rights and responsibilities, and there was a discussion of school resources. The members completed a written evaluation and discussed the effectiveness of the program.

OUTCOMES OF THE PROGRAM

Results   According to Huey, the program was a tremendous success. The overall group rating was 9.5 on a scale of 10 when the members were asked if the group had been helpful to them. The young men wanted the group to last longer, and they considered it very helpful. They had shared their feelings of anger, guilt, frustration, confusion, and fear. They explored concerns about their situation and the impact it might have on their future and the future of their baby.

Follow-up   At one- and two-year follow-ups, none of this first group had fathered a second child, and all were progressing toward their career goals as they had imagined that they might be without a child. Three were in college or technical school, two were in the military, two were working full time, and one was still in high school. None of them had married the mother of his child; in fact, only two were still dating her a year later. All of them were contributing something toward the support of their child, and those close enough to visit were seeing the baby on a regular basis.

SUMMARY

This group is another example of a specific program designed to meet the needs of a particular population. Such a group can be replicated in a community agency. The steps taken to set up this program and the general structure of the sessions can suggest a model for other specialized short-term groups for adolescents. This group illustrates the possibilities involved in combining an *educational* program (one designed to impart certain information) with a *therapeutic* program (one geared to helping members explore their feelings, attitudes, and values and make decisions).

A SYSTEMWIDE PROGRAM FOR COUNSELING YOUNG PEOPLE IN GROUPS

This chapter has thus far described the formation of specific counseling groups for adolescents in schools and agencies. Now we consider organizing a group-counseling project on a larger scale for adolescents in senior and junior high school and for children in the elementary grades. The project to be described demonstrates that it is possible to set up a program, including training and supervision of professional group counselors, on a systemwide scale.

BACKGROUND OF THE PROGRAM

Project Group Work* was initiated in Bettendorf, Iowa, to train group counselors working with elementary and secondary students. The focus of the original training was on school social workers, psychologists, and teachers serving behaviorally disordered youths. Since the project's inception in 1984, the training has been expanded to include elementary and secondary counselors who provide service to "at-risk" students. At-risk students include those who are depressed, suicidal, homeless, or abused and those who have experienced significant losses in their lives. In reaction to the crisis element involved in working with these students, the project has incorporated crisis-management training.

This project is noteworthy in that it:

- emphasizes group counseling with special-education and at-risk regular-education students in the elementary through secondary grades
- provides supervised training in group work in a school setting
- emphasizes the importance of therapeutic relationships between group leaders and students
- uses a discussion approach in identifying problematic issues and devising solutions
- establishes a peer support system
- uses classroom teachers as co-leaders
- blends concepts from a variety of group-counseling theories
- incorporates crisis-management techniques as a part of group-counseling training

The groups are viewed as therapeutic discussion groups. Their purpose is to provide a safe environment in which students feel comfortable discussing issues that are interfering with their educational functioning. The groups, with a range of 6 to 12 students, meet for a minimum of one class period a week.

Topics or issues discussed in the group include academic difficulties, adolescent/adult relationship problems, feelings associated with having a disability, value conflicts, family problems, and child abuse. The students are often poorly motivated or exhibit behavioral difficulties in school

*For additional information about Project Group Work, contact Phil Piechowski, Supervisor, School of Social Work Services, Mississippi Bend Area Education Agency, 729-21st Street, Bettendorf, IA 52722; telephone (319) 359-1371. The Iowa Department of Education has put together a booklet, *Project Group Work: An Innovative Approach to Counseling in Schools,* edited by Piechowski and Ciha (1988). Use the above contact for information on this booklet.

because of their personal stress. For them the group becomes a place for expressing feelings, learning to care for oneself and others, and gaining insight into healthy ways of coping.

BASIC ELEMENTS OF THE GROUP EXPERIENCE

Phil Piechowski and Tom Ciha, directors of Project Group Work, report that the following elements have been found to be essential in conducting school counseling groups:

- **Fostering hope**. The at-risk student generally feels a sense of hopelessness. Participants in the group must be helped to see that positive change is possible.
- **Developing a sense of belonging.** At-risk students perceive themselves as alienated from the "mainstream" of school activities. Participation in a group promotes a feeling of togetherness and fosters a desire to be included in desirable social roles.
- **Focus on the here and now**. Although an understanding and discussion of the student's past history is helpful, the student is encouraged to identify goals for the present and future.
- **Reinforcement system.** A system for reinforcing appropriate social skills is often necessary in the initial stage of the group.
- **Changing an image.** Many at-risk students have either poor self-esteem or an inflated ego. Students participating in the group are encouraged to explore their feelings of self-worth and to evaluate their feelings against objective information about their accomplishments.
- **Teacher participation.** The involvement of a student's teacher as a co-leader with the counselor, social worker, or psychologist is important. The teacher adds significantly to the group because he or she is involved with the student daily and can lend support throughout the week. The teacher's capacity for understanding and accepting these students is increased because he or she becomes aware of some of the students' personal struggles through the group sessions.

TRAINING GROUP LEADERS

Since the project's inception in 1984, hundreds of counselors, teachers, school social workers, and psychologists have received intensive training in crisis management and group counseling. The training has included developing practitioners' skills in crisis intervention, group leadership, and using group dynamics to establish a cooperative learning experience. No single theoretical model is promoted; these practitioners have been exposed to a variety of counseling theories. The group training involves establishment of a peer support system and supervision by a knowledgeable group leader. Groups are observed, and practitioners videotape sessions for review of their leadership skills.

The practitioners meet regularly for peer support and consultation. On attaining the desired degree of proficiency, each group leader assists in training additional professionals.

CONCLUSIONS

Project Group Work has been well received by counselors, teachers, social workers, psychologists, and students. Schools have not only started counseling groups for students with special needs and at-risk regular-education students but have also developed crisis-intervention plans to respond to a variety of situations. Many schools are better prepared, because of the training received through Project Group Work, to respond effectively to suicidal crises, the sudden death of a student or faculty member, and other severely stressful events experienced by adolescents.

Project Group Work practitioners have found that students who are offered the opportunity to discuss personal concerns begin to view the school as a more caring institution. This project has demonstrated that students' behavior and school work improve when they perceive the school as supportive.

WHERE TO GO FROM HERE

Skills for Living: Group Counseling Activities for Young Adolescents (Morganett, 1990), is a very useful resource guide. This is a practical group leader's manual that presents guidelines for conducting skill-building group counseling activities for young adolescents. The book presents ways of getting groups for adolescents off the ground, and the chapters are organized around developmental concerns of adolescents. Morganett has pretests and posttests for each topic and a variety of sample forms (needs assessment; parental consent form; and letters to students, faculty, and parents). This manual will provide many ideas for those who want to set up a group for adolescents. *Skills and Techniques for Group Work with Children and Adolescents* (Smead, 1995, formerly Morganett) deals more with skills and techniques that can be applied to groups for adolescents.

Another useful resource for group work with adolescents is *Working with Children and Adolescents in Groups* (Rose & Edleson, 1987). This excellent book presents a specific guide for the multimethod approach to treating adolescents in groups. Many examples cover children in all age groups, but most of the illustrations are drawn from the preadolescent and early adolescent periods. Separate chapters deal with topics for each stage of a group.

Two useful resources by Paperbacks for Educators that list a wide variety of books for adolescents are *School Counselor Catalog, 6–12,* and *Bibliotherapy for Children and Teens.* These catalogs can be obtained by contacting Paperbacks for Educators, 426 West Front Street, Washington, MO 63090; telephone (800) 227-2591.

For a review of research on groups with adolescents, see *Group Psychotherapy with Children, Preadolescents, and Adolescents* (Dagley, Gazda, & Eppinger, 1994).

REFERENCES AND SUGGESTED READINGS*

*Aronson, S., & Scheidlinger, S. (1994). Group therapy for adolescents. *Directions in Mental Health Counseling, 4*(2), 3–11.

Azima, F. J., & Richmond, L. H. (Eds.). (1989). *Adolescent group psychotherapy.* Madison, CT: International Universities Press.

*Black, C. (1987). *It will never happen to me!* New York: Ballantine.

Corey, G. (1995). *Theory and practice of group counseling* (4th ed.). Pacific Grove, CA: Brooks/Cole.

*Corey, G., & Corey, M. (1997). *I never knew I had a choice* (6th ed.). Pacific Grove, CA: Brooks/Cole.

Dagley, J. C., Gazda, G. M., & Eppinger, S. J. (1994). Group psychotherapy with children, preadolescents, and adolescents. In A. Fuhriman & G. M. Burlingame (Eds.), *Handbook of group psychotherapy: An empirical and clinical synthesis* (pp. 340–360). New York: Wiley.

Elkind, E. (1984). *All grown up and no place to go: Teenagers in crisis.* Reading, MA: Addison-Wesley.

*Kiselica, M. S., Rotzien, A., & Doms, J. (1994). Preparing teenage fathers for parenthood: A group psychoeducational approach. *Journal for Specialists in Group Work, 19*(2), 83–94.

*Moore, J., & Herlihy, B. (1994). Groups for adolescent girls living in father-custody families. *Journal for Specialists in Group Work, 19*(1), 11–16.

*Morganett, R. S. (1990). *Skills for living: Group counseling activities for young adolescents.* Champaign, IL: Research Press.

*Newbauer, J. F., & Hess, S. W. (1994). Treating sex offenders and survivors conjointly: Gender issues with adolescent boys. *Journal for Specialists in Group Work, 19*(2), 129–135.

Paperbacks for Educators. (1995). *Bibliotherapy for Children and Teens.* Washington, MO: Paperbacks for Educators.

Paperbacks for Educators. (1995). *School Counselor Catalog, 6–12.* Washington, MO: Paperbacks for Educators.

*Entries marked with an asterisk are recommended for further reading.

*Piechowski, P. A., & Ciha, T. E. (Eds.). (1988). *Project group work: An innovative approach to counseling in schools.* Des Moines, IA: State of Iowa, Department of Education.

*Rose, S. D., & Edleson, J. L. (1987). *Working with children and adolescents in groups: A multimethod approach.* San Francisco: Jossey-Bass.

*Smead, R. (1995). *Skills and techniques for group work with children and adolescents.* Champaign, IL: Research Press.

CHAPTER 11

GROUPS FOR ADULTS

Introduction

Theme-Oriented Groups

Groups for College Students
Current Practices of Group Work at University
   Counseling Centers
Common Topics in College Groups
A Cautionary Note

Groups for Weight Control
Review of Selected Literature on Weight-Control Groups
A Group Program for Repeat Dieters

The AIDS Crisis as a Challenge for Group Workers
How Groups Can Help
An Educational Focus in AIDS Groups

**One Counselor's Story: Starting an HIV/AIDS
   Support Group**
How the Group Began
Help and Support
Format
Group Issues
Personal Concerns
Looking Ahead

Group Work with Men

A Men's Group in a Community Agency
Background and Purpose of the Group
Structure of the Group
Follow-Up and Outcomes

A Domestic Violence Group

Context of the Group
Resistance to Group Work
A Case Illustration
Format and Goals of the Group
Developing Topics for Group Interaction
Suggestions for Leading a Domestic Violence Group
Some Personal Reactions

A Women's Support Group for Victims of Incest

Purpose and Rationale
Setting up the Group
Structure of the Group
Follow-Up and Evaluation
Resources for Incest Groups

A Long-Term Therapy Group for Survivors of Sexual Abuse

Groups as the Treatment of Choice
Basic Information on Incest
Rationale for Long-Term Group Therapy
Selection of Group Members
Group Process
Leadership

Where to Go from Here

References and Suggested Readings

INTRODUCTION

This chapter describes a variety of special-interest groups for adults. We try to be as practical as possible, so you will be able to incorporate our suggestions in your practice. This chapter begins with some observations on a theme-oriented approach to adult groups. We describe several special-interest groups for college students that can be formed in public and private agencies as well as in college counseling centers. Also described are groups for weight control, AIDS support groups, a domestic violence group, a men's group, a women's support group for victims of incest, and a long-term therapy group for incest survivors.

THEME-ORIENTED GROUPS

Theme-oriented groups have many advantages for adults. If topics reflect the life issues of the participants, they can be powerful catalysts. It is good to consider several factors if you decide to structure your groups around topics.

Think about the common developmental life concerns characteristic of the group membership. If the group you are leading is made up largely of adults in their early 20s, they are likely to be involved in choosing a career, choosing a lifestyle, revising their life plan, seeking meaning in life, and wrestling with unresolved dependence/independence issues. If your group is composed of people making the transition from their late 20s to their early 30s, you can expect such concerns as changes in their values and beliefs, parent/child issues, job difficulties, and depression over not having met goals they've set for themselves.

For groups made up of middle-aged participants, leaders can structure the group around such themes as coping with the pressure of time, adjusting to children's growing up and leaving home, marital crises, changing roles of men and women, coping with aging, the death of one's parents, divorce and separation, stagnation in work, changing one's occupation or career, finding meaning in life apart from rearing a family, creatively coping with stress, and facing loneliness.

Who decides on the themes for a group? This depends on many factors, including your leadership style and the level of sophistication of your group. You and the members can cooperatively develop themes that will provide direction for the sessions. You need to consider the readiness of members to fully explore these themes. Death, loneliness and isolation, anger, depression, and other potentially intense topics can trigger feelings that have been repressed for many years, and both the leader and the members must be able to handle the emotional intensity generated. If members select the themes, rather than being pushed into exploring a given topic, there is a greater chance that they will be able to face them.

GROUPS FOR COLLEGE STUDENTS

A common complaint we hear is that it is easy to feel isolated on a university campus. With the emphasis on intellectual development, students often feel that relatively little attention is paid to their personal development. From our work in counseling centers at universities, we have come to realize that many students seek counseling services not only because of serious problems but also because they want to develop aspects of their personalities in addition to their thinking abilities. These students are hungry for personal nourishment, and they actively seek group experiences in which they can be nourished and can grow by nourishing others. In a weekly group with fellow students, they can formulate goals, explore areas of themselves they've kept hidden that are causing them difficulties in interpersonal relating, and identify the internal blocks impeding the full utilization of their capabilities. By dealing with their personal problems, students free themselves of certain emotional blocks to learning, and become far better students, approaching their studies with a sense of enthusiasm and commitment.

When we speak about college students, we are not restricting ourselves to a population of those in their late teens or early 20s. The groups we've led and co-led on university campuses draw a cross-section of students composed of people in their 20s and 30s as well as many middle-aged people—women returning to college after their children leave home, and men and women preparing for major changes in their careers and lives. A diversity of special needs on the college campus can be explored through a group experience.

CURRENT PRACTICES OF GROUP WORK AT UNIVERSITY COUNSELING CENTERS

Group counseling might well be the treatment of choice for college students who present concerns dealing with autonomy, relationships, and self-esteem. In their national survey, Golden, Corazzini, and Grady (1993) found the following:

- Most groups were co-led, met once each week for an average of 90 minutes, and had 5 to 8 members. Co-leaders generally met about 10 minutes before the group and about 30 minutes following the group session.
- Prospective members were screened 96% of the time. Reasons for excluding a person from a group included: severe psychopathology,

lack of fit with other group members, personality disorder, and actively suicidal. Inclusion criteria included: compatibility with the group focus, motivation for group, ego strength, interpersonal problems, and verbal skills.

- Preparation for the group members was provided by 76% of the counseling centers. Most group leaders used verbal explanations. Other methods of pregroup preparation included written explanations, in vivo/video preparation, and a combination of methods.
- The most frequently offered type of group was a time-limited, structured topic group (66%), in which the group leaders have a planned agenda (such as assertiveness training). Process-oriented therapy groups were offered by 59% of the centers. Time-limited process-oriented topic groups without a planned agenda were offered by 35% of the sample. Only 5% of the counseling centers offered sensitivity-encounter groups.
- The majority of respondents rated their group programs as either fairly successful (58%) or very successful (25%).

Golden and her colleagues concluded that although group therapy is a commonly practiced therapeutic modality in university counseling centers, therapeutic groups are not being used as frequently as other treatment approaches. Their recommendations for ways to increase utilization of therapy groups in college counseling centers include: attempting to ameliorate anxiety about group leader skills, providing ongoing training, and increasing administrative support for groups as a primary treatment modality.

COMMON TOPICS IN COLLEGE GROUPS

As is evident in the national survey conducted by Golden, Corazzini, and Grady (1993), time-limited groups with structured topics or themes are most commonly offered in university counseling centers. This makes sense because counselors frequently say they have difficulty promoting open-ended process groups. Instead, groups are most often formed by an emerging need or client populations with specific concerns. On any college campus a number of students are likely to be victims of violence, rape, sexual abuse, sexual harassment, racism, or discrimination. The themes that emerge from a group often reflect the unique composition of that group.

A variety of structured groups are frequently offered at college and university counseling centers: therapy and support groups for adult children of alcoholics, anxiety management groups, veteran's groups, family issues groups, living under the influence groups, stress management groups, cultural identity groups, nontraditional age student groups, groups for those with relationship concerns, gay and lesbian support groups, self-esteem groups, groups for survivors of childhood sexual abuse, and personal identity groups. These groups are typically short term, lasting from four weeks to the entire term, and are aimed at meeting a variety of special needs by combining a therapeutic focus with an educational one. The scope of the topics for structured groups is limited only by the needs of the population, the creativity of the counselor, and the effort it takes to promote the group. If you are a counselor in a college setting, a good place to begin is to conduct a needs survey. Once you know the special needs of your potential clientele, you can plan a group program around a set of topical themes.

A CAUTIONARY NOTE

Although there are clear advantages to topical or structured groups, some leaders may develop special-interest groups as a way of working on their own unresolved issues. For example, a male leader with resentment toward women may form a men's group and use it as a forum for his own catharsis. Leaders do not have to be completely free of their own problems before they lead a group, but if leaders use session time to grind an ax over some personal issue, they are not facilitating participants' growth. This problem can be avoided by careful supervision during the leader's training period as well as continual self-examination and in-service training for those who lead groups.

If a group is too tightly structured and driven primarily by a concern with presenting information, it is likely that participants will not have an opportunity to bring up their own emerging concerns. Even when there is keen interest in exploring a particular theme, the topics should not become more important than the pressing needs of the members of a group. For meaningful sharing of ideas on a topic, members need to feel free to express their reactions to one another. A balance between content and process is important for a successful group experience. An interpersonal, process-oriented focus will increase the chances that members will feel trusting enough to discuss topics in a personal way.

GROUPS FOR WEIGHT CONTROL

Although weight control and body image are concerns regardless of gender, women especially feel pressured to have an "ideal body," because there is a strong social bias against "overweight" women in our society. Women tend to internalize societal messages to be unrealistically thin, and if they are not, there are psychological and social prices to pay. Many overweight women experience chronic depression and low self-esteem (McNamara, 1989a).

REVIEW OF SELECTED LITERATURE ON WEIGHT-CONTROL GROUPS

University counseling centers are increasingly offering groups for people with eating disorders. These groups are often designed for women who are bulimic or anorexic or are compulsive eaters. There is a growing recognition that individuals with eating disorders can benefit from group psychotherapy (Brisman & Siegel, 1985; Hendren, Atkins, Sumner, & Barber, 1987; Roth & Ross, 1988).

Roth and Ross (1988) designed long-term groups using cognitive-interpersonal therapy for people with eating disorders. They contend that most people with eating disorders also suffer from systematic distortions of their personal and social worlds. These clients usually have a number of self-defeating beliefs about weight, eating patterns, body image, sense of autonomy, and self-esteem. Some of the beliefs they commonly hold are:

- "I am fat and ugly."
- "Thinness gives me self-worth."
- "I can restrictively diet without any side effects to my health."
- "I am not able to control my life."
- "I am a worthless person."

Their personal relationships are often dissatisfying because of these assumptions about themselves. They also tend to hold distorted interpersonal beliefs that lead them to feel misunderstood by others. Some of these beliefs are:

- "People are basically untrustworthy."
- "People expect me to be perfect."
- "If people get to know me, they'll find me uninteresting."
- "It is essential that I always please others."
- "It is wrong for me to express my anger directly toward others."

In the long-term cognitive groups that Roth and Ross describe, clients with eating disorders have a forum to address the relationship between dysfunctional cognitions, maladaptive social skills, faulty relationships with others, and eating behaviors. In these groups the focus is on cognitive restructuring and learning a range of social skills. The self-defeating beliefs and behaviors that members manifest can be explored and corrected within the group.

Hendren, Atkins, Sumner, and Barber (1987) describe their experience in treating about 200 people with eating disorders in five open groups combining inpatients and outpatients. Although their groups seemed promising for individuals suffering from bulimia and anorexia nervosa, they emphasized the need for more rigorous and extensive long-term follow-up studies as a prerequisite for making definitive conclusions about the lasting benefits of group therapy for such patients.

Brisman and Siegel (1985) recognized the limitations of therapy groups that meet weekly for people with bulimia. They developed a three-phase, multidimensional group program aimed at increasing the cohesion of the group, which was thought to accelerate the therapy process. The program they describe began with an intensive weekend workshop, at which the members developed contracts in which they pledged to change their behavior. There was a follow-up session at which the members were able to deal with problems they had encountered in fulfilling their contracts. They also reported their successes, and these were reinforced. In the final phase, the members met without their therapists to offer support to one another, to reevaluate their contracts, and to share their feelings about the progress of their treatment. In general, the authors found that modified group therapy was a viable treatment, which might be considered before resorting to psychiatric approaches.

Zimpfer (1990b) reviewed studies on the outcomes of groups for the treatment of bulimia. He concluded that group work was a preferred treatment for this population. He found a noticeable increase in the number of follow-up studies of group treatment. All of the follow-ups except one revealed effectiveness in maintaining overall reduction in binge/purge behavior. Also, all but one showed effectiveness in maintaining psychological improvement. In every study reviewed, there was a reduction or elimination of binge/purge behavior, depression was reduced, and body image was improved.

McNamara (1989a) did a study of group counseling for overweight and depressed college women comparing behavioral and cognitive-behavioral group programs aimed at weight control. She found that both of these approaches were effective in producing weight reductions as well as alleviating depression, easing the fear of negative evaluations, and reducing social avoidance and distress. She concluded that the addition of the cognitive-restructuring component did not improve the efficacy of the behavioral weight-control program.

A GROUP PROGRAM FOR REPEAT DIETERS

McNamara (1989b) conducted a structured group program for women who were repeat dieters and who were potentially at risk of developing more serious eating disorders. These groups were composed of eight to ten college women who met for eight weeks for 90-minute sessions. This group is an example of programs that can be organized both for teaching purposes and for supporting the participants in their attempt to change their eating patterns.

The program consisted of structured group meetings designed to accomplish two main goals: (1) replace dieting with healthier eating patterns and a regular exercise program and (2) improve self-esteem and body image by encouraging self-acceptance and the resistance of unrealistic societal expectations for thinness. The leaders recruited group members by making announcements in large introductory psychology classes. Some screening was done, and potential participants were informed about the purpose of the group. They were assisted in deciding whether they were motivated to meet the goals of the program. Individual members developed their own personal goals, which was an integral part of the ongoing group process. Those who joined the groups expressed their frustration with their prior attempts at dieting and their desire to feel better about their bodies.

The eight sessions included some brief lectures, structured exercises, cognitive-restructuring strategies, opportunities for sharing reactions and behavior, and discussing assigned homework at following meetings. The first three sessions of this group program focused heavily on eating behavior, although the structure was designed to gradually facilitate deeper levels of self-disclosure and self-exploration. Beginning with the fourth meeting, the topics tended to shift away from food and eating habits to internal factors that contribute to negative body image and excessive preoccupation with food and weight. Following are some of the issues and tasks for each of the eight sessions.

Session 1: Introduction   After the members get acquainted with one another, the leaders emphasize the importance of confidentiality and ask the members for their reasons for dieting. A brief lecture focuses on the risks associated with repeat dieting and the vicious circle of dieting. The goals of the group are clarified, and members are invited to discuss their reactions about replacing their dieting behavior with healthier habits. For homework, the members are asked to keep a food diary that consists of recording their food intake and their feelings both before and after eating.

Session 2: Changing Eating Behavior   This session focuses on eating behavior, weight, and calories. Emphasis is given to setting a realistic goal for a target weight. Members are then helped in determining how many calories they can consume to maintain their weight goal. They are asked to begin a regular exercise program, which they choose, for at least 30 minutes, three times a week. They are also asked to stop dieting and to start establishing a healthy eating style.

Session 3: Changing Thought Patterns   This session opens with a report on how each person did with her homework assignment for the previous week. The leaders encourage participating and providing encouragement and support. They also look for common themes, especially the feelings, struggles, and accomplishments the women share. By this time, there is a growing cohesion within the group because of these common experiences. This allows for the introduction of goal-oriented, problem-solving strategies. Members are introduced to the circular relationship that exists between thoughts, feelings, and behaviors. They are shown how dysfunctional thinking tends to lead to dysfunctional eating behavior. The leaders ask the members to share with others their thoughts and feelings about the experiences, both before and after eating, that they have recorded in their diaries. The leaders comment on common themes the participants raise and encourage further group interaction. Participants are also taught how to identify negative thoughts and how to replace them with constructive coping responses. The members are asked to work on one new coping response during the week and to record their efforts in their food diaries.

Session 4: Perfectionism, Depression, and Self-Esteem   At this time in the group's development, the members are unified by the common goal of adopting healthy eating habits. Because of the trust and cohesion that have generally been established by this meeting, the participants are ready to reveal more personal aspects of themselves. The members have some opportunity to discuss the new coping techniques they have tried during the previous week. The topic of perfectionism is then introduced with an exercise, and a brief lecture deals with the relationship between perfectionism, depression, and self-esteem. Members learn that women who have eating and body-image problems tend to be perfectionistic and to experience depression when they do not live up to their unrealistically high ideals. The women learn how to challenge the underlying assumptions of this perfectionism and how to replace their "shoulds" and "oughts" with more realistic goals. They also learn how to nourish themselves without food. The homework assignment consists of taking home a small, attractive box that the group leaders distribute and taking out nourishing activities or thoughts when they feel down and are tempted to use food as their defense.

Session 5: Anger and Assertiveness   The topics of this session follow from the previous discussion of how perfectionism leads to depression. Anger and assertiveness are introduced by asking women in the group to look at situations in which they might be reluctant to assert themselves. Members are asked "What price do you pay for being nonassertive?" They generally recognize the relationship between their feelings of frustration and anger and their eating patterns. Because anger is considered unfeminine in this society, many women report that they seek food as an outlet for their feelings of anger or resentment. The co-leaders explore with the members the difficulties they encounter in being assertive, especially at times when they feel angry. The members are encouraged to challenge one another's self-defeating thoughts and behaviors and to support self-enhancing behaviors.

Session 6: Societal Standards of Thinness and Beauty   An exercise introduces the members to a discussion of how society places unrealistic pressures on women to be thin. Members are asked to list the qualities of the "perfect woman." These characteristics are then discussed, and the leaders encourage group interaction on the topic of the cultural pressures to be "superwomen." The group explores the messages in magazine advertisements that have been brought in by the leaders. For homework the members are asked to have a man they know identify a woman he finds attractive. They are instructed to ask him what he finds attractive about her and to listen for qualities other than weight that he mentions. The purpose of this exercise is to challenge the belief that women must be superthin to be considered attractive. Members are also asked to bring in a magazine photo of a woman whose body looks like theirs and one whose body they wish they had.

Session 7: Improving Body Image   This session opens with a mirror exercise that introduces the topic of body image. Members form triads and are given a full-length mirror. They are instructed to take turns standing in front of the mirror. Starting at the top of her body and moving down, each woman comments only on what she likes about her body. After the exercise, participants talk about what they felt during the exercise, including what made them feel uncomfortable, what they felt good about, and how they felt in the triad. The leaders ask the members what they would be losing if they were to like their bodies. Later in this session the focus is on correcting distortions in body image. The women also discuss what the men they talked to during the previous week reported that they found sexy and attractive in women.

Session 8: Termination   At this time members are helped to consolidate the gains they have made in the group sessions with respect to acquiring healthy eating behaviors and improving their body image. They are reminded that this is the final meeting, and each person is asked to say what she considers to be most valuable about the group and what the most important thing is that she learned about herself. The members are encouraged to exchange feedback concerning positive changes they have observed in one another. Each person is asked to complete this sentence: "The one thing I want to continue to work on when I leave this group is . . ." Members are given referral resources for additional counseling if they feel the need for this service.

McNamara reports that the participants concluded that the group had been effective in reducing repeat dieting and improving body image. The results suggest that this kind of program is an efficient preventive strategy for women who may be at risk for developing more serious eating problems. This program is probably best presented as a short-term preventive group for people with eating problems, but it could be lengthened for clients with more serious eating disturbances. If these modifications were made, the sessions might focus on the dysfunctional family dynamics that frequently underlie eating disorders. Male and female co-leaders might work together in a more expanded version of this program to deal with the fears, anger, and likely transferences that the participants might have toward the male leader.

This group program was based on the work of Weiss, Katzman, and Wolchik (1985) with bulimic individuals. McNamara revised their work to meet the needs of repeat dieters and others at risk for an eating disorder. If you are interested in further information about this group program, refer to the articles describing group approaches to weight control (McNamara, 1989a, 1989b). You can also contact Kathleen McNamara, Ph.D., Psychology Department, Colorado State University, Fort Collins, CO 80523; telephone (303) 491-6061.

THE AIDS CRISIS AS A CHALLENGE FOR GROUP WORKERS

Acquired immune deficiency syndrome (AIDS) has become a critical health problem facing contemporary society. AIDS already affects a wide population and will certainly become an increasing problem. It has been called an "equal opportunity disease" that strikes at diverse populations. As a counselor you will inevitably come in contact with people who have AIDS, with people who have tested positive and are carriers of the human immunodeficiency virus (HIV), or with people who are close to them. You simply cannot afford to be unaware of the many issues surrounding the AIDS epidemic. You will not be able to educate those with whom you come in contact unless you learn about the problem yourself. We encourage you to explore your own attitudes, values, and fears about working with AIDS patients, with HIV-positive clients, and with those who have been affected by the AIDS epidemic.

HOW GROUPS CAN HELP

People afflicted with AIDS often stigmatize themselves and perpetuate beliefs such as "I feel guilty and ashamed," "I feel that God is punishing me," "I am a horrible person, and therefore I deserve to suffer," and "I am to blame for getting this disease." Indeed, they often accept what they have heard from others that "you got what you deserved." A support group can provide a safe place for the participants to deal with the impact of this social stigma and vent their anger, enabling them to form a new perspective on their situation. In the supportive climate of a group, these people can openly talk about the burdens of carrying the stigma and can begin to challenge self-destructive beliefs. Instead of blaming themselves, they can begin to forgive themselves and decide how to make the most of the time they do have.

By sharing their fears, these participants can find some measure of hope by realizing that they are not completely alone in facing an uncertain future. The fact that others are waging a common struggle brings about a high level of cohesiveness in this kind of support group. The participants have many physical, psychological, and spiritual challenges to meet, and a group can be of major help.

Bruhn (1989) offers the following guidelines for those who lead HIV/AIDS support groups:

- Determine the mental status of the client. Is the client HIV-positive? Has he or she been diagnosed with AIDS?
- Determine the nature of the client's fears, including whether they are real or imagined.
- Determine the client's current needs in all areas.
- Determine realistic goals. It is useful to explore hopes, expectations, and wishes regarding family, spouse, and work.
- Determine both short-term and long-term counseling needs and strategies for meeting these needs.

Applying these guidelines can help group leaders create an atmosphere of acceptance and concern in which clients can voice their most pressing concerns and learn as much as possible about what is known about the disease.

The issues that are typically talked about in a support group for people with HIV/AIDS include feelings of helplessness, social stigmatization, guilt, shame, isolation, anger, and anxiety and concerns related to the clients' identity and intimacy with a partner (Grant, 1988). For instance, when clients initially learn that they are infected with the virus, they frequently feel powerless to change their situations. The social stigma associated with the disease is an added burden on gay youths who often already feel isolated by the lack of a supportive social network. Clients also experience anxiety over their prognosis. Most youths are making decisions about furthering their education and establishing their careers; a positive HIV diagnosis tends to cast doubt and uncertainty on these plans. One of the developmental tasks youths face is developing intimacy with a partner; infected youths worry about the rejection they expect if they were to tell a potential partner about their condition. The supportive climate of the group provides these youths with the means for coping more realistically and effectively with their situation.

AN EDUCATIONAL FOCUS IN AIDS GROUPS

It is disconcerting to consider that accurate knowledge about AIDS may not lead people to change their sexual behavior. In a study of college students' knowledge of AIDS and behaviors, Gray and Saracino (1989) found that knowledge alone did not appear to translate into behavioral change.

These researchers emphasize the professional, ethical, and moral obligation of counselors in taking an active stance to combat the spread of HIV. Some procedures they suggest are:

- Provide young adults with explicit sexual terms for discussing sexual behavior and values.
- Use role-playing approaches and sexual decision-making strategies to bridge the gap between what young people know cognitively and what they do behaviorally. Help sexually active clients develop and use specific and personal "safer sex" strategies.
- Discuss sexual behavior from an integrated and personal perspective. Include topics such as personal values, relationship status, religious influence, and decision-making skills.

The supportive environment of a group provides an ideal means of reinforcing and maintaining behavior change. This kind of group can be aimed at helping young people translate what they know into specific actions. But there must be a plan to include information in a meaningful way. In HIV/AIDS support groups it is important that there be an educational component as well as a therapeutic focus. People in these groups, as well as their friends and family members, often labor under a host of myths and misconceptions about both HIV and AIDS. As a responsible practitioner, you must dispel these misconceptions and help people acquire realistic knowledge and attitudes. For example, a major misconception is that HIV/AIDS affects only the gay population and that if you are not gay you have no need to worry about being infected. In fact, heterosexuals have become infected through blood transfusions, through needle sharing by illicit drug users, and through sexual contact with members of the opposite sex who themselves are carriers of the virus. The truth of the matter is that the AIDS epidemic does affect many of us, either directly or indirectly.

Education of various target groups is the key in preventing sharp rises in the number of people who become infected. To be able to educate members of your groups, you need to have current information. This certainly includes an awareness of the values, mores, and cultural background of the various clients you serve. In attempting to change the habits of racial, cultural, and religious groups, you are likely to run up against considerable resistance unless you are able to "speak their language." Furthermore, in educating the general public, it is important to realize that victims of AIDS and those who are HIV-positive can easily become the scapegoat of people's projections of their unconscious fears and hatred.

In his support groups for youths with the AIDS virus, Grant (1988) focuses on education as well as offering support to members at each session. These sessions begin with crisis intervention aimed at encouraging those clients who feel upset and isolated to talk about their feelings. Using a flexible approach, Grant gauges the reactions of the members to determine when it is appropriate to move into teaching. These topics of discussion include the use of condoms, sexual bargaining, and learning to set limits. Some time is devoted during the sessions to providing information on a wide range of subjects such as nutrition, stress management, strategies for making behavioral changes, and methods of modifying substance abuse. Grant reports that the group encourages individuals to practice safer sex to avoid infecting others and to make the necessary lifestyle changes that could increase the chances of maintaining their physical and emotional health.

Spector and Conklin (1987) organized a therapy group for AIDS patients around the principles of supportive psychotherapy. They reported that the terminal patients in their group typically experienced feelings of isolation, both psychological and physical. These clients felt alone in their existential dilemma, especially when those close to them and caretakers distanced themselves from them as they approached death. The primary therapeutic goal of their group was to restore some measure of lost support and compassionate contact that could come about through the cohesive group. Spector and Conklin reaffirmed their belief in group psychotherapy as providing a valuable support system for people with AIDS. They list the following suggestions for group therapists who are interested in conducting a group for people with AIDS:

- In selecting members, it is good to group individuals at similar stages of the disease. The co-therapists found that mixing patients whose disease was far advanced with those in a relatively early stage led to intolerable fears in the latter.
- It is essential that the group leaders be as knowledgeable as possible in all aspects of the disease, as the members often bring the information they receive from the media, relatives, and friends to the group sessions for clarification.
- Group therapists need to regularly monitor the mental status of each patient to detect any psychological changes.
- The co-leaders must be comfortable discussing sexuality, drug use, and sexual techniques aimed at safer practices.
- It is useful for the therapists to be prepared to offer clear, up-to-date information concerning resources such as social services, long-term care facilities, and local support groups.

In summary, it seems clear that support groups for people with AIDS offer valuable therapeutic and educational functions. Members in these groups can learn the truth about the facts surrounding their disease, and they can acquire a range of cognitive and behavioral strategies for enhancing the quality of life. The acceptance and caring within the group can foster an increased sense of hope and can facilitate development of their inner resources to create a meaningful existence.

If you want to know more about group work with HIV-infected persons and persons with AIDS, we suggest the following resources: Barrows and Halgin (1988), Bruhn (1989), Castronovo (1990), Dworkin and Pincu (1993), Grant (1988), Gray and Saracino (1989), Jones (1996), Norsworthy and Horne (1994), Smith (1994), Spector and Conklin (1987), Stokes and Damon (1995), and Tunnell (1991).

In the following section one counselor tells how he began organizing HIV/AIDS support groups and why he continues doing them. His personal account applies many of the principles of group work outlined in this book and describes some unique challenges in conducting counseling groups with this population.

ONE COUNSELOR'S STORY: STARTING AN HIV/AIDS SUPPORT GROUP

Steven I. Lanzet is a licensed professional counselor at the Boise Counseling Center and is the HIV testing and counseling program director at Planned Parenthood of Idaho. He has taught in the counseling and psychology programs at Albertson College of Idaho and Boise State University and was support services coordinator for the Idaho AIDS Foundation. He provides on-going training and clinical assistance to the foundation and other HIV service providers in the Northwest. The discussion that follows is written from the perspective of Steven Lanzet.*

HOW THE GROUP BEGAN

In 1987, after a doctor told me that I was suffering from an illness that could be associated with HIV disease, I decided to take an HIV test. I had grave fears that I was going to test positive and wouldn't have long to live. If indeed I was going to die, I needed to make some plans. This crisis proved to be the catalyst for clarifying my values and making decisions about changing my life.

Later, I received word that I had tested negative. I experienced a great deal of emotional turmoil while waiting for the results, and I suspected that others went through a similar experience. Being a group counselor and believing in the power of the group process, I decided to begin a support group for people who were dealing with HIV/AIDS. Although most people said that they thought the group was a good idea, they felt it was highly unlikely that anyone would come to the group, because I work in a very conservative community. There was a chance that victims would not attend for fear of discovery. It did not take long for me to realize that there were two epidemics, one called AIDS, and the other called AFRAIDS.

*For further information on this topic, contact Steven I. Lanzet, Boise Counseling Center, 815 Park Boulevard, Suite 310, Boise, ID 83712; telephone (208) 345-4660.

I met a nurse epidemiologist at the local health department who was administering the HIV tests, Linda Poulsen, and discovered that many people were testing positive. Linda also had the idea that a support group would be helpful. Together we sat down and planned our ideal group. We decided that whether or not people showed up, we would sit there every time for at least an hour each session. We were very surprised to find out in our first group that eight people showed up for what turned out to be a powerful session. Most of these people had many things in common, best captured by the statement "I felt as if I was the only one who was going through this."

HELP AND SUPPORT

As we started to reach out, we realized that, unfortunately for us (in 1987 in Boise, Idaho), there wasn't a lot of support from the medical community. In designing the group, however, I found Linda, who was able to answer the questions of group participants about the physiological aspects of HIV/AIDS. The health department is often a good place to look for help and a co-leader when you decide to start a group. These people have direct knowledge and experience in dealing with the virus. In addition to the department, our major source of support is the Idaho AIDS Foundation. To find out what help is available in your community, call the National AIDS Hotline at (800) 342-AIDS.

One of our first tasks was to find a suitable location. Even though churches are abundant in our community and available for this kind of purpose, many gay people aren't welcomed in some of the mainline denominations. We also ruled out the use of the health department, because it was the place where many people had found that they were HIV-positive, and we thought they would have negative associations to it. We wanted a space that was comfortable, relaxed, and as noninstitutional as possible. Eventually, we decided to use the YWCA. It was very flexible and had a reputation of being open to new ideas.

Another source of support was the local gay community. The Gay Community Center put us in touch with various gay organizations, and we were able to put out the word that we were starting the group. After a few months, we sent a flier to health-care providers, psychologists, counselors, and social workers about the services we could offer. I found out quickly that if we showed some flexibility, many people in the community were willing to work with us and to share their knowledge. We invited guest speakers to every other group session.

FORMAT

From the outset, I decided that it would be best to use trained group leaders rather than to rely on volunteers. Professionals expressed interest in working with people with HIV/AIDS, and I provided ongoing coordination.

The format for these groups was the result of trial and error. When we began, we decided on an open support group to include a variety of people with AIDS, people who had tested HIV-positive, friends, family, parents, and those who were worried about being infected. In addition, health professionals and volunteers could attend.

I was concerned that we would get people who were in such advanced stages of the disease that it would be very difficult for me or the other clients to relate to them. But we found real benefit in having "advanced stage clients," because the participants who were relatively healthy saw that it could happen to them and also were provided with a source of strength. The members could begin to anticipate how to build a support system to solve problems that others were discussing. I have come to believe that a heterogeneous group including people dealing with all stages of the disease is advisable. Some people, however, felt uncomfortable having participants in the group who were at stages considerably different from theirs. In a large community it is possible to create groups that are more homogeneous. The categories of people could be:

- family and friends
- those who have not tested HIV-positive but who are worried about being carriers of the virus
- women only
- HIV-positive youth group
- caregivers
- groups for various minority groups conducted in language of origin
- newly diagnosed clients
- those who are HIV-positive without symptoms
- those who are HIV-positive with symptoms
- those with terminal-stage AIDS

I quickly found out that we were better off with a heterogeneous approach as groups build up a genuine cohesiveness and are very resistant to making a switch. I recommend that you assess your situation and decide what works best for you and your group members.

At our first and second meetings we asked people to brainstorm with us about what topics would be most interesting and relevant to deal with in the group. We did this exercise a number of times in different groups and combined the needs assessment lists. They became the foundation for the guest speakers we asked to our groups. Some of the topics that came up were:

- the grief and loss process
- assertiveness training (dealing with doctors and other professionals)
- family issues

- spirituality
- medication and other health-care concerns
- nutrition and exercise
- learning about how to be sexually safer
- coping with homophobia and other forms of discrimination
- living wills and other legal issues
- coping with depression and other mental-health concerns

We typically begin a group session with a quick go-around. The importance of confidentiality is emphasized at the beginning of each session. If the members care to, they talk about what has brought them to the meeting that night. Often they go into their history, how they came to be HIV-positive, and what their experience has been before and after that time. As early as possible in each group meeting, the group leaders help members to identify common concerns and link the work of members. Before people come to these groups, their overwhelming feeling is that "I am all alone with this issue." It is difficult to maintain this defense when they see other people dealing with similar concerns.

Later in the session, we invite questions and comments from the participants. We also bring in outside resources to lead the group on a particular question raised by the members. These guests have been well received, and this practice also introduces members to the resources available in the community.

At each meeting we encourage members to bring up personal concerns they want to explore. Typical concerns are:

- "I told my mother about my health."
- "My lover left me."
- "I have this purple blotch on my skin, and I don't know what to do."
- "I've been in jail since I last saw you."
- "I'm feeling good [I'm feeling bad]."

The role of the co-leaders at this time is to help people express themselves and to encourage people to speak to one another in the group rather than through the leaders. People are allowed to respond to what others say, but we ask them to be nonjudgmental, to use "I" language, and to speak directly to the other person.

The group ends with some sort of ritual. One of our early rituals was standing in a circle and giving a mutual shoulder rub. I assumed that many of the participants in our group had stopped getting touched after they were diagnosed and that if they came to the group they could be guaranteed a little bit of nonsexual body contact such as a couple of hugs. We encourage people to give and get hugs if they so desire. At some groups, participants have asked if people would be willing to share names and phone numbers so they could develop a network outside of the group.

GROUP ISSUES

Over the years that I have been running these groups, a number of issues resurface, one of which is confidentiality. We continually need to redefine confidentiality, answer any questions about it, discuss it fully, and get everybody to agree to abide by this practice. At times, we have spent as much as half of a meeting discussing confidentiality and trust.

When an individual has knowingly broken confidentiality, the members tell the person that he or she is no longer welcome at the group. The group has been consistent with this norm. I stress that no one can confirm an individual's HIV status except that person. Nevertheless, group members remain afraid of disclosure and have faced serious consequences when their status was disclosed.

Dealing in the group with people who are ill is a matter that must be addressed. Our members have depressed immune systems, and we ask those who are contagious not to come to the group that evening. We have had people come to the group when they were very ill yet noncontagious. Certain other members have had a variety of reactions, which need to be dealt with in an open fashion.

When a new member enters the group, we encourage the returning members to share more about their stories before asking the new client to participate. In telling their stories, returning members often relate what their life was like before they were HIV-positive, what it was like to test positive, and what their subsequent experience has been. They also tend to talk about what the group has meant to them. By the time we come around to the new individuals, it is much easier for them to express themselves. We then say, "You probably have some questions that you would like answered, and this would be a good time to do it." A typical question is: "I'm feeling very depressed too. Tell me about that and what you have done about it." Or: "I haven't told my parents, and you said you haven't told your parents. I'm curious who has told their parents." This practice helps the new member get involved with the group and feel connected.

There is a lot of humor in our groups. At first, people who are new to the group are somewhat put off by the laughing, but eventually most of them learn the value of humor in putting concerns into perspective. The leaders must remember to accentuate the feelings that go along with the laughter and to look for the pain as well as the humor.

Dealing with grief and loss is a recurring theme. We are constantly reminding people about the grief cycle. Probably the most common reaction we get in the group is members experiencing an emotion and feeling as if they're going crazy or are out of control. It is essential to teach people to identify where in the grief cycle they are so when their anger erupts, they see it as a natural and necessary process. Almost always there is someone else in the group who has experienced the same kind of feeling and can speak to this issue.

When a member of the group either becomes very ill or dies, it is essential to explore the feelings evoked in other members. We spend some time at the meeting following the member's death in remembering him or her and talking about things that we liked about that person. Of course, along with this process comes dealing with the members' feelings about dying and grief. Usually there is talk about the funeral, which sometimes leads to a discussion about what others hope their memorial service will be like. We encourage this kind of talk, because it helps to reveal some of the members' own issues and helps them to discuss their own mortality.

PERSONAL CONCERNS

As a result of leading these groups, I have learned to cope with anger at me. The first time someone in the group got mad at me, I didn't know how to respond. I eventually understood that anger was sometimes directed at me because the clients felt more comfortable with me than with other people. One of the doctors in our area who deals with people with HIV/AIDS told me he had many patients who were angry with him. As we talked, I began to realize the pattern. A great deal of anger is associated with AIDS, but people have few places to vent their anger. The client knows that I'm a safe and nonrejecting target. I try to help the client redirect some of the anger and find ways to work through it.

Perhaps the greatest anxiety I experienced was feeling that the time I have to work in the HIV/AIDS area is limited. I realize that no matter how hard I try to fight it, burnout is always tapping at my shoulder. The toll of running a group like this and losing so many group members to this disease has been high. The best way to deal with our personal reactions is for leaders to meet outside the sessions to talk about our feelings. Providing support for group leaders is imperative.

I ran the HIV support group for four years. This was possible because I took periodic breaks from facilitating groups and reduced the frequency of the groups that I led. Having a co-facilitator is very helpful and highly recommended. Also, it is important to help other counselors become involved so you can take short or extended breaks. The support groups I have developed with other counselors who don't deal primarily with AIDS continue to be a key way to prevent burnout.

LOOKING AHEAD

Our plans for the future include doing a statewide needs assessment, providing more training and supervision for group leaders, maintaining a follow-up system, and expanding the number of groups to include more members of minority groups and rural residents. I urge any trained group facilitator to learn more about HIV/AIDS to help meet urgent community needs and to consider starting or helping with an HIV/AIDS support group. It is both very demanding and very rewarding.

GROUP WORK WITH MEN

Traditional forms of individual talk therapy are probably not the best way to reach men. David Jolliff (1994) suggests that a better way to deliver counseling services to men is through therapy groups that allow men to tap their masculine power and energy, utilizing it in their own healing process. One such group, designed to help men explore ways they experience and express their gender roles, contained both a psychoeducational component and an interpersonal, process-oriented dimension. Hetzel, Barton, and Davenport (1994) provide an overview of their men's group.

The group was conducted for two hours once a week for ten sessions. The first six sessions were structured around these themes:

- men and masculinity
- men and emotions
- men and work
- men, intimacy, and sexuality
- men and family of origin (lasting for two sessions)

The last four sessions were unstructured and emphasized concerns raised by the members. The group was co-led by a female and a male therapist, both doctoral students. Based on feedback from the members during the group sessions and information gathered from postgroup interviews, the co-leaders made the following recommendations for counselors who are interested in conducting all-male counseling groups:

- Be aware of your own thoughts and feelings about men and masculinity and be willing to explore them.
- Be knowledgeable about the psychological development of men and the ways societal expectations influence their behavior.
- Because men are socialized to be independent, they may find it difficult to participate in traditional counseling that stresses introspection and expression of feelings. Be careful not to label this behavior as pathological.
- Be flexible and creative in the way you structure the group and in the techniques you employ.
- Don't scale down your expectations for male clients. It is important to both accept and challenge the assumptions and beliefs that men hold, providing them with opportunities to explore and experiment with new thoughts, feelings, and behavior.
- Anticipate issues of premature termination that may arise in an all-male counseling group. Both during the pregroup screening and dur-

ing the sessions, help men talk about ways they might deal with discouragement and discuss the tendency to quit.

- Create a climate within the group that invites members to discover commonalities and facilitates developing meaningful relationships with other members.
- Consider both the advantages and disadvantages of using a mixed-sex versus single-sex co-leadership model.
- Advertise your group widely, and solicit referrals from other counselors.

Hetzel, Barton, and Davenport (1994) conclude that if counselors adopt a gender-sensitive approach, it is possible to reframe behaviors traditionally perceived as problematic in male clients: resistance to expressing feelings, being overly task-oriented, and withdrawing from intimacy. A gender-sensitive leadership style can provide male clients with a fuller understanding of how gender role expectations and their socialization have influenced their lives. Even more important, the group can help them discover a greater sense of freedom and expression.

If you want to learn about groups for men, begin with the excellent book *Man Alive: A Primer of Men's Issues* (Rabinowitz & Cochran, 1994), which offers rich material that can be incorporated into group sessions. Rabinowitz and Cochran provide consciousness-raising activities and personal development exercises, many of which could be adapted for group work with men. Other resources that may be helpful in forming groups for men include Alberti and Emmons (1995), Dougherty (1990), Hetzel, Barton, and Davenport (1994), Kimmel (1987), Moore (1990), Moore and Leafgren (1990), and Wilbur and Roberts-Wilbur (1994).

A MEN'S GROUP IN A COMMUNITY AGENCY

Randy Alle-Corliss, a clinical social worker in a department of psychiatry in a large health maintenance organization (HMO), designed and co-leads a men's group in the agency where he works with co-leader Abran Esquibel, a clinical social worker. The following discussion is written from the perspective of Randy Alle-Corliss.*

BACKGROUND AND PURPOSE OF THE GROUP

The purpose of the group is to provide men coming to a psychiatric counseling center with an opportunity to work together on common issues such as depression, stress, marital and relationship difficulties, parenting

*For further information about this group, contact Randy Alle-Corliss (private practice), 440 W. Baseline Road, Claremont, CA 91711; telephone (909) 920-1850.

concerns, work-related issues, loneliness, and isolation. No mens' groups were being offered in our area, but we believed men could profit from talking about life struggles in a safe and supportive group. We assumed that exploring deeply personal concerns would lead to a reduction of isolation and increase the bonding among men. Many of our male clients did not have significant male friendships; if they had friends, they were often distant from them. We felt personally challenged to begin a group for men, which we did more than five years ago. To date we have conducted about 15 of these groups.

Since we were working for a large HMO, we knew the number of group sessions would be limited. The group format, whereby more clients could be seen in a shorter amount of time, at a greater frequency, could serve the needs of the clients and at the same time serve the needs of the organization. And we were convinced that the group would have other therapeutic benefits in addition to the cost-effectiveness factor. We assumed that the group would offer a place for men to discover universal themes, to ventilate feelings they had stored up, and to practice skills they could carry outside of the group and apply in various settings in everyday life.

We began by writing a proposal and presenting it to the administration. We developed a memorandum describing the purpose of the group and sent it to other clinicians, asking them to recommend appropriate candidates for this type of group. We excluded from the group candidates who were psychotic or suicidal, in extreme crisis, and those who lacked the psychological strength required for sustained group interaction.

STRUCTURE OF THE GROUP

The group meets for 90 minutes each week for a total of 16 weeks. In addition, the co-leaders meet regularly for 15 minutes before each session and 15 minutes afterward. The group is topically oriented, educationally and therapeutically focused, and combines a variety of techniques. At times it takes longer than one session to cover a particular topic.

The Initial Session   We start the group with general introductions from each member and ourselves. We also cover the basic ground rules in the first meeting, including confidentiality, attendance, and basic HMO policies. During this first meeting, we explore gender-related issues such as what it means to be a man, the messages the men received in growing up, and how these messages affect them today. We typically discuss a number of norms pertaining to being a man. The members are invited to share their reactions to adhering to or breaking these norms and how these norms influence their daily behavior. Typical topics discussed at other sessions are described next.

Relationships with Father and Mother   We examine relationships with parents, particularly with fathers, since this seems to be a central influence in the lives of most men. Many of the men are disappointed by their father's absence or are angry about the excessive force and aggression their fathers used to discipline them. We also explore their relationships with their mothers, especially as it relates to how they handled their feelings around them. We typically invite members to write letters to their parents, which they share in the group. Initially we used a videotape by Robert Bly discussing mens' issues, but as we gained more experience it became clear that more than enough material emerged within the here-and-now context of the group sessions.

Relationships with Significant Others   It is clear to us that the men in our groups often experience difficulty simply recognizing, let alone expressing, their feelings. One reason some men join the group is because they have trouble expressing feelings and behaving assertively. Members have opportunities to talk about their relationships with significant others, especially with women. Some of them may be going through a divorce or having marital difficulties. We broadened our description of relationships to include gay relationships. Our experience in working with some gay men in these groups has taught us the importance of using language that is free of bias with respect to sexual orientation. Regardless of one's sexual orientation, the men in our groups typically discover that they have a great deal in common.

Developing and Maintaining Friendships   We include discussion about friendships with other men and women, for we continue to find that men receive conflicting messages about appropriate gender roles. We also find that men have difficulty initiating friendships and maintaining intimacy. They tend to be quite isolated from other men, and one purpose of the group is to provide them with rich sources of support. We encourage the men in the group to get together outside of the group and to develop other sources of support, especially with other men. However, we caution the members about subgrouping in a way that could detract from group cohesion.

Relationships with Children   We typically examine relationships with children, as many of the men enter the group with concerns about being an effective parent. We discuss the importance of men's relationships with their children. We teach assertiveness skills to assist the men in setting limits and following through on consequences with their children. We often have the men write letters to their children, which they read in group, to help them express and explore unrecognized feelings.

Relationship to Work   Those members who have lost a job often struggle with feeling devastated over not working. The members talk about how

work affects their lives at home, especially with their partners and children. Men often struggle with working too much, setting limits, and frustration on the job. Many men report feeling overly responsible and
stressed when assuming the role of provider. By talking about the importance of work, many of the men learn that there is more to life than simply providing and working. In addition to working, the men come to
realize the importance of a balance between work and play.

Sexuality   Most of the men have a host of concerns regarding sexuality.
However, they tend to be reluctant to discuss such concerns openly. We
have small handouts to spur the mens' thinking on particular topics, such
as sexual performance, feelings of attraction to other people, impotence,
differences in sexual appetites, and aging. Due to the commonalities
among the members, men can explore fears regarding their sexuality and
sexual practices in ways that allow them to gain a deeper understanding
of their sexuality.

Closing the Group   We end the group with good-byes and reminiscing
among members and leaders. Valuable feedback is given, and the members evaluate their experience. We reinforce any gains the members have
made and give them tangible items to take with them to remind them of
their participation in the group. We have given out certificates of attendance with the statement: "It is okay to be a man." We encourage the
members to continue their new behaviors. We also point out to them
potential pitfalls they are likely to encounter in applying what they
learned in the group to everyday living.

FOLLOW-UP AND OUTCOMES

It is critical to assist the members in evaluating the impact of the group
experience. Toward this end, we arrange for a postsession group, which
we call the "reunion group." Between the ending of a 16-week group and
the beginning of a new group, we have the members from the previous
group meet again. Reminders are sent to all the members urging them to
attend. The reunion group gives members a chance to take another look
at what the group meant to them. We place special emphasis on how they
have been applying their learning in their everyday lives. The men have
an opportunity to discuss any problems they've encountered in imple-
menting a new style of behavior. In addition to providing support, we also
challenge the members to take further risks where it seems appropriate.
The follow-up group gives these men a way to establish a plan for putting
their new goals into action now that the group has ended.
      The members' evaluations of their experience at the follow-up session
are typically positive and constructive. Many of the men say they had
been looking for this kind of group for years. They often report that they
greatly valued the opportunity to discuss personally significant topics in

a group setting. They report feeling less depressed, less isolated, and being more able to recognize and communicate their feelings. Some men return to the group later when their benefits allow them the opportunity for continuing their treatment.

Men report that the group has helped them to manage their anger more effectively, to develop more male friends, and to become more assertive. Many of the men are able to utilize the feedback they receive in immediate ways by becoming more aware of their feelings and more communicative in their relationships. They begin to think of themselves and other men more positively. In general, they say that they feel more content with themselves, they feel a wider range of emotions, and they are able to laugh and have more fun.

A DOMESTIC VIOLENCE GROUP

Paul Jacobson, a licensed marriage and family therapist, has designed and conducted a group for men with a history of domestic violence. What follows is an account of this group from Paul's perspective.*

CONTEXT OF THE GROUP

Most group counseling is aimed toward people seeking help. However, the domestic violence group I describe here was for a specialized involuntary population. The men who came to this group were ordered into treatment by court judges or probation officers. Most of these group members typically arrived with attitudes of resentment, blaming of others, and operating under the conviction they did not need counseling. The techniques and strategies for relating to this type of resistance differ somewhat from those used with a voluntary population.

RESISTANCE TO GROUP WORK

An individual assessment interview was conducted for all members prior to attending any group meetings. This was deemed essential to both reduce their potential for disruptive hostility and to ease them into the more stressful group situation. During this time, an attempt was made to support the individual, explore the circumstances of the abusive behavior and his arrest, challenge his defenses in a moderate manner, and gain his cooperation through suggestions of therapeutic need.

*For further information on this group, contact Paul Jacobson, P. O. Box 2352, Idyllwild, CA 92549; telephone (909) 659-4484.

The assessment interview was also essential to begin developing a therapeutic relationship. The importance of establishing an honest relationship with the facilitator cannot be over-estimated. Without this, self-disclosure in a group of guarded strangers would be very unlikely. The design of this group was based on the assumption that, when given the opportunity, participants would willingly apply personal information to themselves, even without initially accepting responsibility for their actions.

I agree with Edleson and Tolman (1994), who contend that men who are prone to violence must accept responsibility for their actions if a treatment approach is to succeed. In my own groups for men who are violent, I have observed the same dynamics that Edleson and Tolman describe. Men who batter often begin group counseling in a state of denial. They typically externalize the source of their problems, and they rarely attribute their problems to their violent behavior. However, for change to occur, these men need to understand their own dynamics and take responsibility for their behavior. If they do not eventually recognize and accept their own problematic behavior, it is unlikely they will change. Nor will they understand the impact of their behavior on their partners, their relationships, and themselves.

A CASE ILLUSTRATION

To give a concrete idea of how this resistance influences a member's participation in a group, let me use Jerome as an example. Jerome arrived for this meeting 20 minutes late complaining that he had totally forgotten the appointment that he made two days prior. Jerome, like all the group members, had been ordered into the program following plea bargaining in which he agreed to attend counseling rather than spend 45 days in jail. His charges had been reduced from felony spousal abuse to a misdemeanor.

Although Jerome had chosen the group alternative, he insisted that he did not need counseling and preferred the quicker remedy of jail. He blamed the public defender for getting him into this program, rather than pursuing this choice. As we talked, his initial agitation diminished somewhat. But when he described the situation of abuse with his wife, he again become loud, animated, and emotional. Jerome told about coming home late one night after having a few beers and getting angry because his wife had not made him dinner. When he ordered her to do so, she responded with "Make it yourself." With this he apparently lost control and claimed he wasn't aware of what he was doing. However, he insisted he never hit her with a closed fist. Jerome was adamant that if she'd only made dinner none of this would have happened. Thus, it was her fault. He further blamed her friends for putting "uppity" ideas into her head.

In exploring other anger experiences, Jerome admitted that it bothered him a little when he became violent, and he wanted to control himself better. This statement was one of the first signs of a more personal stake for participating in the group. Further questioning found Jerome glad to be working again after several months of unemployment, and he admitted that his drinking had increased a little while he was unemployed. Jerome was clearly removed from his emotions, unaware of his own stress level, and unaware of his dependency on alcohol. Furthermore, he did not take responsibility for his actions or his feelings.

FORMAT AND GOALS OF THE GROUP

Each group session began with a didactic presentation. The group was designed to address both educational and therapeutic goals. Following the didactic segment of the initial session, members were given a written multiple-choice questionnaire. This allowed individual responses without the pressures inherent with group verbalization. Then a go-around was used to stimulate discussion. Jerome became more involved at this point and actively verbalized his answers, interacted with other members, and demonstrated an understanding of the concepts. Verbal participation was one of the facilitator's main goals for each group member.

Member Goals   Since the group members had each been arrested for violence against their partners, goals were developed to assist in more optimal relational functioning. Some goals were agreed upon during the assessment interview, but most were selected by the leader for individual treatment plans. Following is a list of some group goals:

- Develop behavioral alternatives to physical violence.
- Learn cognitive techniques for anger management.
- Discuss abusive events and behavioral alternatives.
- Gain an overview of relationship dynamics, expectations, and the development of physical abuse.
- Learn about physiological reactions as correlates of stress and stress reduction methods.
- Develop a recognition of feelings and emotional processing.
- Increase self-disclosures, personal discussion, and assertive communication.
- Increase personal responsibility.
- Stop or decrease alcohol/drug use and recognize use patterns.

Format   All but one series of the 15-week program were conducted using an open group format. Participants were added intermittently throughout the group's duration. The major advantage was to maintain an adequate number of members in the face of high dropout rates. The main disadvantage was difficulty developing group cohesion and trust. Only one 15-week series utilized a closed group format, which seemed far superior.

Some Ground Rules   A few of the group members appeared extremely impulsive and easily frustrated or angered. Several individuals were excluded from the group due to alcohol/drug problems, and many used these substances. Members were told of the group rule of abstinence from drugs prior to meetings during the initial interview. If someone arrived intoxicated, they were not allowed into the group. Two such occurrences meant termination. The only other requirement was attendance, and several individuals were terminated for missing more than the allowable three sessions.

DEVELOPING TOPICS FOR GROUP INTERACTION

Meetings were structured around topics deemed relevant to group goals. The topics themselves were arrived at through several trials of alternatives and could have evolved differently with other geographic and socioeconomic populations. Discussions of these topics were designed to educate, gain involvement, convey information, and confront issues relevant to this population. For instance, Jerome gained valuable insight through the topics of stress and substance abuse. He realized that his own unemployment had led to a high unconscious stress level, which, in turn, aggravated his alcohol use. Unfortunately, Jerome believed that since he was now employed he no longer needed to worry about this. If Jerome faces a similar situation in the future, we hope he will remember the stress reduction techniques he was taught.

The topics presented to the groups were loosely divided into areas of interpersonal and intrapersonal experience. Intrapersonal topics included education concerning human physiology and endocrine systems functioning, cognitive techniques for emotional processing, relaxation methods, drug and alcohol effects, stress and stress reduction, and anger. As many members appeared to have underlying issues about personal adequacy, other topics included meaning in life and the benefits of goal accomplishment. The interpersonal topics involving relationships included communication theories, problem-solving techniques, sex roles, relational expectations, human needs and differences, values, and family experiences.

The topics overlapped considerably, which afforded members an opportunity to explore interpersonal issues in several ways. For example, most communication issues were mentioned under the topics of transactional analysis, assertion training, and problem solving. In many of these groups, written worksheets, scripted role-playing, or other activities were used to encourage member participation. If personal experiences were forthcoming, these were also used to explore and demonstrate relevant issues.

In one group, Jerome and other members practiced rewording their communications into assertive statements. The premise was that if members could learn the ideas and concepts through practice in relatively anxiety-free situations, they could more easily apply them to the conflict-laden areas in everyday life. After Jerome practiced role-playing as a co-worker and relating assertively to an imagined check-out clerk, he was able to discuss his assertive attempts with his wife. At this point he was not only applying the concepts to his own life but also reporting his attempts in group. This progress not only demonstrated his greatly increased trust and openness but also allowed him to receive the support and feedback usually necessary for behavior change.

It should be mentioned that some of the group goals were broad and more suited for long-term treatment; yet many members showed observable progress. To remain personally invested in working with this difficult population, it became necessary to notice small incremental changes and regard these as signs of success and progress. Additionally, the continual training and use of the topics provided a great deal of facilitator development as well. Although perhaps toward an extreme, these issues are relevant within the modern-day "men's movement."

SUGGESTIONS FOR LEADING A DOMESTIC VIOLENCE GROUP

- Know your motivation for organizing and facilitating a domestic violence group.
- Be aware of your own stress level and reactions.
- Try to maintain equanimity and respond rationally.
- Learn to verbalize theoretical ideas in common everyday language.
- Remember that commonly accepted therapeutic concepts are not universally understood or recognized.
- Discover your own similar issues with group members.
- Expect resistance and avoid taking it personally. Respect resistance and work with it therapeutically by encouraging the clients to explore any resistance.
- Use any medium at your disposal to teach and intervene (such as art, video, and handouts).
- Learn to recognize small incremental changes as progress toward discrete, obtainable therapeutic goals.
- Develop a good support system for yourself.

SOME PERSONAL REACTIONS

Facilitating this group has been a major challenge, both rewarding and frustrating. Leading this group forced me to seriously evaluate my statements, style, countertransference, and motivations continually. I discovered related issues of my own and made significant insights into the functioning of this population in general. The development of this program utilized the best of my theoretical beliefs and therapeutic skills, while its evolution reflects my changing perspectives on treatment. I maintained motivation to seek new information and education to accomplish this, which in itself is rewarding. A few individuals expressed gratitude, and others showed improvement without acknowledging it, also providing a source of reinforcement.

For me, working with this population was trying. Many continued to blame significant others for their situation throughout the group. My numerous and varied interventions often seemed ineffective, which I found frustrating and disappointing. Likewise, my educational content was repeatedly challenged, degraded, or dismissed. I was often the target for hostility, expressed directly or indirectly, which affected me greatly. Last, even collecting my small fee was difficult, since many group members were unemployed or barely surviving. Some never paid, and many only gave me a partial payment.

The greatest weakness of this program was the absence of spousal involvement. Although attempts were made in this direction, deep-seated relational dynamics, the lack of a co-therapist, and the actual court mandate wording contributed to difficulties in accomplishing this. An open-ended support group was also needed following the structured program. Several members voiced a desire for a continuing group, which showed progress in and of itself. Also, as mentioned, the preferred modality would be a closed-group format, which more easily results in cohesion, trust, and productive therapeutic work.

If you want more information on this topic, two helpful resources are Edleson and Tolman (1994) and Grusznski and Bankovics (1990).

A WOMEN'S SUPPORT GROUP
FOR VICTIMS OF INCEST

Sexual abuse of children by family members continues to come to the attention of mental-health professionals. Approximately 10% of white, middle-class women in the United States indicate that they had a childhood sexual experience with an older male relative (Herman & Schatzow, 1984). A sexual encounter with a trusted family member not only typically results in a major psychological trauma itself but also frequently leads to emotional problems for the victim later in life. Some of the common problems include impaired self-esteem, negative identity formation, difficulty in intimate relationships, sexual dysfunction, and repeated victimization (Herman, 1981; Meiselman, 1978, 1990).

One of our friends and colleagues, Lupe Alle-Corliss, is a licensed clinical social worker in a psychiatric department who leads groups for women with a history of incest. When she initially designed these support groups years ago, her intent was to structure a time-limited therapy group that would allow women to begin the process of working through unresolved issues related to their incestuous past. Today, with the rapidly changing state of mental-health care, being able to conduct time-limited groups is even more advantageous because it is cost-effective, efficient, and fits the demands for short-term treatment.

The following description, written from the perspective of Lupe Alle-Corliss, highlights key features of the many groups she has conducted.*

PURPOSE AND RATIONALE

A group approach, or a combination of group and individual therapy, is generally considered to be the treatment of choice for victims of incest. In providing a safe and therapeutic environment for incest survivors, the main goal is to empower these women by helping them get past the molestation and the "victimization" role. Other objectives are to help women share their secret and recognize that they are not alone, understand the current impact of this experience, and begin to work through and resolve feelings associated with their trauma and make changes. In a group situation women find a commonality and a basis for identification, and a new type of family can emerge, one that is different from the client's original family, which may have been dysfunctional.

SETTING UP THE GROUP

I have learned the value of recruiting potential members for my groups by publicizing them within my own agency by way of memos, announcements, and personal contact with colleagues. In considering members for the women's support group, I seek clients who display a readiness to deal openly with the trauma of incest. Typically, these women are in individual therapy. For women who are involved with another therapist, I ask for a release form so I can consult and coordinate with the individual therapist.

I meet regularly with each potential member for the purpose of assessing their readiness and appropriateness, orienting them to the group process and goals. Through screening I also determine how well they are likely to fit with other potential group members. Sometimes, prospective members will verbalize their eagerness to be part of the group yet non-

---

*For further information about these groups, contact Lupe Alle-Corliss at her private practice: 10620 Town Center Drive, Suite 124, Rancho Cucamonga, CA 91730; telephone (909) 920-1850.

verbally they may be saying otherwise. They might be extremely uncomfortable with certain questions regarding the incest that are sure to come up in the group. Others may indicate, either directly or indirectly, that they want to be in the group because they have been referred. It is important to assess their true motivation, for some clients may not be completely ready to involve themselves in this type of intense group. They may be acting on the basis of pressure or the need to please others. Also, based on the emerging composition of the group, it might become clear that a particular client may not be a compatible member in a specific group.

Clients are asked why they want to be in such a group, and an attempt is made to determine how ready the individual is to talk in a group setting about the incest and its impact. Other questions sometimes asked during the screening include: "If there is any previous group experience, what was this like for you?" "Were you, or are you now, involved in individual therapy, and what was this experience like?" "What are your personal goals for the group?" "What are your expectations, hopes, and fears about participating in the group?" Applicants are also encouraged to ask me questions about the group and to interview me, including inquiring about my style of conducting the group.

It is critical that members possess the ego strength to deal with the material that will be explored during the sessions. Members need to have adequate interpersonal skills to deal with others in a group situation. People with suicidal and extremely self-destructive tendencies and people who do not have adequate contact with reality are screened out. Also, clients with recent drug addictions may be at a vulnerable place in their recovery process and therefore may not be ready to enter into such an emotionally demanding group. Care is taken not to include family members or friends in the same group. Also excluded are those who are not ready or willing to talk openly about their experiences. Thompson and Renninger (1995) list other criteria for appropriate clients for short-term groups: a person who was victimized in childhood or adulthood; one who is committed to attending the group regularly; and an individual who is motivated to complete weekly homework assignments, communicates effectively, and functions relatively well in daily life.

Herman and Schatzow (1984) employ the following three criteria for inclusion in a group: (1) the clients must express generally positive feelings about participating in a group with others who have experienced incest; (2) the potential participants must not be in a crisis state; that is, they must be functioning reasonably well in daily life; and (3) they must have an appropriate ongoing relationship with an individual therapist.

STRUCTURE OF THE GROUP

The group is closed and meets for 75 minutes for a 12-week period. This time limitation is designed to facilitate bonding and to produce a reasonable degree of pressure necessary to work through the members' resistances. Although each group has its own process, these groups generally go through the phases to be described.

Initial Phase   The initial phase involves getting to know one another, establishing ground rules, and identifying personal goals. This stage is crucial in the development of trust and rapport and in giving members permission for catharsis and ventilation. A signed contract is used to encourage commitment and help the clients feel that their participation is valued and important.

As a continuation of the orientation process, at the first group meeting I emphasize the importance of regular attendance, being prompt, confidentiality, the limitations of time, and bringing any unresolved issues back to the group rather than dealing with them outside of the group. A date for the postgroup meeting, which is typically about three months after termination, is established at the first session. In the early phase of the group, members express empathy with one another over the difficulty of sharing the incest issue. The following guideline questions are provided to help them deal directly with the impact of incest on them: "How did the molestation happen?" "Who molested you?" "How old were you?" "How long did it go on?" "How did you deal with it?" "How did you feel toward the people who were in a position to protect you from the molestation but failed to do so?"

Much of the initial phase is focused on identifying personal and specific goals in writing and then discussing them. The procedure allows all in the group to know of each person's goals and provides a direction for the sessions. The goals for my group are similar to those identified by Thompson and Renninger (1995) in their short-term therapy groups with survivors of sexual abuse, which include:

- providing education, validation, and support via other survivors of sexual abuse;
- exploring past sexual abuse and its effects on current life functioning and behavior;
- decreasing isolation and increasing self-esteem;
- increasing ability to trust oneself and others;
- instilling a sense of empowerment; and
- decreasing secrecy, shame, and stigmatization associated with the abuse.

Members generally feel much anxiety and apprehension at first. A member often feels that she is the only one with such a terrible burden, and she may feel that she would be an outcast if others knew about her secret. As the women realize that they have a common experience, they begin to open up and find the support available in the group useful. By sharing the incest experience, the women free themselves to look at how it continues to have an impact on them. The focus of the sessions is not merely on reporting the details of the specific acts but also on exploring their feelings, beliefs, and perceptions about what happened. Although it is important for these women to share their stories about what occurred in their past, it is essential that they deal with the effects the incest continues to have on their lives. They need to acquire present coping skills that will empower them and enable them to move forward.

As well as gaining insight into her own dynamics, a woman learns that she can be of help to others through her disclosures. Initially, a woman might show resistance by becoming the "helper" or "caretaker" of others in her group. Herman and Schatzow (1984) observed that the increased risk taking involved in discussing feelings and beliefs about the incest story led to an increase in the group's cohesiveness. They found that discharging and sharing intense emotions resulted in bonding, mutual supportiveness, and a safe climate that allowed exploration of the common themes of secrecy, isolation, shame, helplessness, fear, hurt, and anger.

Middle Phase   During the middle phase, focus is on accomplishing the goals of individual members. Connections are made between a woman's past behavior and her present behavior. In this way she begins to see patterns and to understand her own dynamics. For instance, a woman might have chosen men who dominated her, abused her, or in some way took advantage of her. She sees with greater clarity her own part in allowing this type of treatment to continue. A group is a good way to help such a woman become aware of and challenge her faulty belief systems. Through the group process, these women can rid themselves of destructive beliefs and can learn to create functional self-statements. Themes in an individual's life are typically identified. A number of therapeutic strategies can promote change in feelings, attitudes, and behaviors. Some specific techniques include: providing reassurance for women that they behaved normally in an abnormal situation; reading books in a personal way; keeping a diary or journal that includes thoughts, feelings, and behaviors in certain situations; writing letters that are not sent; talking to other family members; and recording and sharing dreams. A very useful way of helping these women express their emotions is through artwork. By asking them to draw the abused child within them, insights unfold surrounding their ordeal. Participating in art often enables them to face the total impact of their molestation. There is some support in the literature for the therapeutic value of these expressive techniques. According to Thompson and Renninger (1995), art and drawing assist clients in arriving at an emotional understanding of their past experiences. Along with cognitive/behavioral techniques, visual exercises facilitate positive change.

Women are encouraged to continue to work on recovering memories and to deal with flashbacks that are so often a common occurrence for the incest survivor. Much needed support and validation is provided, and clients are assisted in recognizing maladaptive defense patterns and developing healthier coping styles.

Final Phase   Toward the end of the group the women are reminded of the upcoming termination. I assist the members in reviewing what happened in the group as a whole as well as what they individually learned and how they can now continue to apply their insights and newly acquired behaviors to situations outside of the group. Role playing helps in this consolidation process. I give a structured questionnaire to help the members pull together and assess their learning. The members evaluate their progress and determine future plans, including what work they still need to do. They write down and give feedback to one another, and they identify certain people in the group whom they are willing to contact should they feel a need for help and support. Although the women cognitively know that the group will be ending, it is a common reaction for them to say that they do not want it to end. Members are asked how they want to celebrate the ending of the group. I find that it is therapeutic to have the members share food as well as participate in a "Personal Poster" in which each member can give individual support and constructive feedback to every group member. The rationale for this exercise is that each member is able to take with her some constructive feedback or supportive comments and can use this experience for support and encouragement. This serves as a reminder of their gains through the group experience.

In their description of a short-term group for incest survivors, Thompson and Renninger (1995) see the use of referrals in the community as a critical piece of the final stage of group. They encourage their members to join another therapy group, join a community support group, or pursue healing through individual therapy. I also encourage the women in my group to remain open to further therapeutic work if they are not already concurrently in individual or group therapy.

FOLLOW-UP AND EVALUATION

Building follow-up procedures into your design provides a basis for understanding the longer term value of the group experience as well as improving the design for future groups. In the short-term groups reported on by Herman and Schatzow (1984), the results of a six-month follow-up survey of 28 women supported their assumption that this therapeutic approach was particularly effective in resolving the issues of shame, secrecy, and stigmatization associated with incest. The single most helpful factor was the contact with other women who had been incest victims.

In the case of my groups, several follow-up meetings are scheduled to help the members make the transition from the weekly groups to being on their own and relying on the supportive networks they have developed. Part of the purpose of this follow-up is to reinforce what was learned and provide renewed support. Follow-up sessions are scheduled 6 to 12 weeks later. During these sessions, the clients are given a postevaluation that asks questions such as:

- What did you like best about the group?
- What did you like least about the group?

- How do you feel that you have changed as a result of being in this group?

The members are also asked to rate themselves as "better," "worse," or "the same," in regard to the following areas: work, friendships, relationships with family members, intimate relationships, feelings about sex, feelings about oneself, and the ability to protect and take care of oneself.

Based on many follow-up group meetings with the members of these groups, it is clear that a well-developed group format with proper screening can result in a therapeutic group experience. Overall, I have found that such a group greatly enhanced treatment of incest survivors as it allowed clients to be seen on a regular basis and provided them with continuity and the support needed for healing. Furthermore, such clients developed a very strong support network that provided them with the strength and courage to begin to resolve past issues, overcome old, negative patterns and set healthy, challenging goals for their future. Perhaps the greatest message they received was that they "deserve" to feel good about themselves and lead more productive lives.

RESOURCES FOR INCEST GROUPS

If you are interested in learning more about designing groups with women with a history of incest, there are many excellent articles and books on the subject. You might begin by reading the articles by Herman and Schatzow (1984) and by Thompson and Renninger (1995). Other useful resources listed at the end of this chapter include: Bass and Davis (1994), Butler (1978), Courtois (1988), Courtois and Leehan (1982), Finklehor (1984), Forward and Buck (1978), Goodwin (1982), Hall (1992), Hardy and Lewis (1992), Herman (1981), Justice and Justice (1979), Laidlaw, Malmo, and Associates (1990), Maltz (1991), Maltz and Holman (1987), Mandell and Damon (1989), McBride and Emerson (1989), Meiselman (1978, 1990), Rush (1980), and Sprei and Goodwin (1983).

A LONG-TERM THERAPY GROUP FOR SURVIVORS OF SEXUAL ABUSE

Sandi Burns, a psychotherapist in Billings, Montana, has been conducting long-term groups for incest "survivors" for more than 15 years. Her type of group offers an alternative to the preceding illustration of a short-term group. The discussion that follows is written from the perspective of Sandi Burns.*

*For further information on these groups, contact Sandi Burns, 2912 Laredo Place, Billings, MT 59102.

GROUPS AS THE TREATMENT OF CHOICE

While in a community agency setting in 1978, I began seeing women who had been sexually abused as children. I eventually went into private practice and have continued to run groups for people who were sexually abused as children. Although there are some differences between individuals who seek counseling through a community mental-health agency and through private practice, I have maintained the basic structure of the group.

In an agency setting, where people with little income were seen, there were waiting lists of people to be admitted to the group. Consequently, I tended to screen for those who needed the services the most—those who had been most traumatized. This usually meant that the group consisted of individuals who were sexually abused over long periods of time, and in many cases, women who had multiple perpetrators.

In a private practice setting, my clients tended to have a higher income level, were highly verbal, and functioned relatively well in their daily lives. As a general rule, they tended to be less traumatized than persons seen in the agency setting.

I continue to find longer term group therapy preferable for people who have experienced sexual abuse. However, with the advent of managed health care, insurance companies are dictating the length of treatment. This trend certainly does not favor long-term group therapy.

BASIC INFORMATION ON INCEST

When incest occurs, there is a violation of one's most private self. However, the physical act is but a small part of the dynamics that occur. First of all, children who are sexually abused by a family member feel betrayed and generally develop a mistrust of others who could potentially take advantage of them. Second, the sexual abuse is often just one of several dysfunctions within these families. There may also be physical abuse of children, spousal abuse, substance abuse, or a multitude of other family problems. Third, the perpetrators use many distortions to persuade children to participate in the sexual abuse or to allow them to continue taking advantage of them. Most victims, even by adulthood, have no idea how this happened. They usually only recall the sexual contacts. Thus, they are unaware of how emotionally abusive this situation was, not just between themselves and the perpetrators but within the whole family.

Victims of sexual abuse tend to repeat the psychodynamic patterns in their adulthood. A parent perpetrator may teach the child to be very submissive, have no privacy, and that only the needs of that parent are important. Many grow into adulthood with these same distortions they were taught, enter further abusive relationships, and continue to be victimized. Because incest cannot continue unless the secret of it is kept, victims learn to keep many secrets. Also, most victims of incest stop their emotional development at the age at which the incest begins. Thus, even though they may have sexual knowledge way beyond their chronological age, they have been conditioned to blunt their feelings about the abusive situations.

RATIONALE FOR LONG-TERM GROUP THERAPY

When people have been sexually abused as children, they have been betrayed, and they learn to mistrust others. Particularly with incest, the child tends to distrust others because they feel they were left unprotected and used and betrayed by the significant persons in their lives. Thus, these individuals tend to bring this sense of mistrust into a therapy group. In time-limited groups, many are never able to develop enough trust to deal with the issues by the time a group ends. Also, many fear opening themselves up when they know a group will end in a brief period of time.

A long-term group is helpful because it allows members to proceed at their own pace in developing trust in the leaders and other members. Also, in a long-term group, individuals can work on their own time frame to deal with issues pertinent to them, getting past faulty distortions and behavior patterns they may have learned from the abusive situation.

In a homogenous group, members can identify with others and for the first time may not feel so "different" or "alone." Also, for them to disclose about their abuse helps break the cycle and the "secret" that they may have lived with for so long. In a safe environment with identification and support from others, they can begin to receive feedback that challenges the distorted beliefs they hold and the distorted childhood messages they received.

Sexually abused survivors often need a great deal of validation, support, and consistency to enable them to delve into the issues of abuse. This process takes time. Time is also needed for more extensive working through of the trauma. In a long-term group, participants are not only able to learn to identify their faulty distortions and behavior patterns but are given enough time to practice new, more emotionally healthy styles of relating and behaving.

SELECTION OF GROUP MEMBERS

Assessment   A six-month commitment is required, so persons will not "drop in" while in crisis only to flee prematurely. The commitment seems to bring only those who feel motivated at that time to be in a group. Each member admitted to the group must be able to function in her everyday life. In making an assessment, I look for factors such as ego strength, motivation, interpersonal skills, and level of current functioning.

Intake Interview   All potential members are interviewed at least once before group participation. This interview is aimed at assessing their readiness for participating in a long-term group, level of motivation, current coping skills, and emotional stability. Also, the leader tells the client of the purposes of the group, its structure and functioning, and the ground rules. Although every new client is apprehensive in joining such a group, the anxiety is usually gone after the first meeting. For those who may appear to be acceptable in the assessment process but who feel undecided, several other individual sessions will be planned. Some may decide to continue some individual therapy with later consideration of group participation. Generally, a mutual decision is reached between the screening therapist and the client.

During the intake interview, the ground rules are explained and clarified:

- Confidentiality is very important to those who have experienced incest because of the past secrecy, the shame they feel, and the many issues of trust.
- Attendance at all sessions is important so that the group members can develop a safe environment that will allow disclosure of such emotional and personal issues.
- Members are asked to make a six-month commitment, which will allow an exploration in some depth of these traumatic issues.
- If people are chemically dependent, they are not admitted to the group. Such clients are encouraged to get involved in drug treatment, self-help, or both.
- Individuals who are in a crisis are not accepted, for they will probably need more individualized attention than the group could provide.
- Individuals who exhibit a high degree of denial by insisting that they have no current problems coping with their past childhood trauma are not admitted to the group.
- Socialization with other members outside the group is not permitted. This practice has proved to be more harmful than helpful to the members.
- A requirement for termination is that members devote at least two sessions in working through the termination with all group members. This process also gives members good practice for other termination issues in their lives.

GROUP PROCESS

Although the commonalities within this homogenous group help build cohesion, at the same time, acceptance of individual differences is emphasized. Each person needs to be accepted at whatever level she is currently functioning, and she needs to work at her own pace. All members' experiences and reactions are accepted without condemnation.

One of the benefits of these group experiences is an increased empathy for others.

I also began a group for partners or spouses of people who were in my two groups for adults molested as children. This group was educational and helped them understand what their partners were experiencing, both as a result of the sexual abuse and in their therapy. The majority of the time, the partner does not know how to handle situations surrounding the lingering effects of the abuse. The group for partners was beneficial both to the survivors and to the partners in opening communication channels and fostering understanding.

Control and boundaries are key therapeutic issues in incest groups. As children being victimized, clients seldom felt they had any control. Now as adults, they need to be able to make choices and attempt to exert control. If a person is feeling frightened, needs time out, or wants to quit talking because her emotions are becoming too tense, this wish is respected. Also, victims of incest often fear a "loss of control" over the emotions. In our groups, considerable work is done in teaching the women deep breathing, body awareness, and other methods of releasing pent-up emotions. This work is reinforced through guidelines and boundaries. Incestuous families have few boundaries to follow. The therapist must set these boundaries in the group—for example, by intervening in harmful interaction between members. Certain boundaries are emphasized throughout the duration of the group, such as not harming yourself or another person or destroying property. Clients are encouraged to express their emotions in a safe, constructive, and nonthreatening way.

Many victims of incest feel rather powerless and have low self-esteem. This issue is addressed near the beginning of group and throughout as new clients enter. Members are taught that if they want time in the group to talk, need some attention from others, or want responses from others, they need to speak up and ask, breaking one of the patterns of incest victims.

Some members have adopted "caretaking" patterns and have consistently placed others' needs above their own. They have the task of learning how to take care of themselves. They must also learn to avoid rescuing others or taking away others' responsibilities. Skills of negotiation, feedback, and conflict resolution are modeled by the therapist and encouraged among members.

LEADERSHIP

To run a group for incest survivors, leaders need two essential forms of knowledge: (1) knowledge about group process and dynamics, and (2) knowledge about sexual abuse, incest, and the incestuous family dynamics. The victims may have "blind spots" in their present lives. They require a skilled and knowledgeable leader to help them discover and work through their distortions. At the same time, leaders must be careful not to re-create abusive situations. They need to establish firm and appropriate boundaries, which were often lacking in the clients' backgrounds.

It is essential to understand and be aware of transference issues throughout the life of the group. Incestuous families lack clear boundaries. Some are too rigid, and some are too loose. The survivors oftentimes parallel these dysfunctional patterns in their behavior, expectations, and communication in the group.

The therapist's function is to be a process facilitator, educator, observer, parental role model, alter ego, and limit setter. The group leader needs a balance between warmth and firmness. The members of a sexual abuse group need to experience gentleness, understanding, nurturing, and reliability.

These groups can be rewarding and, at times, draining, for the therapist. I find it rewarding to witness some major positive changes in people who have participated in long-term group therapy. Many of them go on to live happy, satisfying, and full lives. However, this highly painful, depressing, and anger-laden trauma work becomes difficult to sustain without continued peer support and helpful supervision for the leader.

If you have an interest in this kind of long-term group for incest victims, I highly recommend *Healing the Incest Wound: Adult Survivors in Therapy* (Courtois, 1988).

WHERE TO GO FROM HERE

Since groups for adults represent such a wide variety of special interests, it is difficult to list one or two books as a place to begin. Depending on your interests, you might find the following books particularly helpful in getting ideas for your groups.

A very useful book that provides a step-by-step approach for group work is *Working with Adults in Groups* (Rose, 1989). Written from a cognitive/behavioral perspective, this book provides guidelines for starting and conducting groups, using cognitive/behavioral intervention strategies in small groups, and techniques for assisting members to carry their learning beyond the group sessions.

Group leaders who work with adults can find an excellent discussion of both the theory and practice of therapy groups in the works of Irvin Yalom. His classic work is *The Theory and Practice of Group Psychotherapy* (1995). *Existential Psychotherapy* (1980) provides an outstanding discussion of the ways themes of death, freedom, isolation, and meaninglessness can be integrated into clinical practice and group work. *Inpatient Group Psychotherapy* (1983) is highly readable for group practitioners who work with both higher and lower level inpatient groups. Yalom integrates techniques with relevant research findings.

The theme-oriented approach to group work was described in this chapter. If you want to do further reading in topics that can be applied to groups, see *I Never Knew I Had a Choice* (Corey & Corey, 1997), which deals with existential concerns that people bring to groups. The book contains many exercises and activities leaders can use for their groups. Each chapter is followed by numerous annotated readings appropriate for developing themes and topics for adult groups.

If you want to read further about the ways of creating your own techniques in working with various adult groups, see *Group Techniques* (Corey, Corey, Callanan, & Russell, 1992), which describes various techniques for all the stages of group development.

REFERENCES AND SUGGESTED READINGS*

Alberti, R. E., & Emmons, M. L. (1995). *Your perfect right: A guide to assertive behavior* (7th ed.). San Luis Obispo, CA: Impact Publishers.

Apolinsky, S. R., & Wilcoxon, S. A. (1991). Adult survivors of childhood sexual victimization: A group procedure for women. *Family Therapy, 18*(1), 37–45.

Axelroth, E. (1991). Retrospective incest group therapy for university women. *Journal of College Student Psychotherapy, 5*(2), 81–100.

Barrows, P. A., & Halgin, R. P. (1988). Current issues in psychotherapy with gay men: Impact of the AIDS phenomenon. *Professional Psychology: Research and Practice, 19*(4), 395–402.

Basow, S. A. (1992). *Gender: Stereotypes and role* (3rd ed.). Pacific Grove, CA: Brooks/Cole.

*Bass, E., & Davis, L. (1994). *The courage to heal: A guide for women survivors of child sexual abuse* (3rd ed.). New York: Harper Perennial.

Brisman, J., & Siegel, M. (1985). The bulimia workshop: A unique integration of group treatment approaches. *International Journal of Group Psychotherapy, 35*(4), 585–601.

*Bruhn, J. G. (1989). Counseling persons with a fear of AIDS. *Journal of Counseling and Development, 67,* 455–457.

*Butler, S. (1978). *Conspiracy of silence: The trauma of incest.* New York: Bantam Books.

*Castronovo, N. R. (1990). Acquired immune deficiency syndrome education on the college campus: The mandate and the challenge. *Journal of Counseling and Development, 66,* 578–580.

*Corey, G. (1995). *Theory and practice of group counseling* (4th ed.). Pacific Grove, CA: Brooks/Cole.

*Corey, G., & Corey, M. (1997). *I never knew I had a choice* (6th ed.). Pacific Grove, CA: Brooks/Cole.

*Corey, G., Corey, M., Callanan, P., & Russell, J. M. (1992). *Group techniques* (2nd ed.). Pacific Grove, CA: Brooks/Cole.

*Courtois, C. A. (1988). *Healing the incest wound: Adult survivors in therapy.* New York: Norton.

*Entries marked with an asterisk are recommended for further reading.

*Courtois, C., & Leehan, J. (1982). Group treatment for grown-up abused children. *Personnel and Guidance Journal, 60*(9), 564–566.

Dougherty, P. (1990). A personal perspective on working with men in groups. In D. Moore & F. Leafgren (Eds.), *Problem solving strategies and interventions for men in conflict* (pp. 169–182). Alexandria, VA: American Association for Counseling and Development.

Dworkin, S. H., & Pincu, L. (1993). Counseling in the era of AIDS. *Journal of Counseling and Development, 71,* 275–281.

*Edleson, J. L., & Tolman, R. M. (1994). Group intervention strategies for men who batter. *Directions in Mental Health Counseling, 4*(7), 3–16.

*Finklehor, D. (1984). *Child sexual abuse: New theory and research.* New York: Free Press.

*Forward, S., & Buck, C. S. (1978). *Betrayal of innocence: Incest and its devastation.* Los Angeles: J. P. Tarcher.

*Golden, B. R., Corazzini, J. G., & Grady, P. (1993). Current practices of group therapy at university counseling centers: A national survey. *Professional Psychology, Research and Practice, 24*(2), 228–230.

Goodwin, J. (1982). *Sexual abuse: Incest victims and their families.* Boston: John Wright.

*Grant, D. (1988). Support groups for youth with AIDS virus. *International Journal of Group Psychotherapy, 38*(2), 237–251.

*Gray, L. A., & Saracino, M. (1989). AIDS on campus: A preliminary study of college students' knowledge and behaviors. *Journal of Counseling and Development, 68,* 199–202.

Gregg, C. (1994). Group work with single fathers. *Journal for Specialists in Group Work, 19*(2), 95–101.

Grusznski, R., & Bankovics, G. (1990). Treating men who batter: A group approach. In D. Moore & F. Leafgren (Eds.), *Problem solving strategies and interventions for men in conflict* (pp. 201–212). Alexandria, VA: American Association for Counseling and Development.

Hall, Z. M. (1992). Group therapy for women survivors of childhood sexual abuse. *Group Analysis, 25,* 463–475.

Hardy, J., & Lewis, C. (1992). Bridging the gap between long-term and short-term group psychotherapy: A viable treatment model. *Group, 16*(1), 5–17.

Hendren, R. L., Atkins, D. M., Sumner, C. R., & Barber, J. K. (1987). Model for the group treatment of eating disorders. *International Journal of Group Psychotherapy, 37*(4), 589–602.

Herman, J. (1981). *Father-daughter incest.* Cambridge, MA: Harvard University Press.

*Herman, J., & Schatzow, E. (1984). Time-limited group therapy for women with a history of incest. *International Journal of Group Psychotherapy, 35*(4), 605–616.

*Hetzel, R. D., Barton, D. A., & Davenport, D. S. (1994). Helping men change: A group counseling model for male clients. *Journal for Specialists in Group Work, 19*(2), 52–64.

Isely, P. J. (1992). A time-limited group therapy model for men sexually abused as children. *Group, 16*(4), 233–246.

Jolliff, D. (1994). Guest editorial: Group work with men. *Journal for Specialists in Group Work, 19*(2), 50–51.

*Jones, L. (1996). *HIV/AIDS: What to do about it.* Pacific Grove, CA: Brooks/Cole.

Justice, B., & Justice, R. (1979). *The broken taboo: Sex in the family.* New York: Human Sciences Press.

Kimmel, M. S. (Ed.). (1987). *Changing men: New directions in research on men and masculinity.* Newbury Park, CA: Sage.

*Laidlaw, T. A., Malmo, C., & Associates. (1990). *Healing voices: Feminist approaches to therapy with women.* San Francisco, CA: Jossey-Bass.

Lott, B. (1994). *Women's lives: Themes and variations in gender learning* (2nd ed.). Pacific Grove, CA: Brooks/Cole.

*Maltz, W. (1991). *The sexual healing journey: A guide for women and men survivors of sexual abuse.* New York: Harper Collins.

*Maltz, W., & Holman, B. (1987). *Incest and sexuality: A guide to understanding and healing.* Lexington, MA: D. C. Heath and Company (Lexington Books).

*Mandell, J. G., & Damon, L. (1989). *Group treatment for sexually abused children.* New York: Guilford.

*McBride, M. C., & Emerson, S. (1989). Group work with women who were molested as children. *Journal for Specialists in Group Work, 14*(1), 25–33.

*McNamara, K. (1989a). Group counseling for overweight and depressed college women: A comparative evaluation. *Journal for Specialists in Group Work, 14*(4), 211–218.

*McNamara, K. (1989b). A structured group program for repeat dieters. *Journal for Specialists in Group Work, 14*(3), 141–150.

*Meiselman, K. (1978). *Incest: A psychological study of cause and effects with treatment recommendations.* San Francisco: Jossey-Bass.

*Meiselman, K. (1990). *Resolving the trauma of incest: Reintegration therapy with survivors.* San Francisco: Jossey-Bass.

*Moore, D. (1990). Helping men become more emotionally expressive: A ten-week program. In D. Moore & F. Leafgren (Eds.), *Problem solving strategies and interventions for men in conflict* (pp. 183–200). Alexandria, VA: American Association for Counseling and Development.

*Moore, D., & Leafgren, F. (Eds.). (1990). *Problem solving strategies and interventions for men in conflict.* Alexandria, VA: American Association for Counseling and Development.

*Norsworthy, K. L., & Horne, A. M. (1994). Issues in group work with HIV-infected gay and bisexual men. *Journal for Specialists in Group Work, 19*(2), 112–119.

Rabinowitz, F. E. (1994). The impact of an interpersonal encounter-group class for North American college students studying abroad. *Journal for Specialists in Group Work, 19*(1), 38–42.

*Rabinowitz, F. E., & Cochran, S. V. (1994). *Man alive: A primer of men's issues.* Pacific Grove, CA: Brooks/Cole.

Rich, K. D. (1994). Outpatient group therapy with adult male sex offenders: Clinical issues and concerns. *Journal for Specialists in Group Work, 19*(2), 120–128.

*Rose, S. D. (1989). *Working with adults in groups: Integrating cognitive-behavioral and small group strategies.* San Francisco: Jossey-Bass.

Roth, D. M., & Ross, D. R. (1988). Long-term cognitive-interpersonal group therapy for eating disorders. *International Journal of Group Psychotherapy, 38*(4), 491–510.

Rush, F. (1980). *The best kept secret: Sexual abuse of children.* Englewood Cliffs, NJ: Prentice-Hall.

*Seligman, M. (1993). Group work with parents of children with disabilities. *Journal for Specialists in Group Work, 18*(3), 115–126.

*Smith, D. (1994). A "last rights" group for people with AIDS. *Journal for Specialists in Group Work, 19*(1), 17–21.

*Spector, I. C., & Conklin, R. (1987). AIDS group psychotherapy. *International Journal of Group Psychotherapy, 37*(3), 433–439.

*Sprei, J., & Goodwin, R. (1983). Group treatment of sexual assault survivors. *Journal for Specialists in Group Work, 8*(1), 39–46.

*Stokes, J., & Damon, W. (1995). Counseling and psychotherapy for bisexual men. *Directions in Mental Health Counseling, 5*(8), 3–15.

*Thompson, N., & Renninger, S. (1995). Short-term group treatment for survivors of sexual abuse: A psychoeducational approach. *Directions in Mental Health Counseling, 5*(6), 4–11.

Tunnell, G. (1991). Complications in group psychotherapy with AIDS patients. *International Journal of Group Psychotherapy, 41,* 481–498.

Weiss, L., Katzman, M., & Wolchik, S. (1985). *Treating bulimia: A psychoeducational approach.* Elmsford, NY: Pergamon Press.

*Wilbur, M. P., & Roberts-Wilbur, J. (1994). Group work with men's beliefs. *Journal for Specialists in Group Work, 19*(2), 65–82.

*Yalom, I. (1980). *Existential psychotherapy.* New York: Basic Books.

*Yalom, I. (1983). *Inpatient group psychotherapy.* New York: Basic Books.

*Yalom, I. (1995). *The theory and practice of group psychotherapy* (4th ed.). New York: Basic Books.

Zimpfer, D. G. (1990a). Groups for divorce/separation: A review. *Journal for Specialists in Group Work, 15*(1), 51–60.

Zimpfer, D. G. (1990b). Group work for bulimia: A review of outcomes. *Journal for Specialists in Group Work, 15*(4), 239–251.

CHAPTER 12

GROUPS FOR
THE ELDERLY

Group Outcomes
A Personal Commentary
Resources for Bereavement Groups

Where to Go from Here

References and Suggested Readings

INTRODUCTION: PERSONAL OBSERVATIONS*

America is moving from its "greening" to its "graying" as the elderly population increases rapidly. There are more than 30 million people 65 years and older in the United States today, more than 12% of the total population. This share is expected to increase to 21% by the year 2030 (Wright, Coley, & Corey, 1989). In the next 40 years, the number of elderly will almost double, with the number of persons 85 years and older increasing most rapidly (Blazer, 1989). Given this reality, it is essential that mental-health professionals design effective therapeutic strategies to help the elderly cope with the challenges of aging. Group workers have an opportunity to create a wide range of support groups, psychoeducational groups, and counseling groups for elderly people.

In the 1970s, when I first started working with the elderly, there was little interest in addressing the needs of the elderly. People, even old people, asked me "Why does a young person like you want to work with old people?" But the graduate students of today are unlikely to get these reactions. In the 20 years since the first edition of this book, several trends have emerged:

- There are a lot more elderly in this country.
- There is an increased interest in working with the elderly.
- There are many innovative groups designed to meet the needs of the elderly.
- Many graduate students in the helping professions have an interest in specializing in gerontology.
- Americans are beginning to perceive old people as vital members of society and to treat them with more respect.

The elderly have special needs and problems that should not be ignored by any helping professional. Group workers of the future will increasingly be held accountable for developing programs to help the elderly find meaning in their lives and be productive after retirement. As mental-health professionals become involved with the elderly, their challenge is to do more than add years to a person's life—they must help individuals lead fuller and better lives. Counselors need to develop special programs for the elderly, and they must continue their efforts to find the means to reach this clientele.

Much of this chapter is based on a description of my group work with the elderly in institutions. Counselors often encounter obstacles when organizing and conducting groups for the elderly. Some of the barriers are due to the unique characteristics of this population, but other obstacles are found within the system or the institutions themselves—for example, lack of interest in therapeutic work for the elderly, lack of administrative

*This chapter is written from the perspective of Marianne Corey.

support for group work, lack of cooperation from staff workers, and lack of proper training in working with the elderly for graduate students. Molinari (1994) suggests that some professionals who want to specialize in gerontology have concerns about not being valued by their colleagues because of the unglamorous status of older clients. Such biases are perpetuated by graduate programs in clinical and counseling psychology that offer inadequate training in working with the elderly. Another obstacle is the difficulty reaching the elderly as a target population.

UNIQUE CHARACTERISTICS OF THE ELDERLY

A liking for old people does not alone make a good counselor. This unique population requires special skills and knowledge. Leaders who are forming their first groups for the elderly will find some definite differences from their work with other age groups. They need to be aware of the particular life issues faced by older people. I have made the following observations over the years as a result of my personal and professional contact with the elderly.

- The attention span of some elderly people may be short because of physical or psychological difficulties. Consequently, the pace of the group needs to be slower.
- The elderly are often taking medications that interfere with their ability to be fully present.
- With some who are in advanced stages of senility, reality orientation becomes a problem. Sometimes they simply forget to come to sessions.
- Regular attendance at group sessions can be problematic because of physical ailments, transportation problems, interruptions in the schedules of institutions, and conflicting appointments with doctors and social workers.
- Older people often need support and encouragement more than they need confrontation. Therefore, group work is oriented less toward radical personality reconstruction and more toward making life in the present more meaningful and enjoyable. However, never to challenge or confront older people could be seen as patronizing and may be based on the distorted belief that they cannot change.
- The elderly have a great need to be listened to and understood. Respect is shown by accepting them through hearing their underlying messages and not treating them in a condescending way. The elderly often suffer from "conversation deprivation." To be encouraged to share and relate with others has therapeutic value in itself (Burnside, 1984b).
- Some older people are more difficult to reach. They may be resistant and skeptical about the effectiveness of counseling, and it may take more time to establish trust. It is very important to carefully consider the titles you use in describing your services for the elderly, because older people

are more sensitive to feeling stigmatized when they seek out a mental-health professional. Stone and Waters (1991) indicate that there are certain advantages to developing peer group counseling programs for older adults. Because peer counselors tend to be perceived as friends rather than professionals, they may be less threatening to those clients who view a need for traditional forms of counseling as a sign of weakness.

• Themes more prevalent with the elderly than with other age groups include: loss; loneliness and social isolation; poverty; feelings of rejection; the struggle to find meaning in life; dependency; feelings of uselessness, hopelessness, and despair; fears of death and dying; grief over others' deaths; sadness over physical and mental deterioration; and regrets over past events.

• Loss is probably the central theme of growing old. Anxiety, low self-esteem, and somatic complaints are typical responses to the losses faced by elderly persons (Hern & Weis, 1991). People live most of their adult years with an internal locus of control, but as they age they have to adjust to an increasingly external locus of control when confronted with losses over which they have little control. Physical disabilities and sensory impairments contribute to the social isolation experienced by very old people (Myers, 1990).

PRACTICAL AND PROFESSIONAL CONSIDERATIONS FOR GROUP WORK WITH THE ELDERLY

ISSUES IN THE GROUP PROCESS

The issues addressed in Part Two of this book pertaining to stages in the development of a group have some applicability to designing and conducting groups for the elderly. This section provides brief examples of practical issues for you to think about in forming specialized groups for older people.

The Group Proposal   It is especially important to develop a sound proposal, because you may encounter resistance from agencies dealing with the elderly. Refer to Chapter 4 for the elements that might be included in a proposal for groups for the elderly.

Screening and Selection Issues   The needs of the elderly are diverse, so you need to consider the purposes of the group in determining who will or will not benefit from the experience. The decision to include or exclude members must be made appropriately and sensitively. For example, to mix regressed patients with relatively well-functioning older people is to invite fragmentation. There may be a rationale for excluding people who are highly agitated, are delusional, have severe physical problems that could inhibit their benefiting from the group, or display other behaviors that are likely to be counterproductive to the group as a whole.

Purpose of the Group   Elderly people generally need a clear, organized explanation of the specific purposes of a group and why they can benefit from it. Some of them are more closed to the potential values of group participation than are other populations. In short, it is important to be able to present a positive approach to the members. The anxiety level may be high among an elderly group, which calls for a clear structure and repetition of the goals and procedures of the group.

Practical Issues   Practical considerations regarding the size, duration, setting, and techniques to be used depend on the level of functioning of a particular group. For example, more members could be included in a well-functioning group than in an organic brain syndrome group. The attention span of a group of outpatients would be longer than that of patients who are out of contact with reality. It is essential for you to have a good understanding of the members' mental and physical capabilities.

Confidentiality   Institutional life is often not conducive to privacy. Elderly group members may be suspicious when they are asked to talk about themselves, for they may fear some sort of retaliation by the staff or fellow members. Take great care in defining the boundaries of confidentiality to ensure that confidences will not be broken and to provide a safe and nonthreatening environment.

Labeling and Prejudging Group Members   Institutions are quick to diagnose and categorize people, and they are slow to remove such labels when they no longer fit. In working with the elderly, you must be careful not to be rigidly influenced by what you hear or read about a given member. Remain open to forming your own impressions, and be willing to challenge any limiting labels imposed on your elderly clients.

Visitors to Groups   As is often the case in institutions, visitors and other staff members may wish to attend a particular group session. A good practice with even severely regressed patients (who may not be aware of another's presence) is to announce visitors in advance of their attending a session and again at the beginning of the session. In addition, the purpose of their visit should be mentioned to lessen suspicion.

Value Differences   A good understanding of the social and cultural backgrounds of your members will enable you to work with their concerns in a sensitive way. As was true in my case, you may be younger than the members, and this age span can represent significant value differences. For example, a group leader in her early 20s might consider living together as an unmarried couple an acceptable norm, whereas a member in her mid-70s might suffer guilt and shame for doing so. This leader needs to take this member's anxiety seriously and not simply reassure her that she has no need to feel guilty. You are likely to assume that there is therapeutic value in discussing personal problems and conflicts openly. However, revealing personal matters may be extremely difficult for some elderly people because of their cultural conditioning. Respect members' decisions to proceed at their own pace in revealing themselves.

The Issue of Touching   Aging people have a special need for being touched. They may be alone, and you and others in their group may be their only source of touching. Your own comfort level with touching will be a vital factor in determining how free members feel to exchange touches. It is also critical that you not misinterpret an older person's touching.

The need for touching among the elderly was vividly expressed during a visit to the respected home for the elderly in China. I observed an elderly woman lying on her bed, mumbling to herself and looking extremely withdrawn. As I stood near her bed, I struggled with myself over the appropriateness of touching her, not knowing if it would be accepted in a different cultural setting. I gave in to my urge to hold the woman's hand, and she reciprocated immediately by pressing my hand and turning toward me. She slowly began to talk, and I asked our tour guide to translate. He introduced my daughters and me to her, and she showed great interest in where we were from and what we were doing. She kept repeating how lucky I was to have such daughters. She touched my daughters and me again and again. Within a short time this woman sat up on her bed and began laughing and talking. She had been an artist, and my daughters and I shared our interest in art with her. The young tour guide, who had never been in a home such as this, told me how surprised he was by her intellectual sharpness. When he initially saw her lying on her bed, he thought that she might be dying. The attending nurse mentioned that this woman had indeed been very withdrawn and depressed, and the nurse was surprised by the woman's excitement and interest in us. Within a span of 20 minutes she had become completely animated. This episode reminded me again of how much we can communicate with a touch or a smile.

My own intuitions about the therapeutic value of touch in working with elderly persons are supported by the literature. In their review of the literature of groups for older persons, Myers, Poidevant, and Dean (1991) encourage counselors to provide physical contact including hugging and touching, but only when this contact is deemed acceptable by older clients. In their discussion of group work with the very old, Hern and Weis (1991) found the use of touch to be one of the most effective forms of positive reinforcement. Even a pat on the hand or the joining of hands appeared to increase feelings of belonging.

Difficult Group Members   You may encounter many types of difficult members in this age group. Some may refuse to speak or make any contact, some may never stop talking or interrupting, and some may be highly agitated and hostile. Learn to set firm limits, and deal with these members nondefensively. Members who display problematic behaviors should not be labeled and categorized. The challenge is to understand the broader meaning of the behaviors that these members are manifesting in the group, rather than simply labeling them "resisters."

Some Cautions   The following are a few cautions in your practice of group work with the elderly:

- Be careful not to treat people as frail when they are not.
- Don't keep your members busy with meaningless activities.
- Don't insult their dignity, intelligence, and pride.
- Don't assume that every elderly person likes being called by their first name, "honey," or "sweetie."
- Make use of humor appropriately. Avoid laughing at your members for failing to accomplish tasks, but laugh with them when, for instance, they have created a funny poem.
- Be careful not to change your way of speaking with them. Avoid talking to them as if they were small children.
- Allow your members to nag and complain, even if there is nothing you can do about their complaints. You don't need to burden yourself with the feeling that you should do something about all of their grievances. Sometimes it is enough to simply let them get the problems off their chest.
- Avoid probing for the release of strong emotions that neither you nor they can handle effectively in the group sessions.
- Determine how much you can do without feeling depleted, and find avenues for staying vital and enthusiastic.

ATTITUDES AND SKILLS OF LEADERS

It is critical to be aware of how your own feelings and attitudes will affect your work with the elderly. You will need to find ways to successfully deal with the emotions generated within you as a result of their work. If you want to work effectively with the concerns of the aged, it is necessary to acquire special skills and knowledge. Your range of life experiences, as well as your basic personality characteristics, can either help or hinder you in your work. (This would be a good time to review the personal characteristics of effective group leaders discussed in Chapter 3.) I consider the following as important assets for group work with the elderly:

- genuine respect for old people
- a history of positive experiences with old people

- a deep sense of caring for the elderly
- a respect for the elderly person's cultural values
- an understanding of the ways in which the individual's cultural background continues to influence present attitudes and behaviors
- an ability and desire to learn from old people
- an understanding of the biological aspects of aging
- the conviction that the last years of life can be challenging
- patience, especially with repetition of stories
- knowledge of the special biological, psychological, and social needs of the aged
- sensitivity to the burdens and anxieties of old people
- the ability to get old people to challenge many of the myths about old age
- a healthy attitude regarding one's own eventual old age
- an understanding of the developmental tasks of each period of life, from infancy to old age
- an appreciation for the effects that one period of life has on other stages of development
- a particular understanding of how one's ability to handle present life difficulties hinges on how well one dealt with problems in earlier stages
- a background in the pathology of aging
- the ability to deal with extreme feelings of depression, hopelessness, grief, hostility, and despair
- personal characteristics such as humor, enthusiasm, patience, courage, endurance, hopefulness, tolerance, nondefensiveness, freedom from limiting prejudices, and a willingness to learn
- an ability to be both gentle and challenging
- the sensitivity to know when it is therapeutic to provide support and when to challenge
- a working knowledge of the group process along with the special skills needed for group work with the elderly
- a willingness to touch or be touched

SPECIAL TYPES OF GROUPS FOR THE ELDERLY

Not all old people can be placed in the same type of group. Leaders must take into account the special needs of potential group members. Some groups that are commonly offered include those with an emphasis on reminiscing, physical fitness, body awareness, grief work, occupational therapy, reality orientation, music and art therapy, combined dance and movement, preretirement and postretirement issues, remotivation, preplacement (preparing people to move from an institutional to a community setting), organic brain syndrome, education, poetry, health-related issues, family therapy, and assertion training. This is certainly not a complete list, and leaders can invent ways to bring their particular talents into a group setting to promote interaction among elderly members. An example in this chapter is a group composed of adolescents and the elderly. Leaders who have artistic hobbies can have members do something with their hands. In the process of creating products, the members often talk about themselves in spontaneous ways. Groups that entail the members' doing something specific can promote more interaction than groups limited to discussion.

I want to share an example of a group that naturally evolved from an exercise class at a senior citizens' center in our community. Jerry and I were invited by a 70-year-old man to attend the class, which was very physically challenging. The leader of this class, May, was also an elderly person who had several talents that she combined fruitfully and shared with her group. May not only directed activities designed for physical fitness but also provided a climate that fostered meaningful personal and social interactions. For example, she was very patient with members who interrupted the exercises by talking about problems that were preoccupying them that day. Sometimes they described the details of an enjoyable weekend, at times they listed numerous complaints ranging from home problems to world problems, and often they engaged in nonmalicious community gossip. If May had held to a rigid notion of what an exercise class should be, many of these spontaneous interchanges would not have evolved. Her talent and enthusiasm inspired both humor and seriousness of purpose. May had a special gift of gently pushing and confronting the members to exceed what they thought were their physical limits. Thus, people typically left feeling both physically rejuvenated and psychologically uplifted.

Burlew, Jones, and Emerson (1991) assert that combining an exercise program with group counseling can provide a way to address physical aging and psychological well-being, and can result in higher compliance rates for participation in exercise programs. Exercise can combat the depression that so frequently is associated with loss in the elderly person's life.

Reminiscence therapy that encourages members to recall and re-experience the past is another useful kind of group for the elderly. This therapy approach can help the elderly build bridges to bring vitality into their present existence. Reminiscence was once viewed as an unproductive escape into the past. However, the literature reveals that it is now considered a most useful therapeutic strategy in promoting psychological integration with elderly clients. Singer, Tracz, and Dworkin (1991) point out that a reminiscence group provides elderly participants with an opportunity to communicate with others who share similar concerns and experiences. Because depression over loss and changes is such a central theme in the lives of elderly people, a group offers a safe place for them to express their feelings of loneliness and hopelessness. Clearly, reminiscence groups facilitate socialization, which is a crucial ingredient in overcoming isolation.

Creanza and McWhirter (1994) make use of life themes as a way to stimulate participants in recalling and reliving past experiences. They designed a pregroup screening and orientation method utilizing life themes such as: childhood memories, working life, psychological stress, and gender issues. They found that inviting seniors to reminisce about their past was an ideal way to structure the pregroup interview. Doing so gave members a comfortable way of getting to know one another, it provided common themes for exploration in future sessions, and it enhanced the attractiveness of the group.

According to Molinari (1994), a therapeutic life review group can be beneficial by assisting elderly clients in the process of putting life events into a new perspective. Molinari designed a six-session life review group structured around the following topics:

- Introduction: How can the use of reminiscence reveal who you are and how you feel about yourself?
- Family history: Describe the family members who have influenced you the most.
- Developmental stages: Make an outline of your life, dividing it into significant periods.
- Life crises: Describe some of the major crises in your life, how they have affected you, and how you have coped with them.
- Experiences with death: Share examples of personal encounters with death and your present concerns about dying.
- Meaning of life: Discuss the evolution of your life goals from past to present. To what degree do your goals provide you with meaning in your life today?

Molinari contends that groups can help elderly clients integrate current life changes into an overall developmental perspective. In a group, elderly members are encouraged to reflect on who they are, where they have been, and to identify future goals. The group provides an ideal forum for socialization that allows members to share their concerns over aging in a supportive context with their peers.

A PROGRAM FOR INSTITUTIONALIZED ELDERLY PEOPLE

Many different types of groups are available to elderly people. The number and types of groups possible is limited only by the imagination of the counselor and the counselor's willingness to create groups to meet the special needs of elderly clients. I co-led two groups in a psychiatric hospital and they are described next.

THE PREPLACEMENT GROUP

The preplacement group consisted of individuals in an institutional setting who were going to be released into community settings—returning home or to board and care residential facilities. As with other group populations, it is necessary to give careful consideration to the selection of members. A group is not likely to function well if severely disturbed and hallucinating members are mixed with clients who are psychologically intact. It is a good practice, however, to combine talkative and quiet people, depressed and ebullient types, excitable with calmer clients, suspicious with more trusting individuals, and people with different backgrounds. The size of the group is determined by the level of psychological and social functioning of the participants. A group of ten relatively well-functioning people is much easier to manage than even a smaller number of regressed clients.

The preplacement group that my co-leader and I formed consisted of three men and four women—a good balance of the sexes and a workable number for two leaders. Before the first meeting I contacted the members individually and gave them a basic orientation to the group. I told them the purpose of the group, what the activities might be, and where, when, and for how long the group would meet. I let each person know that membership was voluntary. When people seemed hesitant to attend, I suggested that they come to the initial session and then decide whether they wanted to continue.

Before the first session my co-leader and I decided on a few general goals for the group. Our primary goal would be to provide an atmosphere in which common concerns could be freely discussed and in which members could interact with one another. We wanted to provide an opportunity for members to voice complaints and to be included in a decision-making process. We felt strongly that these people could make changes and that the group process could stimulate them to do so.

The group met once a week for an hour in the visitor's room. Before each group session I contacted all the members, reminded them that the group would meet shortly, invited them to attend, and accompanied them to the group room. I learned that it was difficult for them to remember the time of the meetings, so individual assistance would be important in ensuring regular attendance. Those who were absent were either ill or involved in an activity that couldn't be rescheduled, such as physical therapy. The group was an open one; members would occasionally be discharged, and we encouraged newly admitted patients to join. This didn't seem to bother the members, and it didn't affect the cohesion of the group. As leaders, we also attempted to make entrance into the group as easy as possible. We always allowed some time for the new members to be introduced and to say anything they wanted to about being new to the group, and we asked current group members to welcome them.

The Initial Stage   During the initial sessions the members showed a tendency to direct all of their statements to the two leaders. In the hope that we could break the shell that isolated each person in a private and detached world, my co-leader and I immediately began to encourage the members to talk to one another, not to us. When members talked about a member, we asked them to speak directly to that member. When members discussed a particular problem or concern, we encouraged others to share similar difficulties.

In the beginning the members resisted talking about themselves, voicing complaints, or discussing what they expected after their release from the institution. Their usual comment reflected their hopelessness: "What good will it do? No one will listen to us anyway." Our task was to teach them to listen to one another.

The Importance of Listening and Acting   My co-leader and I felt that one way of teaching the old people to listen would be by modeling—by demonstrating that we were really listening to them. Thus, when our clients spoke of problems related to life on the ward, my co-leader and I became actively involved with them in solving some of these conflicts. For example, one member complained that one of the patients in his room shouted for much of the night. We were able to get the unhappy member placed in another room. When some members shared their fears about the board-and-care homes they were to be released to, we arranged to take them to several such homes so that they could make an informed choice of placement. One woman complained that her husband did not visit her enough and that, when he did take her home, he was uncaring and uninterested in her sexually. On several occasions my co-leader and I held private sessions with the couple.

Some men complained that there was nothing to do, so we arranged for them to get involved in planting a garden. Another group member shared the fact that she was an artist, so we asked her to lead some people in the group and on the ward in art projects. She reacted enthusiastically and succeeded in involving several other members.

Our philosophy was to encourage them to again become active, even in a small way, in making decisions about their lives. We learned *not* to do two things: (1) encourage a patient to participate in an activity that would be frustrating and thereby further erode an already poor self-image, or (2) make promises we couldn't keep.

Listening to Reminiscences   In addition to dealing with the day-to-day problems of the members, we spent much time listening as they reminisced about sadness and guilt they had experienced, their many losses, the places they had lived and visited, the mistakes they had made, and so on. By remembering and actively reconstructing their past, old people can hope to resolve the conflicts affecting them and decide how to use the time left to them. In addition, they enjoy remembering happy times when they were more productive and powerful than they are now. I believe that this life review is an important and healthy process and that old people need to experience it.

Most agencies that work with the elderly offer reminiscence and life review groups. According to Lewis and Butler (1984), the life review is seen as a universal psychological process associated with increased awareness of one's finiteness. The myth of immortality gives way to an acceptance of one's death. The life review involves a progressive return to consciousness of earlier experiences, a resurgence of unresolved past conflicts, and bringing up memories that have been deeply buried in the unconscious. Although some older people are aware of a need to put their entire life into a meaningful perspective, others avoid this type of review as a protection against painful memories.

The Use of Exercises   My role as a leader of this group differed from the roles I had played in other types of group. I found that I was more directive, that I was much less confrontive and much more supportive, and that I spent a lot of time teaching the members how to express themselves and listen to others. My co-leader and I designed a variety of exercises to catalyze member interaction. The exercises often succeeded in getting meaningful discussions started, and sometimes they were just plain fun. We always began by showing how an exercise could be done. Some of the exercises we assigned the group were as follows:

- Go on an imaginary trip, and pick a couple of the other group members to accompany you. (Although you may have to deal with feelings of rejection expressed by those not chosen, this exercise is very helpful for people who are reluctant to reach out to one another and make friends.)
- If you could do anything you wanted, what would it be?
- Bring a favorite photograph, and share it with others in the group.
- Bring a picture of you and your family, and talk about your family.
- Describe some of the memories that are important to you.
- Tell what your favorite holiday is and what you enjoy doing on that day.

Another exercise that helps the elderly focus and contributes to member interaction is the sentence-completion method for low-level clients (Yalom, 1983). Incomplete sentences can be structured around a variety of themes, such as:

- self-disclosure (One thing about me that people would be surprised to know is . . .)
- separation (The hardest separation that I have ever had is . . .)
- anger (One thing that really irritates me is . . .)
- isolation (The time in my life when I felt most alone was . . .)
- ward events (The fight on the ward last night made me feel . . .)
- empathy (I feel touched by others when . . .)

- here-and-now interactions (The person whom I am most like in this room is . . .)
- personal change (Something I want to change about myself is . . .)
- stress (I experience tension when . . .)

Working with incomplete sentences can trigger intense emotions. Thus, the group leader needs to be skilled in dealing with these feelings.

We used exercises as simple means of getting group interaction going. One of our group sessions fell on the day before Thanksgiving. We asked the participants to remember a special Thanksgiving day from the past— to recall all the people who were with them and everything that happened. The members received these instructions enthusiastically, and everyone participated. My co-leader and I pointed out to them that the fun and excitement they had experienced during past holidays was due partly to their interaction with people and could certainly be experienced again if they made a special effort this Thanksgiving to reach out to and make contact with one another. The Thanksgiving celebration did, in fact, go well for the group members. Several of them made a point of sitting together, and they reported at the next session the fun they had had.

By encouraging the members to express themselves, these exercises led to their getting to know one another, which led in turn to a lessening of the "what's the use" feeling that was universal in the beginning.

Debunking Myths   My co-leader and I explored some myths and attitudes that prevail regarding the aged to challenge the members' acceptance of these myths. The following are some of the beliefs we considered:

- Old people can't change, so it's a waste of time and effort to try to help them with counseling or therapy.
- All people who retire become depressed.
- It is disgraceful for an old person to remarry.
- Young people are never forgetful; old people always are.
- Forgetfulness is a sign of senility.
- Old people cannot contribute to society.
- There are many child molesters among the aged.
- Most young people want to neglect the elderly members of their family.
- Old people are always emotional and are financial burdens, whether their children take them into their home or not.
- People should retire at 65.
- Old people are not creative.
- An elderly person will die soon after his or her mate dies.
- Becoming old always means having a number of serious physical problems.
- Old people do not understand the problems of younger people.
- Old people are no longer beautiful.
- Old people are dependent and need to be taken care of.

- Most old people are lonely.
- There is a high degree of alcoholism among the aged—higher than among younger people.
- Old people are no longer interested in sex.
- Old people are not afraid to die.

Molinari (1994) states that, contrary to popular belief, the elderly are able to benefit from psychotherapy. He lists the following as myths regarding mental illness in the elderly:

- Most old people become senile and are not suitable candidates for psychotherapy.
- Most old people live in institutional settings and have limited access to mental-health facilities.
- Depression is a natural consequence of aging.
- Preoccupation with death and dying is typical of older adults.
- Treatment of emotional problems in the elderly is not effective.

Anyone working with elderly people needs to differentiate between myths and facts surrounding what it means to grow old. According to Molinari, both professionals and lay people alike harbor a host of misconceptions about the elderly. The facts are that the elderly can and do learn and change. Creative and informed professionals can do much to enhance the lives of their elderly clients, thereby helping to dispel the myths that have acted as a barrier to providing quality services for the elderly.

Outcomes To work successfully with the elderly, one must take into account the basic limitations in their resources for change yet not adopt a fatalistic attitude that will only reinforce their sense of hopelessness. Had my co-leader and I expected to bring about dramatic personality changes, we would soon have been frustrated, because the changes that occurred were small and came slowly. Instead, we expected to have only a modest impact, and so the subtle changes that took place were enough to give us the incentive and energy to continue. The following are some of the outcomes we observed:

- Members realized that they were not alone in experiencing problems.
- The participants learned from one another's feedback.
- People in the group felt an acceptance of their feelings and realized that they had a right to express them.
- Members said that they liked coming to the meetings, and they told this to patients who weren't members.
- The group atmosphere became one of trust, caring, and friendliness.
- The members continued the socializing that had begun in the group outside group sessions.
- The members learned one another's names, which contributed to increased interaction on the ward.

- Participants engaged in activities that stimulated them rather than merely waiting for their release.
- The members began to talk more personally about their sorrows, losses, hopes, joys, memories, fears, regrets, and so on, saying that it felt good to be listened to and to talk.
- The enthusiasm of the members and the staff led to the formation of another group for ward members.
- The nurses reported seeing a change in the patients and expressed a desire to learn the skills needed to facilitate such groups.
- Staff members noticed positive changes, such as elevated spirits, in some of the members.
- Staff members became involved in thinking of appropriate activities for different members and helped the members carry them out.

My co-leader and I encountered some frustrating circumstances during the course of the group. For instance, the members occasionally seemed very lethargic. We later discovered that this occurred when the participants had received medication just before the group session. Still, it was difficult to discern whether a member's condition was due to the medication or to psychological factors. It was not uncommon to find a member functioning well one week and feeling good about herself and then to discover, the next week, that she had had a psychotic episode and was unable to respond to anyone.

Some small changes that occurred in the group sessions were undone by the routine of ward life. On the one hand, some of the members resisted making their life on the ward more pleasant for fear of giving the impression that their stay would be a long one. It was as though they were saying "If I communicate that I like it here, you might not let me go." On the other hand, some members resigned themselves to institutional life and saw the ward as their home, expressing very directly that they did not want to leave.

Termination   I was to be co-leader of this group for only three months, and I prepared the members for my departure several weeks in advance. After I left, my co-leader continued the group by himself. On occasion I visited the group, and I was remembered and felt very welcome.

A GROUP FOR PATIENTS WITH ORGANIC BRAIN SYNDROME

Some of the patients on the ward had severe dementia due to organic brain syndrome (OBS), and my co-leader and I decided to form a group with these people that would provide them with some sensory stimulation. The group would have the same format as the preplacement group, but the activities would be somewhat different.

The group consisted of three men and three women, and the sessions lasted from half an hour to an hour. We felt successful after a session if members had not wandered off or fallen asleep. I sat in front of the group and touched the members to make sure they could see and hear me. Each week I told them who I was, where they were, why they were there, and who was present. I moved around a lot, making physical contact with each member; I called them by name. The other leader and I developed a routine of opening the session by providing chocolate candy or, in some cases, a cigar, and the members very much enjoyed this ritual. Once I brought in a bottle of perfume, let everyone smell it, and helped the women put it on, which brought many giggles. This allowed for touching, which these people very much needed. The members sat holding hands and sang favorite old tunes while one of them plucked away at a guitar. It was a touching experience to see these people enjoying singing an old and much-loved song; they still remembered the words but had to struggle with their physical handicap to sing them. I can still hear the group singing "You Are My Sunshine."

We generated another activity in the OBS group by bringing in a beach ball and encouraging the members to throw it to one another and to go through the struggle of retrieving it. This stimulated the members into activity. We brought in large, colorful pictures and had the members describe what they saw. The members had a tendency to talk very little, so we encouraged them to notice one another's presence and address one another. We brought a tape recorder to some sessions, recorded the songs, and then listened to everyone's voice. We brought in clay one day, but this proved to be a disaster because several members started eating it. This problem could have been prevented, though, had we paid closer attention to what was going on. Bringing my two daughters and introducing them to each member of both my groups delighted my children as well as the group members. This was a natural catalyst; afterward there was much talk among the members about the fun they had had with my children. Weather permitting, we took the members on walks, having them touch and smell flowers, trees, and shrubs. In all of these ways we encouraged members to employ all of their senses, so that they could be more alive.

Obviously, the goals of this group were more limited in scope than those of the preplacement group. Few changes were observed outside of the group; members continued not to react to or recognize one another much of the time. However, I felt that it did them good to be aroused from their lethargy, if only for short periods of time. The following are notes I made after the second session:

> The OBS group was slow. In the beginning, two people insisted on going to sleep. One member kept wandering off. Later, some talked about a birthday party and shared the fun they had. Everyone sang some songs and held hands. I contacted everyone in group, touching and talking with each one. It is difficult not to get discouraged, and I have to continually keep my goal—

to get any of them to converse or react about anything—in mind. As I did last time, I made a point of saying good-bye to each of them individually.

With this particular group, it was rewarding to see even the most minute changes. It was exciting for me to hear one 87-year-old man, who usually showed no responsiveness, giggle when I put some perfume behind my male co-leader's ear. During the initial sessions he had never uttered a word; now, slowly, he began to talk and sing with the rest. One lady who had not allowed anyone to touch her reached out one day and held another member's hand.

I visited this group three months after I had left it, not expecting to be remembered. I was touched when some members approached me in recognition and reminded me that I had not been to the group meetings!

GROUPS FOR FAMILIES OF THE ELDERLY

I see a pressing need for therapy groups for people who have aged relatives in an institution. Very often a family's feelings of guilt, anger, failure, and hopelessness will keep them away from their hospitalized member, depriving him or her of the joy of visits. Or the family members may visit but transmit their negative feelings to the old person. In either case, everyone suffers from the loss of true contact. By allowing families to share their concerns with other families, groups can relieve much of the tension that normally results from the responsibility of caring for a loved one who is old.

My co-leader and I experimented with this idea by holding several sessions with one member and his entire family. The family members talked about the shame they felt over having one of their relatives committed to a mental institution, and the patient expressed the anger he felt over being ignored by his family. After expressing their feelings, the family members made the decision to visit the institutionalized member more often.

There is a trend toward providing support groups for the caretakers of the elderly. Dobson and Dobson (1991) describe ways of setting up a group for caretakers that provides support for adult children struggling to adjust to aging parents. They also describe the content of the group and the techniques they employ. Hinkle (1991) describes a support group for caregivers of people with Alzheimer's disease. He addresses the particular needs of caregivers and the special issues facing these families.

PERSONAL REACTIONS AND OBSERVATIONS

Working with the elderly can be very rewarding; however, at times it can be draining and demanding. Sometimes I felt depressed, hopeless, and angry. These feelings were seldom directly connected with my activities with the patients; the smallest changes I observed in them were rewarding and gave me an incentive to go on. I felt annoyed when I saw student psychiatric technicians or other staff members show disrespect for the patients. These students often called an elderly person by his or her first name yet insisted that they themselves be addressed by their surname. Occasionally, an agitated patient would be restrained physically or with medication without ever being asked what had made him or her so upset in the first place. Another upsetting sight was a patient in a wheelchair being pushed around and not being told where he or she was going.

Sometimes patient behavior was treated as crazy when in reality there was a good reason for it that could have been discovered if anybody had tried. One day a student brought a blind member of my OBS group to the meeting, and he proceeded to take off his shoes. The student shouted at him to put them back on. I approached Mr. W. and kneeled in front of him. "Mr. W., you are taking your shoes off in our group session," I said. "How come?" He apologized, saying he thought he was being taken to the physical therapy room.

In another case, a 75-year-old patient kept taking his shoes off all day long, always gathering up newspaper to put around his feet. Everyone considered this behavior bizarre. I remembered that during my childhood in Germany I was often told in the winter to put newspaper into my shoes to keep my feet warm. After spending some time with this man, I found that this "strange" behavior was based on the same experience. I learned to be careful not to judge a patient as bizarre or delusional too quickly but rather to take the time to find out whether there was a logical reason for a peculiar behavior.

I felt challenged when I had to struggle with the heavy diagnostic language used by the staff members to record the patients' behavior in their official records. I often found it difficult to understand the notes in the records, and I was concerned that the simple language I was using to describe the members' behavior in group might be considered inappropriate. A number of staff members apparently had reservations about the use of technical language too. One day, during an important hospital meeting, it was decided that from then on a minimum of labeling of patients would be used. Instead, patient behavior would be described in a way that anyone could understand. Instead of labeling a patient withdrawn, staff members would describe the behavior of the patient that led them to conclude that he or she was withdrawn. This would, of course, be more time consuming, and several staff members resisted it.

Patients were sometimes discouraged or made to feel shameful when they physically expressed affection for another ward member. Sensuality was perceived by the staff as bad because of "what it could lead to." I had several very good discussions with staff members about our attitudes toward the sexuality of the aged. By dealing with our own attitudes, misperceptions, and fears, we were able to be more understanding and helpful to the patients.

It was also sad to see the elderly describe themselves as ugly, having accepted the standard that only the young are beautiful. In our groups my co-leader and I talked about attitudes toward old people's physical appearance. We were able to work with the members on accepting and liking themselves.

WORKING WITH HEALTHY AGING PEOPLE

Although the preceding section focuses on group programs for institutionalized elderly people, it is a mistake to assume that groups have value only to the frail or ill elderly. Groups are a most effective approach in addressing developmental issues of aging and the challenges of finding meaning in later life. In working with the *well* elderly, the social support mechanisms of a group help members understand the universality of their struggles. Many elderly people who are not institutionalized have problems coping with the aging process. These people have to deal with the many losses associated with old age in addition to the pressures and conflicts that the younger generation experiences, and they can profit from personal-growth groups that serve people of all ages. Here are a few suggestions for helping healthy, well-functioning elderly people:

- Combine a group of people over 65 with a group of adolescents and have them explore their common struggles—their feelings of uselessness, difference, and isolation from the rest of society.
- Aging people can be employed or asked to volunteer as teacher aides in elementary and secondary schools.
- High school or college students learning to speak a foreign language can visit homes for the aged that include people who speak the language the student is learning. In addition to helping the student, this provides some badly needed stimulation for the elderly person.
- Groups can be formed to explore such themes as love, sex, marriage, meaning in life, death, failing health, and body images. Many of the myths surrounding these issues for elderly people can be examined in depth.
- Teachers can invite elderly people to be guest speakers in their classes and ask them to discuss historical events they experienced that are being studied by the students.
- People in senior citizen centers can be asked to teach young people arts and crafts and other skills.

A COMBINED GROUP FOR THE
ELDERLY AND ADOLESCENTS

Michael Nakkula conducted an innovative group combining older people with adolescents. Nakkula's group, originally designed as a master's thesis project, was aimed at assessing members' changes in attitude as a result of their experiences in eight group sessions. Results from that study, which were shared in the prior two editions of *Groups: Process and Practice,* have inspired other graduate students to conduct similar intergenerational group research. In addition, the group structure and process outlined here have been replicated by practitioners in a variety of educational and mental-health settings.

BASIC ASSUMPTIONS

Nakkula's study was based on a review of the literature, his personal observations on the developmental tasks of the young and the old, and his experience as a group leader for the elderly and for adolescents separately. In particular, he found his group work with the elderly consistently reverting back to discussions of children, whether it be a desire to have more contact with grandchildren, reflections on their own youth, or concerns about the youth of today. This repetition of child-oriented themes sparked the idea of constructing an intergenerational format. Some of his key assumptions were:

- Part of maintaining health in the elderly is staying in contact with all age groups.
- The old need to have an opportunity to pass on their wisdom to the younger generation.
- The young need exposure to the elderly to gain wisdom.
- The elderly can become a "living history book" to young people.
- There is a need to bring these two age groups together to exchange elderly wisdom and youthful vitality.
- Older people benefit from the knowledge that their investment in society can live on beyond their own lives.
- Adolescents need role models for their developing value systems.
- The benefit of interaction between the young and the old is based not only on what they can learn from their differences but also on what they can learn from their similarities.
- Contact between the two age groups can lead to less fear and more realistic attitudes about the aging process among adolescents.
- The two age groups display a striking resemblance in their struggle to understand the purpose of their lives.
- Both groups suffer from apparent alienation within our social structure.
- The elderly are stifled in their attempt to realize their full potential; adolescents are stifled by their limited power and control and lack experience in using the power they do have.

Based on these assumptions, Nakkula hypothesized that combining the two age groups would result in positive changes in attitude toward members of the opposite age group due to increased knowledge and understanding. He also hypothesized that the group experience would lead to an increase of self-esteem in the elderly.

STRUCTURE OF THE GROUP

Participants were divided into two groups, each consisting of five junior high school students, aged 12 and 13, and five elderly people, all of whom lived in a nursing home. They met for eight sessions; sessions were structured as follows:

Session 1. The purpose of the group was explained. The members were asked to interview one another and later introduce one another to the rest of the group.

Session 2. The objective was to help members look at their similarities and differences. Classical music was played, and they were asked to think about the most critical task in their life. The differences and similarities of these tasks were then discussed in the group.

Session 3. The goal was to discuss what factors would lead to personal strength and, in turn, to personal happiness. The members were asked to think about their assets and how they thought their strengths contributed to their happiness. They were asked to choose a strength from the other age group they would like to possess.

Session 4. The purpose was to assist the elderly in putting their life experiences into perspective and to teach adolescents that life is an ongoing process that demands work. Members brought to the session photographs of themselves at different points in their lives. They talked about their favorite picture, explaining why it was associated with special meaning.

Session 5. The aim was to examine how the young and the old were represented in the media. Members shared and discussed news articles. They also identified adjectives used by the media in describing the young and the old.

Session 6. The purpose was to examine the messages found in music and to compare yesterday's with today's music, as well as to look for common themes. After listening to select pieces of music, members discussed the feelings that were aroused and the people and situations they associated with each piece. They also talked about what was happening in the world at the time these songs were written. All the members sang a song known to everyone.

Session 7. The elderly were given an opportunity to share the significance of their heritage with the young, and the young had an opportunity to realize the importance of the elderly in connecting them with their roots. The members discussed their ethnic backgrounds. Adolescents discussed what they knew about their heritage. The elderly talked about how their families had come to the United States and what it had been like for them, their parents, and their grandparents from the beginning.

Session 8. The purpose was to say good-bye and to leave one another having earned mutual respect. The members divided into pairs and talked about what they had learned from and enjoyed about each other. They also identified at least one misconception they had had about the other age group and how it had been clarified. They exchanged names and addresses so that they might stay in touch.

OUTCOMES

This study used a pretest and posttest design with treatment and comparison groups to assess adolescent attitudes toward the elderly and to assess the degree to which the elderly felt useful in society. The young people who participated in the discussion group changed many of their attitudes or biases toward the elderly from pretest to posttest, whereas those in the nonparticipant comparison group did not. Changes included an increase in the perception of elderly people as wise, and a decrease in the perception of them as senile; an increase in the perception of them as interesting, and a decrease in the perception of them as boring; and an increase in the belief that the elderly are an attribute, rather than a burden, to society. The elderly who participated in the study showed a general increase in self-esteem, whereas those in the comparison group did not. Connected with the change in self-esteem was the chance to socialize with curious and enthusiastic youngsters who seemed to genuinely enjoy listening to their reminiscing about these experiences.

IMPLICATIONS AND COMMENTARY

Through his work in Harvard University's new Risk and Prevention Program, Nakkula has begun to think of his elderly-adolescent group in terms of risk and protective factors. *Risk factors* increase the likelihood of negative life outcomes. *Protective factors* bolster the individual in the face of life's difficulties. Surviving or thriving through difficult experiences builds strength or resiliency, which in turn serves as one of life's essential protective factors. The elderly-adolescent groups can serve as a protective factor for both the old and the young.

For the elderly, the groups can serve as protection against depression, which often stems from loneliness, isolation, and feelings of worthlessness. Many elderly people experience multiple losses over short periods of time, including the loss of a spouse, of friends, of their health, and, in the case of those living in senior citizens' centers, of their homes. This array of losses places the elderly at high risk for depression and apathy, which depletes them of the energy required to remain physically and emotionally healthy. Involvement in a discussion group or related activity with children or early adolescents gives the elderly something to look forward to, and it gives them an important role in a society where many young people are in desperate need of guidance and mentoring. Nakkula views this role as a vital protective factor against the risks of loss and isolation.

For the adolescents, the groups can help to build character, a primary form of resiliency. The opportunity to make a meaningful contribution to the well-being of another person is missing for many youth. When the adolescents begin to feel their value in the lives of their new elderly friends, it can fill them with a sense of pride and importance. For some, this experience is an initiation into the world of community involvement and human responsibility. Such an experience serves as protection against feelings of alienation, which are common when the adolescent search for meaning in life goes unfulfilled.

In my talks to the elderly I encourage them to spend time with young people, especially those who are significant to them. My message to them is not to underestimate the tremendous power and influence they could have in the lives of young people. In my adult therapy groups I often hear about a grandparent who had a significant impact on a person's life when a parent was too busy.

Groups combining old and young provide an economical response to the mental-health needs of the increasing elderly population while also creating a vehicle through which young people can contribute something valuable to the community. They target precisely what lies at the core of distress and despair for many old and young people alike: loneliness.

An example of having older people live with younger people is Advent Christian Village, a retirement, nursing, and child-care community in Dowling Park, Florida. A friend of mine who was orphaned grew up in the village. She fondly remembers her interaction with the older people who lived there. The elderly attended to the needs of the younger residents and in many cases became substitute parents. The younger residents were able to offer meaningful companionship to the elderly residents. It is remarkable that the village, which was founded in 1913 as a home for orphans and retired preachers, has managed to keep pace with the ever-changing concerns of contemporary society. It provides:

- professional care for neglected youths
- a serene and secure environment for active retirees
- competent care for impaired and frail elderly residents

At the time this chapter was first written in 1977, a place like the village was certainly the exception. By contrast, I now often hear of projects involving some creative combination of the young and the old. At St. Elizabeth Senior Day Care Center in Pompano Beach, Florida, for example, the elderly gather with preschoolers for activities like barbecues or finger painting with colored shaving cream. The director of this center commented: "It's an unwritten love agreement. The little ones—their parents have to work, so they're not here to give them warmth. The seniors are in the same situation, so we bring them together to fulfill the needs of both" ("A Home," 1990, p. 57). For more information on day-care centers in which the aged are involved, write to the National Council on the Aging, Department Y, 600 Maryland Avenue, SW, Washington, DC 20024.

There are many possibilities for designing programs that combine the elderly and the young. It is up to the creativity of the group practitioner to come up with variations. For more detailed information about the group discussed here, contact Michael Nakkula, 30 Lake Avenue, Newton Centre, MA 02159; telephone (617) 244-6462.

BEREAVEMENT GROUPS

THE THERAPEUTIC VALUE OF GRIEF WORK

Grief is a necessary and natural process after a significant loss. However, many forces in our society make it difficult for people to completely experience grief. Social norms demand a "quick cure," and other people often cannot understand why it is taking "such a long time" for a grieving person to "get back to normal." As is the case with any emotion that is not expressed, unresolved grief lingers in the background and prevents people from letting go of losses and forming new relationships.

Hospice centers help the terminally ill deal with their impending death and also help survivors who have lost a loved one feel their full range of emotions during bereavement. These hospices typically offer both closed groups and time-limited groups, as well as short-term groups with changing membership. Many survivors need the reassurance that they are not "going crazy."

Kübler-Ross (1969) made a significant contribution in describing the stages a dying person tends to go through, from denial to acceptance. But as she emphasized, all people who are dying do not conform to sequential stages in a neat and tidy way. Likewise, people who are working through a loss also grieve in their own way, and they do not necessarily proceed from denial to acceptance of their losses. Some are never able to accept the death of a child or a spouse. They may get stuck by denying their feelings and by not facing and working through the pain over the loss. Those therapists who work with grieving clients know full well the therapeutic value of fully experiencing the pain. At some point in the grief process, people may feel numb, as if they were functioning on automatic pilot. Once this numbness wears off, the pain seems to intensify. People who are going through this pain need to learn that they may well get worse before they feel better. To put to rest unresolved issues and unexpressed feelings, people need to express their anger, regrets, guilts, and frustrations. When they attempt to deny their pain, they inevitably wind up being stuck, for this unexpressed pain tends to eat away at them both physically and psychologically.

Unresolved grief accounts for many of the referrals for counseling and psychotherapy. This grief may be over many types of losses besides a death, such as the breakup of a relationship, the loss of one's career, or children leaving home. In learning to resolve grief, regardless of its source, people need to be able to talk about what they are telling themselves internally and what they are feeling. They typically need to bewail the lack of fairness in their situation. They may eventually face up to the fact that there is no rational reason that will explain their loss.

THE ADVANTAGE OF THERAPEUTIC GROUPS FOR LOSS

Groups can be instrumental in helping people feel less isolated as they move at their own pace in their own way in working through their grief. The group process can be used to therapeutic advantage by individuals who are struggling to adjust to many of the changes that confront them because of their loss. Certainly this is not a task reserved for older people, since loss and grief can affect people regardless of their age. However, bereavement is a particularly critical developmental task that older people must often cope with, not only because of the loss of others who are close to them but also because of the loss of some of their capacities. Although death strikes at children as well as the elderly, facing one's own death and the death of significant others takes on special significance with aging.

If people who are experiencing bereavement are able to express the full range of their thoughts and feelings, they stand a better chance of adjusting to a new environment. Indeed, part of the grief process involves making basic life changes and experiencing new growth. If people have gone through the necessary cycle of bereavement, they are better equipped to take on a new purpose and a new reason for living. Group counseling can be especially helpful to people at this time.

AN ELDERLY BEREAVEMENT GROUP

The following is a description of an elderly bereavement group designed and conducted by Alan Forrest, a professor of counseling at Radford University. This account is written from the perspective of Alan Forrest.*

GUIDELINES FOR ESTABLISHING THE GROUP

One of the primary goals of a bereavement group is to educate the mourner to the reality that grief is a process that is measured in years, not months. It does not proceed the same for everyone; as one widow stated, "You never really get over the loss, but the challenge is learning how to

*For further information about bereavement groups, contact Alan Forrest, Ed.D., Department of Counselor Education, P. O. Box 6994, Radford University, Radford, VA 24142; telephone (540) 831-5214.

live with it." The following guidelines are suggested for beginning a group and making it work effectively.

Be clear about the purpose and structure of the group. A bereavement group for the elderly should have a psychoeducational focus, including elements of education, emotional support, and encouragement for social interaction. The group can serve as a catalyst for meeting the members' emotional needs, dispelling myths and misconceptions of loss responses, and for enhancing the ability to develop new relationships outside the group. This has the tendency to assist the grief process and nurture self-esteem. To achieve a high level of group cohesion and trust, my co-leader and I decided on a closed, time-limited group. I followed an 8- to 10-session format, meeting once a week for two hours. Because clients have a strong need to talk about their losses, I limited the group to 6 to 8 members, thereby allowing adequate time for each member to have the opportunity to share.

The screening and selection process is a central factor contributing to the success of the group. It is essential to have a clear sense of who will likely benefit from a group in making the determination of whom to include. When working with the elderly, there will generally be more widows than widowers. However, it is useful to have at least two widowers present so the first does not feel alone. Another consideration is recency of the loss. I did not include people whose loss had occurred less than 12 weeks ago. This early into their bereavement, most people are not ready for a group experience. Some groups have potential members wait until six or nine months after the loss before beginning a group. Lastly, and perhaps most important of all, it is essential to rule out candidates who exhibit serious pathology, as they are likely to impede the group process and take precious time from the other group members.

Group leaders have a responsibility to identify and define expectations. It is a good group policy to clearly define the ground rules and boundaries of the group in the screening process and again in the initial group meeting. At the first group meeting, I ask members to state their expectations. This serves the dual function of being an icebreaker and also of clearing up misinterpretations about the purpose of the group.

Leadership style and the activity level of the leader are important considerations for a bereavement group. A high degree of leader activity is effective during the early stages of group. But as the group evolves into a cohesive unit, I tend to become less active. A co-leader format is useful. The intensity of an individual's emotions frequently has an impact on other members. One co-leader can concentrate on helping an individual express and work through a painful experience while the other co-leader pays attention to members reacting to this pain. A co-leadership style facilitates bringing several members into a given member's work.

Disruptive behaviors can impede the group process. It is important for co-facilitators to address disruptive behavior as soon as it occurs. For example, it is not unusual for a group member to express the attitude that "my loss is greater than your loss." I handled this by saying, "We are not here to compare losses. Everyone's loss is unique. We are here because of losing someone, and everyone's loss is important in this group." Other disruptive behaviors to be aware of include the person who habitually gives advice but rarely engages in personal sharing; the person who gives moralistic advice and uses "shoulds," "musts," and "have tos"; the member who typically observes but seldom participates in personal sharing; the person who makes irrelevant comments; and the person who continually interrupts other group members when they are working on their loss issues. Other disruptive behaviors should be addressed as they emerge.

IMPLEMENTING THE BEREAVEMENT GROUP

Norms and Expectations   During the initial session of the group, I discuss the norms and expectations for the group, including beginning and ending on time and socializing outside of the group. I address members' questions about how the group functions. Ending sessions on time can be difficult, because it is hard to accurately gauge the length of time it takes for the expression of the intense emotions that are elicited. But it is helpful for participants to have a sense of the beginning, middle, and ending phases of each session so they can make maximum use of the time.

Socializing outside of most counseling groups is generally discouraged. Subgroups may form, and this can have a negative effect on the cohesion and process of the group. However, while leading bereavement groups for the elderly, I don't adhere to this norm. There are advantages to outside contact among members, such as helping them deal with loneliness and social isolation that are a part of the bereavement experience.

Participant Introductions   At the first group meeting, I ask participants to introduce themselves and share something personal about themselves. I monitor these disclosures, so that each member has approximately equal time to share. The introductions provide each member with the opportunity to be the focal point of the group and also facilitates the universality of the feelings and expression of grief. Introductions are generally limited to name, circumstances of the loss, fears and anxieties participants have, and anything else they want others to know about them. One useful technique is to have each group member share what they were thinking and feeling while they were driving to this first meeting. The commonalities are noted, which begins a linking process. Due to the excessive anxiety many individuals experience, it is sometimes necessary to do the above exercises in dyads prior to introductions to the entire group.

Sharing Personal Loss and Bereavement Experiences   At some point in the first group session, each participant is given the opportunity to discuss in detail their loss and bereavement experiences up to this point in their lives. Introductions allow for some of this to occur, and as group members become more comfortable with one another they are more receptive to discussing their losses in greater detail and in more personal ways.

Learning about the Grief Process   Perhaps the single most important gift counselors can give to bereaved individuals is an accurate understanding of the grief process, so individuals no longer believe that their grieving is abnormal or that they are "going crazy." Areas typically discussed are: descriptions of the grief process, possible reactions such as physical symptoms, suicidal ideation, increased dependence on medication, depression, typical behaviors, and the reactions of others to one's loss.

Topical Issues   Topics generally addressed in the group include guilt, loneliness, a changing identity, fear of letting go of the deceased, changed social and interpersonal roles, important dates (birthdays, anniversaries, holidays), existential issues, rituals, the influence of family members on the grieving process, nutrition and physical exercise, and termination of the group itself, which is another loss that participants will need to address. Although the group facilitator may bring any of these themes up for discussion, it is also important to be open to topics group members want to explore.

Photographs and Memories   In an effort to make the deceased real and concrete to the other group members, I encourage members to bring in and share photographs. Additionally, each group member is given the opportunity to tell the group about that person. This exercise assists group members to feel a deeper sense of each other's loss and gives each mourner the chance to share a memory, thereby reaffirming his or her relationship with the deceased. Each photograph is passed around, and group participants can be encouraged to ask questions or share their observations of the person in the photograph.

Addressing Secondary Losses   Secondary losses are frequently ignored in the bereavement process despite the fact that they can be as powerful as the loss itself. A secondary loss—a loss that occurs as a consequence of a death—may take many forms and can affect a group in dramatic fashion. For example, one widow, whose husband had died very suddenly and unexpectedly shortly after taking early retirement, was struggling not only with him physically being gone but also with the loss of all the hopes, plans, and dreams they had shared. It was difficult for her to discuss moving on with her life, because her future plans were so intertwined with those of her husband. It was not until she examined her secondary losses that she could open up, engage in the group, and receive group support. Clients need to identify and anticipate secondary losses so they can be prepared for and grieved.

Emotional Intensity   A bereavement group contains a high level of emotional intensity, but many clients are unable or ill-prepared to deal with the breadth and depth of emotions they will encounter in themselves or in others. A degree of vulnerability accompanies the expression of emotions, and many participants may not be ready for it. Others may perceive this vulnerability as a sign of weakness. Therefore, these concerns must be repeatedly addressed throughout the group experience. Some group members will weep from the start to the end of each group session, which clearly communicates how difficult the group is for them. These members' crying is acknowledged, but it may not be immediately addressed. They may require time to process their emotions before feeling comfortable in verbally expressing them. These individuals receive support from the group by others respecting their need, for a period of time, to maintain some emotional distance.

Confidence and Skill Building   Many of the bereaved elderly, particularly widows, had been very dependent on their spouses. It is possible that some of this dependency may be transferred to their adult children. Although these individuals are grieving and in emotional pain, they have the capacity to develop new skills. Doing so can bring increased confidence and self-esteem. One group participant whose husband died shared, with much embarrassment, that she was having difficulty balancing her checkbook because her husband had always attended to family financial matters. When others in the group shared similar situations of being dependent on their spouses, she was encouraged and went to her bank to learn how to balance the checkbook. This particular woman gained so much confidence in herself that by the final group session she shared that she had bought a new car, something that her husband had always done for her. It is important to remember that confidence and self-esteem are just as essential for the elderly as for anyone else.

Multiple Losses   When a group member appears to be stuck and not moving through the grieving process, it can be an indication that the current loss has stimulated previously unresolved loss issues. With age comes an increased number of losses: friends, family, and other losses such as retirement, declining health, home, and for some, mental and cognitive functioning. All of these life transitions, in addition to losses through death, need to be grieved and are areas to be addressed. In the context of the group, the universality gained from discussing these issues is invaluable.

The Use of Touch   Many of the elderly, particularly men, who have lost a spouse, have a strong need to be touched. Without a spouse, it is difficult to get this need met. If a counselor is comfortable with the use of therapeutic touching, it is a way to meet the need of being touched on the part of the client and also a way for the counselor, or other group member, to physically make contact with another. It is paramount that the counselor be clear as to the appropriateness of the touching and whether or not the client is willing to be touched. A word of caution in using touch with a grieving individual: the touch may be countertherapeutic if it is used to communicate or is interpreted as "Don't cry, everything's going to be all right." The counselor and other group members are unable to take away another person's grief. Crying is part of the healing process, so group facilitators need to carefully attend to the participants and take their lead from them.

Termination   Termination of the bereavement group provides participants with another opportunity to learn how to deal with loss in a healthy manner. Members are encouraged to address any unfinished business toward the deceased or toward other group members or the facilitators. The members can anticipate how it will be to no longer have a group, explore what the group experience has meant to them, and examine their plans for continued support. Rituals can be effectively utilized throughout the group experience and can be powerful tools to increase self-awareness, especially during the termination process. One technique that has proven to be a powerful group ending experience is to have each participant light a candle that represents the deceased. Participants share with the group any thoughts about what they learned or about their deceased or what the group has meant to them. This exercise has the effect of engaging the group in a final shared experience, provides an ending ritual, uses light as a metaphor for insight and illumination, and leaves each participant with something concrete (the candle) to take home with them. Group members have found this to be a highly emotional and healing experience.

COUNSELOR SELF-AWARENESS

To function successfully as a grief counselor requires an awareness of self and one's own experiences of loss. The issues that encompass grief and loss are very emotional and touch our deepest fears as human beings. As a counselor, one has a desire to be helpful to other people, yet the anguish and pain the counselor witnesses cannot be removed from the grieving individual. This may result in discomfort and frustration on the part of the counselor. If the counselor is not aware of personal loss issues, the grief work with clients experiencing loss will be seriously affected and compromised.

The experience of bereavement necessitates that the counselor examine, at least minimally, three personal areas. First, working with the bereaved increases one's awareness of one's own losses. Examining personal issues (past and present) surrounding loss and bereavement is a difficult task, filled with profound sentiments. What is important is not that counselors have completely resolved all the loss issues they have experienced but rather that they be aware and actively involved in working on them. If a client is experiencing a loss similar to that of a recent loss in the life of the counselor, it may be difficult, if not impossible, to therapeutically help the client.

Secondly, grief may interfere in working with clients with regard to a counselor's own feared losses. Although all counselors have experienced losses in the past, there may be apprehension over future losses. Counselors may encounter personal anxiety when thoughts of losing their own children, partners, or parents enter into their work with clients. This is usually not problematic unless the loss a client presents is similar to the one we fear most. For example, if the counselor has an elderly parent, he or she may have difficulty facilitating an elderly bereavement group. If the counselor's parent is seriously ill, it will be even more difficult (if not impossible) to work with this population.

A third area involves the counselor's existential anxiety and personal death awareness. Death is a part of the cycle of life, and working with bereaved individuals is a constant reminder of the inevitability of one's own life and the lives of those we care for deeply. Most of us think about our own mortality and, in varying degrees, experience anxiety about it. However, it is possible to acknowledge this reality and not allow it to hamper our work with clients. How we choose to respond to the losses in our own lives will determine how effective we are in providing comfort and growth experiences in the lives of others.

GROUP OUTCOMES

How effective are elderly bereavement groups? No empirical outcome studies have been done on the elderly bereavement groups I have facilitated; however, there is some interesting anecdotal information.

Some group participants begin the group but after two or three sessions prematurely and suddenly terminate. Follow-up interviews indicate that their reasons for leaving include: the group is too emotionally threatening, too intimate, too sad; and the belief by some that they "should" be able to cope with their loss on their own. It is important to be cognizant of generational, cultural, and gender differences when working with an elderly population. Separately, or together, each will have an effect on whether or not one chooses to remain in the group.

A primary goal of an elderly bereavement group is to reduce the isolation and loneliness that may be the result of a loss, particularly when someone has lost their spouse of many years. At the conclusion of one of the groups, all the participants agreed to meet twice a month on Tuesday evenings for an evening out for dinner at a restaurant. They used this time to check in with one another, socialize, and share a meal together. In another group, all the members exchanged phone numbers and would periodically meet informally for emotional and social support. And still another group contracted with me to meet once a month, for three months, in what we referred to as an "aftercare group" following formal termination of the group. In each of these groups, all members had been strangers at the beginning of the group.

Two women who participated in one of the groups were there because each had experienced the death of one of their adult children. Regardless of how old one becomes, the loss of a child is a devastating experience. These two women formed a strong connection that continued long after the group ended. Some years later, I read in the newspaper that they had started a support group for older persons who had an adult child die. They had grown through their grief and were now reaching out to help others.

A PERSONAL COMMENTARY

Before I began facilitating loss and bereavement groups I was filled with enthusiasm, excitement, and altruism, tempered somewhat by numerous fears, anxieties, and insecurities. What could I give to those who were experiencing intense emotional pain and psychic distress? Would I have the "right" answers? Would I be good enough? How could I provide relief from the suffering of a spouse who lost her husband of 50 years?

I discovered that I didn't need to have all the answers and that if I trusted the group process, I would never be disappointed. There are times when no words can express the intensity of feelings in the group. That's how I learned the value of therapeutic silence and how one's presence can be healing.

To hear and truly feel another person's pain is not without effort. And knowing you can't take away that pain can be frustrating and depressing. The first group session is usually the most difficult because each group member relates the circumstance of his or her loss. The hurt, suffering, and pain can be overwhelming; but there is also comfort in knowing that one does not have to be alone. I have shared tears, and I have shared laughter working with bereaved elderly groups. It may seem paradoxical, but I have learned more about the process of living from facilitating these groups than I have about dying and grieving. Wisdom, courage, and strength of character cannot be taught in graduate school, but I have profited from some wise, courageous, and strong individuals—my clients.

When people learn that I work with death, loss, and bereavement, their initial reaction is generally "that must be terribly depressing." But what I have discovered about life and living, meaning and purpose, and my reason for being more than compensates for any sadness, pain, and distress it causes me. Facilitating an elderly bereavement group is life affirming and personally enriching. I have learned to celebrate each day as a precious gift and to deeply value my personal relationships. As one widow shared in group one evening, "The heart is a home with many rooms. Always keep the door open. That way the love fire burning and the warmth that is generated will spread to others. And, if your flames ever dim and all that remains are the glowing embers of the yesterdays of your life, then reach out and allow the warmth of another heart to touch you."

RESOURCES FOR BEREAVEMENT GROUPS

The following references may be helpful for learning more about designing and conducting a bereavement group with the elderly: Folken (1991), Lund, Diamond, and Juretich (1985), MacLennan (1988), Nachmias (1988), Poey (1985), Rando (1984), Redburn and Juretich (1989), Schwab (1986), Stone (1988), Worden (1991), Yalom and Vinogradov (1988), and Zimpfer (1991).

WHERE TO GO FROM HERE

If you are interested in working with the elderly, it would be a valuable experience to become involved with older people and their families. It is important that you explore your feelings about responsibilities toward older family members, which can help you understand the struggles of the members of the groups you lead. You can take a number of other steps to better prepare yourself to work with the elderly:

- Take courses dealing with the problems of the aged.
- Get involved in fieldwork and internship experiences working with the elderly.
- Visit agencies for the care of the elderly, both in your own country and on any trips you take abroad.
- Attend conventions on gerontology, a mushrooming field.
- Investigate institutes and special workshops that provide training in leading groups for the elderly.
- Explore your feelings toward your own aging and toward older people in your life.
- Read the literature in group work with the elderly.

A good reference for group workers is the special issue of group work with the aging and their caregivers in the *Journal for Specialists in Group Work* (Vol. 16, No. 3, September 1991). Most of the articles in this special issue are listed in the References and Suggested Readings for this chapter.

Irene Mortenson Burnside has had a valued impact on our views about working with the elderly. *Working with the Elderly: Group Processes and Techniques* (1984b) is a must for any person considering group work with the aged. Many people with experience working with the elderly are contributors to this book, and it contains a wealth of practical information on subjects such as training and supervision of group workers, suggestions for contracts in working with older people, group membership issues and procedures, responsibilities of group leaders, special groups, guidelines for group workers, and the future of group work with the aged.

For practical strategies in working with the elderly in groups, see *Inpatient Group Psychotherapy* (Yalom, 1983). It has especially good points on ways of helping group members work in the here and now and transfer group learning to everyday life. And Yalom's *Existential Psychotherapy* (1980) provides a superb philosophical foundation for the practice of group work.

REFERENCES AND SUGGESTED READINGS*

Birren, J. E., & Deutchman, D. (1991). *Guiding autobiography groups for older adults: Exploring the fabric of life.* Baltimore: The Johns Hopkins University Press.

Blazer, D. (1989). The epidemiology of psychiatric disorders in late life. In E. W. Busse & D. G. Blazer (Eds.), *Geriatric psychiatry* (pp. 235–260). Washington, DC: American Psychiatric Press.

*Burlew, L. D., Jones, J., & Emerson, P. (1991). Exercise and the elderly: A group counseling approach. *Journal for Specialists in Group Work, 16*(3), 152–158.

*Burnside, I. (1984a). Self-help groups. In I. Burnside (Ed.), *Working with the elderly: Group process and techniques* (2nd ed.) (pp. 234–247). Belmont, CA: Wadsworth.

*Burnside, I. (Ed.). (1984b). *Working with the elderly: Group process and techniques* (2nd ed.). Belmont, CA: Wadsworth.

*Butler, R., & Lewis, M. (1991). *Aging and mental health: Positive psychosocial approaches.* St. Louis: C. V. Mosby.

*Creanza, A. L., & McWhirter, J. J. (1994). Reminiscence: A strategy for getting to know you. *Journal for Specialists in Group Work, 19*(4), 232–237.

Dennis, H. (1984). Remotivation therapy. In I. Burnside (Ed.), *Working with the elderly: Group process and techniques* (2nd ed.) (pp. 187–197). Belmont, CA: Wadsworth.

Dobson, J. E., & Dobson, R. L. (1991). Changing roles: An aging parents support group. *Journal for Specialists in Group Work, 16*(3), 178–184.

Folken, M. H. (1991). The importance of group support for widowed persons. *Journal for Specialists in Group Work, 16*(3), 172–177.

*Hern, B. G., & Weis, D. M. (1991). A group counseling experience with the very old. *Journal for Specialists in Group Work, 16*(3), 143–151.

Hinkle, J. S. (1991). Support group counseling for caregivers of Alzheimer's disease. *Journal for Specialists in Group Work, 16*(3), 185–190.

A home away from home. (1990, July 2). *Newsweek,* pp. 56–58.

*Kübler-Ross, E. (1969). *On death and dying.* New York: Macmillan.

*Kübler-Ross, E. (1975). *Death: The final stages of growth.* Englewood Cliffs, NJ: Prentice-Hall.

*Entries marked with an asterisk are recommended for further reading.

*Lewis, M. I., & Butler, R. N. (1984). Life-review therapy: Putting memories to work. In I. Burnside (Ed.), *Working with the elderly: Group process and techniques* (2nd ed.) (pp. 50–59). Belmont, CA: Wadsworth.

Lund, D. A., Diamond, M. F., & Juretich, M. (1985). Bereavement support groups for the elderly: Characteristics of potential participants. *Death Studies, 9,* 309–321.

MacLennan, B. W. (1988). Discussion of "bereavement groups." *International Journal of Group Psychotherapy, 38*(4), 453–458.

Martin, A. (1984). Family sculpting: A combination of modalities. In I. Burnside (Ed.), *Working with the elderly: Group process and techniques* (2nd ed.) (pp. 225–233). Belmont, CA: Wadsworth.

*Molinari, V. (1994). Current approaches to psychotherapy with elderly adults. *Directions in Mental Health Counseling. 4*(3), 3–13.

Myers, J. E. (1990). Aging: An overview for mental health counselors. *Journal of Mental Health Counseling, 12*(3), 245–259.

*Myers, J. E., Poidevant, J. M., & Dean, L. A. (1991). Groups for older persons and their caregivers: A review of the literature. *Journal for Specialists in Group Work, 16*(3), 197–205.

Nachmias, S. (1988). The group technique as a means of social rehabilitation through self-help for widows. In E. Chigier (Ed.), *Grief and bereavement in contemporary society* (Vol. 2) (pp. 156–163). London: Freund Publishing House.

Nakkula, M. J. (1984). *Elderly and adolescence: A group approach to integrating the isolated.* Unpublished master's project, University of Minnesota, Duluth.

Poey, K. (1985). Guidelines for the practice of brief, dynamic group therapy. *International Journal of Group Psychotherapy, 35,* 331–354.

Price, G. E., Dinas, P., Dunn, C., & Winterowd, C. (1995). Group work with clients experiencing grieving: Moving from theory to practice. *Journal for Specialists in Group Work, 20*(3), 159–167.

Rando, T. A. (1984). *Grief, dying, and death.* Champaign, IL: Research Press.

Redburn, D. E., & Juretich, M. (1989). Some considerations for using widowed self-help group leaders. *Gerontology and Geriatrics Education, 9*(3), 89–98.

Robison, F. F. (1993). A training and support group for elderly diabetics: Description and evaluation. *Journal for Specialists in Group Work, 18*(3), 127–136.

Schwab, R. (1986). Support groups for the bereaved. *Journal for Specialists in Group Work, 11*(2), 100–106.

*Singer, V. I., Tracz, S. M., & Dworkin, S. H. (1991). Reminiscence group therapy: A treatment modality for older adults. *Journal for Specialists in Group Work, 16*(3), 167–171.

*Stone, M. L., & Waters, E. (1991). Accentuate the positive: A peer group counseling program for older adults. *Journal for Specialists in Group Work, 16*(3), 159–166.

Stone, W. N. (1988). Commentary on "bereavement groups." *International Journal of Group Psychotherapy, 38*(4), 447–452.

Waters, E. B. (1990). The life review: Strategies for working with individuals in groups. *Journal of Mental Health Counseling, 12*(3), 270–278.

Weiss, J. C. (1994). Group therapy with older adults in long-term care settings: Research and clinical cautions and recommendations. *Journal for Specialists in Group Work, 19*(1), 22–29.

Worden, J. W. (1991). *Grief counseling and grief therapy: A handbook for the mental health practitioner.* New York: Springer.

Wright, J., Coley, S., & Corey, G. (1989). Challenges facing human services education today. *Journal of Counseling and Human Service Professions, 3*(2), 3–11.

*Yalom, I. (1980). *Existential psychotherapy.* New York: Basic Books.

*Yalom, I. (1983). *Inpatient group psychotherapy.* New York: Basic Books.

*Yalom, I. D., & Vinogradov, S. (1988). Bereavement groups: Techniques and themes. *International Journal of Group Psychotherapy, 38*(4), 419–446.

Zimpfer, D. G. (1991). Groups for grief and survivorship after bereavement: A review. *Journal for Specialists in Group Work, 16*(1), 46–55.

NAME INDEX

Alberti, R. E., 381
Alle-Corliss, L., 309, 381, 391
Alonso, A., 7
Anderson, B. W., 44
Aronson, S., 325
Arredondo, P., 18, 76, 78
Atkins, D. M., 365
Atkinson, D. R., 17
Aubrey, M., 30
Austin, K. M., 44

Banawi, R., 78
Bankovics, G., 390
Barber, J. K., 365
Barrows, P. A., 373–374
Barton, D. A., 380, 381
Bass, E., 396
Bednar, R. L., 89, 90, 91, 127, 166,
    214,254, 255, 257, 258
Bennett, B. E., 44
Black, C., 343, 344
Blazer, D., 408
Bly, R., 383
Bond, L., 257, 258
Borgers, S. B., 127
Bowman, V. E., 127
Brisman, J., 365, 366
Brown, L. K., 315
Brown, M., 315
Bruhn, J. G., 371, 374
Bryant, B. K., 44
Buck, C. S., 396
Burlew, L. D., 415
Burlingame, G. M., 127, 162, 213, 214, 253,
    254, 258
Burns, S., 396
Burnside, I., 409, 440
Butler, R. N., 419
Butler, S., 396

Callanan, P., 37, 40, 144, 402
Castronovo, N. R., 374
Chu, J., 78
Ciha, T., 354, 355
Cochran, S. V., 381

Coleman, N. C., 78
Coleman, V. D., 17, 42, 78
Comas-Diaz, L., 78
Conklin, R., 373, 374
Conyne, R. K., 9, 85
Corazzini, J. G., 362–363
Corey, G., 7, 37, 40, 44, 90, 91, 187, 189,
    339, 402, 408
Corey, M., 37, 40, 187, 189, 301, 402, 408
Courtois, C., 396, 401
Creanza, A. L., 416

D'Andrea, M., 17, 18, 24
Dagley, J. C., 357
Damon, L., 396
Damon, W., 374
Daniels, J., 17, 18, 24
Davenport, D. S., 380, 381
Davis, L., 396
Dean, L. A., 412
DeLucia, J. L., 78, 127
Diamond, M. F., 440
Dies, R. R., 12, 89, 90, 91, 165, 166, 213,
    214, 256, 257
Dobson, J. E., 424
Dobson, R. L., 424
Dougher, M. J., 30
Dougherty, P., 381
Draguns, J., 17
Dufrene, P. M., 78
Dworkin, S. H., 374, 415

Edleson, J. L., 319, 356, 386, 390
Emerson, P., 415
Emerson, S., 396
Emmons, M. L., 381
English, N. C., 110–111, 345, 349
Eppinger, S. J., 357
Esquibel, A., 381
Evans, N. J., 90, 91

Fassler, D., 315
Finklehor, D., 396
Folken, M. H., 440
Forrest, A., 28, 44, 432

SUBJECT INDEX

TO THE OWNER OF THIS BOOK:

We hope that you have enjoyed this book and found it useful. We would like to know as much as possible about your experiences with *Groups: Process and Practice* (Fifth Edition), so that we can take your reactions into consideration in future editions. You can write your comments on this form and send it to us care of Brooks/Cole Publishing Company. Many thanks for your help.

School: _____

Your Instructor's Name: _____

1. In what class did you use this book? _____

_____

2. What did you like *most* about *Groups: Process and Practice?* _____

_____

_____

3. What did you like *least* about the book? _____

_____

_____

4. How useful were the exercises at the end of the chapters in Parts One and Two? Did you use any of them in class? _____

_____

5. How useful and informative were the chapters on specific groups in Part Three? Were there any chapters in this section that you did not read? _____

_____

6. In the space below, or in a separate letter, please make any other comments about the book you'd like. For example, what were your general reactions to the book? Were any chapters *or* concepts particularly difficult? Do you have any suggestions for future revisions? We'd be delighted to hear from you!

_____

_____

_____

Optional:

Your name: _____ Date: _____

May Brooks/Cole quote you, either in promotion for *Groups: Process and Practice* (Fifth Edition) or in future publishing ventures?

Yes: _____ No: _____

Sincerely,

Marianne Schneider Corey and Jerry Corey

FOLD HERE

FOLD HERE

Brooks/Cole is dedicated to publishing quality books for the helping professions. If you would like to learn more about our publications, please use the mailer to request our catalogue.

Name: _____

Street Address: _____

City, State, and Zip: _____